ARIZONA
100 BEST PLACES TO VISIT
BUCKET LIST

ISBN: 9798884936065

ABOUT ARIZONA

Arizona, a constituent state of the United States of America, holds the sixth position in terms of size among the country's states. The majority of its population has been concentrated in urban areas, especially since the mid-20th century, leading to rapid urban and suburban growth at the expense of rural areas. The origin of the state's name is debated among scholars, with some suggesting it comes from a Basque phrase meaning "place of oaks," while others attribute it to a Tohono O'odham (Papago) Indian phrase meaning "place of the young (or little) spring." Arizona gained statehood on February 14, 1912, becoming the last of the 48 contiguous United States to be admitted to the union.

Arizona presents a landscape filled with contradictions. Despite its reputation for a hot, low-elevation desert adorned with cacti and creosote bushes, over half of the state is situated at an elevation of at least 4,000 feet (1,200 meters) above sea level, boasting the largest stand of evergreen ponderosa pine trees globally. While Arizona is renowned for its arid desert regions, the presence of numerous large man-made lakes means it has more shoreline than commonly believed. Notable natural features like the Grand Canyon and the Painted Desert have become international symbols of the region's rugged beauty, yet the state's environment is delicate and faces significant pollution threats, surpassing those of major cities like New York City and Los Angeles. Despite its romanticized image as a wild desert and a haven of old-fashioned simplicity, Arizona's economic shift towards industrial and technological sectors occurred long before it embraced a pastoral or agrarian identity, starting in the 1860s.

Arizona is situated in the southwestern portion of the contiguous states, sharing borders with California to the west, Nevada to the northwest, Utah to the north, New Mexico to the east, and the Mexican state of Sonora to the south. The Colorado River serves as the dividing line with California and Nevada. The state's capital and largest city, Phoenix, are located in the south-central region. Arizona covers an area of 113,990 square miles (295,233 square km). As of 2020, the population stands at 7,151,502, with an estimated population of 7,431,344 in 2023.

The remarkable topography of Arizona is largely shaped by plate tectonics, involving the movement of large, relatively thin segments of the Earth's crust, and stream erosion. The interaction of the Pacific Plate and the North American Plate played a crucial role, generating significant tectonic forces that uplifted, folded, and stretched Arizona's geological crust. This process gave rise to the state's mountain ranges, basins, and high plateaus. Over the course of countless years, rivers and their tributaries have intricately carved distinctive landforms across these surfaces.

Arizona is geologically characterized by two primary divisions: the Colorado Plateau and the Basin and Range Province, with geologists including the Transition Zone (or Central Highlands) in their classification. The northeastern 40% of the state falls within the picturesque Colorado Plateau, featuring tablelands that are less rugged than the adjacent Utah portions. These Arizona plateaus, labeled as mesas and plateaus, primarily consist of plains occasionally interrupted by step-like escarpments. While the general terrain is traversable, the Grand Canyon of the Colorado River stands out as a remarkable exception. The highest points in the state, Humphreys Peak (12,633 feet or 3,851 meters) in the San Francisco Mountains and Baldy Mountain (11,403 feet or 3,476 meters) in the White Mountains, are forest-clad volcanic mountains atop these plateaus.

The southern border of the Colorado Plateau is demarcated by the Mogollon Rim, a series of massive escarpments spanning over 200 miles (320 km). South and west of the rim, numerous streams flow through narrow canyons or wide valleys, transitioning from the Transition Zone into the Basin and Range Province. The Transition Zone is characterized by separated plateau blocks, rugged peaks, and isolated rolling uplands that remained largely unexplored until the late 19th century. Serving as an ecological boundary between low deserts and forested highlands, the zone features a blend of elements from both regions, such as the Spanish bayonet of the Sonoran Desert alongside the juniper typical of higher elevations.

In the southern and western third of the state, the Basin and Range region houses the majority of the population but lacks the prominent canyons and mesas for which Arizona is renowned. This area primarily consists of expansive, open-ended basins or valleys with gradual slopes. Northwest-to-southeast-trending mountain ranges emerge as isolated features within the desert plain.

Contrary to common desert stereotypes, Arizona's landscape is characterized by the scarcity of sand dunes, and stony desert surfaces are rarely visible except in the far southwestern part of the state. River floodplains boast younger soils, providing more favorable conditions for agriculture.

Practically the entirety of Arizona is encompassed within the Colorado River drainage system. The Gila River, along with its major feeder streams—the Salt and the Verde—stands as the primary tributary of the Colorado River in Arizona.

The Salt River is sustained by the Black, White, and Verde rivers, functioning as its principal perennial tributaries. It converges with the Gila River southwest of Phoenix. Only during sporadic and occasionally destructive flood events does runoff water manage to flow downstream past the numerous dams established along the Salt's system. Originating in the western part of the Mogollon Rim in western New Mexico, the Gila River includes another smaller Mogollon Rim tributary, the San Francisco River. In southern Arizona, the intermittent streams of the Santa Cruz and San Pedro rivers flow northward into the Gila, while the Agua Fria and Hassayampa rivers, also intermittent, drain central Arizona southward into the Gila. Due to dams and irrigation systems, the Gila River remains dry for a significant portion of its length, except during rare occasions.

The Little Colorado River, draining the leeward side of the Mogollon Rim and flowing from southeast to northwest into the Colorado River between Marble Canyon and the Grand Canyon, draws limited water from its extensive watershed. The rain shadow effect on the leeward side of the Mogollon Rim results in the Little Colorado being mostly a trickle and frequently drying up. Various other small and intermittent streams, including the Bill Williams River, drain a sizable yet arid region in western Arizona.

Approximately half of Arizona is characterized as semiarid, with one-third being arid, while the remaining portion falls under a humid classification. The Basin and Range region features an arid and semiarid subtropical climate, making it a popular destination for winter visitors and new residents. In Phoenix, January days receive more than four-fifths of possible sunshine, with a mean maximum temperature of 65 °F (18 °C). Light frosts are occasional in most locations in the Basin and Range during winter, and some precipitation breaks the exceedingly dry springs and mildly dry falls. In July, daily maximum temperatures in Phoenix average 106 °F (41 °C), while nighttime temperatures drop to an average of 81 °F (27 °C).

Moisture-laden air from the Gulf of California and the eastern Pacific Ocean arrives in July, bringing more than two months of irregular but sometimes heavy thundershowers known locally as the "summer monsoon." Phoenix and Tucson typically receive about 1 inch (25 mm) of precipitation in July and approximately 3 inches (75 mm) throughout the summer. Winter rains in this region originate from the Pacific.

The Colorado Plateau experiences cool to cold winters and a semiarid climate. The average mile-high elevations, coupled with direct exposure to polar air masses, can result in January mean high and low temperatures diverging significantly, such as 46 °F (8 °C) and 19 °F (-7 °C) in Winslow. Year-round temperatures in Flagstaff are generally 30 °F (17 °C) cooler than those in Phoenix. Most areas in the region receive between 10 to 15 inches (250 to 375 mm) of precipitation annually, with the Mogollon Rim and White Mountains having the highest average at 25 inches (625 mm).

Due to the diverse relief within the Transition Zone, climatic conditions vary widely over small areas. A significant portion of Arizona's humid region falls within this zone and the adjacent high southern edge of the Colorado Plateau. Perennial streams flowing through shaded riparian corridors contribute to atmospheric moisture, resulting in temperatures several degrees cooler than those in nearby deserts.

Given the diverse relief and climate found in Arizona, it is not surprising to encounter a wide range of vegetation across the state. Approximately one-tenth of Arizona is covered by forests, one-fourth by woodlands, one-fourth by grasslands, and the remaining portion is characterized by desert shrub. Elevations exceeding 6,000 to 7,000 feet (1,800 to 2,100 meters) support forests primarily composed of ponderosa pine, with Douglas and other firs, spruces, and aspen appearing in the highest areas. In the northern half of the state, ranging from 4,500 to 7,500 feet (1,375 to 2,300 meters), piñon pine and juniper dominate, while evergreen oak and chaparral thrive between 4,000 and 6,000 feet (1,400 and 1,800 meters) in the central mountains. Plains grasses cover approximately one-third of the Colorado Plateau, and Sonoran or desert grass carpets the higher elevations of the basins. Mesquite trees have encroached upon many former grasslands in the south. Cacti are prevalent throughout the state, with the greatest variety found below 2,000 feet (600 meters). Foothills in the Tucson-Phoenix area boast giant saguaro cacti characteristic of the Sonoran Desert, while the northwest Basin and Range areas feature striking stands of Joshua trees. Shrubs dominate the lowest portions of all regions, including big sagebrush and saltbush in the Colorado Plateau, and creosote bush in the Basin and Range.

Arizona's animal life is equally diverse, representing various ecological communities from the Rocky Mountains, Great Plains, and Mexican regions. Significant larger mammals include black bears, deer, desert bighorns, antelope, and wapiti (elk). The tropical coatimundi, a raccoon-like mammal, has expanded northward into Arizona, and the javelina, or peccary (wild pig), is a popular game animal in the southern part of the state. Among the several cat species, the bobcat and the mountain lion (puma) are the most characteristic in Arizona. Coyotes, skunks, and porcupines are abundant, as are cottontails, jackrabbits, and various fox species. The state's southern border, positioned along a major flyway, is rich in birdlife, attracting thousands of birdwatchers. Game birds include turkeys and a variety of quails, doves, and waterfowl. Native fish species include the Arizona trout and the Colorado squawfish. Venomous animals such as rattlesnakes, scorpions, and Gila monsters are also present.

The indigenous peoples of Arizona are celebrated for their diverse cultural heritage. However, since the 19th century, the urbanized regions of the state have served as cultural outposts reflecting tastes, fashions, speech, religious preferences, political attitudes, and lifestyles from various locales like Chicago, New York City, Washington, D.C., San Francisco, and Los Angeles.

Up until the latter part of the 19th century, with the exception of small and scattered indigenous groups, central and northern Arizona remained largely uninhabited. Spanish occupation was limited due to the constant threat posed by actively hostile Apache bands, confining their presence to intermittently occupied missions, presidios, and ranches in the Santa Cruz valley, south of Tucson.

Upon Arizona's acquisition by the United States in 1848 (as part of New Mexico, as per the Treaty of Guadalupe Hidalgo), there were fewer than 1,000 people of Hispanic origin residing in the state. The number of Hispanic residents in Arizona surged in the 20th century, mostly Mexicans or their descendants who arrived since 1900. Relations between Mexican Americans and Anglos in Arizona have sometimes been strained, but in general, the two ethnic groups have a history of cordiality uncommon in other border states. While some communities have Mexican barrios, most Mexican Americans in

Arizona live in diverse neighborhoods and actively participate in the state's business, political, and social life, with intermarriage with Anglos being common. Although elements of Mexican culture have been incorporated into the Arizona lifestyle, the majority of the population, largely newcomers from other parts of the country, have been influenced only superficially. The Mexican American population in Arizona, for the most part, aligns with mainstream American culture.

Despite the historical subjugation, exploitation, and mistreatment, the Native American peoples in Arizona have endured, and their culture remains prominent, comprising less than one-tenth of the total population. Native Americans are organized into 15 tribes across 17 reservations, ranging in size from the 85-acre (34-hectare) Tonto Apache reserve to the 23,400-square-mile (60,600-square-km) Navajo reserve (nearly three-fifths of which lies in Arizona). The Navajo tribe, with about 100,000 members in Arizona, actively directs the development of its land and people, with the tribal government taking complete responsibility in various aspects of Navajo social and economic life. Other well-known tribes include the Apache and the Hopi, while the Tohono O'odham and the Akimel O'odham (Pima) have received significant attention in anthropological and historical literature. Less familiar tribes include the Havasupai, residing at the bottom of the Grand Canyon, as well as the Hualapai, Yaqui, and Yavapai. The African American population in Arizona constitutes a small proportion of the state's total, often concentrated in predominantly African American neighborhoods due to de facto housing segregation. Arizona voluntarily desegregated its schools in the early 1940s. Asians and Pacific Islanders are growing in numbers but remain the smallest minorities in the state.

Contrary to the romanticized perception of Arizona as a region filled with charming ghost towns, mining camps, remote ranches, Native American reservations, and idyllic cotton and citrus farms, the reality is that the majority of its population is concentrated in urban settings. A significant portion, about three-fifths, resides in Maricopa

County, notably in Phoenix. Six out of the 15 counties in the state collectively house approximately four-fifths of Arizona's total population. The number of individuals living on farms and ranches is relatively small, and most towns and cities exhibit low population densities.

In the southern parts of Arizona, older inhabited areas feature buildings constructed from adobe. In contrast, Flagstaff and Prescott, cities in northern Arizona settled by New Englanders in the 1860s and '70s, showcase Victorian-style houses that mirror the traditions and preferences of their initial inhabitants.

Phoenix serves as the primary trade center of the state, driven by its central location, robust agricultural economy, and appealing vacation and retirement offerings. Consequently, it has evolved into one of the largest and fastest-growing urban areas in the Southwest. Tucson, although older and smaller compared to Phoenix, acts as a gateway to Mexico and maintains strong commercial and medical ties with Sonora and other northern Mexican states. Since 1970, Tucson's population growth rate has been comparable to that of Phoenix.

In the early 21st century, Arizona witnessed a remarkable surge in its population, growing at nearly three times the national rate. Slightly over a quarter of the population fell under the age of 18. Among the newcomers were "snowbirds," retirees who sought refuge from winter in the warm desert and returned to their primary residences when the weather turned hot, continuing a trend observed in the past. Another contributing factor to the population growth was the phenomenon of "white flight" from California and the migration of individuals from declining industrial areas in the Midwest and Eastern United States, particularly those in the working-age bracket. Additionally, individuals were drawn to the state by promising opportunities in metropolitan areas, where economies were evolving to offer desirable high-paying jobs. A significant but unquantifiable portion of the newcomers entered the state illegally, with the majority hailing from Mexico and Central America. These individuals often filled roles in the state's low-paid service and agricultural sectors. The overall population was projected to reach 10 million by the year 2027.

Before World War II, Arizona's economy primarily revolved around primary production activities such as mineral extraction, lumbering, cattle raising, and crop cultivation. However, since the late 1940s, there has been a notable shift towards manufacturing industry and services. This transformation aligns the state's economy more closely with the growing affluence and technological advancements observed nationwide. This transition is particularly evident in the Phoenix area, where a dynamic high-technology economy has flourished.

Favorable conditions such as good soil, ample irrigation water, and a lengthy growing season empower Arizona to cultivate various crops, including cotton, alfalfa, a range of grains, vegetables, fruits, and nuts. Arizona consistently ranks among the leading cotton producers in the country. Citrus growing has been a significant and expanding sector of the state's economy for many years, and more recently, wine producers have found success in cultivating various grape varieties. Livestock production encompasses beef, dairy products, poultry, and eggs. Notably, the average size of farms in Arizona surpasses that of any other state, and farmers and ranchers utilize over four-fifths of the state's water resources.

Historically, metallic ores like copper, zinc, and, to a limited extent, silver and gold have been significant contributors to Arizona's revenue. The extraction of coal from the Black Mesa area in Native American reservations in northeastern Arizona holds importance, particularly because coal-fired stations in the region generate a substantial portion of electricity for the southwestern United States. This northeastern area also yields a small amount of petroleum and considerable quantities of uranium.

Since the 1880s, the extensive stands of ponderosa pine in northern Arizona have fueled a robust lumber and pulp-paper industry within the state. The presence of rich alluvial soils, especially in Yuma, Pinal, Pima, and Maricopa counties, has supported extensive and lucrative agricultural activities. Arizona's appealing climate and landscape are also recognized as valuable resources.

The natural geographic corridor formed by the Colorado Plateau, along with its Mogollon Rim escarpment, has facilitated irrigation projects and most of the state's hydroelectric power, including that generated by the Roosevelt, Hoover, and Glen Canyon dams. Approximately a dozen dams collectively regulate the runoff from the Mogollon Rim, storing and redirecting water to provide flood control and create lakes for water storage. This hydrological pattern has led to significant political and legal challenges for Arizona, including prolonged litigation with California over water rights from the Colorado River system. Internally, water distribution poses a major concern as groundwater depletion, particularly around Phoenix and Tucson, has occurred, and there are no new sources of surface water. To address this issue, cities have had to purchase water rights from distant areas, leading to increasing litigation involving municipalities, Native American tribes, and federal agencies over water rights.

Between 1880 and 1950, copper production stood as the predominant industry in Arizona. While the state remains the leading copper-producing state in the country, manufacturing has emerged as the primary basic industry, especially in electronics, communications, aeronautics, and aluminum. This shift has led to one of the most dynamic and prosperous economies in the nation. Despite this economic prosperity, many of Arizona's peripheral counties, particularly those with substantial Native American populations, persist as some of the poorest areas in the United States.

The expansion of urban and industrial areas has caused significant pollution in major parts of Arizona, eroding its historical status as a refuge for individuals seeking pristine air. Nevertheless, the state's climate, picturesque scenery, and relaxed lifestyle continue to draw millions of visitors annually, and Arizona has become a favored retirement destination, particularly in the lower desert regions. Noteworthy retirement communities like Sun City near Phoenix and Green Valley near Tucson have experienced continuous growth.

Similar to other western states, Arizona has not prioritized the development of mass transit systems, leading state and municipal governments to grapple with the challenge of constructing adequate roads to accommodate the growing population. This historical trend dates back to the state's earliest service industry, which involved long-distance cartage across challenging desert and mountain terrain. In contemporary times, the five interstate highways traversing Arizona are often congested with heavy trucks. These highways generally trace historic routes, many of which originated along Native American trade paths and were later adapted for stagecoaches and freight carriers. Railroads were introduced in the late 19th century, primarily along established east-west routes in southern and northern Arizona, with limited service to the rugged interior. However, there has been a noticeable shift towards mass transit development in the larger cities of the state in the early 21st century. Phoenix introduced a light-rail system serving the city and its environs in 2008, while Tucson initiated a streetcar service in 2014.

Surface transportation in Arizona typically follows the model of southern California, featuring streets laid out in a grid pattern interconnected by freeways and highways. Some effort has been made to develop bicycle paths within the cities. Phoenix's Sky Harbor International Airport offers nonstop international and domestic flights, while Tucson International Airport provides a more limited selection of nonstop flights. Airports in Flagstaff and Yuma have even fewer nonstop flights, and numerous smaller towns have airports capable of accommodating small jet aircraft. Additionally, there are several military airfields across the state.

While traditionally recognized for Native American folk arts and crafts, Arizona has not developed circles of painters and writers comparable to those in neighboring New Mexico. However, interest in various forms of art, including painting, crafts, drama, music, and publishing, has grown alongside the increasing population. Architecture and graphic arts have been notably influenced by Southwestern regional themes. Notably, few of the state's artists are native-born. Prominent writers associated with Arizona include Zane Grey, Edward Abbey, and Barbara Kingsolver. Some native-born 20th-century writers, like Marguerite Noble, Alberto Ríos, and Eva Antonia Wilbur-Cruce, have contributed to a genre emphasizing the region's hardships and austere beauty. Active contemporary Native American writers, although mostly born outside Arizona, include Leslie Marmon Silko, N. Scott Momaday, Luci Tapahonso, Laura Tohe, Simon Ortiz, and Ofelia Zepeda.

Contemporary Native American arts and crafts, executed within tribal traditions, gain global recognition. Particularly, Hopi and Navajo artists in painting, silver and jewelry craftsmanship, weaving, basket making, and pottery produce highly sought-after and expensive works.

No single city dominates as an art center, but Scottsdale, Tucson, Sedona, and Tubac host colonies of working artists. Flagstaff and Tucson have respected photographers. The Phoenix Art Museum houses permanent collections of Western American, Asian, Latin American, and European art, along with a fashion design collection. Other notable institutions, such as the Arizona State Museum in Tucson, the Heard Museum in Phoenix, the Sharlot Hall Museum in Prescott, and the Museum of Northern Arizona in Flagstaff, showcase archaeological and traditional collections of Indian arts and crafts. Phoenix and Tucson strongly support symphony orchestras, theaters, ballets, and opera.

Architecture serves as a distinctive blend of regional Southwest traditions and modern international trends. Examples include Frank Lloyd Wright's work, such as his residence at Taliesin West, and Paolo Soleri's futuristic city, Arcosanti. Various structures in the Spanish style, like the Heard Museum, stand out. The Nogales Public

Library synthesizes Spanish Southwestern and contemporary styles. The San Xavier del Bac Mission, near Tucson and completed in 1797, is one of the most photographed buildings in Arizona.

The University of Arizona Press, the state's leading book publisher, releases scholarly and popular titles with a Southwestern focus. The Arizona Historical Society supports a journal- and book-publishing program. "Arizona Highways" magazine is widely recognized for bringing diverse features of Arizona to a global audience. Popular sources of news and editorials include the daily "Arizona Republic" and weekly "New Times," both published in Phoenix.

Various sports and recreational activities provide entertainment and leisure in Arizona. Professional sports teams include the Arizona Cardinals (football), Phoenix Suns (men's basketball), Arizona Diamondbacks (baseball), Arizona Coyotes (hockey), and Phoenix Mercury (women's basketball). The diverse terrains attract hunting, fishing, camping, hiking, and amateur prospecting enthusiasts. Arizona boasts more national parks and monuments than any other state, including the Grand Canyon, Saguaro, Petrified Forest, Chiricahua, Montezuma Castle, and Organ Pipe Cactus. The Arizona–Sonora Desert Museum near Tucson is a renowned living museum dedicated to the natural world of the Sonoran Desert. Rodeos occur in cities and on larger Native American reservations. Various festivals are sponsored by towns and cities, such as Helldorado Days in Tombstone, Rex Allen Day in Willcox, and the White Mountain Festival in Pinetop.

History of Arizona

Although the physical environment of the region may seem challenging for habitation and sustenance, Arizona boasts some of North America's oldest records of human occupation. Artifacts from material culture indicate that humans likely inhabited Arizona over 25,000 years ago. Throughout much of this prehistoric era, these early inhabitants lived in caves and engaged in hunting practices, targeting species that are no longer present today. The Cochise culture, comprised of individuals residing in what is now southeastern Arizona, is believed to have originated over 10,000 years ago and persisted until 500 BCE or even later.

Over the past 2,000 years, prehistoric societies in Arizona demonstrated high levels of organization and advancement. Many of these Native American groups established durable masonry villages known as pueblos, a term derived from the Spanish word for "town" or "village." Arizona has become a focal point for archaeological research in the New World, particularly during this period. Notable prehistoric cultures that emerged during this time include the Hohokam, Ancestral Pueblo (Anasazi), Mogollon, Sinagua, Salado, Cohonina, and Patayan. The nomadic Apache and Navajo likely arrived in the region between 1100 and 1500 CE.

The documented history of European explorers and settlers in the region traces back to the 1530s in Mexico when Spaniards began writing about the legend of Eldorado and the Seven Golden Cities of Cíbola. In 1539, Fray Marcos de Niza, a Franciscan priest, entered Arizona in search of wealth and hoping to convert Native Americans to Christianity. Faced with hostility from indigenous people, Fray Marcos returned to Mexico and provided misleading reports about the places he had visited. The following year, Francisco Vázquez de Coronado led a well-armed expedition to Arizona, aiming to claim the American Southwest for Spain. Unlike Marcos's reports, Coronado spoke favorably about the area, particularly in communications with Viceroy Mendoza, the ruler of New Spain. Members of Coronado's expedition explored the Grand Canyon and Hopi pueblos, while Coronado himself journeyed as far as eastern Kansas before returning to Mexico.

In 1583, members of the Hopi tribe guided the Spanish explorer Antonio de Espejo to the site of present-day Jerome, where he was disappointed to find copper and other nonprecious metal ores instead of gold. By 1675, Franciscan missionaries had established themselves at the Hopi villages. However, five years later, the Hopi revolted during the Pueblo Rebellion, driving the Spaniards out. In the early 1700s, Roman Catholic missionaries built churches in the upper Santa Cruz valley in southern Arizona. Despite Hispanic settlers being confined to the valley by Apache raiders, priests visited various parts of northern Arizona, including the Hopi villages, in the 18th century, but made no serious attempts at religious conversion.

After Mexico gained independence from Spain in 1821, the new government ordered the closure of missions in Arizona. Arizona was ceded to the United States as part of New Mexico in 1848 and gained independence from New Mexico in 1863. Following the Gadsden Purchase in 1853, when Mexico sold Arizona's southernmost region to the United States, only a few scattered and isolated Mexican American ranches remained, primarily near the Mexican border.

Until the Mexican-American War (1846–48), only a handful of Americans, such as explorers, soldiers, trappers, and sheep drivers, ventured into Arizona. In 1851, the U.S. Army Corps of Engineers initiated multiple expeditions into Arizona with the aim of identifying a suitable route for constructing a wagon road to California. To safeguard travelers, miners, and settlers from potential conflicts with Native Americans, the U.S. government began establishing army posts at strategic locations. In 1883, the Atchison, Topeka and Santa Fe Railway was completed across northern Arizona, connecting St. Louis, Missouri, to California. Simultaneously, the Southern Pacific Railroad finished a line from New Orleans to Los Angeles, passing through Tucson and Yuma in that same year.

Copper, which dominated Arizona's economy until the 1950s, saw its initial mining activities in the state commence at Ajo in 1854. Around the same time, the Planet mines were established on the Colorado River banks. The Clifton-Morenci district in eastern Arizona saw the emergence of two significant mining operations by 1876. Copper mining operations in Globe and Jerome, located in central Arizona, experienced rapid growth, along with silver mines in Tombstone. The most significant copper discovery, however, took place in Bisbee in 1877, situated in southeastern Arizona near the Mexican border. By

1880, advancements in electrical engineering on a national and international scale, coupled with available investment capital, created a robust demand for copper. Arizona quickly became a major supplier, continuing to mine and process approximately two-thirds of the copper produced in the United States.

During the 1870s, several homesteaders, including a significant number of Mormon immigrants from Utah, made efforts to establish farming economies along the limited streams and rivers in Arizona. However, the challenges of droughts, floods, and the substantial capital required highlighted the need for large-scale, well-organized, and technologically advanced commercial farming in the state. Central Arizona's agricultural interests devised comprehensive plans incorporating costly dams and extensive canal systems for water storage and flood control. The completion of the Salt River Project in 1911 marked a significant milestone, providing water to farmers in the Phoenix area, now recognized as the state's agricultural hub. Despite this, water shortages persisted, leading to a protracted legal battle with California. In 1963, the U.S. Supreme Court affirmed Arizona's right to approximately 2.8 million acre-feet (3.5 billion square meters) of water annually from the Colorado River and the entire flow of the Gila River. In 1968, following extensive and contentious discussions, the U.S. Congress approved the Central Arizona Project—a vast system of pumps and canals designed to transport water from the Colorado River to the Phoenix and Tucson areas. The project reached completion in 1993.

Range cattle played a pivotal role in Arizona's economy from the 1860s until World War II, with the prominence of large feedlots emerging during that period. However, these feedlots have gradually diminished, and today, the cattle raised in Arizona contribute only a small fraction to the nation's edible beef supply.

After gaining statehood in 1912, Arizona quickly promoted itself as the home of the "five Cs": copper, cattle, cotton, citrus, and climate. The state's clear, clean, and dry air earned a reputation for providing relief from respiratory ailments, attracting health seekers from across the country. This influx of migrants and visitors contributed significantly to the state's economy. In the 1920s, the rise of "motor courts" (motels), dude ranches, and resorts catered to the growing numbers of tourists, winter residents, and retirees. Arizona, strategically located away from the coasts, housed several World War II flight schools and military bases, fostering further development.

Post-war, a notable migration wave, especially from the Midwest, transformed Phoenix into one of the fastest-growing urban areas in the United States. The advent and widespread use of refrigeration and air conditioning played a pivotal role, making Arizona more attractive and habitable. Despite its romanticized image, Arizona has not been immune to the challenges of urban industrialization. Technological advancements, such as railroads, copper smelters, nuclear reactors, automobiles, refrigeration, computers, and hydroelectric turbines, have been crucial for sustaining the state's population.

While newcomers often envision a land of personal fulfillment, Arizona grapples with issues like high rates of bankruptcy, crime, and divorce. Striking a balance between modern society in an arid environment and preserving the state's stunning natural landscape poses a significant challenge. The primary concern for Arizona lies in managing its growing population in a way that safeguards the characteristics that initially made the state attractive.

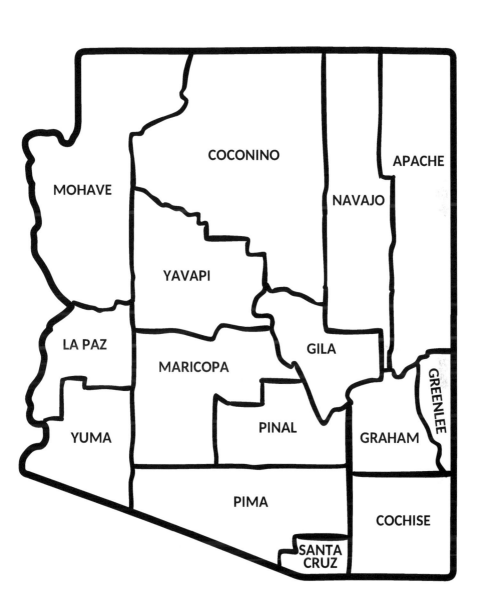

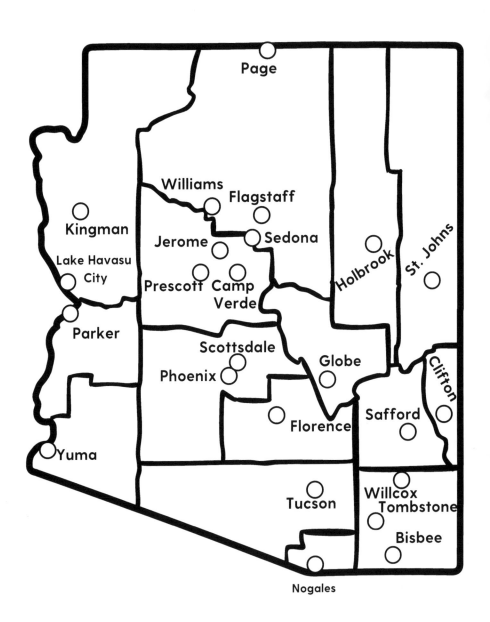

Page

Williams
Flagstaff
Kingman
Jerome
Sedona
Lake Havasu
City
Holbrook
St. Johns
Prescott
Camp
Verde
Parker
Scottsdale
Globe
Clifton
Phoenix
Safford
Florence
Yuma
Tucson
Willcox
Tombstone
Bisbee
Nogales

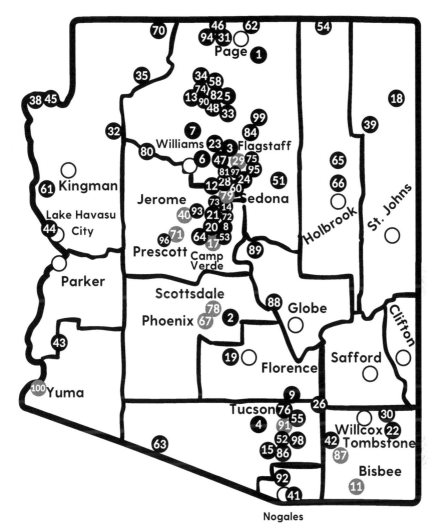

Page 1

Williams 70 35 32 46 94 31 62 54

34 58 74 13 90 82 5 48 33

99 84

7 23 3 Flagstaff 18

80 6 47 29 75 39

81 97 95 65

12 28 24 51 66

73 79 60 Sedona

Jerome 40 93 14

21 72 Holbrook St. Johns

96 71 64 20 8 89

17 53

Kingman 61 38 45

Lake Havasu 44 City

Prescott Camp Verde

Parker 43

Scottsdale

78 Globe Clifton

Phoenix 67 2 88

19 Safford

Florence

Yuma 100 9 26 30

Tucson 76 Willcox 22

4 55 Tombstone

63 91 42

52 98 87

15 86 Bisbee 11

92

41

Nogales

● Bisbee

25

● Phoenix

16 **27** **36** **37** **56** **57** **68** **83**

● Tombstone

10 **59**

● Scottsdale

49 **50** **85**

● Tucson

69 **77**

1	Antelope Canyon	**33**	Grand Canyon Desert View Watchtower
2	Apache Trail	**34**	Grand Canyon National Park
3	Arizona Snowbowl	**35**	Havasu Falls
4	Arizona-Sonora Desert Museum	**36**	Heard Museum
5	Beamer Trail	**37**	Hole in the Rock
6	Bearizona Wildlife Park	**38**	Hoover Dam
7	Bedrock City	**39**	Hubbell Trading Post National Historic Site
8	Bell Rock	**40**	Jerome
9	Biosphere 2	**41**	Juan Bautista de Anza National Historic Trail
10	Bird Cage Theatre	**42**	Kartchner Caverns State Park
11	Bisbee	**43**	Kofa National Wildlife Refuge
12	Boynton Canyon Trail	**44**	Lake Havasu State Park
13	Bright Angel Trail	**45**	Lake Mead National Recreation Area
14	Broken Arrow Trail	**46**	Lake Powell
15	Butterfield Overland National Historic Trail	**47**	Lowell Observatory
16	Camelback Mountain	**48**	Mather Point
17	Camp Verde	**49**	McCormick-Stillman Railroad Park
18	Canyon de Chelly National Monument	**50**	McDowell Sonoran Preserve
19	Casa Grande Ruins	**51**	Meteor Crater National Landmark
20	Cathedral Rock	**52**	Mission San Xavier del Bac
21	Chapel of the Holy Cross	**53**	Montezuma Castle National Monument and Tuzigoot
22	Chiricahua National Monument	**54**	Monument Valley Navajo Tribal Park
23	Coconino Lava River Cave	**55**	Mt. Lemmon Scenic Byway
24	Coconino National Forest	**56**	Musical Instrument Museum
25	Copper Queen Mine Tour	**57**	Mystery Castle
26	Coronado National Forest	**58**	North Kaibab Trail
27	Desert Botanical Garden	**59**	O.K. Corral
28	Devil's Bridge Trail	**60**	Oak Creek Canyon
29	Flagstaff	**61**	Oatman Ghost Town
30	Fort Bowie	**62**	Old Spanish National Historic Trail
31	Glen Canyon National Recreation Area	**63**	Organ Pipe Cactus National Monument
32	Grand Canyon Caverns and Grotto	**64**	Out of Africa Wildlife Park

PLACE NAME	CITY	COUNTY	VISITED
Antelope Canyon	Page n.c.	Coconino	
Apache Trail	Apache Junction	Maricopa, Pinal	
Arizona Snowbowl	Flagstaff n.c.	Coconino	
Arizona-Sonora Desert Museum	Tucson n.c.	Pima	
Beamer Trail	Flagstaff n.c.	Coconino	
Bearizona Wildlife Park	Williams n.c.	Coconino	
Bedrock City	Williams n.c.	Coconino	
Bell Rock	Sedona n.c.	Yavapai	
Biosphere 2	Oracle	Pinal	
Bird Cage Theatre	Tombstone	Cochise	
Bisbee	Bisbee	Cochise	
Boynton Canyon Trail	Sedona n.c.	Coconino	
Bright Angel Trail	Flagstaff n.c.	Coconino	
Broken Arrow Trail	Sedona	Yavapai	
Butterfield Overland National Historic Trail	Tucson n.c.	Cochise, Maricopa, Pima, Pinal, Yuma	
Camelback Mountain	Phoenix	Maricopa	
Camp Verde	Camp Verde	Yavapai	
Canyon de Chelly National Monument	Chinle n.c.	Apache	
Casa Grande Ruins	Coolidge	Pinal	
Cathedral Rock	Sedona n.c.	Yavapai	
Chapel of the Holy Cross	Sedona n.c.	Yavapai	
Chiricahua National Monument	Willcox n.c.	Cochise	
Coconino Lava River Cave	Flagstaff n.c.	Coconino	
Coconino National Forest	Flagstaff n.c.	Coconino, Gila, Yavapai	
Copper Queen Mine Tour	Bisbee	Cochise	
Coronado National Forest	Tucson n.c.	Cochise, Graham, Pima, Pinal, Santa Cruz	
Desert Botanical Garden	Phoenix	Maricopa	
Devil's Bridge Trail	Sedona n.c.	Yavapai	

*n.c. - nearest city

PLACE NAME	CITY	COUNTY	VISITED
Flagstaff	Flagstaff	Coconino	
Fort Bowie	Willcox n.c.	Cochise	
Glen Canyon National Recreation Area	Page n.c.	Coconino	
Grand Canyon Caverns and Grotto	Peach Springs	Mohave	
Grand Canyon Desert View Watchtower	Flagstaff n.c.	Coconino	
Grand Canyon National Park	Flagstaff n.c.	Coconino, Mohave	
Havasu Falls	Peach Springs n.c.	Mohave	
Heard Museum	Phoenix	Maricopa	
Hole in the Rock	Phoenix	Maricopa	
Hoover Dam	Kingman n.c.	Mohave	
Hubbell Trading Post National Historic Site	Holbrook n.c.	Apache	
Jerome	Jerome	Yavapai	
Juan Bautista de Anza National Historic Trail	Nogales	Pima, Pinal, Santa Cruz	
Kartchner Caverns State Park	Benson n.c.	Cochise	
Kofa National Wildlife Refuge	Yuma n.c.	La Paz, Yuma	
Lake Havasu State Park	Lake Havasu City	Mohave	
Lake Mead National Recreation Area	Kingman n.c.	Mohave	
Lake Powell	Page n.c.	Coconino	
Lowell Observatory	Flagstaff	Coconino	
Mather Point	Flagstaff n.c.	Coconino	
McCormick-Stillman Railroad Park	Scottsdale	Maricopa	
McDowell Sonoran Preserve	Scottsdale	Maricopa	
Meteor Crater National Landmark	Flagstaff n.c.	Coconino	
Mission San Xavier del Bac	Tucson n.c.	Pima	
Montezuma Castle National Monument and Tuzigoot	Camp Verde n.c.	Yavapai	
Monument Valley Navajo Tribal Park	Page n.c.	Navajo	
Mt. Lemmon Scenic Byway	Tucson n.c.	Pima	
Musical Instrument Museum	Phoenix	Maricopa	

*n.c. - nearest city

PLACE NAME	CITY	COUNTY	VISITED
Mystery Castle	Phoenix	Maricopa	
North Kaibab Trail	Jacob Lake n.c.	Coconino	
O.K. Corral	Tombstone	Cochise	
Oak Creek Canyon	Sedona n.c.	Yavapai	
Oatman Ghost Town	Oatman	Mohave	
Old Spanish National Historic Trail	Page n.c.	Apache, Coconino, Mohave, Navajo	
Organ Pipe Cactus National Monument	Ajo n.c.	Pima	
Out of Africa Wildlife Park	Camp Verde	Yavapai	
Painted Desert	Holbrook n.c.	Navajo	
Petrified Forest National Park	Holbrook n.c.	Navajo	
Phoenix	Phoenix	Maricopa	
Phoenix Art Museum	Phoenix	Maricopa	
Pima Air and Space Museum	Tucson	Pima	
Pipe Spring National Monument	Fredonia n.c.	Mohave	
Prescott	Prescott	Yavapai	
Red Rock Scenic Byway	Sedona n.c.	Coconino, Yavapai	
Red Rock State Park	Sedona n.c.	Yavapai	
Rim Trail	Flagstaff n.c.	Coconino	
Route 66	Flagstaff n.c.	Apache, Coconino, Mohave, Navajo, Yavapi	
Sabino Canyon	Tucson n.c.	Pima	
Saguaro National Park	Tucson	Pima	
Scottsdale	Scottsdale	Maricopa	
Sedona	Sedona	Coconino, Yavapai	
Seligman	Seligman	Yavapai	
Slide Rock State Park	Sedona n.c.	Coconino	
South Kaibab Trail	Flagstaff n.c.	Coconino	
South Mountain Park	Phoenix	Maricopa	
Sunset Crater Volcano National Monument	Flagstaff n.c.	Coconino	

*n.c. - nearest city

PLACE NAME	CITY	COUNTY	VISITED
Taliesin West	Scottsdale	Maricopa	
Titan Missile Museum	Sahuarita	Pima	
Tombstone	Tombstone	Cochise	
Tonto National Monument	Globe *n.c.*	Gila	
Tonto Natural Bridge State Park	Payson *n.c.*	Gila	
Trail of Time	Flagstaff *n.c.*	Coconino	
Tucson	Tucson	Pima	
Tumacácori National Historical Park	Nogales *n.c.*	Santa Cruz	
Tuzigoot National Monument	Cottonwood *n.c.*	Yavapai	
Vermilion Cliffs National Monument	Page *n.c.*	Coconino	
Walnut Canyon National Monument	Flagstaff *n.c.*	Coconino	
Watson Lake	Prescott	Yavapai	
West Fork Oak Creek Trail	Sedona *n.c.*	Coconino	
Wineries in Southern Arizona	Tucson *n.c.*	Pima	
Wupatki National Monument	Flagstaff *n.c.*	Coconino	
Yuma	Yuma	Yuma	

*n.c. - nearest city

COUNTY	CITY	PLACE NAME	VISITED
Apache	Chinle n.c.	Canyon de Chelly National Monument	
Apache	Holbrook n.c.	Hubbell Trading Post National Historic Site	
Apache, Coconino, Mohave, Navajo	Page n.c.	Old Spanish National Historic Trail	
Apache, Coconino, Mohave, Navajo, Yavapi	Flagstaff n.c.	Route 66	
Cochise	Tombstone	Bird Cage Theatre	
Cochise	Bisbee	Bisbee	
Cochise	Willcox n.c.	Chiricahua National Monument	
Cochise	Bisbee	Copper Queen Mine Tour	
Cochise	Willcox n.c.	Fort Bowie	
Cochise	Benson n.c.	Kartchner Caverns State Park	
Cochise	Tombstone	O.K. Corral	
Cochise	Tombstone	Tombstone	
Cochise, Graham, Pima, Pinal, Santa Cruz	Tucson n.c.	Coronado National Forest	
Cochise, Maricopa, Pima, Pinal, Yuma	Tucson n.c.	Butterfield Overland National Historic Trail	
Coconino	Page n.c.	Antelope Canyon	
Coconino	Flagstaff n.c.	Arizona Snowbowl	
Coconino	Flagstaff n.c.	Beamer Trail	
Coconino	Williams n.c.	Bearizona Wildlife Park	
Coconino	Williams n.c.	Bedrock City	
Coconino	Sedona n.c.	Boynton Canyon Trail	
Coconino	Flagstaff n.c.	Bright Angel Trail	
Coconino	Flagstaff n.c.	Coconino Lava River Cave	
Coconino	Flagstaff	Flagstaff	
Coconino	Page n.c.	Glen Canyon National Recreation Area	
Coconino	Flagstaff n.c.	Grand Canyon Desert View Watchtower	
Coconino	Page n.c.	Lake Powell	
Coconino	Flagstaff	Lowell Observatory	
Coconino	Flagstaff n.c.	Mather Point	

*n.c. - nearest city

COUNTY	CITY	PLACE NAME	VISITED
Coconino	Flagstaff n.c.	Meteor Crater National Landmark	
Coconino	Jacob Lake n.c.	North Kaibab Trail	
Coconino	Flagstaff n.c.	Rim Trail	
Coconino	Sedona n.c.	Slide Rock State Park	
Coconino	Flagstaff n.c.	South Kaibab Trail	
Coconino	Flagstaff n.c.	Sunset Crater Volcano National Monument	
Coconino	Flagstaff n.c.	Trail of Time	
Coconino	Page n.c.	Vermilion Cliffs National Monument	
Coconino	Flagstaff n.c.	Walnut Canyon National Monument	
Coconino	Sedona n.c.	West Fork Oak Creek Trail	
Coconino	Flagstaff n.c.	Wupatki National Monument	
Coconino, Gila, Yavapai	Flagstaff n.c.	Coconino National Forest	
Coconino, Mohave	Flagstaff n.c.	Grand Canyon National Park	
Coconino, Yavapai	Sedona n.c.	Red Rock Scenic Byway	
Coconino, Yavapai	Sedona	Sedona	
Gila	Globe n.c.	Tonto National Monument	
Gila	Payson n.c.	Tonto Natural Bridge State Park	
La Paz, Yuma	Yuma n.c.	Kofa National Wildlife Refuge	
Maricopa	Phoenix	Camelback Mountain	
Maricopa	Phoenix	Desert Botanical Garden	
Maricopa	Phoenix	Heard Museum	
Maricopa	Phoenix	Hole in the Rock	
Maricopa	Scottsdale	McCormick-Stillman Railroad Park	
Maricopa	Scottsdale	McDowell Sonoran Preserve	
Maricopa	Phoenix	Musical Instrument Museum	
Maricopa	Phoenix	Mystery Castle	
Maricopa	Phoenix	Phoenix	
Maricopa	Phoenix	Phoenix Art Museum	

*n.c. - nearest city

COUNTY	CITY	PLACE NAME	VISITED
Maricopa	Scottsdale	Scottsdale	
Maricopa	Phoenix	South Mountain Park	
Maricopa	Scottsdale	Taliesin West	
Maricopa, Pinal	Apache Junction	Apache Trail	
Mohave	Peach Springs	Grand Canyon Caverns and Grotto	
Mohave	Peach Springs *n.c.*	Havasu Falls	
Mohave	Kingman *n.c.*	Hoover Dam	
Mohave	Lake Havasu City	Lake Havasu State Park	
Mohave	Kingman *n.c.*	Lake Mead National Recreation Area	
Mohave	Oatman	Oatman Ghost Town	
Mohave	Fredonia *n.c.*	Pipe Spring National Monument	
Navajo	Page *n.c.*	Monument Valley Navajo Tribal Park	
Navajo	Holbrook *n.c.*	Painted Desert	
Navajo	Holbrook *n.c.*	Petrified Forest National Park	
Pima	Tucson *n.c.*	Arizona-Sonora Desert Museum	
Pima	Tucson *n.c.*	Mission San Xavier del Bac	
Pima	Tucson *n.c.*	Mt. Lemmon Scenic Byway	
Pima	Ajo	Organ Pipe Cactus National Monument	
Pima	Tucson	Pima Air and Space Museum	
Pima	Tucson *n.c.*	Sabino Canyon	
Pima	Tucson	Saguaro National Park	
Pima	Tucson	Tucson	
Pima	Tucson *n.c.*	Wineries in Southern Arizona	
Pima	Sahuarita	Titan Missile Museum	
Pima, Pinal, Santa Cruz	Nogales	Juan Bautista de Anza National Historic Trail	
Pinal	Oracle	Biosphere 2	
Pinal	Coolidge	Casa Grande Ruins	
Santa Cruz	Nogales *n.c.*	Tumacácori National Historical Park	

*n.c. - nearest city

COUNTY	CITY	PLACE NAME	VISITED
Yavapai	Sedona *n.c.*	Bell Rock	
Yavapai	Sedona	Broken Arrow Trail	
Yavapai	Camp Verde	Camp Verde	
Yavapai	Sedona *n.c.*	Cathedral Rock	
Yavapai	Sedona *n.c.*	Chapel of the Holy Cross	
Yavapai	Sedona *n.c.*	Devil's Bridge Trail	
Yavapai	Jerome	Jerome	
Yavapai	Camp Verde *n.c.*	Montezuma Castle National Monument and Tuzigoot	
Yavapai	Sedona *n.c.*	Oak Creek Canyon	
Yavapai	Camp Verde	Out of Africa Wildlife Park	
Yavapai	Prescott	Prescott	
Yavapai	Sedona *n.c.*	Red Rock State Park	
Yavapai	Seligman	Seligman	
Yavapai	Cottonwood *n.c.*	Tuzigoot National Monument	
Yavapai	Prescott	Watson Lake	
Yuma	Yuma	Yuma	

*n.c. - nearest city

ANTELOPE CANYON

COUNTY: COCONINO   CITY: PAGE *n.c.*

DATE VISITED:	WHO I WENT WITH:

RATING: ☆ ☆ ☆ ☆ ☆   WILL I RETURN? YES / NO

Antelope Canyon, a breathtaking marvel of nature and a popular destination for tourists, is renowned for its sleek, undulating sandstone walls that shimmer in the sunlight streaming from above. Located in the heart of the American Southwest, this narrow and deep slot canyon was formed over countless years as water carved its way through the rock.

Located in the northernmost region of Arizona, Antelope Canyon is situated within the expansive Navajo Nation, covering an area roughly equivalent to the size of West Virginia. It holds a central position in the Grand Circle, a region that encompasses other breathtaking attractions such as Monument Valley, the Grand Canyon, and Zion National Park.

Antelope Canyon consists of two distinct segments: Upper Antelope Canyon, referred to as "The Crack," and Lower Antelope Canyon, known as "The Corkscrew." The mesmerizing, undulating formations of the sandstone, shaped by erosion over thousands of years, showcase captivating patterns of colors, lights, and shadows. This spectacle draws photographers and nature enthusiasts from across the globe. A visit to Antelope Canyon provides a unique opportunity to immerse oneself in the natural beauty of the Earth while also granting convenient access to other iconic wonders in the surrounding area.

Antelope Canyon holds profound historical and cultural importance for the Navajo community, whose ancestral lands encompass the canyon. Beyond being a striking geological wonder, it is a sacred site embodying the enduring traditions and spiritual beliefs of the Navajo Nation.

The Navajo designation for Upper Antelope Canyon is "Tsé bighánílíní," signifying "the place where water runs through rocks," reflecting the canyon's formation through the gradual erosion caused by flash floods over numerous centuries. Lower Antelope Canyon, or "Hazdistazí," translates to "spiral rock arches," encapsulating the unique shapes and curves intricately carved into the sandstone. The English name "Antelope Canyon" originates from the presence of herds of Pronghorn Antelope that once roamed the region.

For the Navajo people, Antelope Canyon holds spiritual significance. The fluid contours of the sandstone, the interplay of light and shadow throughout the day, and the serene, secluded atmosphere within the slots collectively create a feeling of reverence and tranquility. The canyon is regarded as a monument to the potency of natural forces and the relentless passage of time, themes deeply ingrained in Navajo culture.

Antelope Canyon, akin to other slot canyons, underwent a prolonged formation spanning millions of years, shaped by a dual process of erosion. The Navajo Sandstone constituting the canyon initially experienced erosion through flash floods laden with debris, akin to sandpaper, cutting through the layers of rock. This prolonged action over time carved the canyon's deep and narrow passages. Rainwater, particularly during monsoon seasons, rushes into the vast basin above the sections of the slot canyon, gaining momentum and carrying sand as it flows into the narrow passages, gradually deepening and sculpting them.

The second phase, known as subaerial erosion, involves the natural weathering of rock faces exposed to wind and thermal stress. Over the course of thousands of years, these processes synergize to produce the smooth, undulating shapes and 'waves' in the rock that have become the hallmark of the canyon's renown.

When contemplating a visit to Upper versus Lower Antelope Canyon, there are several factors to take into account.

Upper Antelope Canyon, also known as "The Crack," stands out as the more frequently visited option, primarily because of its ground-level entrance that requires no climbing. The canyon walls soar to a height of 120 feet above the stream bed, rendering it impressively deep but relatively short in length. Direct sunlight penetrates the narrow canyon, casting a luminous glow on the contoured sandstone walls and generating mesmerizing light beams during specific times of the day and year.

On the other hand, Lower Antelope Canyon, referred to as "The Corkscrew," involves some maneuvering, including staircases and narrow passages. It boasts a longer, narrower, and more intricate layout compared to the upper section. In Lower Antelope Canyon, sunlight tends to be diffused and indirect, producing a subtler, glowing effect on the sandstone walls.

Each section offers distinctive perspectives and experiences, making the choice between them often dependent on personal preferences, physical fitness level, and photography interests.

The ideal time to visit Antelope Canyon depends on the type of experience you're seeking—whether you're an avid photographer in pursuit of perfect lighting, a nature enthusiast looking to avoid crowds, or a first-time visitor eager to witness the canyon's overall beauty.

Antelope Canyon witnesses hot, dry summers and cool winters. Spring (March to May) and Fall (September to November) are considered the most comfortable seasons, featuring mild temperatures that enhance the enjoyment of exploration. Summer (June to August) can be notably hot, with temperatures occasionally exceeding 100°F. Winter

(December to February) brings colder conditions, with temperatures potentially dropping below freezing, especially during the night.

The period from June to September marks the monsoon season in the region, introducing the possibility of thunderstorms and heavy rainfall. Flash floods pose a risk during this time, occasionally leading to the closure of the canyon due to safety concerns.

For photography enthusiasts, the time of day significantly influences the quality of images. In Upper Antelope Canyon, the most sought-after moment occurs around midday when sunlight directly penetrates the canyon, highlighting the swirling patterns in the rock and creating dramatic light shafts. This phenomenon typically takes place from late March to early October. Lower Antelope Canyon offers more diffused and consistent light throughout the day, resulting in stunning photographs.

The peak tourist season at Antelope Canyon spans from late spring to early fall, aligning with optimal photographic conditions. During this period, the canyon can become quite crowded, and tours may sell out quickly. Nevertheless, Lower Antelope Canyon has a one-way traffic system, and group sizes are limited to 15 people at a time.

Reaching Antelope Canyon is a straightforward process once you familiarize yourself with the available options.

Airports:

Page Municipal Airport (PGA): Situated in Page, Arizona, this airport is the closest to Antelope Canyon. However, it has very limited flight options and few (if any) rental cars.
Flagstaff Pulliam Airport (FLG): Located in Flagstaff, Arizona, approximately 135 miles from Antelope Canyon.
Phoenix Sky Harbor International Airport (PHX): Situated in Phoenix, Arizona, approximately 280 miles from Antelope Canyon.

Car rentals are accessible at all these airports, but availability may be scarce or expensive during peak seasons. The drive duration varies from 2 to 4 hours, depending on the chosen airport.

As Antelope Canyon is within the Navajo Nation Reservation, independent exploration is not permitted. Visitors MUST be accompanied by an authorized guide.

Consider opting for Grand Canyon Adventures' daily guided Antelope Canyon tour, which also includes a visit to Horseshoe Bend. Departing from Flagstaff, this excursion allows you to witness two of the most spectacular sights in the Southwest. With transportation taken care of, professional guides accompany you throughout the journey. The Antelope Canyon & Horseshoe Bend tour covers entrance fees, lunch, drinks, and even a stop at Glen Canyon Dam for a stunning view of the Colorado River and Lake Powell. Booking this tour well in advance is advisable, especially during busier periods (generally March to September), as they are likely to sell out.

Antelope Canyon, although breathtaking, presents natural hazards and safety considerations that visitors should be mindful of.

Flash Floods: The canyon is susceptible to flash floods, particularly during the monsoon season from July to September. Tours are canceled if there's a risk of flooding, and while re-entry into the canyon is generally possible within a day or two, it is advisable to plan for additional time and flexibility during the monsoon season.

Stay Hydrated: The Arizona desert can be intensely hot and dry. It is recommended to bring at least double the amount of water you anticipate needing.

Dress in Layers: Desert temperatures can vary significantly between day and night. Dressing in layers is advised to be prepared for the hot midday sun and potentially cool early mornings and evenings. During the summer, it's recommended to wear light, breathable clothing that covers your skin for sun protection. Additionally, a wide-brimmed hat, sunglasses, and sunscreen are essential.

Footwear: Wear durable, comfortable shoes, as the terrain involves walking on sandy and uneven surfaces. Opt for hiking boots or sports shoes with good grip for the best experience.

It's important to note that Lower Antelope Canyon requires navigating several metal staircases, and both canyons entail walking through narrow passageways. Individuals with mobility issues should take this into account when planning their visit. Neither Upper nor Lower Antelope Canyon is wheelchair accessible.

APACHE TRAIL

COUNTY: MARICOPA, PINAL | **CITY:** APACHE JUNCTION

DATE VISITED: | **WHO I WENT WITH:**

RATING: ☆ ☆ ☆ ☆ ☆ | **WILL I RETURN?** YES / NO

Arizona's Apache Trail is a treasure trove of tourist opportunities, offering a variety of experiences such as a scenic desert drive, family outings, or a day by the lake.

The trail derives its name from the Apache Indians, who initially used it for navigation through the Superstition Mountains. Evolving into a stagecoach route in the early 1900s, the trail now meanders through both the Superstition Mountains and Tonto National Forest.

Officially designated as Arizona State Route 88, the Apache Trail spans a 40-mile journey, commencing in Apache Junction and concluding at Theodore Roosevelt Dam. The road features numerous twists, switchbacks, and sharp turns, warranting caution for inexperienced drivers. Upon reaching the trail's end, visitors can choose to retrace their route or proceed onto the circle route, guiding them back through Globe.

It's essential to be aware that the trail is only partially paved, although well-maintained. Most reliable vehicles should be able to navigate the drive, but it's advisable to avoid taking RVs beyond Tortilla Flat due to the challenging terrain.

The 40-mile stretch of the Apache Trail is dotted with numerous scenic stops and engaging activities, offering the flexibility of being a short afternoon outing or a full-day adventure, depending on the chosen stops. Here are recommendations for stops along the trail, listed in the order they appear:

Goldfield Ghost Town (4.5 miles from Apache Junction): A reconstructed 1890s ghost town with attractions such as tours of a defunct gold mine, Old West gunfights, a history museum, gold panning, a narrow-gauge train, and a reptile exhibit. Some attractions may have a small fee, but access to the ghost town is free. The Mammoth Steakhouse and Saloon offer a nostalgic dining option.

Lost Dutchman State Park: A 320-acre state park with trails into the wilderness surrounding the Superstition Mountains. A small entrance fee per car is applicable. Popular for hiking, camping, and RVs, named after a legend about a lost gold mine.

Canyon Lake: The most scenic of the three man-made lakes along the trail, featuring a large marina, sandy beaches, an RV park, and campgrounds. Surrounded by dramatic red rock cliffs, providing opportunities to spot bighorn sheep or bald eagles. Activities include boat rentals and Dolly Steamboat tours.

Tortilla Flat: Founded in 1904 as a stagecoach stop, retaining its historic charm with a saloon, restaurant, country store, and mercantile shop. Known for prickly pear gelato and claims a population of six people. Recommended turnaround point for inexperienced drivers or those preferring paved roads.

Fish Creek Hill: A challenging yet scenic drive from Tortilla Flat to the Fish Creek Hill Viewpoint, offering dramatic Sonoran Desert vistas.
RVs and large trailers are discouraged, and caution is advised.

Apache Lake: Less crowded than Canyon Lake due to its isolated location, offering a scenic overlook, fishing, and camping grounds.

Theodore Roosevelt Dam: Marks the end of the Apache Trail, a massive cement structure constructed between 1905 and 1911 to control the Salt River flow. Turnaround point to head back via the Apache Trail or continue east on Arizona State Route 188 toward Globe.

Tonto National Monument: Along AZ 188 toward Globe, passing Tonto National Monument in Tonto National Forest. Features two ancient Native American cliff dwellings dating back 700 years. The Lower Cliff Dwelling is open year-round, accessible via a steep, 0.5-mile paved path. The Upper Cliff Dwelling is accessible only by guided tour from November through April on weekends.

Tips for Your Visit:

Spring is arguably the optimal time to drive the Apache Trail when wildflowers are abundant, weather permitting. However, the trail remains open year-round.

Be cautious about inclement weather, as certain trail sections are prone to flash flooding. If adverse weather is forecasted, consider rescheduling for a drier day.

Due to being a popular tourist attraction, expect varying levels of driving experience on the trail. Utilize viewing points and turn-offs, keeping the road clear, and exercise caution as some sections are steep, winding, and feature cliff drop-offs.

Access to AZ 88 is free, and most trail attractions do not have entrance fees.

For water recreational activities, Canyon Lake is recommended, offering facilities and accessibility for various vehicles and trailers.

While there are no hotels along the Apache Trail, there are excellent campgrounds. Nearby accommodations can be found in Apache Junction or Globe.

Getting There:

The Apache Trail commences about 50 minutes east of downtown Phoenix, just outside Apache Junction. Continuing beyond the trail's end and heading east onto AZ 188 leads to the city of Globe, completing a 120-mile circle route.

ARIZONA SNOWBOWL

DATE VISITED: | WHO I WENT WITH:

RATING: ☆ ☆ ☆ ☆ ☆ | WILL I RETURN? YES / NO

Arizona Snowbowl is an expansive ski resort sprawled across the San Francisco Peaks, boasting an elevation of 11,500 feet. Offering a diverse range of ski runs, gondola rides, and forest trails for hiking, the resort is a haven for outdoor enthusiasts. The annual snowfall averages 260 inches, and the ski season extends from November to April, providing a perfect winter playground for families and thrill-seekers alike.

For both novice skiers and seasoned snowboarders, the resort presents 32 runs, catering to different skill levels with green, blue, and black diamond paths. Beginners can commence their skiing journey at the Little Spruce conveyer belt, progressing to the Hart Prairie lift for wider spaces with fewer crowds. Advanced winter athletes can ascend the Humphrey's Peak lift, unlocking exhilarating ski excursions. The Snowbowl's trail map allows visitors to customize their adventure.

The Snowburners program offers skiing and snowboarding classes for children aged four to 12, ensuring a fun and educational experience. Adult classes, including a free Snow Experience lesson for first-time skiers aged 13 and older, are also available.

Situated just a 7-mile drive from Flagstaff, Arizona Snowbowl is easily accessible via Highway 180 and Snowbowl Road. The resort has two parking lots at the base locations —Hart Prairie and Agassiz base areas. Overnight parking is permitted for visitors engaged in hiking the surrounding outdoor trails.

The Mountain Line Express Shuttle provides complimentary transportation to Snowbowl from downtown Flagstaff, offering a convenient direct ride service during winter months.

Lift entry costs vary with the ski season, and visitors can purchase tickets in advance or at the base areas. Season passes offer various multi-day features and discounts on online tickets, while children aged ten and under receive free season passes. March is recommended for ticket purchases, providing discounts on lift admission, classes, and rentals. Operating from 10:00 a.m. to 4:00 p.m. daily, Arizona Snowbowl provides a range of amenities, including delectable dining options, high-quality rental equipment, and public lockers.

For a more immersive experience, consider staying at the Basecamp at Snowbowl cabins, featuring gas fireplaces and charming front porches. Preparing for your winter adventure is made easy with a selection of onsite restaurants, sports shops for skiing gear, and nearby casual eateries in Flagstaff.

ARIZONA-SONORA DESERT MUSEUM

COUNTY: PIMA   CITY: TUCSON *n.c.*

DATE VISITED: WHO I WENT WITH:

RATING: ☆ ☆ ☆ ☆ ☆   WILL I RETURN?   YES / NO

The Arizona-Sonora Desert Museum is not your typical indoor museum; it combines elements of a natural history museum, aquarium, botanical garden, zoo, art gallery, and the replication of a natural landscape all within one location. Spanning two miles of walking paths through desert habitats, the museum features approximately 230 animal species, over 1,200 types of plants, and an extensive mineral collection. Located in the Tucson area, this destination is a must-see and ranks among the top museums nationwide.

Established in 1952, the museum's history celebrates the uniqueness and beauty of the desert. Diverse exhibits, including the Walk-In Aviary, Cat Canyon, Cactus Gardens, Warden Aquarium, Hummingbird Aviary, and Packrat Playhouse, provide a comprehensive experience. Visitors can also enjoy Stingray Touch, the Riparian Corridor, and the Desert Loop Trail during their museum visit. Live animal demonstrations are regular occurrences, showcasing raptors in flight and offering educational presentations about big horn sheep, snakes, parrots, and other desert animals.

With about 85 percent of the museum outdoors, it's advisable to plan visits during the early morning or late afternoon, particularly between May and September, to avoid the heat of the day. Spring, when cacti are in bloom, is a particularly delightful time to explore. Free sunscreen is conveniently provided in most museum restrooms. Please note that pets are not permitted on the museum grounds or in the parking lot, so it's recommended to leave them at home in a comfortable environment with proper ventilation.

The Art Institute at the museum showcases numerous art exhibits and offers art classes, drawing inspiration from the captivating desert landscapes that have inspired artists worldwide. After exploring the exhibits under the sun, visitors can enjoy refreshments at various dining options within the museum, such as Ironwood Terraces, Ocotillo Café, Phoebe's Coffee Bar, and the Cottonwood for drinks and ice cream. The museum welcomes visitors every day of the year, operating from 8:30 am to 5 pm between October and February, and from 7:30 am to 5 pm between March and September. Due to the extensive offerings, plan to allocate at least two hours for your visit.

BEAMER TRAIL

At river mile 61.5, the Little Colorado River converges with the primary flow of the Colorado River. Since John Wesley Powell's pioneering exploration in 1869, this confluence has marked the conclusion of Marble Canyon and the official beginning of the Grand Canyon itself – the gateway to Powell's "Great Unknown." The scenery at this junction is extraordinary. When untouched by floodwaters, the Little Colorado mirrors the hue of the sky. Majestic, unbroken expanses of vibrant vertical stone rise 4000 feet to the rim, where two monumental canyon systems seamlessly unite. While the Grand Canyon is renowned for its routine extraordinariness, the Beamer Trail leading to the mouth of the Little Colorado River stands out as an exceptional example of canyon scenery.

Named after Ben Beamer, a pioneer, farmer, and miner active in eastern Grand Canyon during the early 1890s, the Beamer Trail pays homage to his endeavors. Beamer's attempts to cultivate crops and establish a residence near the mouth of the Little Colorado were unsuccessful. The mouth of Palisades Creek serves as a backdrop to various historical human activities. The infamous Horsethief Route, a river crossing downstream, facilitated the movement of stolen livestock from Utah to Arizona during the low water of winter before the construction of dams. Seth Tanner, renowned for the Tanner Trail, discovered and maintained silver and copper mining claims on both sides of the river. Other early pioneers, like George McCormick, joined these efforts, with optimistic name changes such as renaming the mine from Tanner to Copper Blossom.

The stretch between the Tanner Trail and Palisades Creek provides an opportunity to observe some of the oldest exposed sedimentary rocks in the Grand Canyon. Known as the Grand Canyon Supergroup, these rocks and dark lava flows boast vibrant colors and are estimated to be between 800 million and 1.2 billion years old. Identifiable by their distinct 20-degree tilt, the Supergroup adds a geological dimension to the rich history of this region.

The Colorado River stands as the sole dependable source of high-quality drinking water in the area. Access to the shoreline is available at various points between the Tanner Trail and Palisades Creek, as well as near the mouth of the Little Colorado River. However, the Colorado River often carries a substantial sediment load, posing challenges in purification. Despite the Little Colorado having permanent water in its lower stretches, the high mineral and sediment content renders it practically undrinkable.

The Beamer Trail falls within the "at-large" use area BA9, and it is encouraged to utilize existing campsites whenever feasible. There is one exception: the vicinity around the mouth of the Little Colorado River, within a ¼ mile of the confluence, is closed to overnight use to protect sensitive wildlife habitat. Optimal campsites are situated between the Tanner Trail junction and Palisades Creek, particularly on the beaches along the Colorado River. However, campsite options along the Tapeats rim between Palisades Canyon and the Little Colorado River are limited for small parties and non-existent for larger groups.

Visitors camping along the Colorado River are advised to urinate directly into the river to avoid fouling beaches for other hikers, as the scent of urine and associated algae growth can quickly become unpleasant. Human feces should be buried in a cat hole, 4-6 inches deep and at least 200 feet away from water, campsites, and trails. It is crucial to carry out all toilet paper and other trash to maintain the pristine condition of the environment.

The southward access to the area is facilitated by the Tanner Trail, while the Beamer Trail intersects with the Tanner Trail just above Tanner Rapids. Although it is feasible to reach the north end of the Beamer Trail via the Little Colorado River, navigating rim-to-river routes in this rarely visited gorge is consistently challenging and potentially perilous. The Little Colorado River drains a significant portion of northeastern Arizona and has the potential to generate floods with substantial sediment loads. Safe travel through this confined and flood-prone canyon system requires a current weather report, careful campsite selection, a conservative approach, and vigilant attention to the sky. Visitors utilizing Little Colorado River routes will need a permit to cross Navajo land.

Embarking on the Tanner Trail towards the river and proceeding upcanyon, one may encounter minor obstacles in the form of small outcroppings of Dox Sandstone, which generally have straightforward solutions. The path between Tanner Canyon and Palisades Creek is generally uncomplicated, with riparian vegetation denser near the shoreline, prompting the trail to veer slightly above the waterline where the brush transitions to rocky slopes.

The nature of the Beamer Trail undergoes a notable transformation at Palisades Canyon. What was once a relatively easy, straightline walk across sandy slopes becomes a challenging journey along narrow, exposed ledges at the brink of high cliffs. Tapeats Sandstone outcrops emerging from deep water necessitate a climb of about 300 vertical feet up the talus immediately north of the mouth of Palisades to reach the top of the Tapeats. This slope provides the only break in the sandstone cliff in the surrounding area, making it an obvious starting point. The top of the Tapeats serves as the route all the way to the Little Colorado. The trail is eroded, narrow, and, in some sections, remarkably exposed at the edge of an impressive precipice, requiring hikers to exercise caution. Those with a known fear of heights may find this trail segment challenging, resembling a junior version of the Tonto Trail as it contours around numerous small, steep gullies draining Palisades of the Desert. While the trail is generally well-defined, potential route-finding challenges may arise where the trail crosses drainages. Although it's possible to scramble down to walk the shoreline a quarter-mile below the confluence, the main trail adheres to the Tapeats rim all the way to the Little Colorado River.

BEARIZONA WILDLIFE PARK

COUNTY: COCONINO   CITY: WILLIAMS *n.c.*

DATE VISITED: WHO I WENT WITH:

RATING: ☆ ☆ ☆ ☆ ☆   WILL I RETURN? YES / NO

Amidst the ponderosa pines in Kaibab National Forest, Bearizona Wildlife Park provides a captivating spectacle as black bears, Alaskan tundra wolves, bighorn sheep, arctic wolves, jaguars, and bison freely wander, leaving human spectators in awe.

Situated approximately 33 miles west of Flagstaff, Bearizona offers an outdoor retreat featuring a 3-mile drive-thru route for observing its diverse collection of North American animals. Additionally, visitors can explore the 20-acre walk-thru area named Fort Bearizona.

Fort Bearizona serves as the residence for three grizzly cubs—Hanna, Sky, and Crockett. These cubs arrived at the park in the summer of 2020 under unfortunate circumstances. Their mother was shot by a hiker in a surprising encounter, leading to her euthanization due to severe injuries. After approval from Montana Fish, Wildlife & Parks and the U.S. Fish and Wildlife Service, Bearizona took on the responsibility of caring for these orphaned grizzly cubs, marking the park's first acquisition of grizzly bears.

The rapidly maturing cubs now inhabit the specially designed 29,000-square-foot Kinder Cubs habitat, featuring a waterfall, stream, and cave. This enclosure serves as their temporary residence while the construction of the Grizzly Encounter exhibit is underway. Anticipated to open in 2022, the new exhibit aims to be the "best grizzly bear enclosure in the country," boasting multiple levels, a 200-foot-tall cliff, two waterfalls, and underwater viewing areas, as envisioned by Animal Director Dave O'Connell.

Bearizona has made adjustments during the COVID-19 pandemic, closing certain attractions to facilitate social distancing. While Wild Ride Bus Tours and the petting zoo remain closed indefinitely, the Birds of Prey show has been replaced with "random surprise and delight encounters throughout the day." The gift shop and restaurant have reopened after a temporary closure last year.

Notably, ATVs and open-top vehicles are prohibited in the drive-thru area, emphasizing the importance of staying inside one's vehicle for safety.

Animal enthusiasts can encounter a variety of creatures, including black bears, Alaskan tundra wolves, arctic wolves, bighorn sheep, reindeer, bison, jaguars, pronghorn, javelina, foxes, and otters.

Bearizona operates from 8 a.m. to 7:30 p.m. daily, with the last cars admitted at 6 p.m. Visitors are encouraged to check the website for seasonal hours. For optimal wildlife viewing, mornings and late afternoons are recommended, especially during the hot summer months. Weekdays are preferable to avoid crowds, as Fridays, Saturdays, and Sundays tend to be more crowded.

Visitors have the flexibility to explore Bearizona at their preferred pace. The park suggests allocating approximately three hours for a comprehensive visit, although some guests choose to extend their stay.

Situated approximately 170 miles northwest of central Phoenix, Bearizona is located at 1500 E. Route 66 in Williams. To reach the park from Phoenix, take Interstate 17 to Flagstaff, then head west on I-40 to Exit 165 at Williams.

BEDROCK CITY

COUNTY: COCONINO   CITY: WILLIAMS   *n.c.*

DATE VISITED: WHO I WENT WITH:

RATING: ☆ ☆ ☆ ☆ ☆   WILL I RETURN?   YES / NO

Carved in stone and proudly displaying its prehistoric charm, Bedrock emerges as one of Arizona's most captivating roadside attractions, guaranteed to evoke a sense of nostalgia.

While the legendary Grand Canyon and the iconic Arizona Interstate 40, commonly known as the historic Route 66, draw masses of visitors to this region, there's a hidden gem just a short journey from the canyon that many are unaware of—one that both kids and adults find delightful.

Travelers exploring the Grand Canyon's South Rim and those cruising along Route 66 should be on the lookout for one of the country's most unique roadside attractions. Here, Instagrammable scenes and entertaining activities add a whimsical touch to the journey. If fantastic photo opportunities and a trip down memory lane sound appealing, consider adding Bedrock City to the itinerary for an ultimate dose of nostalgic feels.

Bedrock City, sometimes known as Flintstones Park, was constructed by Francis Jerome Speckels and opened its doors for the first time in 1972. It stands as a historic amusement park inspired by the popular cartoon, The Flintstones. The Flintstones, a globally acclaimed children's show, graced primetime television screens from 1960 to 1966, with reruns continuing for several decades. Even today, episodes of the series are still broadcasted by numerous global networks.

Featuring colorful buildings in vibrant hues, cartoon-like Paleolithic characters, and typical Flintstones vehicles with rock wheels, Bedrock City is a tangible representation and recreation of the beloved TV show. It preserves the legacy of The Flintstones in a wholesome way, offering families over the decades a special piece of Arizona history. Generations of children have had the chance to experience the likeness of their favorite prehistoric animated characters' home setting not just on the screen but in real life.

Similar Bedrock City attractions once existed near Mount Rushmore in South Dakota, opening in 1966 and closing for good in 2015. However, enthusiasts of The Flintstones can still explore Bedrock City in Arizona, making it the sole remaining place globally to stroll through the fictional abode of America's beloved ancient cartoon characters. Nonetheless, the journey wasn't without its challenges, and the cherished Bedrock was on the brink of being lost—almost.

In 2019, after five decades of existence, the Flintstones-themed Bedrock City was sold to Troy Morris and Ron Brown. The duo acquired the property from its original owner, who decided to retire. Initially, Morris and Brown intended to demolish Bedrock City and replace it with their own venture, Raptor Ranch—a sanctuary for captivating winged creatures such as eagles, falcons, owls, hawks, and more. True to their plans, Morris and Brown successfully opened Raptor Ranch, offering visitors demonstrations, flight shows, and insights into wildlife conservation and raptors from knowledgeable experts.

Despite the introduction of Raptor Ranch, Bedrock City continued to attract numerous tourists, leading the new owners to reconsider. In response to persistent visitor interest, they opted to keep Bedrock City open indefinitely alongside their newly established birds of prey operation. The outcome is Raptor Ranch, seamlessly blending wildlife experiences with nostalgic nods to childhood cartoons. It's a worthwhile stop on the way to or from the Grand Canyon, offering more than just 'yabba-Dabba-doos' and 'cuck-kaw!' cries. Moreover, Raptor Ranch features one of the closest campsites to the Grand Canyon outside the park's boundaries, making overnight accommodation a viable option for campers.

Visitors to the authentic Bedrock City should not anticipate a pre-packaged, manufactured experience akin to those offered by the United States' top amusement parks, such as Disney and Universal Studios. Instead, enthusiasts of Barney and friends are in for a trip down memory lane, traversing the dusty streets of Bedrock City to immerse themselves in a quirky yet familiar atmosphere—one that authentically captures the fun essence of the old Hanna-Barbera cartoon.

While park-goers revel in the excitement of Raptor Ranch and its impressive birds of prey, they can conclude the day by strolling through Bedrock's iconic landmarks, eliciting genuine feelings of nostalgia and providing ample opportunities for fun and memorable photo ops. From the prehistoric market, Bedrock School, and primitive train rides to Bedrock Post Office, the rudimentary Bedrock Jail, and Bedrock's Beauty Salon, the famed features of the fictional Old Stone Age town are faithfully reproduced in concrete or wood, contributing to the place's paleo-period charm.

Visitors can explore Fred and Wilma's house, along with numerous other Flintstones-themed replica homes adorned in vibrant, cartoon-like colors, each furnished with caveman décor that stays true to the original series. Stone-and-rock Flintstones vehicles are also on display throughout Bedrock, though their drivability remains questionable. Spread across three acres of desert landscape, other highlights include life-sized reproductions of beloved characters like Fred, Wilma, Barney, Betty, and Dino, as well as stone-age characters and dinosaurs scattered across the land.

No visit to Bedrock would be complete without a stop at Fred's Diner for some hearty grub. While the menu may not feature 'Bronto burgers' or 'brontosaurus ribs,' the funky eatery compensates with tasty American treats such as hot dogs, burgers, chicken tenders, pizza, onion ring baskets, and quesadillas.

Flintstones enthusiasts in the Grand Canyon National Park vicinity are in for a treat;

Raptor Ranch and its nostalgic counterpart, Bedrock City, are conveniently located just 24 miles or approximately half an hour's drive from the South Rim Entrance. Spotting this fantastic Arizona attraction is a breeze—simply keep an eye out for the prominent Flintstones signs along the route.

Visitors to the Grand Canyon, Bedrock City, and Raptor Ranch have various accommodation options, including stays within the Grand Canyon or nearby cities such as Flagstaff, Williams, or Tusayan. For the ultimate Flintstones and Raptor experience, there's the Raptor Ranch Campground and RV Park. Here, campers can overnight in a tent, RV, or travel trailer for a nominal fee, which includes admission to Bedrock City, raptor flight demonstrations, WiFi, laundry room access, and campfire rings.

The campground offers amenities like an on-site convenience store, showers, a gift shop, and overflow parking. With 32 RV sites and over 25 tent sites, there's ample space for those seeking an affordable night's sleep just 20 minutes from the Grand Canyon's South Rim entrance.

Bedrock City at Raptor Ranch is open seven days a week from 8 am until sunset, providing visitors with ample time to explore this quirky destination.

BELL ROCK

DATE VISITED: WHO I WENT WITH:

RATING: ☆ ☆ ☆ ☆ ☆   WILL I RETURN?   YES / NO

Bell Rock in Sedona stands as one of the city's most iconic rock formations, making it a prominent sight for travelers entering Sedona via Highway 179. Positioned just off the road, Bell Rock is not only a visually striking landmark but also an excellent location for hiking. Located south of downtown Sedona off Highway 179, the trailhead parking is approximately 3.6 miles south from the Route 89A and 179 intersection, around Milepost 309. If approaching from the Village of Oak Creek, travelers should head north on Highway 179, turning right onto Bell Rock Boulevard to access the main trailhead. The journey from Phoenix takes about 2 hours.

Despite the popularity of the Bell Rock hike, parking can be challenging due to its high demand. Visiting during early morning or late afternoon hours increases the likelihood of finding a parking spot. The parking lot experiences quick turnover, making it more manageable for patient visitors.

While the parking lot may be full, the trails themselves are not excessively busy, providing hikers with a relatively uncrowded experience. Passing occasional fellow hikers, visitors often find they have the trail to themselves.

There are three primary parking locations to access the Bell Rock Trail.

Bell Rock Trailhead North (Courthouse Vista Parking Lot):

Closest parking lot to Bell Rock, recommended as the primary choice. Considered a sizable parking area, albeit popular. Requires a Red Rock Pass or America the Beautiful Pass for parking. Red Rock Pass can be purchased on-site using a credit card. Amenities include vault toilets at this trailhead.

Yavapai Vista Point (Overflow Parking for Bell Rock Trailhead North):

Located about half a mile north of Bell Rock formation on the left side of the road. Offers a relatively large parking area, increasing the chances of finding a spot. Also serves as a parking area for Cathedral Rock, another popular Sedona hike. Requires a parking pass for access. Vaulted toilets are available. To reach Yavapai Vista Point, drive north along Highway 179, take the roundabout for Back O Beyond Road, and return along Highway 179 to the parking lot. The walk from Yavapai Vista Point to the Bell Rock Trail in Sedona takes approximately 10 minutes, requiring a crossing of Highway 179.

Bell Rock Trailhead South:

Positioned on the south side of Bell Rock, just north of Oak Creek. Offers parking with a 1-mile hike along the Bell Rock Pathway to reach Bell Rock. Farthest parking lot from Bell Rock. Requires a parking pass for access. Vaulted toilets are available. Choosing between these parking locations depends on factors such as proximity, availability, and preferences. Visitors should be aware of the specific requirements, including the need for parking passes and the availability of facilities at each trailhead.

Trail Information:

Bell Rock Climb and Courthouse Butte Loop Trail:

Distance: 4.5 miles
Elevation Gain: 750 feet
Difficulty: Moderate
Hiking Time: 2 to 3.5 hours

Bell Rock Climb:

Distance: 1 mile
Elevation Gain: 625 feet
Difficulty: Moderate
Hiking Time: 1 to 2 hours

If you choose to embark on the climb up Bell Rock only, the duration typically ranges from one to two hours, contingent on your hiking pace and the time spent at the summit.

For those inclined to hike up Bell Rock in Arizona and traverse the Courthouse Butte Loop trail, it's advisable to allocate three to four hours for the entire excursion.

The primary challenge lies in finding suitable spots to scramble up the red rocks since there isn't a clearly defined Bell Rock Trail.

Trails in the Vicinity of Bell Rock:

A climb up Bell Rock in Sedona can be seamlessly combined with other trails in the surrounding area, with notable options being the Bell Rock Pathway and the Courthouse Butte Loop.

Bell Rock Climb

The Bell Rock hiking trail is a delightful and favored choice for kids. If you park at the Bell Rock Trailhead North, head towards Bell Rock in Arizona and be on the lookout for the

"Bell Rock Climb" sign.

The initial section of the climb features baskets filled with rocks, serving as trail markers, guiding you for about a quarter-mile up Bell Rock before reaching higher levels. The last basket is beyond a large rock that requires climbing. Once past the markers, the trail becomes less defined, but it's easy to find your own path. Follow other hikers to the top, utilizing the worn-away sandstone for hand and footholds.

The central Slide area is a popular route up Bell Rock, with a second trail on the east side of the slide leading to the top of one of the spires. Caution is advised, as this is a steep and potentially dangerous hike, particularly beyond the markers, considered a Class 3 hike.

Bell Rock Trail/Bell Rock Pathway

The Red Rock Trail or Bell Rock Pathway stretches between the North and South parking areas for Bell Rock, running alongside Highway 179. Ideal for walking or biking, this 3.6-mile trail has a predominantly wide and hard surface, except for rougher sections near Bell Rock. If parking at the southern trailhead, follow the Bell Rock Trail to access the Bell Rock climb.

Courthouse Butte Loop

Also known as the Bell Rock Loop Trail, the Courthouse Butte Loop encircles Bell Rock and Courthouse Butte, two prominent rock formations in Sedona. Many trails branch off, but using Bell Rock as a marker ensures the correct direction, keeping Bell Rock on your right when hiking clockwise. The Courthouse Butte Trail is a wide gravel trail, offering views of the Sedona Valley, Bell Rock, and Courthouse Butte. Trail signs at crossroads, some labeled as Big Park Loop, assist navigation.

Bell Rock in Sedona Vortex

Bell Rock stands out as one of Sedona's well-known vortex sites, particularly the area known as the Upflow or Electric area. Recognized for its ability to evoke serenity and spiritual energy, it is a popular spot for yoga and spiritual activities. Classified as a powerful and full-energy vortex, the Bell Rock Vortex attracts those seeking a heightened spiritual experience.

On your climb up the Bell Rock trail in Sedona, you will turn to the right between the 10th and 11th rock baskets. This will take you across a large flat rock, and then you will see a place to climb up to what is known as the Meditation Perch. There is a bit of a scramble to get there. This is where the Bell Rock Vortex is.

The Bell Rock hiking trail remains open year-round, offering an enjoyable experience at any season. However, the optimal times for hiking are during the spring and fall due to favorable weather conditions. Although it tends to be busier during these seasons, the comfortable temperatures make for a pleasant experience.

Summer hiking offers fewer crowds but comes with warmer temperatures. Since there is no shade along the trail, it's essential to be well-prepared with sun protection and an ample water supply.

BIOSPHERE 2

COUNTY: PINAL   CITY: ORACLE

DATE VISITED: WHO I WENT WITH:

RATING: ☆ ☆ ☆ ☆ ☆   WILL I RETURN? YES / NO

Biosphere 2 enhances our comprehension of both natural and human-created ecosystems through comprehensive research. This research not only contributes to the exploration and creation of interventions that enhance the resilience and sustainability of Earth systems but also strives to improve the quality of human life. The Biosphere 2 conduct pioneering research in distinctive facilities, engage in interdisciplinary science education, and promote leadership initiatives with a focus on developing scalable solutions for both our planet and beyond.

The University of Arizona took ownership of Biosphere 2 in July 2011, and the Philecology Foundation generously supports its operations and certain research projects. Additionally, various grants and awards, primarily from the National Science Foundation, provide further backing for research endeavors.

In the 1800s, the Biosphere 2 property was part of the Samaniego CDO Ranch. Undergoing several ownership changes, it transformed into a conference center in the 1960s and 1970s, initially for Motorola and later for The University of Arizona. Space Biospheres Ventures acquired the property in 1984, initiating the construction of the current facility in 1986 to explore and develop self-sustaining space-colonization technology.

Between 1991 and 1994, two missions sealed Biospherians within the glass enclosure to assess survivability. Beyond being a highly publicized endeavor, this exercise yielded valuable research that contributed to ecological understanding. Former crew members have published various firsthand accounts offering different perspectives on the experiment.

In 1994, Decisions Investments Corporation took control of the property, and Columbia University managed it from 1996 to 2003. Columbia reconfigured the structure for a different approach to scientific research, including a study on the impact of carbon dioxide on plants. Classrooms and housing for college students of earth systems science were also built during this period.

The property was sold on June 4, 2007, to CDO Ranching and its development partners. They leased the property to UArizona from 2007 to 2011. Currently, the enclosure serves as a valuable tool supporting ongoing research by UArizona scientists. As a laboratory for large-scale projects, such as the Landscape Evolution Observatory, the university's stewardship of Biosphere 2 enables the undertaking of crucial experiments aimed at quantifying the consequences of global climate change.

Biosphere 2 Overview:

Biosphere 2 is a 3.14-acre research facility with a 40-acre campus, situated at an elevation of 3,820 feet above sea level. The facility is enclosed by sealed glass, comprising 6,500 windows and covering 7,200,000 cubic feet. Its highest point reaches 91 feet, and it is sealed from the earth below by a 500-ton welded stainless steel liner. The campus includes 300,000 square feet of administrative offices, classrooms, labs, conference center, and housing. Since 1991, Biosphere 2 has welcomed over 3,000,000 visitors, including more than 500,000 K-12 students. The name "Biosphere 2" reflects its model after Earth, referred to as Biosphere 1.

Biomes under Glass:

Biosphere 2 encompasses various biomes under glass, including the Ocean, Mangrove wetlands, Tropical rainforest, Savanna grassland, and Fog desert.

Mechanics of Biosphere 2:

The basement area, known as the technosphere, covers nearly 3.14 acres and houses all electrical, plumbing, and mechanical systems. The technosphere includes 26 air handlers that control air temperature, remove particles, maintain humidity, and generate condensate water. The Energy Center complex, with five arched segments and three towers, is crucial for continuous power to support living organisms and experiments. Two large generators, using natural gas and diesel fuel, are present in the Energy Center for power backup. Boilers and chillers inside the building heat and cool water, while the towers aid in cooling air by passing it over a water column.

Biosphere 2 is situated at 32540 South Biosphere Road in Oracle, AZ, located northwest of Tucson. The facility is open every day, regardless of weather conditions, from 9:00 am to 4:00 pm, except on Thanksgiving Day and Christmas Day. During winter, tours are available from 9:00 am to 3:30 pm, and during summer, tours are available from 8:00 am to 2:00 pm. Self-guided tours, lasting approximately 1 hour and 30 minutes, are offered daily, and tickets can be purchased online.

Biosphere 2 aims to be inclusive and accessible to all visitors. While much of the campus is wheelchair accessible, certain areas with steep terrain and stairs may not be. The majority of biomes, including the desert, savanna, ocean, and rainforest, are accessible by wheelchair or scooter. The Biosphere 2 team is available to assist visitors in accessing public areas. Questions can be directed to BIO2-INFO@ARIZONA.EDU or by calling 520-621-4800.

Visitors are advised to dress according to the weather, as some parts of the tour are conducted outdoors. Layers are recommended, especially in areas that may be humid or warm. Comfortable walking shoes are essential, as the tour involves approximately 150 stairs (up and down), covering a round-trip distance of just under one mile. It is advisable to bring water bottles. While food is not allowed on the premises, visitors may want to bring snacks or a small cooler since the facility is a considerable distance from the city center. Outside food is permitted on the Biosphere 2 campus, and picnic tables are available in the parking lot. However, it is recommended to eat before or after arrival, as the facility is located quite a distance from dining options, requiring a 15-30 minute drive. All ages are welcome, but the nature of the facility is best suited for an older child and adult audience, with a suggested minimum age of 8 and up.

BIRD CAGE THEATRE

COUNTY: COCHISE   **CITY:** TOMBSTONE

DATE VISITED: **WHO I WENT WITH:**

RATING: ☆ ☆ ☆ ☆ ☆   **WILL I RETURN?** YES / NO

The Bird Cage Theatre commenced operations on December 26, 1881, under the ownership of Lottie and William "Billy" Hutchinson, the latter being a variety performer. Initially aspiring to present respectable family shows, akin to those in San Francisco, the couple organized a Ladies Night for the respectable women of Tombstone, allowing free attendance. However, the economic realities of Tombstone led to the cancellation of Ladies Night, prompting a shift towards baser entertainment appealing to the rough mining crowd.

The Bird Cage's walls bore witness to the impact of gunshot holes, testament to clashes between gunfighters and local miners on the American frontier. The theatre featured 12 balcony boxes where prostitutes operated, and within its confines stood the notorious Bird Cage Poker Table, hosting the longest poker game in history.

Among the early acts were Mademoiselle De Granville (Alma Hayes), known as the "Female Hercules," the Irish comic duo Burns and Trayers, comic singer Irene Baker, serious opera singer Carrie Delmar, and comedian Nola Forest. Entertainment included masquerade balls with cross-dressing entertainers, enabling miners to revel in drinking and dancing throughout the night.

Cornish wrestling competitions and magic shows, where one magician claimed to catch bullets with his teeth, were popular attractions. The basement hosted the record-setting poker game, attracting notable players like George Hearst, Diamond Jim Brady, Adolphus Busch, Doc Holliday, Bat Masterson, and Wyatt Earp. This continuous poker marathon lasted eight years, from 1881 to 1889, with approximately $10 million exchanged and the Bird Cage retaining a ten percent share.

In March 1882, the Grand Central Mine faced water influx at 620 feet, eventually submerging the sought-after silver ore deposits. Hutchinson sold the Bird Cage to Hugh McCrum and John Stroufe, who, along with Bignon, managed the Theatre Comique in San Francisco. Bignon refurbished and renamed it the Elite Theatre, introducing new acts, including his wife, "Big Minnie," a 6ft tall, 230lb performer donning pink tights and showcasing singing, dancing, and piano skills.

While Cornish engines temporarily kept the mines dry, the Grand Central Mine's hoist and pumping plant burned on May 26, 1886. Subsequent economic downturns, marked by a drop in silver prices, led to mine closures and workforce layoffs. Many Tombstone residents departed, and the Bird Cage Theatre closed its doors in 1892.

A minimum of 26 individuals met their demise within the confines of the theater, their tragic fates stemming from fatal falls during performances, heated disputes leading to shootings while engaged in poker games, and the desperate acts of prostitutes driven to suicide. Many of these departed souls are believed to linger within the theater, a phenomenon embraced by the new owners. Visitors often report experiencing an eerie feeling or encountering peculiar scents, but some have even claimed to witness apparitions.

The Great Hall stands out as the most haunted section of the theater, often accompanied by the recurring scents of cigar smoke and whiskey. Visitors have reported hearing unexplained singing, despite no live performance on stage. Auditory phenomena include disembodied laughter, conversations, the sounds of rolling dice, and the shuffling of cards. Mysterious noises emanate from the balconies, and certain areas carry an overwhelming sense of despair. Apparitions in vintage attire have been observed reveling in the Great Hall, while a ghostly stage assistant, clad in black and white striped pants and holding a clipboard, diligently continues his spectral duties.

Objects within the theater exhibit a penchant for disappearing and reappearing. For instance, a $100 poker chip mysteriously appeared on the basement poker table, only to vanish when placed in a safe for examination by an expert. The chip later reappeared in the top drawer of a desk. In the wine cellar, witnesses have reported sightings of a woman in old-fashioned attire and a forlorn man searching aimlessly.

The presence of statues, particularly a life-sized figure of cowboy Wyatt Earp placed on one of the balconies, adds to the theater's paranormal narrative. Initially positioned on a different balcony, the statue had to be swiftly relocated when strange occurrences, such as Wyatt Earp's cowboy hat consistently found on the floor each morning for six months, began to transpire. On one occasion, the statue was even found completely turned around. Subsequent to the relocation, these unsettling events ceased.

Despite its haunted reputation, the Bird Cage Theatre remains open to the public, preserving its original features that transport visitors back to the era of the Old Wild West. The current owners assert that the spirits within the Bird Cage Theatre harbor no malicious intentions.

BISBEE

COUNTY: COCHISE   CITY: BISBEE

DATE VISITED: WHO I WENT WITH:

RATING: ☆ ☆ ☆ ☆ ☆   WILL I RETURN? YES / NO

Situated just over a mile high in elevation in the Mule Mountains, Bisbee, located in picturesque Cochise County, is only 11 miles away from the US/Mexico border. While there are various districts and suburbs within the city limits, Old Bisbee and Lowell are the two areas most favored by visitors. Spending several days in Bisbee is recommended to fully appreciate the historic town's offerings, but given its proximity—an hour and a half drive south of Tucson—it also makes for an excellent day trip.

In 1877, a group of U.S. army scouts and cavalrymen was dispatched to the Mule Mountains to track down renegade Apaches. However, instead of finding the Apaches, civilian tracker Jack Dunn discovered signs of mineral deposits suggesting the presence of lead, copper, and potentially silver. This discovery led to the establishment of the first mining claim in what later became the City of Bisbee. The filing of this claim attracted prospectors and speculators to the Mule Mountains, hoping to strike it rich. Numerous ore bodies were discovered, earning Bisbee the nickname "Queen of the Copper Camps."

Mining in the Mule Mountains proved highly successful, making Bisbee one of the world's wealthiest mineral sites. The town produced nearly three million ounces of gold, over eight billion pounds of copper, as well as significant amounts of silver, lead, and zinc. By the early 1900s, driven by the thriving mining industry, Bisbee had become the largest city in the Arizona territory, boasting a population of over 20,000 in 1910. It was considered one of the most cultured cities in the west, home to the nation's arguably oldest ballfield (Warren Ballpark) and Arizona's first golf course (Turquoise Valley, now an RV park). The Copper Queen, the state's first community library from that period, is still in operation.

Despite its cosmopolitan character, Bisbee retained the rough, colorful elements of its mining camp days, notably in the notorious Brewery Gulch, known for its saloons and brothels. At its peak, the Gulch had nearly 50 saloons and was considered one of the liveliest spots in the west. The historic taverns in the area still reflect the rich character and boom-town atmosphere of that period.

However, not all of Bisbee's history is positive. The Bisbee Deportation of 1917 was a significant event in Arizona's history, with repercussions on labor activities nationwide. This anti-labor incident involved the illegal abduction and deportation of around 1,300 striking mine workers, their supporters, and bystanders by a deputized posse of 2,000 members on July 12, 1917. Orchestrated by Phelps Dodge, the major mining company in the area, the action was a response to the miners' attempts to organize for better working conditions and wages. The company, aiming to prevent unionization, falsely accused the workers of being members of the Socialist-affiliated Industrial Workers of the World (IWW or Wobblies).

The arrested individuals were initially held at Warren Ballpark before being transported in cattle cars for a 16-hour journey, covering 200 miles (320 km) to Tres Hermanas in New Mexico, through the desert without food or water. Upon arrival, the deportees, many of whom lacked money or transportation, were sternly warned against returning to Bisbee.

Starting in 1917, open-pit mining was successfully implemented to fulfill the increasing demand for copper during World War I. Over the course of nearly a century of mining activity, Bisbee produced 8 billion pounds of copper, 102 million ounces of silver, and 2.8 million ounces of gold, in addition to substantial quantities of zinc, lead, and manganese. By 1974, the ore reserves were exhausted, leading to the announcement in December of the imminent closure of mining operations in Bisbee. Phelps Dodge scaled back open-pit operations in that year and discontinued underground operations in 1975.

Bisbee continued to be a thriving mining community until the mid-1970s. The closure of the mine marked a significant demographic shift, as many mining workers and their families departed to seek employment elsewhere. Simultaneously, an influx of creative individuals, drawn by the historic charm and affordability of Bisbee's district, settled in the area to pursue artistic endeavors.

Today, Bisbee has transformed into a culturally vibrant community with a diverse and active population. The town maintains its welcoming atmosphere, offering visitors a blend of art, music, history, architecture, outdoor activities, dining, and nightlife.

The Smithsonian-affiliated Bisbee Mining and Historical Museum has hosted and educated over half a million visitors in recent decades. Among its exhibits is "Bisbee: Urban Outpost on the Frontier," providing an in-depth exploration of the lives of miners and settlers in this unique southwestern region. The renowned Queen Mine Tour offers an immersive experience of the underground world where miners built their community and livelihood out of bedrock.

Yearly events such as the Bisbee 1000, Bisbee Pride Festival, and the Historic Home Tour attract crowds from the region and beyond. Ongoing highlights in Bisbee include the monthly Bisbee After Five art walk and a weekly farmer's market showcasing regional artisanal products.

Originally established as a copper mining town, Bisbee has transformed into a welcoming destination with a lively art scene and a thriving downtown, affectionately known as "Old Bisbee." Main Street is adorned with galleries, live music echoes through the evenings, and the town's rich mining history remains an integral part of its identity. The historical architecture, featuring Victorian-style houses and the elegant Art Deco-designed Cochise County Courthouse, captivates visitors. The Copper Queen Library, located above the historic post office, has received recognition as the best small library in America from the Library Journal, and Bisbee's historic ghost tours transport guests to the town's most "haunted" spots for some eerie stories.

In the southeastern corner of Old Bisbee, the Copper Queen Mine Tour is a highly popular activity for visitors. Over a century ago, this mine was the most productive copper mine in Cochise County, attracting thousands of miners and fostering the growth of Bisbee in the 1880s. Today, tourists can embark on a guided tour of the mine, equipped with a hard hat, miner's lamp, and a yellow slicker, exploring 1,500 feet into the mine while learning about its history, techniques, and dangers. The Queen Mine building also houses the Discover Bisbee visitor center, offering resources, maps, and informative displays about the mine. The gift shop allows visitors to take home a piece of mining history with various gems and minerals available for purchase. Considering the tour's popularity, it's advisable to purchase tickets in advance, especially for weekends.

As one of the first official Smithsonian Affiliates, the Bisbee Mining and Historical Museum invites visitors to experience an interactive journey back in time, exploring the role of this western copper mining town in America's industrialization. Housed in the former headquarters of the Copper Queen Consolidated Mining Company, the museum is open daily from 10 am to 4 pm. The museum showcases impressive minerals, artifacts, photographs, and tools, providing a comprehensive understanding of Bisbee's mining history.

Heading south from Old Bisbee, you'll navigate around the Lavender Pit, a former open-pit copper mine covering 300 acres and reaching a depth of 900 feet. The production of ore at this site exceeded 86 million tons before halting in 1974. A sizable pull-off and parking area lead to the Lavender Pit Mining Overlook, offering a brief yet fascinating stop. Fence cut-outs facilitate unobstructed photos, and informative displays provide insights into the history and mining processes at the site.

In 1899, Frank Hanchett of Lowell, Massachusetts, acquired property, initiating the Lowell and Arizona Copper Mining and Smelting Company. Erie Street, initially established as a business and social center near the Lowell mine, witnessed rapid growth as local mines expanded. However, as the Lavender Pit expanded, over half of Lowell faced imminent development for the massive pit. Consequently, more than 250 homes and businesses had to be relocated. Despite the loss, Erie Street has been preserved by dedicated business owners and locals, forming an outdoor museum that showcases the remnants of this historic neighborhood. The Lowell Americana Project has transformed Erie Street into a living snapshot of the past, continuously restored by a passionate community of residents and volunteers. The Bisbee Breakfast Club supports these efforts through a unique donation "jar" (an old tabletop jukebox), with proceeds benefiting the Lowell Americana Project.

B Active Bisbee serves as a central hub for exploring Bisbee and its surrounding landscapes, offering various enjoyable experiences. Located on Main Street in Bisbee's historic district, B Active Bisbee connects enthusiasts with the outdoors and each other. The shop also provides stylish apparel and gear for activities like hiking, biking, camping, and RVing.

Bisbee is a haven for incredible art, boasting a concentrated collection of folk art that is considered one of the most extensive in America. Murals, sculptures, and art installations adorn the town, including the Broadway Art Stairs, Judy Perry's mural maps, Ben Dale's ironwork, and Fred Albert's mosaic tiles. A Bisbee visit wouldn't be complete without encountering the "Iron Man," a striking statue of the Bisbee Copper Miner crafted by Phillip Sanderson in the 1930s. Numerous galleries offer diverse artistic experiences, with highlights including:

Artemizia Foundation - Artemizia Annex & Gallery 818: Showcasing a dynamic collection of influential contemporary, graffiti, and street artists from around the world, the foundation aims to provoke, inspire, and promote 21st-century art and artists.
Belleza Fine Art Gallery: Featuring the works of over 20 artists in a restored gallery that captures the essence of Bisbee at the turn of the 20th century.
Sam Poe Gallery: A contemporary art space showcasing the work of the husband-and-wife creators Poe & Sam.
Pritchard Gallery: Located in the Copper Queen Library living room, this gallery features multiple Bisbee artists every year.
Subway Gallery: Displaying sculpture, ceramics, photography, paintings, prints, and more.

Constructed in 1909, Warren Ballpark is one of the oldest professional baseball stadiums in the United States. Spectators can access the concrete and adobe brick grandstands where thousands of minor league, semi-pro, high school, and amateur players have competed over the last 110 years.

Where to Stay in Bisbee

Offering spacious one and two-bedroom suites with panoramic verandas, visitors have considered Eldorado Suites their home since 1914. Not only does Eldorado Suites provide some of the best views of Old Bisbee (especially from the 3rd-floor suites), but the property is also just steps away from numerous restaurants, shops, museums, and galleries.

Opposite Castle Rock is where the Muirhead House, now known as The Inn at Castle Rock, was built by Bisbee's first mayor, John Joseph Muirhead, in 1895 in the heart of Old Bisbee. Situated at the foot of Castle Rock, The Inn at Castle Rock is a beautifully eclectic hotel. Inside the lobby, you'll discover the historic Apache Springs Well. The backyard comprises an acre of steep ivy-covered hills with tiled trails, gazebos, and fruit trees.

Built in 1904 and completely renovated in 2016, the Pythian Castle stands as an iconic and historic Bisbee structure. Guests have access to the entire second floor, featuring 3 bedrooms and 3.5 baths, as well as 18-foot tall ceilings in the "great room." This beautiful building is perched above the historic Brewery Gulch District, just steps away from a diverse range of restaurants, shops, and fun activities.

Situated on Main Street in the heart of Historic Bisbee, the Castlerock Casita is a cozy 1-bedroom/1-bath home within walking distance of much that Bisbee has to offer. Amenities include a relaxing patio porch swing and a dedicated parking spot right next to one of Bisbee's historic staircases.

In a town steeped in such a wealth of history and diverse attractions, dining is also a standout feature of any visit to Bisbee.

Bisbee's Table - This well-loved establishment boasts a lively ambiance, and the friendly wait staff serves up American comfort food.

Cafe Roka is a favorite among both locals and visitors, and rightfully so. If you're seeking a unique and delicious fine dining experience, you'll delight in locally sourced ingredients presented in a stunning art deco setting.

Situated on historic Eerie Street in the former pharmacy building, the Bisbee Breakfast Club exudes a fun throwback Americana vibe. The food not only tastes delicious, but the portions are incredibly generous, so bring your appetite. For fellow "Parks & Rec" enthusiasts, there's even a menu option celebrating "Uncle Ronnie Swanson," featuring a double portion of meat and a shot of Lagavulin. An old tabletop jukebox on the front counter allows you to contribute a dollar or two to support the Lowell Americana Project, contributing to their commendable efforts to maintain the vibrancy of historic Erie Street for visitors.

Tips for Your Visit:

1) Plan your dining experiences in advance, as not all restaurants accept reservations, wait times can be substantial, and operating hours vary.
2) As you wander through the streets, staircases, and alleyways admiring the murals and historic structures, be mindful and respectful of local residents, as many of these sights are now on private property.
3) If you're staying in Old Bisbee, particularly near the Brewery Gulch District, be aware that the nightlife can be lively with live music continuing into the late evening. Earplugs are available for guests staying at the Eldorado Suites.
4) For those flying into Arizona, the drive time to Bisbee is 1.5 hours from Tucson International Airport and approximately 3.25 hours from Sky Harbor International Airport in Phoenix.
5) Due to the proximity to the US/Mexico border, anticipate encountering Border Patrol checkpoints along northbound highways in the area.

BOYNTON CANYON TRAIL

COUNTY: COCONINO   **CITY:** SEDONA *n.c.*

DATE VISITED: **WHO I WENT WITH:**

RATING: ☆ ☆ ☆ ☆ ☆   **WILL I RETURN?** YES / NO

Boynton Canyon stands out as one of the premier hikes in Sedona. This trail is relatively easy, leading you along a mostly flat path sheltered from the sun. The hike concludes at the rear of the canyon, where a brief ascent takes you to a viewpoint, providing expansive vistas of Boynton Canyon.

During the hike, there are two optional detours that can enhance your experience. Near the beginning of the trail, take a brief diversion onto the Boynton Vista Trail for breathtaking views of the Enchantment Resort and the iconic red rocks of Sedona.

Additionally, there is a cave and Sinagua ruins worth exploring. Often referred to as the Subway Cave or Boynton Cave, this site is prominently featured on hiking websites (currently ranking as the 3rd most popular hike in Sedona on All Trails) and is listed on Trip Advisor. Many hikers on the Boynton Canyon trail specifically aim to visit the Subway Cave.

BOYNTON CANYON
Trail Type: Out-and-back
Distance: 6.3 miles
Total Elevation Gain: 800 feet
Difficulty: Easy
Estimated Duration: 2.5 to 4 hours

BOYNTON CANYON + THE SUBWAY CAVE
Trail Type: Out-and-back
Distance: 7.1 miles
Total Elevation Gain: 1,100 feet
Difficulty: Moderate
Estimated Duration: 4 to 6 hours

BOYNTON CANYON + THE SUBWAY CAVE + BOYNTON CANYON VISTA TRAIL
Trail Type: Out-and-back
Distance: 7.5 miles
Total Elevation Gain: 1,300 feet
Difficulty: Moderate
Estimated Duration: 4.5 to 6.5 hours

ADDITIONAL DETAILS:
Best Time to Visit: Year-round, with optimal conditions during spring and fall, featuring mild temperatures but higher crowds. Summer entails very hot temperatures but fewer

crowds, while winter brings below-freezing temperatures with reduced crowds.

Location: West Sedona

A Red Rock Pass is required for this hike. Purchase the pass at the trailhead fee machine (credit cards only). Holders of the America the Beautiful Pass can use it instead of acquiring a Red Rock Pass.

HOW TO HIKE BOYNTON CANYON

The primary parking area for this hike is situated on Boynton Canyon Road, near its intersection with Boynton Pass Road. This lot accommodates approximately 25 vehicles and tends to fill up by 7:30 am during busier months. A pit toilet is available in this parking lot. Overflow parking is found on Boynton Pass Road, west of the intersection with Boynton Canyon Road. No designated parking lot exists here; vehicles are parked on the roadside. If utilizing this overflow area, a Red Rock Pass must still be displayed in your vehicle. Depending on your parking location along the road, there is approximately a 0.25-mile walk or longer to reach the trailhead. The trailhead is easily identified within the main parking lot, marked by a prominent trail sign. Before commencing the hike, consider capturing a photo of the trail map with your phone for reference. The initial stretch of the hike is flat and brisk, leading quickly to the first trail junction. To stay on the Boynton Canyon Trail, veer left at this junction, as indicated by a trail junction sign.

BOYNTON VISTA TRAIL

Approximately 0.3 miles into the hike, you'll encounter the junction for the Boynton Vista Trail. The Boynton Vista Trail is a 0.4-mile round trip, offering a moderately strenuous ascent onto the red rocks that proves worthwhile. The views encompass the Enchantment Resort and the crimson-hued mountains of Sedona, providing a splendid perspective of Boynton Canyon, your next destination. This detour takes around 30 to 45 minutes.

THROUGH BOYNTON CANYON

The first mile through Boynton Canyon is picturesque, with massive sandstone cliffs towering to your right and the Enchantment Resort to your left. The trail occasionally opens up, offering a stunning view down Boynton Canyon. While there are a few brief inclines and declines in this section, they are not overly strenuous. About a mile into the hike, you pass the far end of the Enchantment Resort, transitioning to a sandy trail through short, shrubby trees.

THE SUBWAY CAVE

The path leading to the Subway Cave becomes evident at the 2-mile mark (or 2.4 miles into the hike if you've already taken the Boynton Vista Trail). There isn't a sign indicating the trail to the cave, but there is a distinctive tree marking the spot. As you approach the 2-mile mark, be on the lookout for a sizable Alligator Juniper tree situated on the left side of the trail. The spur trail to the Subway Cave commences just across the main trail from this tree, on the right-hand side. Once you reach the tree, follow the trail to the right. Although narrower than the main Boynton Canyon Trail, this trail is easy to navigate. It meanders through the forest, gradually ascending towards the red cliffs. The trail to the Subway Cave spans 0.4 miles, one-way.

Note: If you happen to miss the turnoff for the spur trail, an indication is when you find yourself surrounded by tall pine trees. Just beyond the Alligator Juniper, the forest undergoes a noticeable transformation from short, shrubby trees to a denser forest filled with pine trees. This section looks and smells distinct from the initial two miles of the hike.

While en route to the cave, you will encounter a sign posted by the National Forest Service. Take a moment to read it. You are approaching a sacred site with ancient ruins. It's crucial to show respect for the area, leaving everything undisturbed and refraining from interfering with the ruins or standing on the rock walls.

IN THE SUBWAY CAVE

When viewed from below, the Subway Cave appears as a narrow opening within the sandstone walls. To enter the cave, you'll ascend the sandstone incline, involving a combination of walking and rock scrambling. The incline resembles a sliding board, particularly on the descent. Negotiating this section is the most challenging part of the hike. The incline culminates at the rear of the cave, offering a different perspective upon turning around. It's likely that you'll be sharing this space with other visitors, especially during peak hours, unless you choose an early morning visit or come during the off-season. If you have a fear of heights, it's advisable to stay closer to the back of the cave. To venture to the far end of the cave and proceed to the ruins, you'll navigate a narrow ledge with a drop-off on one side. For a view of the ruins, step onto the ledge on the right side, continue around the bend, and follow the trail along the canyon wall. Numerous excellent photo spots await, but always remember not to disturb the rock walls. Exiting the Subway Cave involves descending the incline at the cave's entrance.

TO BOYNTON CANYON OVERLOOK

Upon rejoining the Boynton Canyon Trail, make a right turn to proceed with the hike towards the conclusion of Boynton Canyon. At this point, it is a little over one mile to reach the trail's endpoint. The trail gradually and consistently ascends towards the rear of the canyon. This last mile is entirely uphill, with the steepest incline occurring in the final half-mile. During this portion of the hike, you will traverse through a forest. Initially, the path leads through a forest adorned with ponderosa pine trees, creating a cooler and delightful-scented environment. As you gain elevation, the ponderosa pine trees gradually give way to maple and oak trees. The ultimate half-mile proves to be the most strenuous part of the hike as you ascend towards the final viewpoint. Expect brief segments where you'll traverse a steep, rocky trail, involving a few stair climbs along the way. The trail concludes at a broad plateau, offering a splendid view back down through Boynton Canyon. To complete the hike, retrace your steps back through Boynton Canyon. Consider adding the Boynton Vista Trail if you haven't already, provided you still have the energy.

TIPS:

1) Commence the hike early, preferably around 7 am, to secure a parking space at the trailhead and avoid the crowds, enjoying the cooler temperatures in the morning.
2) Adhere to Leave No Trace principles, encompassing packing out all your belongings, being considerate of fellow hikers, and leaving archaeological artifacts undisturbed.
3) Allocate at least one hour for the Subway Cave, considering its popularity and potential wait times for photos.

WHAT TO BRING ON THE HIKE

1) While a good pair of walking or running shoes suffices, opting for hiking shoes is recommended, especially if hiking to the Subway Cave. The added traction provides ease and safety during the climb and on the cave ledges.
2) Carry a minimum of 2 liters of water, especially during the summer.
3) Ensure you have sunscreen, a hat, and sunglasses. Although much of the trail is shaded, sun exposure occurs at the Boynton Canyon viewpoint, in the initial mile of the hike, and during the optional Boynton Vista Trail hike.
4) Bring a camera, or a smartphone, to capture the scenic views and memorable moments.

BRIGHT ANGEL TRAIL

COUNTY: COCONINO CITY: FLAGSTAFF *n.c.*

DATE VISITED: WHO I WENT WITH:

RATING: ☆ ☆ ☆ ☆ ☆ WILL I RETURN? YES / NO

The Grand Canyon stands as one of the most frequented National Parks in the United States, yet merely around 1% of visitors venture below the rim. For those yearning to immerse themselves in the Grand Canyon's depths, the Bright Angel Trail emerges as one of the finest day hikes, serving as an accessible entry point for first-time explorers of this remarkable National Park.

Bright Angel Trail Essentials
The provided details pertain to the Bright Angel Trail leading to Indian Garden. Although the trail extends beyond Indian Garden all the way to the Colorado River, venturing further requires thorough preparation with an abundance of water, sun protection, and food. It is strongly advised not to hike beyond Indian Garden during the summer when temperatures typically soar above 100°F.

Difficulty: Strenuous
Trail Type: Out-and-back
Length: 8.9 miles
Starting Elevation: 6,860 feet
Minimum Elevation: 3,800 feet
Total Elevation Gain: 3,034 feet
Dogs Allowed: No
Time: 5-6 hours, factoring in sufficient breaks
Permit Required: No

The optimal seasons for visiting the Grand Canyon and undertaking the Bright Angel Trail are fall and spring, characterized by milder temperatures and relatively smaller crowds, although the Grand Canyon never truly experiences quiet periods.Hiking the Bright Angel Trail during summer is not recommended due to the potential for temperatures exceeding 100 degrees. The trail offers minimal shade, and hiking under such conditions can pose risks of heat exhaustion. Winter presents a viable option for a visit, provided you dress appropriately for colder weather and check the weather forecast for potential snow and rain.

The Bright Angel Trailhead is situated on the South Rim, just west of the Bright Angel Lodge in the Grand Canyon Village. For park residents, the free blue-line park shuttle conveniently stops directly at the trailhead. Day visitors or those who prefer driving themselves can park at the Backcountry Information Center (parking lot D), a short stroll from the Bright Angel Trailhead.

A Brief History

The Bright Angel Trail has served as a route for accessing water at Indian Gardens for centuries. Its name is derived from the Bright Angel Fault, a geological feature creating a rugged break in the sheer cliff walls that would otherwise impede passage to the canyon floor. In the 1800s, the arrival of gold prospectors coincided with the discovery that the native Havasupai people were already utilizing the route from the rim to the canyon floor, where they cultivated crops near Indian Creek. During the 1890s, Ralph Cameron, a miner and entrepreneur, recognized the increasing significance of tourism over mining with the advent of the railroad to the Grand Canyon. He "registered" the Bright Angel Trail, enhancing its infrastructure and establishing a campground at Indian Garden, charging visitors $1 for trail usage. Despite the Grand Canyon receiving National Park designation in 1919, Cameron contested to maintain control over this area. He ultimately lost the legal battle in 1928, compelling him to surrender the trail and campground to the Parks Service. The native Havasupai people endured significant losses during this period. Theodore Roosevelt mandated their departure in 1901, and those who remained were eventually expelled in 1928, relocating to a reservation in Havasu Canyon. After extensive negotiations, the government established the Havasupai Indian Reservation in 1975, recognized as the most remote community in the lower 48 States. This reservation is also where visitors can encounter the breathtaking Havasu Falls.

Key Points Along the Trail

The Bright Angel Trail can be conveniently divided into various sections or milestones, aiding in distance measurement and ensuring a vigilant approach to water consumption, particularly if the hike extends to Indian Garden.

First Switchback – Mile 0.5:
Initiating a series of switchbacks, the first switchback marks the commencement of a rapid descent down the Grand Canyon National Park's canyon walls. The trail quickly loses elevation, accompanied by steep drop-offs along the trail edges, making it a halting point for those averse to exposure.

1.5 Mile Resthouse – Mile 1.5:
Situated at the 1.5-mile mark, this basic stone structure lacks amenities but provides excellent Canyon views. It serves as a suitable turnaround spot for those seeking a shorter hike.

3 Mile Resthouse – Mile 3:
The second resthouse emerges at mile three, with no amenities other than seasonal water. The trail steepens from this point onward, making it a prudent turnaround point for those concerned about the ascent back.

Indian Garden:
Indian Garden, a verdant oasis in the Grand Canyon desert, features a perennial creek

that historically supplied water to Native Americans residing in the canyon for millennia. Presently, Indian Garden hosts a ranger station, a modest visitors center, and the Indian Garden Campground (or Havasupai Garden Campground). Securing a challenging overnight camping permit is essential for those wishing to stay overnight.

Plateau Point:
Located approximately a mile and a half beyond Indian Gardens via the Plateau Point trail, Plateau Point offers a remarkable overlook onto the Colorado River. For day hikers, the round trip to Plateau Point spans 12 miles with an elevation gain of 3,740 feet. This hike is advisable during the cooler spring, fall, and winter months.

The Bright Angel Trail extends beyond Indian Gardens, leading down to the Colorado River. Here, hikers can traverse the river using the Bright Angel Suspension Bridge. On the opposite bank, the trail transforms into the North Kaibob Trail, progressing to Bright Angel Campground, Phantom Ranch (a rustic lodge), and eventually reaching the North Rim of the Grand Canyon.

Be Prepared:

For those contemplating a hike on the Bright Angel Trail to Indian Garden, it is absolutely crucial to bring sufficient water and food for the entire 9-mile round-trip excursion. Since the trail is exposed, adequate sun protection is also essential.

The peril of this trail lies in its deceptively gentle start. Unlike ascending a mountain, where the challenge is immediately evident, this hike descends into a canyon, presenting the easier portion first. This can mislead hikers into believing they can cover more distance than they can realistically manage in a single day. To mitigate risks, it is recommended to arrive at the trailhead before 8 am, equipped with a hydration day pack filled with water and an ample supply of salty snacks.

While there is usually water available at the Bright Angel trailhead, seasonal availability along the trail is not guaranteed from May to September. It is advisable to come fully prepared with a minimum of 3 liters of water per person. Additionally, since there is a river running through Indian Gardens, packing a lightweight water filter is recommended as a precaution.

It's important to remember that uphill hikers have the right of way. Encounters with mule traffic are also possible. If a group of mules is approaching, the park service advises hikers to step off the trail on the uphill side away from the edge, follow the wrangler's instructions, remain quiet and still, and refrain from returning to the trail until the last mule is at least 50 feet (15 meters) past their position. Essentially, giving the mules ample space ensures the safety and well-being of everyone involved.

BROKEN ARROW TRAIL

COUNTY: YAVAPAI   CITY: SEDONA

DATE VISITED: WHO I WENT WITH:

RATING: ☆ ☆ ☆ ☆ ☆   WILL I RETURN?   YES / NO

Sedona's Broken Arrow Trail stands out as one of the most sought-after off-road routes in the region and within the Coconino National Forest. Situated amidst the iconic red rocks of Sedona, Arizona, this trail offers a distinctive blend of hiking, mountain biking, and off-road driving experiences. Renowned for its stunning landscapes, challenging terrains, and an unforgettable adventure, Broken Arrow Trail is a must-visit destination.

Hiking the Broken Arrow Trail:

Length: 3.4 miles round trip
Difficulty:
Hiking: Moderate
Driving: Moderate to Challenging (rated 5.5 out of 10)
Elevation Gain: Approximately 500 feet
Route Type: Out and back
Dog-Friendly: Yes
Hiking Time: 1 to 3 hours
Fee/Permit: Yes, a Red Rock Pass is required for parking at Broken Arrow Trail. The America the Beautiful Pass is also accepted.

Broken Arrow Trail Directions to the Trailhead:

The trailhead for Broken Arrow Trail is situated at the end of Morgan Road, and parking in designated areas requires a Red Rock Pass. To reach it from Sedona, head south on the 179 until you reach the Morgan Road roundabout. Follow Morgan Road until it culminates at the trailhead. Google Maps often designates the Sedona Broken Arrow Trail as Morgan Road. It's worth noting that the experiences differ significantly for those taking an off-road vehicle versus those hiking the trail. While the trail offers beautiful views, it stands out as an exceptional off-road experience, being the premier off-road trail in Sedona.

What to Expect Hiking This Trail:

Hiking Broken Arrow Trail presents a combination of elements found in other popular trails like Devil's Bridge and Cathedral Rock. Resemblances to Devil's Bridge arise because, during the full Devil's Bridge trail, there's a section where side-by-side vehicles and other off-highway vehicles share the trail. The shared portion is wider than the Broken Arrow trail. Approximately half of Broken Arrow Trail features one-way traffic, while the other half accommodates two-way traffic. Certain sections form a loop trail, influencing the type of traffic encountered based on the trail location.

In terms of difficulty, the trail shares similarities with Cathedral Rock, involving some rock scrambling, albeit to a lesser extent. Hikers on Broken Arrow may encounter off-highway vehicles such as side-by-sides, pink jeep tours, or other four-wheel drives. Jeeps traverse the trail slowly due to challenging rock sections, minimizing concerns for hikers. However, hikers should be prepared for some noise and may need to yield to passing jeeps.

For a quieter hiking experience, mornings are recommended, as many jeeps don't start early. If interested in observing vehicles navigating the trail, later in the day is suitable. Larger obstacles on the main trail, particularly the first obstacle, offer vantage points for hikers and kids to spread out and watch 4x4 vehicles pass by.

Driving the Broken Arrow Trail:

Recommended Vehicle Information for the Broken Arrow Trail:

High ground clearance and 4WD vehicles are necessary. Off-road tires and skid plates are recommended. If you have a vehicle similar to a Jeep Rubicon, navigating this trail should be relatively easy. A custom-made vehicle is not a prerequisite for tackling this trail successfully.

Starting Point:
Commence your drive from the trailhead located off Morgan Road, following the well-marked path. Morgan Road essentially terminates at the beginning of the trail, or for those engaging in hiking and mountain biking, it culminates at the parking lot, marking the commencement of the off-road trail.

Trail Difficulty:
The trail is not overly challenging to drive. Some individuals suggest trying a few other trails first, but many alternative off-road trails in the area are characterized by excessive bumpiness and, lack the enjoyable aspects of the Broken Arrow Trail. If you're seeking a fantastic off-road experience, this trail is highly recommended.

Notable Obstacles:

For hikers tackling the trail, these obstacles pose no significant concern. They can be bypassed or ascended slowly. No notable obstacles are worth mentioning for hikers on the trail. However, for those opting to drive, the initial challenge arises right at the trail's beginning. As you commence the trail, you'll encounter a small rock ledge. If uncertainties arise about traversing this minor bump, it might be wise to reconsider continuing. Nevertheless, if you proceed, the first noteworthy obstacle awaits.

Last Chance Climb:
This juncture serves as an opportune spot to assess your readiness for the trail. The obstacle, situated less than half a mile into the trail, involves a steep ascent. It provides a

good preview of what lies ahead. However, your vehicle should encounter minimal difficulty in climbing this segment.

Devil's Dining Room Sinkhole:
While not truly an obstacle, the Devil's Sinkhole serves as a captivating side trip to a unique geological feature, offering an intriguing viewpoint. Some individuals choose to explore this detour, while others may bypass it.

Submarine Rock:
Submarine Rock represents another detour along the route, but it's an enjoyable. The views and the journey to reach it are delightful, featuring satisfying ascents and descents. The name "Submarine Rock" is derived from its resemblance to a submarine when viewed from above.

Chicken Point Overlook
Chicken Point Overlook is situated at the trail's conclusion, providing a stunning vantage point. This overlook point tends to attract a considerable crowd of people capturing photos and maneuvering vehicles, as oncoming traffic converges at this location. Take your time at Chicken Point Overlook and relish the experience. Following this stop, the road transitions into two-way traffic but later reverts to one-way traffic on the route to Mushroom Rock, The Slide, and The Stairs.

Mushroom Rock
Mushroom Rock is a distinctively shaped red rock formation along the trail, resembling a roundabout. Driving around it is enjoyable and not particularly challenging.

The Slide
The Slide, positioned close to Mushroom Rock, involves a steep ascent that can be bypassed if desired. It might present minimal issues for those reaching this point. Exercise caution when deviating from the standard trail, as individuals may become overly confident and inadvertently damage their vehicles.

The Stairs
The Stairs feature a sequence of lengthy, steep rock steps, constituting one of the more thrilling segments of the trail. Engage 4 low and proceed cautiously through these sizable steps.

In summary, this trail is unique and it is strongly recommended to embark on a pink jeep tour, rent a jeep or use your own 4x4 vehicle. It stands out as the best 4x4 trail in the region, often traversed by pink jeeps. While it can be an enjoyable hike, especially for jeep watchers, the trail is ideal for driving a 4x4 vehicle.

⑮ BUTTERFIELD OVERLAND NATIONAL HISTORIC TRAIL

COUNTY: COCHISE, MARICOPA, PIMA, PINAL, YUMA	**CITY:** TUCSON *n.c.*

DATE VISITED: 　　　　　　　**WHO I WENT WITH:**

RATING: ☆ ☆ ☆ ☆ ☆ 　　　**WILL I RETURN?** YES / NO

In 1857, John Butterfield, a businessman and transportation entrepreneur, secured a contract from Congress to establish an overland mail route connecting the eastern United States with the growing settler populations in the Far West. This route, known as the Butterfield Overland Trail, commenced from two eastern termini along the Mississippi River in St. Louis, Missouri, and Memphis, Tennessee. The trail took a southerly course through Missouri, Arkansas, Texas, New Mexico, and Arizona, then turned north through California, concluding in San Francisco. Its sweeping trajectory along the southern rim earned it the moniker "the Oxbow Route," and its southern alignment allowed for year-round service.

From 1858, Butterfield's stagecoaches departed twice a week, transporting passengers, freight, and mail. With an average daily travel distance of around 100 miles, the drivers could reach San Francisco in 25 days or less. Unfortunately, the Butterfield Overland service lasted less than three years, disrupted by the onset of the Civil War and eventually supplanted by telegraph lines and more direct northern routes.

Despite its relatively short existence, the Butterfield Overland Mail played a crucial role in linking the American West more closely to the rest of the country. Prior to its establishment, mail and travel to and from the Pacific Coast relied on a circuitous route across the Isthmus of Panama, with twice-monthly service. Although the Butterfield Overland's operation concluded in 1861, the trail it blazed significantly contributed to shaping and connecting the young United States during a period of territorial expansion and sectional tension.

The Butterfield Overland National Historic Trail (NHT) officially became a part of the National Trails System on January 5, 2023. Stretching across a distance of 3,292 miles and traversing seven states, this trail was designated to commemorate the profound impact of the Butterfield Overland Mail service on shaping the nation's history.

Despite the inclusion of the term "trail" in its name, the Butterfield Overland Trail does not strictly fit the definition of a traditional hiking trail. Approximately 2,000 miles of the original route are now under the management of various private and public entities, and access to specific trail segments is contingent upon the consent of the respective landowner. Availability for public use, such as hiking and other recreational activities, varies depending on the landowner's policies.

Various enjoyable ways to experience the Butterfield Overland Trail exist, encompassing auto-touring, visiting interpretive sites, hiking, biking, horseback riding along trail segments, and exploring museums. The extent to which these activities are feasible depends on the specific segment of the trail you wish to explore, with some segments allowing all or a selection of these activities.

CAMELBACK MOUNTAIN

COUNTY: MARICOPA   CITY: PHOENIX

DATE VISITED: WHO I WENT WITH:

RATING: ☆ ☆ ☆ ☆ ☆   WILL I RETURN? YES / NO

Camelback Mountain, standing at an elevation of 2,704 feet, offers a fantastic hiking or climbing experience in Arizona. Exploring Camelback Mountain is an ideal tourist activity in Phoenix due to its quick accessibility and central location within the Phoenix Valley, providing splendid views. Positioned in the Camelback Mountain Echo Canyon Recreation Area between Phoenix, Scottsdale, and Paradise Valley, Camelback Mountain attracts both local residents and tourists. Designated as a Phoenix city park in 1968, hiking Camelback Mountain ranks among the top 10 things to do in Phoenix according to Trip Advisor. Camelback Mountain derives its name from the distinctive outline it creates on the Valley skyline. Recognized as one of the premier hiking destinations in the country, it draws visitors from all corners of the globe. The prevalent flora on the mountain includes Saguaro Cactus, Ocotillo, Palo Verde, Cholla, Barrel Cactus, and the Creosote Bush. Given the frequent mountain rescues, it is crucial to proceed with caution and be aware of your own limits. Preserving the mountain's environment is essential, so whatever you bring in, make sure to carry it back out. There are two hiking trails, Echo Canyon and Cholla, both presenting challenges; Echo Canyon is steeper, while Cholla is longer. Parking for both trails is permitted only from sunrise to sunset, so plan your visit accordingly. Parking availability at Camelback Mountain trailheads is limited, and parking along most nearby roadways is strictly prohibited. Vehicles in violation of posted signs will be towed at the owner's expense, and visitors idling their vehicles near the trailheads may receive tickets. When hiking, adhere to proper trail etiquette, and keep in mind that ascending hikers have the right of way.

Camelback Mountain faced increasing threats from private development until the 1960s. The Preservation of Camelback Mountain Foundation, led by Barry Goldwater, played a pivotal role in securing the area's protection in 1968. By that time, much of the mountain had already been surrounded by residential development, isolating Camelback Mountain from other natural spaces and consequently limiting the presence of large animals in the area today. However, smaller creatures like cottontail rabbits, lizards, Harris antelope squirrels, various birds, and snakes (including venomous rattlesnakes) are frequently encountered.

Numerous websites categorize the climb as "difficult" or even "extremely difficult," and annual helicopter rescues on the rugged mountainside are not uncommon. Most hikers acknowledge that any trail involves some level of risk, such as a sprained ankle, a fall, or a missed turn. Yet, due to the challenging terrain and unpredictable weather, Camelback presents its own distinct set of challenges.

It should be emphasized that attempting to climb Camelback Mountain during the scorching heat of a desert summer is ill-advised. Phoenix experiences summer temperatures that routinely soar to 110 degrees Fahrenheit and above. Even during the nighttime, there is little respite, with temperatures often remaining at 90 degrees or higher throughout the night. The optimal times for ascending Camelback are late fall, winter, and early spring. In November, the average highs hover in the mid-70s, while December and January see highs in the 60s. February and March are considered among Phoenix's most delightful months, featuring the blossoming of wildflowers and average high temperatures in the 70s. However, it's essential to note that these months are also the most popular with Phoenix's winter and spring visitors, resulting in crowded trails.

In addition to selecting the right season, the timing of your hike on Camelback Mountain is equally crucial for a successful experience. The primary rationale for starting early is the cooler morning temperatures. For instance, in September and October, commencing the hike at 7 a.m. might offer temperatures in the high 70s or low 80s, whereas by 2 p.m., the temperatures could be soaring toward 100 degrees or more. Early starts are also advisable due to the limited parking spaces available. While there has been recent expansion at the base of Echo Canyon, demand still exceeds the available parking spots. Arriving around sunrise when the trailhead opens is recommended to secure a parking space. The Cholla Trail lacks an official parking lot, leading trail users to park along the busy Invergordon Road. On-street parking tends to fill up quickly, and during peak times, hikers may find themselves parking blocks away from the trailhead. Local recommendations include biking or using services like Uber to reach the trailhead, avoiding the hassle of finding parking.

Before embarking on a climb up Camelback Mountain, it is crucial to honestly assess your fitness level. The trail ascends 1,200 to 1,300 feet in just over a mile, introducing hikers to very steep terrain with numerous high step-ups. Additionally, the hike includes segments where the use of hands and arms is necessary to navigate over rocks. Upon completing a Camelback hike, it is common to feel stiffness in the arms and shoulders, underscoring that the hike serves as a workout for both the upper and lower body. Hikers encountering difficulty should recognize that there is no shame in turning back, especially when faced with particularly rocky and steep sections. Many individuals opt to hike the initial, more gradual portion of the Cholla Trail and then decide to turn back as the trail becomes vertical in the final one-third or so. Despite not reaching the summit, they still get to enjoy the splendid views and desert terrain.

There are two primary trails leading to the summit of Camelback Mountain—the Cholla Trail and the Echo Canyon Trail—each with its own advantages and disadvantages. The Cholla Trail spans about 1.5 miles one-way, providing a more gradual ascent. The initial mile follows a path that is relatively easy to navigate. However, the last half-mile involves steep terrain, requiring hikers to engage in rock scrambling. On the other hand, the Echo Canyon Trail is somewhat shorter, covering about 1.2 miles one-way, and consequently, it is steeper. The final climb on this trail necessitates the use of handrails. Unlike the Cholla Trail, the Echo Canyon Trail boasts a trailhead equipped with restrooms, benches, and water facilities. Both hikes offer picturesque views, and the duration for fit hikers to complete either route can range from one to three hours.

While water is available at the Echo Canyon Trailhead, it's important to note that there is no water source along either of the ascent routes, underscoring the importance of carrying an ample supply of water. Even during the cooler winter months, the sun's intensity can be unforgiving. Experts recommend bringing more water than initially anticipated, typically a liter or more per person. Trailside signs emphasize that if you find yourself halfway through your water supply, it's advisable to turn back. Regardless of the hiking season, it's wise to have a snack or two on hand to maintain energy levels. Salty snacks like nuts and pretzels are recommended for an energy boost and to replenish the sodium lost through sweating on the trail.

For navigating the rugged terrain of Camelback Mountain, thick-soled hiking shoes or boots are optimal. Although sturdy hiking sandals may suffice for many Arizona trails, Camelback is an exception where closed-toed shoes are preferable. While some individuals opt for sneakers, they should have a thick sole to guard against sharp rocks, and a good tread is advisable for traction on rocky sections. Wearing a hat or cap is essential for any Arizona trail, and it becomes particularly crucial on Camelback due to the limited shade and the intense Phoenix sun. A bandana around your neck can also be beneficial in managing the heat.

Situated in the heart of the Sonoran Desert, Camelback Mountain serves as a habitat for various wildlife, including snakes and lizards. Rattlesnakes typically remain active in the Arizona desert from approximately April to October, with September being recognized as prime rattlesnake season, characterized by still-hot weather but cooler mornings. To minimize the risk of encountering a rattlesnake, experts recommend consistently watching where you step and refraining from blindly reaching under rocks or into crevices. It's also advisable to avoid wearing earbuds while hiking, as rattlesnakes tend to emit a warning rattle when someone approaches. If a rattlesnake is spotted on the trail, the recommended course of action is to give it a wide berth or, if necessary, turn back. Hikers should also inform others of the potential danger as they proceed along the trail. Lizards are abundant on nearly all Arizona trails, and sightings are common while hiking on Camelback Mountain. Although they may startle you, most Arizona lizards are generally harmless (excluding the venomous Gila monster). The Chuckwalla lizards, distinct in appearance but non-poisonous, are often observed basking in the sun on the rocks along the trail.

On the Camelback trails, you'll encounter several instances where the path narrows, preventing two hikers from passing simultaneously. In such situations, it's essential to adhere to the trail etiquette, which dictates that the uphill hiker has the right-of-way. Therefore, if you are descending, it is customary to move aside, allowing the ascending hiker to pass without interruption. This practice ensures safe and consistent passage along the trail.

Upon reaching the summit of Camelback Mountain, take some time to relish the panoramic views. The summit features various rocks and ledges where you can take a break, enjoy the scenery, and replenish with a refreshing drink of cool water and a salty snack. Despite the sense of accomplishment at reaching the summit, it's crucial to remember that you still have to navigate the descent, which, akin to many steep trails, poses its own set of challenges. The steep rocks that may have seemed strenuous on the ascent can be even more treacherous on the way down. The recommended approach is to proceed with caution, take your time, and rest when the terrain allows. The trailhead operates from sunrise to sunset, so it's important to plan your hike accordingly. Additionally, if you're accompanied by a family pet, keep in mind that dogs are not allowed in any Echo Canyon and Cholla trail areas.

CAMP VERDE

COUNTY: YAVAPAI   **CITY:** CAMP VERDE

DATE VISITED: **WHO I WENT WITH:**

RATING: ☆ ☆ ☆ ☆ ☆   **WILL I RETURN?**   YES / NO

Camp Verde is a town in Yavapai County. Camp Verde, positioned centrally and benefiting from a mild climate throughout the year, offers a prime tourist experience in Arizona. Situated on the picturesque banks of the Verde River, it is conveniently located less than an hour away from major cities like Phoenix, Flagstaff, Prescott, and Payson. The town, along with the surrounding Verde Valley, provides a variety of attractions for history enthusiasts, nature lovers, and those interested in cultural heritage, offering activities such as boating, hiking, biking, and wine tasting. Additionally, visitors of all ages and preferences can enjoy the Out of Africa Wild Animal Park and Cliff Castle Casino.

In 2012, the Town of Camp Verde received recognition as the municipality closest to the geographical center of Arizona, as proclaimed by the governor and determined by the Arizona Professional Land Surveyors. To commemorate this unique status, a monument was erected in Rezzonico Family Park in the same year. The official center, according to APLS, is located near the confluence of the Verde River and East Verde River, approximately 15 miles SSE of Camp Verde in the rugged Mazatzal Wilderness Area.

For those seeking more information or a glimpse into the area's history, the Camp Verde Visitor Center and the Camp Verde Historical Society Museum can be found at 435 S. Main Street. These locations are conveniently situated near the Verde Valley Archaeology Center and Fort Verde State Historic Park. Visitors can drop by to learn about the region's rich past, receive friendly advice to enhance their visit, or simply enjoy a refreshing drink of water.

The Verde Valley, boasting almost 10,000 years of human habitation by diverse cultural groups, holds a profound and extensive history. Archaeologists trace the Valley's initial human inhabitants to the nomadic Clovis culture, succeeded by the more settled Hohokam from the south. The Sinagua, entering from the north, erected the Tuzigoot Pueblo and the cliff dwelling at Montezuma Castle around 1000 A.D., yet abandoned the area in the early 1400s.

Despite ongoing debates about the chronology, archaeologists generally pinpoint the arrival of the Yavapai around 1300, though their oral tradition suggests an earlier period. The Apache people entered the region between 1250 and 1450. In 1582-1583, Spanish soldiers traversed the Camp Verde area, a quarter-century before Jamestown's founding. Apart from mentions of the Verde Valley in travel logs, few artifacts remain from this brief Spanish contact.

White settlers arrived in 1865, initiating farming along the Verde River and its tributaries, starting with a 200-acre settlement at the confluence of the Verde River and West Clear

Creek. Although many settlers came for farming and ranching, a significant mineral discovery in the Black Hills in the late 1870s attracted a new wave of arrivals, leading to the establishment of the towns of Jerome and Clarkdale.

Presently, Fort Verde State Historic Park, the Yavapai-Apache Cultural Department, the Camp Verde Historical Society Museum, and the Verde Valley Archaeology Center are dedicated to preserving and safeguarding the legacies of these diverse cultures.

For over 2,000 years, the fertile Verde Valley in Central Arizona has played a crucial role as a source of sustenance for human communities. The initial cultivators were the Hohokam people, known for their expertise in irrigation systems, a practice they also implemented in Phoenix's Salt River Valley. The intricate network of canals created by the Hohokam transformed the bottomlands of both valleys into thriving agricultural zones, serving as enduring reminders of their connection to the land.

Around 800 AD, the Sinagua people entered the region. While continuing to utilize irrigation canals, they mastered dry-farming techniques for beans, maize, squash, and other crops. Flourishing along the Verde and its tributaries, the Sinagua constructed landmarks like Tuzigoot and Montezuma Castle, which still grace the Verde Valley today. The collapse of the Sinagua culture in 1400 AD paved the way for new settlers, including the Yavapai and Apache peoples. Although primarily hunter-gatherers, these cultures maintained the tradition of utilizing the river's floodplain for cultivating corn and other crops.

In February 1865, non-native farmers from mining camps near Prescott arrived at the confluence of West Clear Creek and the Verde River, following the footsteps of the valley's earliest agriculturalists. They established irrigation canals, applying water to the bottomlands. By the turn of the 20th century, settlers had developed 68 irrigation canals, drawing water from the Verde River and its tributaries to nourish around 8,000 acres of pasture, fields, and orchards.

Today, the agricultural legacy persists, though the water once used for farming now nurtures lawns and trees in the green neighborhoods of Camp Verde. The remaining 40 irrigation ditches still water approximately 6,000 acres of greenspace, including production orchards, farms, and gardens. The Valley is renowned for its sweet corn and luscious tomatoes, attracting visitors to the farmers market and roadside stands throughout the summer.

"Verde Grown" is the brand chosen by Verde Valley farmers, ranchers, food producers, and advocates to share their two-thousand-year-old story of resilience. It represents and celebrates those connected to their agricultural roots and stewardship of the land and river. Verde Grown producers, nurturing crops like fruits, vegetables, cattle, pecans, wine, beer, and wool, contribute to the resilience and economic vitality of the Verde Valley, continuing a tradition that has sustained the region for millennia.

Upon the arrival of white settlers in the Camp Verde region with the intention of establishing farms, they encountered the remnants of ancient cultures. Scattered generously across the valley floor, surrounding hills, and occasional cliff faces were stone pueblos in varying states of decay. The sight of these structures and associated artifacts left the newcomers both amazed and perplexed, leading to the attraction of military and government-funded scientists to the valley. Their goal was to unravel the mystery of who had left such an indelible mark on the landscape.

Over the subsequent decades, archaeologists diligently worked to piece together the narrative of at least two distinct cultures. The initial culture, presumed to be the Hohokam, arrived from the south, followed by the Sinagua, presumed to be from the north. All evidence indicates that these two cultures thrived in the region for approximately 1,200 to 1,500 years before mysteriously disappearing around 1425 AD, reasons for which are still not fully understood.

Three notable cultural sites—Montezuma Castle, Montezuma Well, and Tuzigoot—are now designated National Monuments, protected and interpreted by the National Park Service. North of Flagstaff, a fourth site, Wupatki, is also under the administration of the National Park Service.

Two additional sites, the petroglyph walls at V Bar V Heritage Site and the cliff houses of Honanki and Palatki, are safeguarded and interpreted by the United States Forest Service. However, countless major and minor sites are scattered across the vast landscape, unprotected, in the majority of the Camp Verde area.

Camp Verde is positioned at the southern (downstream) extremity of the Verde Valley, enveloped by a landscape of highlands ranging from 6,000 to 7,000 feet. The surrounding area encompasses nine federal wilderness areas, interlaced with a network of trails leading to some of Arizona's most breathtaking views. Notably, Camp Verde serves as the exclusive gateway to Arizona's two Wild and Scenic Rivers: the lower 40 miles of the Verde River from Beasley Flat to Horseshoe Reservoir and Fossil Creek, featuring a pristine travertine stream fed by a 20,000-gallon-per-minute spring.

Spanning 18 miles of the Verde River, Camp Verde offers a popular destination for a more relaxed trip, whether in a kayak, canoe, or any floating vessel. A network of urban trails guides visitors to nearby bluffs and occasional ancient pueblos. The river serves as the boundary between the Prescott National Forest and the Coconino National Forest, both providing a plethora of amenities, including dispersed and developed campsites, suitable for every season. Moreover, Camp Verde and the surrounding valley host five Arizona State Parks, the 36-mile-long Verde River Greenway, and an upcoming sixth park, Rocking River.

Camp Verde provides a diverse range of dining options, from charming cafes and family-owned bistros to nationally recognized chain restaurants and fast-food establishments. Whether you crave excellent Mexican cuisine, freshly baked bread, or traditional mesquite smoked barbecue, the town offers something to satisfy every palate. Additionally, there is a recent surge in craft brewing and wine tasting venues.

Whether your stay is for a weekend or an extended period, Camp Verde offers numerous excellent places to stay during your visit. All lodging options are conveniently situated near highlighted attractions, making them ideal starting points for outdoor adventures in the Verde Valley. Some accommodations even provide discounts and packaged deals, so it's advisable to inquire before making reservations.

As the ultimate shopping destination in the center of Arizona, Camp Verde caters to both residents and visitors with a diverse shopping experience. The town's charming Main Street features a directory of stores, including unique boutiques, antique shops, and family-owned specialty stores. Hidden treasures and one-of-a-kind items await, making shopping in Camp Verde a joyful experience for everyone.

On June 8, 2018, Camp Verde received official recognition as a dark sky community from the IDA International Dark Sky Association. An IDA International Dark Sky community is a legally organized town, city, municipality, or community that has demonstrated exceptional commitment to preserving the night sky. This commitment is evident through the establishment and enforcement of a quality outdoor lighting ordinance, initiatives in dark sky education, and active citizen support for maintaining dark skies. Camp Verde is the fifth dark sky community in Arizona and the 20th globally to receive this designation. Other dark sky communities in Arizona include Flagstaff (the first in the world), Sedona, Big Park / Village of Oak Creek, and Fountain Hills. In October 2018, the Town of Camp Verde organized its inaugural Dark Sky Festival to commemorate the recognition and celebrate all aspects related to dark skies.

The Verde Valley Archaeology Center provides an enriching opportunity to explore the numerous archaeological sites in the region during your Arizona weekend getaway. Functioning as a hub for preservation, collection, and curation, the center establishes meaningful partnerships within the community it serves. A visit to the center offers a deeper understanding of American Indian history and the science of archaeology. Among the notable exhibits is the Honanki Collection, showcasing various examples of prehistoric basketry and weaving textiles. The Prehistoric Life in Camp Verde exhibit, based on local excavations, provides insights into the town's archaeological findings.

For an African safari experience in the heart of Arizona, consider visiting the Out of Africa Wildlife Park. Renowned as one of the finest wildlife parks or zoos, it offers an opportunity to witness well-cared-for animals in their natural habitats. The Wildlife Preserve, resembling the free-roaming Serengeti, allows visitors to walk or drive through 100 acres of valleys and hills where lions, cheetahs, and other exotic animals roam freely. To learn more about the park's inhabitants, embark on the African Bush Safari, a 40-minute guided tour narrated by expert guides. Additional attractions at the park include the Giant Snake Show, providing an up-close encounter with slithery serpents, the Wonders of Wildlife show featuring grizzly bears at play, and the mesmerizing

Predator Feed, where lions devour 800 pounds of meat.

Fort Verde State Historic Park stands as one of Arizona's well-preserved representations of an Indian Wars period fort. Serving as a crucial base for U.S. Army scouts and soldiers from the 1870s to the 1880s during the Central Arizona Indian Wars, the park offers a glimpse into this historical era. During your visit, you'll encounter four surviving buildings, noteworthy not only for their historical significance but also for their unique architectural aspects. To immerse yourself in the frontier lifestyle, you can participate in various living history tours and demonstrations during your day trip in Arizona.

Declared one of the nation's first National Monuments by President Theodore Roosevelt, Montezuma Castle National Monument stands out as one of the best-preserved prehistoric cliff dwellings in the entire United States. Originally, visitors were permitted to enter the dwelling and view numerous original artifacts left behind. However, due to extensive damage to this cultural landmark, such access is no longer allowed. Nevertheless, you can peer through the windows, gaining insight into the past and the people who once inhabited the dwelling. To reach the side of the limestone cliffs, you'll need to climb a series of ladders, creating a highly memorable excursion.

Embark on an exhilarating ATV adventure through Arizona's rugged desert and mountain terrain with Arizona Offroad Tours (AOT). This provides an excellent opportunity to create lasting memories with family and friends, filled with laughter and excitement. The unforgettable journey will guide you through Verde Valley and Sedona. Alongside riding your own fully-automatic ATV, guided by experienced professionals, you'll gain insights into the surrounding area from a knowledgeable guide. All participants will receive light snacks, ample water, a helmet, goggles, and their personalized AOT bandana.

Situated in the Verde Valley, Hauser and Hauser Farm occupies land once utilized by the Sinagua Indians. The Hauser family, spanning over six generations of farming, has cultivated an incredible rural atmosphere for visitors to enjoy. Younger guests particularly enjoy exploring the farm, observing tractors, and other farming equipment. Opportunities abound to learn about farming methods, irrigation systems, and the day-to-day management of the farm. Depart with some of their delicious sweet corn, each grown with care and perfection, and gather valuable corn-related tips and recipes. Make sure to plan your visit around their renowned annual corn festival.

Operating for nearly two decades, the Cliff Castle Casino is situated an hour away from Phoenix and has consistently earned the title of Arizona's 'Number 1 Casino' for several years. This recognition is well-deserved, drawing people from various locations who flock to enjoy popular slot machines and live table games. What sets Cliff Castle apart is its appeal to the entire family; featuring an arcade, a 20-lane bowling center, live entertainment, a gift shop, and a supervised child care center for the little ones. Additionally, the casino offers various accommodation options for guests staying overnight or for an extended period, along with dining establishments like Johnny Rockets or the Mountain Springs Buffet.

Encompassing over 11,000 acres, the Fossil Creek Wilderness is a designated wilderness area within Arizona's Coconino National Forest. Located at the edge of the Colorado Plateau and nestled at the bottom of a canyon, the wilderness area is renowned for its springs. Exploring the region involves traversing several bodies of water, fostering one of the most diverse ecosystems in the state. Visitors may encounter a variety of flora and fauna, including wildlife such as coyotes, elk, deer, raccoons, foxes, mountain lions, black bears, and skunks. Ornithology enthusiasts will appreciate the wilderness as a habitat for over a hundred bird species, many of which are native to the area.

The Clear Creek Vineyard and Winery, renowned for its Rio Claro wines, is the vision realized by Ignacio Mesa, who delved into viticulture long before turning his dream of owning a winery into reality. With over a decade of grape harvesting and wine aging, the winery offers a diverse array of flavors for enthusiasts to savor. Clear Creek welcomes visitors to sample a glass or two of these delicious handcrafted concoctions. Guests can also embark on a grapevine tour to witness the inception of the winemaking process or gain insights into the production of their varied range of red and white wines.

For those seeking unique vintage and antique items, Sweet Pea Vintage Antiques is the ultimate destination. Covering over 10,000 square feet, this establishment boasts an extensive collection of new and used treasures, ranging from home decor and furniture to jewelry and electronics. The inventory evolves weekly, as numerous vendors contribute to Sweet Pea's eclectic offerings – with a minimum of 40 vendors present at any given time. With over a decade of experience in the vintage and antique industry in Camp Verde, Sweet Pea ensures the discovery of cherished items that you'll hold dear for a lifetime.

Predator Zip Lines offers a guaranteed thrilling and captivating adventure, making it one of Sedona's top tours. This experience of a lifetime involves soaring through Out of Africa's wildlife park on a world-class zip line, passing over some of the planet's most formidable predators. The unforgettable journey includes hovering over incredible animals like tigers, lions, hyenas, wolves, and various other natural predators. For a unique perspective, consider trying the zip line during the night with Predator Zip Lines' Night Flight, providing visitors with breathtaking views of the surroundings and a chance to witness the wild side of Sedona.

Pastor Don Randall Sr. and his family, who spent more than twenty-nine years as missionaries in Northern Ireland, founded the Lighthouse Baptist Church in 2009. This church, a recent addition to Camp Verde, has attracted a growing community of followers seeking an independent, fundamental, Bible-believing congregation. Visitors are encouraged to attend the church and witness the traditional service firsthand, featuring hymn-style singing.

CANYON DE CHELLY NATIONAL MONUMENT

COUNTY: APACHE   CITY: CHINLE *n.c.*

DATE VISITED: WHO I WENT WITH:

RATING: ☆ ☆ ☆ ☆ ☆   WILL I RETURN? YES / NO

Canyon de Chelly National Monument, spanning around 84,000 acres of tribal land in northeast Arizona, is under the joint management of the National Park Service and the Navajo Nation. The monument comprises two canyons: Canyon de Chelly (pronounced "shay") and Canyon del Muerto. Moving southeast from the visitor center is Canyon de Chelly, while Canyon del Muerto extends northeast, creating a "V" shape.

Visitors have the opportunity to observe Ancestral Puebloan pit houses, dating back nearly 5,000 years, along with cliff dwellings integrated into the canyon walls. Additionally, overlooks along the rim provide free access to views of Hogans, traditional Navajo dwellings still inhabited today. However, if you wish to explore the interior of the canyons, hiring a Navajo guide is necessary.

The majority of visitors explore the park by taking the two scenic drives, each offering perspectives of either Canyon de Chelly or Canyon del Muerto. Prior to embarking on the journey, it is recommended to visit the visitor center where you can obtain a map, watch a 23-minute introductory video, and gather information about ranger-led programs. Additionally, at the visitor center, you have the option to hire a Navajo guide who can accompany you on a 4x4, horseback, or hiking tour into the canyon.

Within the confines of the Canyon de Chelly National Monument, the White House Trail stands as the sole hiking trail accessible without the need for a guide. To venture beyond this trail, one must either participate in a ranger-led hike or enlist the services of a Navajo guide. Several trails, including Beehive, Bat, Tunnel, Bear, Baby, Crow, and White Sands, are available for exploration with a guide.

The White House Trail, spanning 2.5 miles as an out-and-back route, commences at the White House Overlook on South Rim Drive. The trail descends 600 feet to the canyon floor via switchbacks and concludes at the White House Ruin. Allocating approximately two hours for the hike is advisable, factoring in additional time to appreciate the ruins and browse through Navajo arts and crafts. Given the limited shade along the trail, it is recommended to wear a hat, generously apply sunscreen, and carry an ample supply of water.

Among the two scenic drives within the park, the South Rim Drive holds the title of being the more popular choice. Tracing the perimeter of Canyon de Chelly, it showcases one of the park's prominent formations, Spider Rock—an 800-foot sandstone monolith believed to be the abode of Spider Woman. However, the North Rim Drive is equally remarkable, providing vistas of Canyon del Muerto, named in remembrance of the 115 Navajo individuals who lost their lives to Spanish soldiers in 1805. Both routes are paved and accessible throughout the year.

The South Rim Drive, spanning 36 miles round trip, commences at the visitor center and concludes at the Spider Rock Overlook. Here, the panoramic view reveals the canyon's vibrant 1,000-foot walls, reminiscent of the Grand Canyon. Along the South Rim Drive, seven overlooks are featured, including the White House Overlook, serving as the starting point for the trail leading to the White House Ruin.

On the other hand, the North Rim Drive, starting from the visitor center, covers approximately 34 miles round trip and includes stops at Antelope House, Mummy Cave, and Massacre Cave overlooks. While this drive offers a less crowded experience, travelers must exercise caution for freely roaming livestock in the area.

With the exception of the White House Trail, entry into the canyon requires the presence of a ranger or a Navajo guide. These guides can be found online through Navajo Nation Parks and Recreation or at the park's visitor center. It is advisable to secure the services of a guide in advance, especially if planning a visit during the peak months from March to October.

Various tour companies offer a range of options, including 4x4 tours, guided hikes, and overnight camping. Some packages combine a guided hike with an overnight stay in a Hogan. If the available options do not meet your preferences, guides often customize experiences upon request.

4x4 tours, typically conducted in Jeeps, vary in duration from three to eight hours, with the three-hour tour being the most common. Stops on these tours include Kokopelli Cave, Petroglyph Rock, First Ruin, Junction Ruin, and White House Ruin. Departures are from hotels in Chinle or the visitor center.

Guided hikes usually require participants to be at least 12 years old and physically fit for a three-hour hike. The level of difficulty can be adjusted based on hikers' preferences.

For those interested in horseback riding, Justin's Horse Rental offers guided rides into the canyons. Located just past the visitor center on South Rim Drive.

Overnight camping options vary, with some companies charging a flat fee, while others charge by the hour or per person. Accommodations typically involve sleeping under the stars, though some companies may offer Hogans as an alternative.

There are two campgrounds in the vicinity, each offering different amenities and managed by different entities. The first, known as Cottonwood Campground, is under the management of Navajo Nation Parks and Recreation. It features 90 individual campsites and two group tent sites, lacking hookups but providing a dump station. The campground is equipped with three restrooms, though showers are not available. Visitors should bring cash to cover the night fee, and campsites are assigned on a first-come, first-served basis at the park campground.

On the other hand, Spider Rock Campground is privately operated by Howard Smith, situated near the Spider Rock Overlook. This campground offers 30 RV and tent camping sites along with a dump station, without any hookups. For those without an RV or tent, there's the option to rent a tent or stay in one of the campground's three Hogans. Reservations are necessary for this campground.

If you prefer accommodations within the park, the sole option available is the Thunderbird Lodge, consisting of 69 rooms and managed by Navajo Nation Hospitality Enterprise. Thunderbird Lodge features pet-friendly rooms and is entirely smoke-free, with a cafeteria-style restaurant that was originally a trading post established in 1896. Additionally, the lodge operates one of the region's leading guide companies.

For those exploring lodging options in the nearby Chinle area, there are several chain hotels with restaurants offering Navajo specialties like fry bread.

Details on nearby hotels include:

Thunderbird Lodge: Located just off US 191 on Indian Route 7, Best Western Canyon de Chelly Inn has 104 smoke-free rooms, an on-site restaurant, and a recently renovated indoor swimming pool.

Best Western Canyon de Chelly Inn: Positioned just off US 191 on Indian Route 7, this Best Western establishment comprises 104 smoke-free rooms, an on-site restaurant, and a recently updated indoor swimming pool.

Holiday Inn Canyon de Chelly: Recognized as the closest hotel to the visitor center, this hotel includes the historic Garcia's Trading Post. It boasts 108 rooms and features an on-site restaurant, considered one of the finest dining options in Chinle.

Directions to Canyon de Chelly National Monument:

If coming from I-40, head north on US 191 to Ganado. Optionally, stop at the Hubbell Trading Post National Historic Site if time allows. Then, take Highway 264 west to Burnside and resume heading north on US 191. Upon reaching Chinle, turn east onto IR 7, and the park entrance is approximately 3 miles from US 191.

Alternatively, exit I-40 at Window Rock and travel around 50 miles north on IR 12 to Tsaile. Turn west at IR 64, following it to Mummy Cave Overlook, which transforms into the North Rim Drive. Avoid using IR 7 between Sawmill and the Spider Rock turnoff, as it is unpaved and unmaintained.

Accessibility:

The visitor center and various overlooks like Massacre Cave Overlook on North Rim Drive, Tsegi, Junction, White House, and Spider Rock overlooks on South Rim Drive are accessible. Note that backcountry trails and areas are not accessible.

Tips:

1) The Navajo Nation observes Daylight Savings Time, while the rest of Arizona (excluding certain tribal lands) does not. Confirm times to avoid missing scheduled tours.
2) Admission to Canyon de Chelly National Monument is free, but a guide is required to explore inside the canyons.
3) Be prepared to make cash or personal check payments, as many guides and Cottonwood Campground may not accept debit or credit cards.
4) Keep in mind that pets are not allowed in the visitor center, on the White House Trail, or during canyon tours. However, leashed pets are permitted at overlooks and in the campground.

CASA GRANDE RUINS

COUNTY: PINAL
CITY: COOLIDGE

DATE VISITED:
WHO I WENT WITH:

RATING: ☆ ☆ ☆ ☆ ☆
WILL I RETURN? YES / NO

Many travelers are drawn to iconic Arizona destinations such as the Grand Canyon and the Saguaro cacti, while the bustling cities of Tucson and Phoenix attract millions of visitors annually. However, nestled between these urban centers lies a relatively small yet significant national park site known as the Casa Grande Ruins National Monument, and its size should not deter exploration. Situated southeast of Phoenix, Arizona, the Casa Grande Ruins National Monument is conveniently located off Highway 287, with its entrance situated on the east side boundary and the sole parking area available at the visitor center. For those interested in visiting Saguaro National Park as well, Casa Grande Ruins National Monument is approximately an hour's drive north from the Tucson Mountain District side of the national park.

The history of this region dates back to around 5500 BCE when the earliest hunting and gathering culture thrived. As the climate shifted to drier and hotter conditions, the ancestral Sonoran Desert people adapted by transitioning to agriculture. Archaeologists have uncovered pottery remains that offer insights into their evolving culture. Around 1500 BCE, these ancestral inhabitants began implementing an irrigation system to bring water from nearby rivers closer to their land. The area became a hub for cultivating crops such as corn, beans, squash, cotton, and tobacco. In the 1100s, a shift occurred from the construction of "pit houses" to above-ground dwellings as the villages became more organized. The culmination of this development was the construction of the Casa Grande.

Based on the most reliable dating methods, it is determined that the Casa Grande was constructed during the Classic Period between 1100 and 1450 CE, likely in the 1300s. The construction, taking into account the significant amount of materials and workforce involved, suggests meticulous planning and organization. This architectural feat provides valuable insights into the advancement of the culture from its early hunter-gatherer origins.

While the specific purpose of the Casa Grande remains uncertain, its construction underscores its significance to the ancestral Sonoran Desert people. Unfortunately, in the late 1300s and early 1400s, this culture vanished. Potential explanations for their widespread depopulation include factors such as drought, flood, disease, invasion, and salinization of farmland. Presently, several Native American groups, including the O'odham, Hopi, and Zuni, can trace their ancestry back to these early inhabitants.

The continuous archaeological endeavors and preservation initiatives focused on the Casa Grande ruins serve to perpetuate the legacy of the ancestral Sonoran Desert people, ensuring that their cultural heritage remains alive and appreciated.

As per the National Park Service statistics report, the Casa Grande ruin received 49,261 visitors in 2021. This reflects a significant decline from the pre-pandemic years, during which the site saw visitation ranging from 62,000 to 76,000 people. However, when comparing recent data to the period between 1970 and 2001, when over 100,000 visitors annually were recorded at the Casa Grande Ruins National Monument, it is evident that the visitor population has decreased in recent decades. For those planning a visit to the national monument, there is an opportunity to incorporate other national park sites into the itinerary. Tonto National Monument, situated approximately 90 minutes to the northeast, can be conveniently explored on the same day. Additionally, the Tucson Mountain District of Saguaro National Park is slightly over an hour south of the Casa Grande ruins, providing further options for exploration.

While visiting the Casa Grande Ruins National Monument, you won't encounter a plethora of activities or a vast expanse to explore, as the site is relatively small, covering only one square mile. However, allocate a few hours to immerse yourself in learning about the culture of the ancestral Sonoran Desert people.

Upon arrival, your first destination at any National Park site should be the visitor center, where you can obtain maps and informative materials guiding you through the site. Park rangers are also available to suggest hikes or address any questions you may have. At the visitor center of the Casa Grande Ruins National Monument, you can delve into museum exhibits and watch a park movie that provides deeper insights into the culture and history of these ancient peoples.

Throughout the park, follow signs directing you to various points of interest, marked as "wayside exhibits." These are illustrated signs offering information about the specific locations you are viewing. Topics covered include farming, life within the walls, engineering and construction, irrigation practices, sacred land, and more. As guided tours are not available, you have the freedom to explore the area at your own pace.

For a pleasant break, the park's picnic area is open daily from 9 a.m. to 4 p.m. Pack a lunch and take advantage of the picnic shelters amid the Arizona landscape. Ensuring responsible environmental practices, the park facilitates proper waste disposal with trash cans and recyclable plastic and can collection stations at the shelter areas. If you bring a pet, keep them on a leash to maintain a Leave No Trace approach.

Exploring the interior of Casa Grande is not permitted, as self-guided tours are restricted due to safety and resource conservation concerns. There are no guided tours available either, as park rangers cannot accompany visitors inside the ruins. The presence of animals such as bats and birds within the ruins poses a potential danger to humans due to their droppings. Moreover, allowing visitors inside could result in permanent damage to the fragile structure of the ruins, as there is not much holding them together. For these reasons, it is strongly advised to appreciate Casa Grande from the outside only.

If you find yourself in the vicinity of Arizona, consider adding Casa Grande Ruins National

Monument to your itinerary. It is easily accessible, with a one-hour drive north from Tucson via I-10 or south from Phoenix. As you explore museums, art galleries, local restaurants, and the nightlife of nearby cities, remember to include visits to the nearby national park sites. Many people cherish the opportunity to experience the history and cultures of ancient peoples, making it a noteworthy addition to vacation memories.

COUNTY: YAVAPAI   **CITY:** SEDONA *n.c.*

DATE VISITED: **WHO I WENT WITH:**

                   RATING: ☆ ☆ ☆ ☆ ☆   **WILL I RETURN?** YES / NO

Embarking on the Cathedral Rock Trail in Sedona is undoubtedly worthwhile, even amidst the vulture-like circling for a parking spot and the demanding ascent to the summit. The trail offers stunning views from various vantage points, ensuring that your efforts are richly rewarded.

Trail Specifications:

Length: 1.0 mile
Trail Type: Out and back
Elevation Gain/Loss: 551 ft.
Difficulty: Moderate with several challenging sections
Kid Friendly: Yes
Dog-Friendly: Yes, but leashes are required.
Accessibility: Limited, with paved parking available

Directions:

To reach the trailhead, take Highway 179 beyond Oak Creek Village, then turn left onto Back O' Beyond Road. Proceed west for approximately 1 mile, and you will find the trailhead on your left. Additional overflow parking is available farther down on Back O' Beyond Rd.

The trail commences directly from Back O' Beyond Road, with a relatively short approach given the total length of the hike being just one mile. Along the way, you'll encounter the junction between Cathedral Rock Trail and Easy Breezy Trail, as well as a small creek to cross before the ascent begins. The path is marked by basket cairns, and the initial climb is relatively straightforward, featuring a well-defined trail and occasional rock staircases. Upon reaching a plateau just before the junction of Cathedral Rock Trail and Templeton Trail, you'll be greeted by a breathtaking panoramic view of Sedona, offering a compelling reason to pause and take it in.

Continuing the hike over a rocky section, you'll reach the base of a crevasse or cleft in the rock. At this point, many hikers might choose to turn around or contemplate whether to proceed. The crack ascends at a 45-degree angle for approximately 40 feet, providing ample hand and footholds that make the climb manageable. However, for those uncomfortable with heights, this segment may pose a challenge. It's important to note that after rainfall, the rocks can become slippery, requiring extra caution.

After conquering the crevasse, the ascent becomes a tad more challenging, albeit with a less steep incline, the elevation gain remains significant. The sandstone surface offers suitable handholds and footholds, often rising in gradations, making certain sections of the climb relatively easy. However, the hike becomes more interesting in two sections where the rock is high and lacks distinctive features. The heavily trafficked trail reveals various approaches as hikers navigate these segments. Some opt for a bit of a running start, with a few cresting over successfully, while others may need assistance from friends. Some simply scramble over the top, using a "smearing" technique to leverage their foot against the rock. Undoubtedly, these sections add an element of fun to the hike.

Upon reaching a second plateau, a popular resting spot, the proximity of the summit becomes apparent. With the most challenging part of the hike now behind you, it's only a matter of time before reaching the top. The remaining stretch of the trail involves a rocky staircase, a few switchbacks past an elegant juniper tree, leading to the ultimate destination. A sign at the summit reading "End of Trail" welcomes you between the two walls of the formation, offering a breathtaking view over the edge. Exercise extreme caution during the descent, as the hike follows an out-and-back route. While descending the crevasse, be mindful of others attempting the climb.

Tips:

1) Parking can be challenging at Sedona trailheads, particularly if you arrive later in the day. Exercise patience, as spaces tend to turn over quickly. In case the designated lots for Cathedral Rock are full, additional overflow parking is accessible at the Yavapai Point Parking Lot, located about two miles south on Highway 179 and on the right-hand side. It's important to note that Yavapai Point has fewer than 20 spots in total and will add nearly 4 miles one way to your hike via the Templeton Trail. This can be an excellent option if you wish to extend your hike.
2) A daily pass for all Sedona trails is available for $5.00, with fee machines at designated trailheads accepting credit cards only. America the Beautiful annual passes are also accepted.
3) Given the limited shade on the trail, use sun protection and ensure you bring an ample supply of water.
4) Completing the hike at sunset is a magnificent experience. If you find yourself on the formation after dark, it is advisable to carry a headlamp for illumination.

CHAPEL OF THE HOLY CROSS

COUNTY: YAVAPAI   CITY: SEDONA *n.c.*

DATE VISITED: WHO I WENT WITH:

RATING: ☆ ☆ ☆ ☆ ☆   WILL I RETURN? YES / NO

If you've ever traveled through the Sedona region in Arizona, you must have been amazed by the stunning red rock formations. The streets are lined with hikers making their way to Devil's Bridge and Cathedral Rock, while downtown echoes with the rumble of ATVs. Sedona is undeniably a popular destination. But, have you ever heard about the Chapel of the Holy Cross?

Perched atop the majestic red rocks of Sedona, Arizona, the Chapel of the Holy Cross stands out as one of the most sought-after attractions in the area. Not only is it visually captivating, but its architectural marvel is truly breathtaking. This chapel is intricately integrated into the famous rocks that define this part of Arizona. Every year, millions of visitors flock to the Chapel of the Holy Cross to witness the 250-foot structure protruding from a thousand-foot rock wall.

The chapel was finished in 1956 and has maintained its original location at 780 Chapel Road in Sedona. It's conveniently less than a 10-minute drive from popular trailheads like Cathedral Rock, Bell Rock, and the well-visited Tlaquepaque shopping center. Due to limited parking spaces, RVs and trailers are not allowed at the Chapel of the Holy Cross, which offers only 45 parking spaces, consistently full throughout the year.

Fortunately, the Chapel of the Holy Cross welcomes visitors throughout the entire year. Regardless of when you decide to explore Sedona, this renowned attraction is accessible. Operating hours are from 9 a.m. to 5 p.m. daily, with the exception of Christmas and Easter when the gift shop remains closed. Moreover, the chapel is actively used for religious services. Mass takes place at 3 p.m. on Wednesdays and Fridays, and a Taize prayer service occurs on Mondays at 5 p.m. Apart from these worship sessions, adoration and confession are offered on Wednesday and Friday afternoons.

Admission to the Chapel of the Holy Cross is free. Upon entering, you'll encounter benches, candles, and an exquisite sculpture of the Living Christ. It's important to be considerate of others as some visitors are there for prayer and meditation, while others may be lighting candles to honor a loved one, or simply appreciating the beauty.

Given the limited parking spaces, it's advisable not to search for the ideal spot but to take the first available one, as the area is highly popular. To avoid crowds, planning an early visit on a weekday is recommended.

For those who find the steep incline to the chapel challenging, there is a golf cart shuttle service available. The uphill walk can be strenuous, so you'll notice golf carts transporting visitors up and down the hill, dropping them off at the ramp leading to the chapel doors.

While the shuttle is a complimentary service, tips are appreciated.

Upon reaching the summit of the hill, whether you ascend on foot or via the golf cart, take a moment to absorb the breathtaking beauty of the surroundings. Many visitors can be seen capturing selfies and posing for photos in the vicinity of the Chapel of the Holy Cross. Therefore, indulge in a few moments to appreciate the spectacular vistas of Sedona.

While the external landscape is awe-inspiring, don't miss the opportunity to step inside the chapel. The interior is equally captivating. The floor-to-ceiling windows immediately draw attention, offering panoramic views of Red Rock Country. Positioned against these windows is the Living Christ sculpture, a remarkable piece of art depicting various symbols of the Christian faith. For instance, the crown of thorns on Jesus' head symbolizes the 99 plus one for the lost sheep from the Gospels' parable. Additionally, you have the chance to light a candle in remembrance of a loved one, with candles lining the front of the sanctuary. The community collectively prays over these lit candles during Friday mass.

After spending a few moments inside the Chapel of the Holy Cross, descend to the basement. The gift shop houses handcrafted items, jewelry, ornaments, and various religious articles. Replicas of the Living Christ sculpture are also available for purchase, and all proceeds contribute to supporting St. John Vianney Catholic Church, the custodian of the chapel.

The Chapel of the Holy Cross is not just a sacred haven of beauty; it also provides trails for exploring the surrounding area. One popular trail is a 3.8-mile loop encompassing the Chapel Trail, Broken Arrow Trail, and Mystic Trail. This moderate hike involves a gain of less than 500 feet in elevation. For those seeking an easier trail, the Mystic, Peccary, Hog Wash Loop is under 3 miles with a 209-foot elevation gain. Both trails traverse the vicinity around the Chapel of the Holy Cross and meander through the captivating red rocks of Sedona, offering splendid views regardless of the chosen path.

While Sedona is a year-round destination, it's advisable to steer clear of the summer months when temperatures can soar above 100 degrees. Late winter and spring are considered optimal, especially for hikers, as these seasons offer cool mornings and comfortable afternoons. However, be mindful that this period is also popular among tourists and snowbirds. If you opt for a visit during the peak season, make it a priority to arrive early at trailheads and attractions such as the Chapel of the Holy Cross.

If you're embarking on a road trip through Monument Valley, heading south to Flagstaff, consider extending your journey a bit further to explore Red Rock Country. If you're spending several days at the Grand Canyon, allocate time for a detour to Sedona. The awe-inspiring scenery of this Southwest region will undoubtedly justify the time and money invested. Don't forget to include a visit to the Chapel of the Holy Cross on your must-do list. If you plan to hike one of the trails, set aside a couple of hours. If your visit is more casual, allow yourself at least 30 minutes to take in the views, explore the interior, and peruse the gift shop.

COUNTY: COCHISE   CITY: WILLCOX *n.c.*

DATE VISITED: WHO I WENT WITH:

RATING: ☆ ☆ ☆ ☆ ☆   WILL I RETURN? YES / NO

Encompassing 12,025 acres in the southern region of Arizona, Chiricahua National Monument stands as the outcome of the eruption of Turkey Creek Volcano millions of years ago. The ash expelled during the eruption gradually cooled, giving rise to layers of rhyolite that eventually eroded into the distinctive formations visible today, such as rhyolite rock pinnacles, balanced rocks, and columns. This monument boasts remarkable landscapes, establishing itself as a sought-after hiking destination in Arizona. Beyond its geological features, the site also encompasses settlers' homesteads and a cemetery. Ranger-led tours provide insight into the lives of early settlers, the Chiricahua Apache who once inhabited the area, and the Civilian Conservation Corps responsible for constructing the park's infrastructure.

The primary activity at Chiricahua National Monument is hiking, with the park offering a variety of trails spanning 17 miles. These trails cater to different preferences, ranging from the relatively flat 0.2-mile Bonita Creek Loop to the more challenging 9.5-mile Big Loop. For those who prefer not to hike, there's the option to drive along the scenic 8-mile Bonita Canyon Drive. Along this route, visitors can make stops to explore Faraway Ranch or enjoy a picnic at one of the five designated picnic areas.

Apart from hiking, the monument also attracts visitors with camping, birding, and stargazing opportunities. Typically, ranger-led programs, including tours of Faraway Ranch, are available, but it's important to note that these programs are temporarily suspended. For the latest information on program availability, interested individuals should check the monument's website.

The monument provides a diverse range of trails suitable for various fitness levels. An interesting incentive for hikers is the opportunity to earn a Chiricahua National Monument "I Hike for Health" pin by hiking at least 5 miles and presenting trail selfies to the visitor center staff.

Echo Canyon Trail stands out as one of the monument's most popular routes, covering a 1.6-mile stretch each way. This trail takes hikers past the Grottoes formation and the imposing Wall Street passage before descending to the forest floor and back up. Completing the loop back to the trailhead can be done via the Hailstone Trail.

For those seeking a water-carved natural bridge, the Natural Bridge trail, although not as visually spectacular as some other hikes in the monument, offers a 4.8-mile out-and-back journey that is considered moderately challenging.

The Heart of Rocks Loop presents views of iconic rock formations, including Duck on a

Rock and Punch and Judy. To reach it, hikers can either start on the Lower Rhyolite Canyon Trail and continue on the Sarah Deming Trail or approach it from Massai Point via Big Balanced Rock Trail. In either case, the round-trip hike will cover a distance of at least 7 miles.

Chiricahua National Monument's sole paved road, Bonita Canyon Road, stretches for 8 miles from the entrance station to Massai Point. Along this route, you'll encounter notable sites, including Faraway Ranch, the historical residence of former Chiricahua Forest Ranger Neil Erickson, the Erickson family cemetery, and vantage points overlooking Bonita Canyon. The journey concludes with scenic views of rhyolite rock pinnacles descending the slopes. Massai Point also features a brief nature trail and picnic tables.

A side road branching off Bonita Canyon Road takes you to the Sugarloaf Mountain Trailhead and additional picnic facilities. Picnicking is also available at various locations, including Massai Point, Echo Canyon, Faraway Ranch, and Bonita Creek.

Chiricahua National Monument features the Bonita Canyon Campground as its sole designated camping area. While there are smaller dispersed campgrounds in the vicinity, these operate on a first-come, first-served basis. For alternative camping options, there is a well-regarded KOA in Willcox, conveniently located off I-10, and another one further away in Benson.

Bonita Canyon Campground, with 25 sites situated near a riparian area, offers amenities such as running water, flush toilets, and picnic tables. However, it lacks hookups and showers. Reservations can be made on Recreation.gov, and early booking is advisable, particularly during the spring, the campground's peak season. It's important to note that vehicles over 29 feet are not permitted at this campground.

For a more remote camping experience, there's the Idlewilde Campground, exclusive for tents and operational from April 1 to September 30. Located on the east side of the Chiricahua Mountains near the New Mexico border, this campground offers nine sites on a first-come, first-served basis, with access to restrooms and running water.

Those seeking a KOA option can consider the Willcox/Cochise KOA Holiday, featuring 62 sites, including many pull-through spaces and rental cabins. The campground provides amenities such as a playground, hand-dipped ice cream for kids, a lighted dog park for dog walking, 38 channels of TV, and Wi-Fi for checking email. Conveniently situated just off I-10, it offers a variety of facilities for both families and adults.

The nearest accommodations to Chiricahua National Monument are located in Willcox, a small Arizona city situated 37 miles northwest of the park. In Willcox, lodging options are primarily budget motels and chain hotels. Sierra Vista, approximately 82 miles southwest of the park, offers a more diverse selection of boutique hotels. Despite the approximately one hour and 45-minute drive from Sierra Vista to Chiricahua National

Monument, the route takes you through the historic town of Tombstone, renowned for the infamous gunfight at the O.K. Corral. Tombstone also provides a few accommodation choices.

OYO Hotel Roses: Despite the modest exterior of OYO Hotel Roses, the interior boasts individually decorated rooms with a boutique ambiance. It's essential to ensure that you book the OYO property on Haskell Avenue, not on Bisbee Avenue.

Holiday Inn Express & Suites: For those who prefer a chain hotel, the Holiday Inn Express & Suites offers clean rooms and complimentary breakfast. Conveniently situated off I-10, just north of the freeway.

Sierra Suites: This boutique hotel in Sierra Vista, featuring terra cotta tiles and wood-beam ceilings, serves as an excellent base for exploring Southern Arizona, including Chiricahua National Monument. It's less than a half-hour from Tombstone and 40 minutes from Bisbee.

Tombstone Monument Ranch: Designed to replicate a Western town with wooden sidewalks, offering themed rooms such as the mining office or bordello, this guest ranch provides three meals a day, along with activities like horseback riding and archery.

Directions:

Chiricahua National Monument is situated approximately 120 miles southeast of Tucson. To reach the monument, take I-10 in either the east or west direction to exit 340 in Willcox, Arizona. Proceed south into the city on Allen Drive, then turn right on Haskell Avenue. Continue until reaching AZ 186, make a left turn, and follow it for 31 miles until reaching AZ 181, where you should turn left. Drive the final 3 miles into the park, and at this point, the state route transforms into Bonita Canyon Road. If traveling from Sierra Vista, take Charleston Road east to Tombstone, following it to Allen Street. Make a right turn, followed by a quick left at 1st Street, and then pick up AZ 80 (East Fremont Street) by turning right. Follow this to Camino San Rafael, turn left, continue for a little over a mile, and turn right on Gleeson Road. Drive 23 miles to US 191 in Elfrida, turn north (left), and go 13 miles to AZ 181. Turn right. Before continuing, refuel in Sunizona, and follow the signs leading to Chiricahua National Monument.

Accessibility:

Chiricahua National Monument provides an accessible visitor center and restrooms. However, the trails leading into the wilderness are not accessible, except for a short, paved section of the Massai Nature Trail. For an opportunity to witness the remarkable rock formations, visitors can drive Bonita Canyon Road and appreciate the landscape from designated overlooks. Those seeking an experience beyond the car can utilize the accessible picnic area at Massai Point. Additionally, the Bonita Canyon Campground offers one accessible campsite, site 8, providing easy access to restrooms, picnic tables, and fire rings.

Tips:

1) There is no gas available within the monument. Depending on your chosen route, ensure you refuel in Willcox or Sunizona before continuing your journey.

2) The monument imposes a 24-foot limit on vehicles, and larger vehicles are not allowed beyond the Faraway Ranch parking lot.

3) Cell service is restricted within the monument. If you plan on hiking, consider carrying a GPS personal locator beacon to signal for help in case of an emergency.

4) Leashed pets are permitted on some lower canyon trails, but they are not allowed on the majority of the monument's trails.

5) Before embarking on any trail, be well-prepared. Bring an ample supply of water (approximately one quart per hour), salty snacks, and electrolytes. Apply sunscreen and wear closed-toed shoes for protection.

COCONINO LAVA RIVER CAVE

COUNTY: COCONINO   CITY: FLAGSTAFF *n.c.*

DATE VISITED: WHO I WENT WITH:

RATING: ☆ ☆ ☆ ☆ ☆   WILL I RETURN? YES / NO

In the Coconino National Forest, located northwest of Flagstaff, Arizona, you have the opportunity to explore ancient lava tubes known as the Lava River Caves.

The Lava River Caves are believed to have originated approximately 700,000 years ago through the solidification of molten rock that emanated from a volcanic vent. As the lava cooled and solidified around the vent, it formed a tube-like structure, now serving as the designated walking trail.

Situated in the heart of the Coconino National Forest, the Lava River Caves maintain a consistently cool temperature, ranging from the 30s to the 40s throughout the year. Given Flagstaff's elevation of around 6,900 feet and the Coconino National Forest's elevation of 9,000 feet near the Lava Caves, it is advisable to bring a coat and pants, as the environment can be chilly regardless of the season.

The entrance to the cave is conveniently located just a short walk from the parking lot, and you'll find helpful signs along the way to guide you, ensuring you don't miss the entrance. Identifying the cave is quite straightforward, as it's a conspicuous hole in the ground situated at the end of the path.

The initial challenge of the hike lies in the ascent into the cave. Once you overcome this hurdle, the rest becomes more manageable. Ensure you have your flashlights ready, keep your phone stowed away, and free up your hands as you venture into the dark abyss. Even before you begin the descent, a chilling breeze welcomes you. Given the cave's cold environment, ice patches on rocks are common during cooler seasons, so exercise caution as you navigate down. Additionally, be mindful of the cave ceiling, which can be quite low in certain areas.

After completing the descent, the trail levels out, transitioning into a slightly uneven but generally flat path. Approximately one-third of the time, you'll find yourself climbing and hopping from one rock to another, adding an element of excitement to the journey. Eventually, you'll reach a fork in the trail. The left path is the easier option, while the right path presents an opportunity to test your limbo skills. If you choose the right path, be prepared for the cave ceiling to lower, leaving only 2-3 feet of standing room. Some people opt to awkwardly squat or crawl through this section, which lasts only a few seconds. The two paths reunite shortly afterward.

If you find yourself in a section of the cave where there are no other hikers in sight or within earshot, consider turning off all your lights. The thickness of the darkness surrounding you is truly surreal, although this might be a bit too eerie for some individuals. As you reach the end of the trail, you'll notice a slight increase in temperature, and you might even find it warm enough to tie your jacket around your waist. The trail concludes at a dead end, prompting you to retrace your steps and head back the way you entered. This hike typically takes anywhere from 1 to 2 hours, but you could extend your stay by bringing snacks and lingering in the cave a bit longer. It's crucial to adhere to the principle of leaving no trace and ensure you pack out everything you brought in.

The cave is pitch black, and the rocks you traverse are not always stable, making stumbling quite likely. It's advisable to think twice about bringing young children on this hike, and under no circumstances should you attempt to bring your dog into the cave.

Directions:

The Lava Tubes are situated approximately 30-45 minutes outside of Flagstaff. Upon turning onto Forest Road 245 from Fort Valley Rd., continue for about 3 miles and then make a left onto Forest Road 171. Proceed for another mile and make a final left onto 171 B. The journey concludes at a decent-sized dirt parking lot at the road's end, and there is no parking fee.

Once you depart from Fort Valley Rd., the remainder of the drive is on a well-maintained dirt road. However, it's important to note that in winter, forest roads may be closed due to adverse weather conditions.

Tips:

1) Ensure each person has at least 2-3 light sources, with headlamps being particularly useful. Check that your flashlights have fresh batteries.
2) Wear appropriate footwear for the hike.
3) Dress warmly, as the cave temperature is typically around 40 degrees, even in summer.
4) Respect the cave environment and other hikers; avoid defacing the cave.
5) Given the low ceilings in some parts of the cave, consider wearing a hat or beanie for protection.
6) While gloves and walking sticks are optional, some hikers find them beneficial.
7) If you are uncomfortable with caves, tight spaces, or darkness, this may not be the ideal hike for you.
8) For those considering camping nearby, it's essential to set up camp at least 1 mile away from the cave's entrance.

COCONINO NATIONAL FOREST

COUNTY: COCONINO, GILA, YAVAPAI   **CITY:** FLAGSTAFF *n.c.*

DATE VISITED: **WHO I WENT WITH:**

RATING: ☆ ☆ ☆ ☆ ☆   **WILL I RETURN?** YES / NO

Encompassing an expansive area of over 1.8 million acres, Coconino National Forest extends from the southern border near Sedona along the Verde River to Sunset Crater National Monument, positioned north of Flagstaff.

As one of the six national forests in Arizona, Coconino National Forest boasts the inclusion of all or parts of 10 designated wilderness areas. Noteworthy features within its boundaries include the summit of Humphreys Peak, the highest point in Arizona, and Mormon Lake, the state's largest natural lake (except during drought conditions). Renowned for its diverse landscapes, the forest showcases a spectrum ranging from red rocks and desert terrain to Ponderosa pine forests and alpine tundra.

This national forest offers visitors a myriad of experiences, such as exploring an ancient Sinagua village, discovering locations where astronauts trained for lunar landings, and engaging in outdoor activities like hiking, biking, fishing, or camping. With several scenic drives traversing Coconino National Forest, it has become a sought-after destination for residents of Phoenix seeking refuge from the summer heat.

Due to its vast expanse, Coconino National Forest offers a plethora of activities for visitors. Embarking on a scenic drive proves to be an excellent way to absorb the park's diverse landscapes, especially for those exploring the area for the first time. The Oak Creek Canyon Scenic Drive, traversing SR 89A between Sedona and Flagstaff, provides a captivating journey through a red-walled canyon and steep switchbacks to Oak Creek Canyon Vista. This vantage point offers stunning views of Coconino National Forest below, making it an ideal starting point.

Another must-try drive is the Volcanoes and Ruins Loop Scenic Drive, commencing 12 miles north of Flagstaff on US 89. Following the Sunset Crater-Wupatki turnoff (Forest Road 545), this route passes through a volcanic field where astronauts trained for lunar landings and continues to Wupatki National Monument, showcasing the remnants of Sinagua pueblos.

For those seeking off-road adventures, Coconino National Forest presents an extensive network of single-track and double-track roads catering to OHVs (off-highway vehicles), ATVs, 4x4s, and dirt bikes. The Cinder Hills Off Highway Vehicle Area near Flagstaff features volcanic terrain, while Sedona boasts 11 OHV routes meandering through red rocks. If you lack an OHV, numerous companies conduct 4x4 tours, especially around Sedona.

The national forest hosts some of the state's finest hiking trails. In Sedona alone, over 90 trails are listed on the national forest website, including notable ones like Devil's Bridge, Courthouse Butte Loop, Boynton Canyon Trail, and West Fork Trail. Flagstaff and the Mogollon Rim region also offer an impressive array of hikes, with Humphreys Trail No. 151 leading to the highest point in Arizona.

Cycling enthusiasts will find satisfaction as many of Coconino National Forest's hiking trails are open to mountain bikes, providing an alternative means to explore the forest's beauty.

Fishing enthusiasts have various opportunities in Coconino National Forest, with locations such as Oak Creek, the Verde River, West Clear Creek Wilderness, Ashurst Lake, Lake Mary, and the C.C. Cragin Reservoir providing habitats for trout, catfish, pike, and other fish species. Boating and paddling experiences are also available, offering the chance to launch a boat at Upper Lake Mary and C.C. Cragin Reservoir or paddle through Marshall Lake.

For those seeking a unique adventure, the Lava River Cave is a lesser-known destination transporting visitors back 70,000 years to a time when a volcanic vent created a mile-long lava tube. While hiking inside, it's essential to bring multiple flashlights and wear warm clothing, as the cave maintains a constant temperature of 42 degrees Fahrenheit, even in the summer.

Elden Pueblo, an ancient Sinagua village similar to Wupatki, is situated on the eastern edge of Flagstaff, just off Highway 89. Visitors can explore the ruins independently and participate in excavation activities during Public Archaeology Days.

Winter sports enthusiasts can indulge in Arizona's premier ski area, Snowbowl, located northwest of Flagstaff. Boasting an average annual snowfall of 260 inches, Snowbowl offers downhill skiing and snowboarding opportunities. The area is also popular among Phoenicians who come to sled after substantial snowfall.

Camping options abound in Coconino National Forest, catering to outdoor enthusiasts with a mix of developed campgrounds, dispersed camping areas, and cabins available for rent. Notable cabins include Crescent Moon and Apache Main in the Sedona area, along with Fernow and Kendrick cabins near Flagstaff.

For those wondering about access, I-17 provides a convenient north-south route through Coconino National Forest, making it easily reachable for visitors from Phoenix or southern Arizona. The majority of the forest lies south of Flagstaff, but to reach the northern portion, take I-40 to Highway 89 and head north, entering the forest near the turnoff for Sunset Crater National Monument. Travelers from the eastern or western part of the state can take I-40 to I-17 and head south. Sedona, surrounded by the Coconino National Forest, is easily accessible for visitors.

A few tips for a visit to Coconino National Forest: Some areas, such as the Red Rock Ranger District near Sedona and Sunset Crater and Wuptaki National Monuments, may have entry fees. However, certain days, like Martin Luther King, Jr. weekend, and special events like Get Outdoors Day, offer free entry to the Red Rock Ranger District. Visitors can acquire more information on special permits and activities by visiting the ranger headquarters in Flagstaff or local district offices in Sedona and Happy Jack. Given the varied elevation ranging from 2,600 feet in the southern part of the forest near the Verde River to 12,633 feet at the summit of Humphreys Peak, it's advisable to check the weather and be prepared for cold nights even in the summer.

COPPER QUEEN MINE TOUR

COUNTY: COCHISE   CITY: BISBEE

DATE VISITED: WHO I WENT WITH:

RATING: ☆ ☆ ☆ ☆ ☆   WILL I RETURN?   YES / NO

Once a prominent copper mine during the early 1900s, the Copper Queen Mine in Bisbee, Arizona, has undergone a transformation into a contemporary and educational tourist attraction. Its origins trace back to 1877 when copper ore was discovered in the Mule Mountains, leading to the establishment of the Copper Queen Mine a year later. The mine operated for nearly a century until its closure in the mid-1970s. After a brief period of closure, it reopened to visitors in 1976 and has since become a popular destination, drawing approximately 50,000 visitors annually.

Visitors are taken deep into the mountain aboard rickety train-carts, providing a glimpse, albeit slightly sanitized, into the life of a real miner. The underground environment, shrouded in darkness but illuminated by modern lights and required headlamps, maintains a constant cool temperature of 47 degrees Fahrenheit year-round, making it advisable for visitors to bring a jacket.

Bisbee's mining history is a captivating narrative marked by unexpected discoveries and unfulfilled promises. In 1877, U.S. Calvary Scout Jack Dunn, tasked with tracking Apache Native Americans and searching for a better water source, accidentally stumbled upon a significant limestone cliff containing lead carbonate in Tombstone Canyon. Reporting his discovery to his commanding officer, they were eager to claim the land but were delayed by the pressing need to track the Apache. Seeking assistance, they enlisted George Warren, with the condition that Dunn be named in all mining claim locations filed by Warren.

However, Warren's journey to the claims station took an unexpected turn. He got sidetracked, got drunk in a saloon, and gambled away the pack provided by Dunn, which contained money, tools, a map, and materials. Finally, 56 days after Dunn's discovery, Warren filed the claim, breaking his promise to name Dunn in all locations and ensuring only his name appeared on the mining claims. This guaranteed Warren a 1/9 interest in the Copper Queen Mine, leaving nothing for Dunn.

Karma eventually caught up with Warren. In Charleston, Arizona, he drunkenly made a bet that he could outrun a man on horseback – a bet he inevitably lost. This loss cost him his undeserved 1/9 interest, estimated to be worth about $20,000 USD at the time, equivalent to $606,000 USD today.

Ownership of the Copper Queen Mine went through several hands, ultimately falling under the control of the Phelps Dodge company in New York City in 1885. Phelps Dodge retained ownership until the mine officially closed in the mid-1970s, and they continue to own it to this day. Throughout its operational years, the Copper Queen Mine stood out as the most productive copper mine in Arizona and one of the best-run copper mines in the United States. Despite the known hazards, dangers, and often unpaid nature of the work within the mine, it remained a sought-after profession due to the stability it offered. The mining industry was the primary catalyst for the population growth of Bisbee, drawing thousands of men and their families from various parts of the country.

The challenging working conditions eventually led to a miner's uprising in 1917, resulting in the formation of a union and a subsequent strike. In response, Phelps Dodge unlawfully employed private police and corrupt sheriffs to arrest over 1,300 miners. They were then forcibly placed on railroad cars and expelled from Bisbee, an infamous event now remembered as the Bisbee Deportation.

In the following decades, particularly after World War II, the demand for copper experienced a significant decline, leading to the formal cessation of operations at the Copper Queen Mine in 1975. Faced with the urgent need for an economic revival, the mayor of Bisbee, along with volunteers, approached Phelps Dodge in 1976, just one year after the mine's closure, with a proposal to reopen it for tourism. Fortunately, Phelps Dodge agreed to the proposal, leading to an economic upturn. Since then, over a million people have visited the Copper Queen Mine, providing a boost to both the mine and the town of Bisbee. The former Phelps Dodge headquarters in Bisbee has been transformed into the Bisbee Mining & Historical Museum, conveniently located across the street from the mine in downtown Bisbee.

Today, the Copper Queen Mine offers daily tours with five different time slots available – 9 am, 10:30 am, 12 pm, 2 pm, and 3:30 pm. The tours typically last around 1 hour and 15 minutes. Children aged 5 and younger are not permitted on the tour. It is highly advisable to book your tour in advance, especially if you plan to visit on a weekend. The 9 am tour is particularly recommended, as it tends to be less crowded compared to later tours. Early morning visitors can enjoy the benefit of a less crowded experience.

During the tour, visitors are required to wear headlamps and bright yellow or orange vests and must be accompanied by a tour guide inside the mine. Open-toed shoes, high heels, and backpacks are not allowed, so it's recommended to bring an extra pair of closed-toe shoes if needed. The tour consists of an 80% cart-style train ride through the mine's deep tunnels and a 20% educational component. The guide makes two stops at different parts of the mine, where visitors disembark from the train, walk with the guide, and gain insights into the history and mining practices. Visitors may be fortunate enough to have a tour guide who worked in the mine during its operational years, providing a unique perspective on the experience.

CORONADO NATIONAL FOREST

COUNTY: COCHISE, GRAHAM, PIMA, PINAL, SANTA CRUZ   CITY: TUCSON *n.c.*

DATE VISITED: _____   WHO I WENT WITH: _____

RATING: ☆ ☆ ☆ ☆ ☆   WILL I RETURN? YES / NO

The Coronado National Forest comprises 15 mountain ranges and eight distinct wilderness districts, which are separated by a vast expanse of desert spanning over 100 miles. Situated across southeastern Arizona, these mountain ranges are commonly referred to as the Sky Islands. These areas offer recreational opportunities year-round, including activities such as hiking, mountain biking, camping, fishing, and more. Mt. Lemmon, in particular, is home to the southernmost ski area in the continental U.S.

Encompassing a total of 1.78 million acres, the forest spans from the Sonoran desert to subalpine forests reaching altitudes of up to 10,000 feet. Due to the diverse landscapes, it is recommended to plan visits to specific regions within the forest, such as the Chiricahua Mountains. Combining various activities, such as hiking one day and enjoying a scenic drive the next, or camping throughout your stay, will allow you to maximize your experience and appreciate the abundance of attractions within the forest.

Visitors predominantly come to engage in activities such as hiking, camping, and enjoying picturesque drives within the Coronado National Forest. While these pursuits can be undertaken in any of the eight wilderness districts, Sabino Canyon, Mt. Lemmon, and Madera Canyon stand out as the most popular destinations.

The Coronado National Forest is renowned for its fishing opportunities. Anglers can cast their lines from the shoreline or small boats on the forest's man-made lakes, targeting species such as rainbow trout, largemouth bass, catfish, and bluegill. Wildlife enthusiasts are drawn to these lakes, where over 400 bird species, some exclusive to the Coronado National Forest, can be observed.

Seasonal activities also attract visitors to the forest. Off-highway vehicles (OHVs) have the option to explore the 25-mile Red Spring Trail, primarily designed for single-track motorbikes when the trail isn't overly muddy. Additionally, winter brings skiers to Ski Valley on Mt. Lemmon.

The Coronado National Forest boasts an extensive network of over 1,000 miles of shared-use trails, catering to a variety of preferences, from short paved nature walks to extensive wilderness hikes. It's crucial to check the weather conditions and ensure you have an ample supply of water before embarking on any trail, even during the winter.

Sabino Canyon offers more than 30 miles of trails, with the 7.4-mile tram route being particularly popular. While visitors have the option to hike the entire route, most choose to take a shuttle to one of the nine stops and then walk to the others. The tram route is paved, and the shuttle is designed to be accessible.

The Madera Canyon Nature Trail, located south of Tucson, presents a 2.4-mile loop crossing Madera Creek and winding through woodlands featuring pinyon, oak, and juniper trees. This trail culminates in a scenic viewpoint of Mt. Livermore, and along the way, hikers may spot some of the more than 240 bird species inhabiting the area.

While Chiricahua National Monument is a distinct entity, it serves as a convenient entry point for exploring the Chiricahua Mountains, boasting over 17 miles of hiking trails. The 9.5-mile Big Loop stands out among experienced hikers, encompassing Echo Canyon, Upper Rhyolite Canyon, Heart of Rocks, Balanced Rock, and more.

The Coronado National Forest features a total of 18 designated scenic drives within its boundaries, each offering a unique and captivating experience. While all of them are worthwhile, some stand out as particularly popular choices.

Catalina Scenic Highway, also recognized as "Mt. Lemmon Highway," serves as the sole paved route leading to the summit of the Santa Catalina Range on the outskirts of Tucson. Renowned for its striking shifts in scenery, this road takes travelers from the Sonoran Desert to the high forests of the Canadian zone, providing panoramic views of the city below.

Pinery Canyon Road presents a more rugged option, requiring a high-clearance vehicle and preferably a four-wheel-drive vehicle. This challenging route rewards adventurers with breathtaking views of the Chiricahua Mountains, featuring notable sites like Cochise Stronghold, once utilized as a hideout by Apache chief Cochise and his people.

Box Canyon Road, situated in the Santa Rita Mountains, meanders through grasslands shaded by mesquite trees before ascending the northern shoulder of the range. During the spring, the road is adorned with blooming flowers, adding to its scenic charm.

Harshaw Road forms a loop through the Canelo Hills, commencing in Patagonia and tracing the path along Harshaw Creek, where gold miners once panned for gold. The journey concludes at AZ-82, two miles north of Nogales, offering highlights such as ghost towns, picturesque canyons, and opportunities to spot wildlife along the way.

Due to its expansive size, the Coronado National Forest offers a variety of camping experiences, catering to different preferences, ranging from RV camping on paved surfaces to primitive tent camping at elevations reaching up to 9,000 feet. For those seeking a more rugged experience, dispersed camping—overnighting in undeveloped areas without amenities like potable water or restrooms—is an option.

Bog Springs Campground, among the most picturesque in the Coronado National Forest, is particularly well-suited for tent camping as it lacks RV hookups. Positioned ideally for exploring Madera Canyon and the Santa Rita Mountains, it offers a scenic and immersive camping experience.

Rustler Park Campground, situated in the Chiricahua Mountains at an elevation of 8,500 feet, provides access to some of the area's finest trails. This campground becomes especially popular in the spring when the surrounding meadow is adorned with vibrant wildflowers.

Molino Basin Campground, unlike other campgrounds in the region that close during winter, opens late in the fall and closes late in the spring. Positioned in the desert, this campground can accommodate trailers and RVs under 22 feet but lacks hookups, providing a unique camping experience in the desert landscape.

Tucson serves as a convenient hub for those looking to explore the more popular regions of the Coronado National Forest. Accommodation options in Tucson are diverse, ranging from luxurious resorts to budget-friendly hotels, with well-known chain hotels providing a solid middle-ground choice. However, if your exploration focuses on the Chiricahua or Dragoon mountains, it's advisable to consider overnight stays in one of the chain hotels located in Willcox.

Loews Ventana Canyon Resort, an iconic Tucson establishment, is situated approximately 15 minutes from Sabino Canyon and roughly 40 miles from the starting point of the Catalina Scenic Highway. Its strategic location makes it an appealing choice for those seeking both proximity to nature and resort amenities.

For a more budget-conscious option, The Downtown Clifton Hotel Tucson is conveniently located just a few minutes from I-10 and downtown Tucson. This reasonably-priced hotel serves as an excellent starting point for day trips to various wilderness areas within the Coronado National Forest.

Tucson serves as the optimal starting point for a journey into the Coronado National Forest, but the directions will differ based on the specific destination within the forest you plan to visit. Here are directions to some of the more popular destinations:

Sabino Canyon: Take Exit 248 for Ina Road from I-10 and head east into Tucson for approximately 15 miles. Ina Road will transition into Skyline Drive, which later becomes Sunrise Drive. Turn left at Sabino Canyon Road, drive half a mile to Forest Road 805, turn right, and 500 feet later, make another right at Upper Sabino Canyon Road. Continue to the parking lot.

Mt. Lemmon: From I-10, take Exit 256 for Grant Road and head east into Tucson. Drive approximately 8 miles to Tanque Verde Road and turn left. After another 3 miles, turn left onto the Catalina Highway. Follow this road for about 28 miles to reach the summit of Mt. Lemmon.

Chiricahua Mountains: Depart from Tucson and take I-10 East for nearly 80 miles to Exit

336, Haskell Avenue. Follow Haskell Avenue for 4 miles into Willcox and make a right at Maley Street/AZ-186. Continue for 31 miles, then turn left at AZ-181. After 3 miles, the road name changes to Bonita Canyon Road. In the next 2 miles, you'll reach Chiricahua National Monument.

Tips:

1) Given the diverse climate, terrain, and activities across the Coronado National Forest, it is advisable to invest time in researching the specific region you intend to explore before embarking on your trip.
2) Keep in mind that certain areas, like Sabino Canyon, may charge a day-use fee. Additionally, if you plan to stay in a developed campground or ski on Mt. Lemmon, be prepared to pay the respective fees associated with these activities.
3) For individuals aged 10 and older planning to engage in fishing within the Coronado National Forest, an Arizona fishing license is mandatory.
4) It's important to note that many campgrounds in the forest operate on a first-come, first-serve basis. Aside from utilizing developed campgrounds, there is also an option for dispersed camping in areas where vehicles are permitted.

DESERT BOTANICAL GARDEN

COUNTY: MARICOPA   CITY: PHOENIX

DATE VISITED: _____ WHO I WENT WITH: _____

RATING: ☆ ☆ ☆ ☆ ☆   WILL I RETURN?   YES / NO

Situated in Papago Park, in close proximity to downtown Phoenix, the Desert Botanical Garden holds the distinction of being a Phoenix Point of Pride and is one of only 24 botanical gardens accredited by the American Alliance of Museums. Diverging from the typical focus of botanical gardens, it concentrates on showcasing plants that thrive in the Sonoran Desert, with a secondary emphasis on the animals and people inhabiting this arid landscape surrounding the city. The expansive 140-acre garden plays host to various activities throughout the year, including concerts, plant sales, art installations, and special events like Las Noches de las Luminarias. Notably, it features the highly acclaimed restaurant, Gertrude's.

Rooted in the Great Depression, the Desert Botanical Garden's origins trace back to Gertrude Divine Webster, a wealthy divorcée facing challenges in raising rare cacti. Seeking advice, she consulted with Swedish botanist Gustaf Starck, leading to discussions that evolved into a vision for a botanical garden dedicated to desert plants in Phoenix. The duo began collecting specimens, with Webster providing financial support and Starck rallying enthusiasts with a sign reading "Save the Desert." In 1939, the Desert Botanical Garden opened its doors to the public. While World War II necessitated a temporary closure, the garden thrived in the 1950s, expanding from 1,000 specimens at the war's end to 18,000 by 1957. Presently, the garden showcases over 50,000 plants, including 485 rare and endangered species, attracting more than 450,000 visitors annually. It stands as one of the Valley's premier attractions, offering a captivating way to appreciate the distinctiveness of the Sonoran Desert.

The Desert Botanical Garden provides a rich array of attractions and activities, featuring five distinct loop trails showcasing native desert plants.

Desert Discovery Loop Trail: Commence your exploration on the Desert Discovery Loop Trail, located just off the Ottosen Entry Garden. The loop is adorned with palo verde trees and a diverse assortment of cacti and succulents from various parts of the world. Notable highlights include the Kitchell Family Heritage Garden, spotlighting plants from Baja California. This trail serves as a starting point for branching off to other trails except for the Desert Wildflower Loop Trail.

Plants & People of the Sonoran Desert Loop Trail: Gain insights into the historical use of plants for food, medicine, and construction materials on this trail. Additionally, discover examples of Tohono O'odham, Western Apache, and Hispanic households.

Desert Wildflower Loop Trail: Experience a burst of colors during spring, with yellow, orange, pink, and purple blossoms adorning the 0.3-mile loop. This trail leads to the Butterfly Pavilion.

Sonoran Desert Nature Loop Trail: Revel in breathtaking views of Phoenix and the surrounding mountains as you traverse this trail.

Center for Desert Living Trail: Explore the theme of sustainability along this trail, delving into practices and principles related to desert living.

Experience the Butterfly Pavilion:

Typically open during various weeks in the fall and spring, the Butterfly Pavilion is home to a multitude of butterflies, including Monarchs indigenous to the Southwest. Visitors have the opportunity to learn about pollinators while enjoying the fluttering presence of butterflies, creating picturesque moments for photographs within the pavilion. An activity book for children can be downloaded in advance. Admission to the Butterfly Pavilion is complimentary with general admission, but it is essential to reserve a designated time for your visit.

Indulge at Gertrude's:

This distinguished restaurant, renowned for its New American cuisine, welcomes guests every day of the week. With a menu that highlights locally-sourced, seasonal ingredients, patrons can savor dishes such as green chili cheeseburgers, duck enchiladas, and lamb curry. Whether you opt for brunch, lunch, or dinner, or simply wish to enjoy a cocktail or two, Gertrude's promises a delightful culinary experience.

Explore Indoor Offerings:

For a break from the sun, discover the garden's 9,000-book library dedicated to native desert plants, and peruse the gift shop for gardening and desert-themed souvenirs.

Attend an Event:

Throughout the year, the garden hosts special events that captivate visitors. Look out for spring and fall music concerts, as well as seasonal gatherings like Boo-Tanical Nights and Agave on the Rocks. Dog Days at the Garden welcomes canine companions for an early walk, while Las Noches de las Luminarias invites families to enjoy holiday-themed activities amidst the glow of 8,000 luminarias along the trails.

The Desert Botanical Garden is situated at 1201 N. Galvin Parkway. If arriving by car, take the 202 to Priest Drive, which transforms into Galvin Parkway. Proceed north through the Van Buren Street intersection, pass through the first roundabout, and at the second roundabout, turn right to reach the parking lot.

Alternatively, you can opt for the Loop 101 to McDowell Road, heading west for six blocks until reaching Galvin Parkway. Take a left, followed by another left at the initial roundabout. Parking at the garden is complimentary.

For those using public transportation, take the light rail to the Washington/Priest Station and transfer to Bus 56 north, with a stop directly in the garden's parking lot.

The Desert Botanical Garden operates daily, excluding Thanksgiving, Christmas, and July 4. Hours are subject to seasonal variations, and early closures may occur for special events, so it's advisable to check the calendar before your visit. Garden members enjoy entry one hour earlier on Wednesdays and Sundays. Regardless of the time of year, come prepared with essentials such as a refillable water bottle (two hydration stations are available) and sunscreen, as it is crucial even in winter. Sunglasses and a hat are also recommended, and since there is no tram service, expect plenty of walking. Wear comfortable shoes.

Combine your visit to the Desert Botanical Garden with a trip to its adjacent neighbor, the Phoenix Zoo, or explore other nearby attractions like the Hall of Flame Museum of Firefighting, located less than a mile away. Another option is a visit to the Arizona Heritage Center, operated by the Arizona Historical Society.

For a picturesque photo opportunity, hike to Papago Park's iconic landmark, Hole in the Rock, visible from Galvin Parkway with an easily accessible parking lot. The short 10-minute hike, with minimal elevation gain, provides stunning sunset views of downtown Phoenix set against a vibrant orange sky.

DEVIL'S BRIDGE TRAIL

COUNTY: YAVAPAI   **CITY:** SEDONA   *n.c.*

DATE VISITED: **WHO I WENT WITH:**

RATING: ☆ ☆ ☆ ☆ ☆   **WILL I RETURN?**   YES / NO

Devil's Bridge stands as the largest natural sandstone arch in the Sedona region, offering a breathtaking sight amidst the area's renowned natural beauty, despite its somewhat ominous name.

Beginning at an elevation of 4,600 feet, the moderately challenging 1.8-mile roundtrip hike involves a mere 400-foot climb in altitude. While the ascent is not overly strenuous, the views awaiting at the summit are nothing short of awe-inspiring.

Catering to both casual hikers and more adventurous outdoor enthusiasts, the trail starts at the parking area, marked by a trailhead guiding you towards Devil's Bridge Trail. Initially designed for jeep travel, the path is smooth and well-defined, leading through juniper-filled washes adorned with prickly pear cactus.

As you progress, the trail gradually inclines, offering captivating scenery along the way. However, the true marvel of Devil's Bridge is yet to unfold.

Approximately three-quarters of a mile from the parking area, the trail diverges. Following the left path leads you to the base of the bridge, allowing for a unique view by standing directly beneath the 50-foot-high arch, gazing skyward.

The upper trail, however, promises the most enchanting experience. Ascend a natural rock staircase to a spacious area with panoramic views. Continuing further, you'll reach an elevated level that provides direct access to Devil's Bridge.

For the daring, walking across the top is an option. Once on the bridge, you'll find the walk is not overly challenging. However, exercise caution and apply common sense, mindful of the height and potential risks associated with the impressive geological formation.

Important Note for Passenger Vehicles: The gravel section of Dry Creek Road (FR 152) necessitates a high-clearance vehicle. If you have a low-clearance vehicle, you can park at the Dry Creek Road trailhead located at the conclusion of the paved road section or at the Mescal Trailhead on Long Canyon Road. The recommended routes are either the Mescal to Chuckwagon to Devil's Bridge trails (covering 4.0 miles round trip) starting from Long Canyon Road, or the Chuckwagon to Devil's Bridge trails originating from Dry Creek Road (covering 5.8 miles round trip). The gravel portion of Dry Creek Road is commonly used as a jeep trail and is not advised for pedestrian use.

Directions: To reach Devil's Bridge, drive 27 miles south from Flagstaff to Sedona on US

89A. Continue through Sedona until you reach Dry Creek Road (FR152) at the west end of the town. Turn right onto Dry Creek Road and drive for two miles until you encounter a fork in FR152; take the right fork, leaving the paved road. Note that this road is rough, requiring high-clearance vehicles. Avoid this route during wet weather. After about 1.3 miles on this road, make a right turn to reach Devil's Bridge Trailhead and parking lot.

Alternate Access for Passenger Vehicles:

The unpaved section of Dry Creek Road (FR 152) demands a high-clearance vehicle.

Via Chuckwagon Trail: For low-clearance vehicles, the option is to park at the Dry Creek Vista Trailhead, situated at the end of the paved section of Dry Creek Road shortly after the mentioned right-hand turn at the fork. This route includes an additional 2.1 miles one-way on a moderately easy rolling trail with spectacular views. The total distance from this trailhead to the bridge is approximately 2.9 miles (making it a 5.8-mile round trip), and the trail signs provide clear directions to Devil's Bridge. (Note: The unpaved portion of Dry Creek Road is a popular jeep trail and is not recommended for pedestrian use.)

Via Mescal Trail: Continue on Dry Creek Road until you reach the stop sign at the intersection of Long Canyon Road. Turn right and travel 0.2 miles to find the Mescal Trailhead on the right. Utilize the signed Mescal-Chuckwagon trail connection to reach the Devil's Bridge Trailhead. The round trip from this trailhead to Devil's Bridge is 4.0 miles.

FLAGSTAFF

COUNTY: COCONINO

CITY: FLAGSTAFF

DATE VISITED:

WHO I WENT WITH:

RATING: ☆ ☆ ☆ ☆ ☆   **WILL I RETURN?**   YES / NO

Affectionately known as "Flag" by its 75,000 residents and frequent visitors, Flagstaff is located approximately a two-hour drive from Phoenix and is recognized as the gateway to the Grand Canyon. Positioned at an elevation of 7,000 feet, the city becomes a sought-after destination for Phoenicians during the summer, providing a respite from the scorching temperatures in the Valley. Residents and visitors alike come to Flagstaff to partake in festivals and explore the surrounding ponderosa pine forest through hiking. In the winter, Flagstaff serves as a central hub for winter sports enthusiasts engaging in activities such as downhill skiing, cross-country skiing, and snowshoeing.

Beyond its appeal to outdoor enthusiasts, Flagstaff invites visitors to delve into its charming shops, peruse artists' studios, experience its burgeoning beer scene, and explore top-rated attractions like Lowell Observatory, the renowned site where the discovery of Pluto took place.

Flagstaff stands out as a year-round destination. During the summer, it offers a cool escape from the triple-digit heat experienced in Phoenix, while in the winter, it becomes a popular hub for those passionate about winter sports. The fall season brings a vibrant display of changing leaves in and around Flagstaff, and spring, though typically chilly, offers a pleasant atmosphere.

The presence of Northern Arizona University (NAU) contributes to the city's dynamic, with the atmosphere being quieter when school is out during the summer or breaks and busier during weekends featuring home football games.

Exploring the boutiques, shops, and galleries in downtown Flagstaff can easily occupy an entire day, but the city offers a rich array of experiences beyond its vibrant urban center. Delve into the history of the region, from prehistoric tribes to early ranchers, the geological wonders of the Grand Canyon, and Flagstaff's connections to NASA, all within the city's museums and attractions. Alternatively, immerse yourself in the natural wonders of the area, ranging from the iconic Grand Canyon to Humphrey's Peak, the highest natural point in Arizona. Flagstaff guarantees a fulfilling adventure, catering to various interests and preferences.

Flagstaff's historical roots extend beyond its formal establishment in 1894. The Museum of Northern Arizona serves as a showcase for the region's geology, Native American history, culture, and arts. Visitors can step inside a replica Hopi kiva or explore prehistoric ruins at the Elden Pueblo Heritage Site. The Arizona Historical Society operates a pioneer museum in Flagstaff, while the state maintains Riordan Mansion, an Arts and Crafts home built in 1904. Exploring more recent history involves driving along

Route 66 or stopping by The Museum Club, a nostalgic watering hole reminiscent of that era.

Nestled at the base of the San Francisco Peaks and enveloped by one of the world's largest ponderosa pine tree forests, Flagstaff offers a stark contrast to the desert landscape of the Valley. Dive into the study of local flora at The Arboretum at Flagstaff and encounter diverse fauna, including bobcats and otters, at Bearizona in nearby Williams. Lowell Observatory, just minutes from downtown, provides insights into the universe, commemorating the discovery of Pluto in 1930 and showcasing astronaut training for lunar landings.

Flagstaff is a haven for outdoor enthusiasts. In the summer, embark on a challenging 9.2-mile hike up Humphrey's Peak or explore the Flagstaff Urban Trail System, some sections leading into national forests. Seek an adrenaline rush at the Flagstaff Extreme Adventure Course, featuring aerial and zip line courses. During winter, over 100 inches of snowfall invites downhill skiing at the Arizona Snowbowl Winter Resort, cross-country skiing at the Arizona Nordic Village, or sledding at Flagstaff Snow Park.

While a long day trip from Phoenix to the Grand Canyon National Park is feasible, a more effective approach is to use Flagstaff as a base. Opt for an overnight stay in the city and venture to the Grand Canyon the following morning, providing ample time to explore the canyon throughout the day. For an efficient route to the national park from Flagstaff, consider bypassing the typical Williams route and take the back route. Head west on Highway 64 from the intersection of Highways 89 and 64 to reach the park entrance. If you lack transportation, a shuttle service is available every four hours from the bus station to Maswik Lodge within the park.

Extending your stay in Flagstaff opens up opportunities to explore various attractions in Northern Arizona. Just 18 miles north of the city lies Sunset Crater Volcano National Monument, offering a chance to hike through otherworldly landscapes. Adjacent to it, Wupatki National Monument preserves Pueblo ruins dating back to the 1100s. Additional Pueblo sites include Walnut Canyon National Monument (11 miles east of Flagstaff) and Montezuma Castle National Monument (57 miles south). Heading less than an hour east on I-40, you'll encounter Meteor Crater, the best-preserved meteor impact site on Earth. For those seeking a nostalgic journey, Route 66 beckons as you drive west on the Mother Road through Williams and Seligman, both inspiring locations for the movie "Cars."

The mountain community boasts over 200 restaurants, offering an overall exceptional dining experience. Casual dining options include wood-fired pizza from Pizzicletta, hearty deli sandwiches from Proper Meats + Provisions, and flavorful brisket from Satchmo's Cajun and Barbecue. For a special evening out, consider Brix Restaurant and Wine Bar, Josephine's Modern American Bistro, Tinderbox Kitchen, and Criollo Latin Kitchen. The influence of the university has brought a global culinary scene to Flagstaff, with options like Karma Sushi Bar Grill and Swaddee Thai Authentic Thai Cuisine for those seeking international flavors.

Flagstaff has a strong affinity for craft beer, evident in its dedicated beer trail. The Flagstaff Brewery Trail features eight breweries within the city (with one brewery having two locations, totaling nine stops on the trail). Highlights include Beaver Street Brewery, the city's first brewery, and its sister property, Lumberyard Brewing Co. Additionally, the original location of Mother Road Brewing Co. is conveniently within walking distance. For those with an adventurous palate, Dark Sky Brewing Company offers experimental beers with unique flavors like churro and peanut butter.

While not part of the brewery trail, Drinking Horn Mead Hall stands out for its alcoholic meads sweetened primarily with fruit juices and occasionally honey. Indulge in flavors like black cherry or lemon ginger for a distinct and refreshing experience.

The most convenient place to stay in Flagstaff is downtown, providing easy access to restaurants, breweries, bars, and shops. Consider booking a room at historic hotels like The Hotel Weatherford or Hotel Monte Vista. For a modern option in downtown, the Residence Inn Flagstaff is a good choice. Additionally, some homes in downtown Flagstaff are available for rent, and chain hotels near the university offer convenient access to Mountain Line buses.

While Flagstaff may not have resorts comparable to Sedona or Scottsdale, the Little America Hotel stands out as a AAA-Four Diamond property situated on 500 acres of ponderosa pine forest. Bed and breakfast options are also available, with The England House Bed and Breakfast being a popular choice near downtown Flagstaff.

For outdoor enthusiasts, accommodations include cabins at Mormon Lake Lodge, Arizona Mountain Inn & Cabins, and Ski Lift Lodge & Cabins, or yurts at the Arizona Nordic Village. Flagstaff/Grand Canyon KOA offers a limited number of cabins as well.

The most straightforward way to reach Flagstaff from Phoenix is by car, with a driving time of approximately two to two and a half hours. If you don't have a car, bus or shuttle options are available.

Tips:

1) Plan to spend at least four hours in Flagstaff during a day trip to explore downtown and enjoy a meal. Allocate an additional hour for each attraction you wish to visit.
2) Dress in layers, including a jacket or sweater, pants, and a long-sleeved shirt, as temperatures in Flagstaff can be around 30 degrees Fahrenheit cooler than Phoenix. Even on warm summer days, temperatures may drop significantly after dark.
3) In winter, be prepared for snow and bring essentials like a coat, gloves, and closed-toe shoes. While chains are generally not required on I-17 from Phoenix to Flagstaff, some remote roads may necessitate chains or close due to weather conditions.
4) Due to Flagstaff's high altitude, stay hydrated and be cautious about alcohol consumption. If engaging in strenuous activities like hiking or biking, consider planning an extra day for acclimatization.
5) Check for events and festivals, especially during the summer and warmer weeks of

spring and fall, as Flagstaff hosts various activities most weekends.

FORT BOWIE

COUNTY: COCHISE **CITY:** WILLCOX *n.c.*

DATE VISITED: **WHO I WENT WITH:**

RATING: ☆ ☆ ☆ ☆ ☆   **WILL I RETURN?** YES / NO

A trip to Fort Bowie National Historic Site in southeastern Arizona demands some effort. The journey involves a lengthy drive into Cochise County, culminating in the final mile on a dirt road. Subsequently, visitors need to embark on a 1.5-mile hike to reach the remnants of the fort. Despite the challenges, the experience promises to be unforgettable.

Nestled in Apache Pass, which lies between the Chiricahua Mountains and the Dos Cabezas Mountains, Fort Bowie played a crucial role as a military outpost on the Arizona frontier. Even today, it retains the same sense of solitude that characterized it in the 1800s, exuding a quiet ambiance. The landscape reveals skeletal remnants – stone walls, pathways, and adobe slabs resembling the fins of ancient creatures emerging from the tall grass.

Throughout the late 1800s, Fort Bowie served as a primary staging area for the U.S. Army's conflict with the Chiricahua Apaches, led by figures such as Cochise and Geronimo. This isolated outpost played a pivotal role in shaping Arizona's history, witnessing clashes between an emerging nation and a resilient, independent people striving to safeguard their land and way of life.

The significance of this secluded location in hosting such conflicts becomes evident when considering Arizona's key factor: water. In the state's history, water scarcity often played a decisive role in various events, and Fort Bowie stands as a poignant testament to this pattern.

In the shade of a leafy canopy, a slender stream cascades down a rocky surface and meanders through the sand. The soft murmur is barely audible amidst the presence of willow, walnut, and velvet ash trees, but appearances can be deceiving. In this dry terrain, the sound of water resonates through the landscape like a thunderous clap. Apache Spring has served as a vital source of sustenance in southeastern Arizona while becoming a focal point of intense conflicts. The spring's water descends through a narrow gorge in Apache Pass, a steep crevice that reaches an elevation exceeding 5,000 feet, encircled by prominent peaks such as Bowie Mountain and Helen's Dome. The lower slopes of Apache Pass are dominated by desert grasses intermingled with brushy chaparral, while higher elevations feature oak, juniper, and piñon woodlands.

For centuries, the Chiricahua Apaches called this area home. As it provided the only water supply for miles, along with essential resources like firewood and grass, Apache Pass became a significant landmark for travelers. Spanish explorers and later Mexican settlers traversed Apache Pass, marking it as a crucial stop on the emigrant trail leading to the California goldfields.

In 1858, the Butterfield Overland Mail Company initiated stagecoach service between St. Louis and San Francisco, utilizing the route through Apache Pass. A station was constructed in the pass to capitalize on the valuable spring water.

During this period, sporadic instances of violence occurred between the Apache people and settlers. The pass and its surroundings did not become part of the United States until the Gadsden Purchase in 1854. Initially, Cochise and the Chiricahua Apaches maintained a fragile peace with the newcomers, allowing the stage line to operate with minimal hindrance for over two years. However, everything took a dramatic turn in the winter of 1861.Lieutenant George Bascom, possibly just following orders, found himself forever linked to the event that ignited America's longest war due to his heavy-handed and rigid approach – an event now known as the Bascom Affair.

In January 1861, Felix Martinez Ward was abducted during an Apache raid on his family's ranch. In February, the inexperienced Lieutenant Bascom led a detachment of 54 men into Apache Pass with orders to rescue Ward and retrieve all stolen livestock.

During a meeting, Bascom accused Cochise of kidnapping and theft, leading to a confrontation. Despite Cochise's protestations of innocence and offers to aid in finding the missing boy, Bascom attempted to arrest him. Employing a knife, Cochise cut through the back of the tent and escaped, while other Chiricahua Apaches, including Cochise's family members, were captured. The soldiers sought refuge in the stone-walled Butterfield stage station.

In the subsequent days and weeks, Cochise took hostages in an attempt to exchange them for his family and warriors. When this effort failed, he resorted to killing the hostages. In retaliation, the Army executed the warriors in their custody. This incident triggered open warfare between white settlers and Chiricahua Apaches, a conflict that raged for the next twenty-five years.

Interestingly, Felix Ward had indeed been abducted by Apaches, but not by Cochise's group. He was traded to the White Mountain Apaches and raised alongside their children, eventually becoming a warrior. As an adult, he worked as a scout and interpreter for the U.S. Army, adopting the name Mickey Free.

The initial construction of Fort Bowie took place in the summer of 1862, constituting a basic, makeshift camp. A more substantial fort was later erected on a plateau approximately 300 yards southeast in 1868, and the remnants of this fort stand today. A brief pathway guides visitors to the location of the original fort.

Fort Bowie National Historic Site stands out as a walk-in park, a unique feature in Arizona. To access it, visitors must embark on a 1.5-mile hike, a measure taken to preserve both natural and historical resources. This hike also enhances the experience, immersing visitors in the solitude and isolation reminiscent of the frontier. Along the trail, the narrative unfolds, revealing each chapter of the site's history.

As visitors traverse the undulating hills, the trail passes by the ruins of the Butterfield Stage Station, a reconstructed Apache wikiup, the post cemetery adorned with grave markers, the original fort, and Apache Spring, which continues to provide a reliable water source.

Informative signs along the route detail significant incidents such as the Bascom Affair and the Battle of Apache Pass, a fierce clash involving Cochise, 150 warriors, and an advance guard of the California Column. The historical events cease to be abstract, as the ground beneath your feet is where they unfolded, where individuals stood, fought, and met their fate.

Upon emerging from the wooded area around the spring, the remnants of Fort Bowie come into view, sprawling across the tablelands and encircled by rising hills.

Pathways meander among the structures, each identified by plaques indicating its original purpose. Additional signs and historic photos enrich the setting, including a photograph of Geronimo and his band after their surrender in 1886. They were briefly brought to the fort before being exiled to Florida and Alabama, marking the conclusion of the Apache Wars. Fort Bowie was ultimately abandoned in 1894.

The visitor center, situated on a slope, features a wraparound veranda with rocking chairs and picnic tables, providing an excellent spot for lunch. The center houses exhibits and artifacts that add depth to the narrative, and a small store offers books and souvenirs.

Upon concluding the visit, one can either hike back the same way or opt for the trail behind the visitor center. This trail ascends Overlook Ridge, a limestone hill, providing stunning views of the fort and valleys below. While this route doesn't increase the distance, it offers a more challenging workout, rewarding hikers with expansive panoramas. The trail descends, rejoining the entrance trail near the Butterfield Station, just half a mile from the trailhead on Apache Pass Road.

How to explore Fort Bowie National Historic Site:

When: The site is open daily from sunrise to sunset. The visitor center welcomes visitors from 8:30 a.m. to 4 p.m. daily, with closures on Thanksgiving and Christmas.

Where: Located southeast of Willcox in southern Arizona. For those traveling from Phoenix, take Interstate 10 east beyond Tucson to Bowie (Exit 362). Proceed east on the I-10 Business Loop and make a right turn onto Apache Pass Road. Travel 12 miles to reach the trailhead parking. The last mile of the road is unpaved, but it is generally navigable with a regular passenger vehicle. Expect to cover a 3-mile round-trip distance on a dirt trail to reach the fort and return. Mobility-impaired visitors can arrange access by contacting the park.

Admission: Entrance is free of charge.

㉛ GLEN CANYON NATIONAL RECREATION AREA

COUNTY: COCONINO   CITY: PAGE *n.c.*

DATE VISITED: WHO I WENT WITH:

RATING: ☆ ☆ ☆ ☆ ☆   WILL I RETURN? YES / NO

Encompassing an expansive stretch from Lees Ferry in Arizona to the Orange Cliffs in Utah, Glen Canyon National Recreation Area sprawls across over 1.25 million acres, sharing boundaries with four other national parks and adjoining 9.3 million acres of Bureau of Land Management-managed land. Within its vast expanse lies Lake Powell, the second-largest manmade lake in the United States, and a segment of the Colorado River. The recreation area boasts six entrances, with Wahweap, Arizona, being the most frequented. Additionally, Glen Canyon National Recreation Area features five marinas, four visitor centers, and two in-park hotels, making it ideal for an extended stay, spanning several days or even a week, to fully explore the diverse landscapes.

Boating stands out as the primary activity within the recreation area. While visitors have the option to bring their own boats to navigate Lake Powell, many choose to rent houseboats, powerboats, and various watercraft from Wahweap, Bullfrog, and Antelope Point marinas. Alternatively, one can explore the waterways through kayaking, embark on a Colorado River rafting adventure through Horseshoe Bend with Wilderness River Adventures, or opt for a scenic boat tour of the expansive lake.

Even for those less inclined towards water-based activities, Glen Canyon National Recreation Area offers a plethora of terrestrial pursuits. Hikers from around the globe are drawn to witness natural arches, slot canyons, and otherworldly landscapes surrounding Lake Powell. For those desiring to cover more ground, designated off-highway vehicle (OHV) trails provide an adventurous option, while road bicycling is another enjoyable way to traverse the area. For those with limited time, a tour of the Glen Canyon Dam near the Wahweap entrance is a worthwhile experience.

Due to its immense size, Glen Canyon National Recreation Area boasts numerous trails for exploration, although only a few receive regular maintenance. It's crucial to be adequately prepared before embarking on these trails. Ensure you carry an ample water supply, especially in the summer, and inform someone about your hiking destination and expected return time.

Horseshoe Bend: Among the most popular hikes in Glen Canyon National Recreation Area, this 1.5-mile round trip takes you to the edge of a horseshoe-shaped canyon carved by the Colorado River, which still flows below. To avoid crowds, consider an early morning or late afternoon visit.

Hanging Gardens Trail: Another highly frequented trail near the Carl Hayden Visitor Center, this 1.5-mile round trip concludes at a fern wall and is suitable for almost any hiker.

Bucktank Draw and Birthday Arch Trail: Covering a 4.2-mile round trip on a sandy trail leading to Birthday Arch with short detours to Mini Arch and a slot canyon, this trail is located north of the Arizona-Utah border just before mile marker 10.

Lonely Dell Ranch: Functioning more as a self-guided tour than a hike, this uneven trail near Lees Ferry passes through ranch buildings, a picnic area, and an orchard where visitors can pick ripe fruit.

Devil's Garden: Offering a relatively easy hike over sandy and rocky terrain, the 1-mile Devil's Garden Trail off Hole-in-the-Rock Road in Utah showcases hoodoos and arches.

If you lack a 4-wheel-drive vehicle, Highways 89 and 89A provide stunning views that are sure to impress. Nevertheless, the scenery becomes even more awe-inspiring once you venture off the paved roads.

Burr Trail: Stretching over 67 miles, this route begins north of Bullfrog Marina at the intersection of UT 1668 (Burr Trail Road) and UT 276, continuing through Capitol Reef National Park towards Boulder, Utah. Comprising a mix of paved and dirt roads, some sections require four-wheel drive, and the trail becomes impassable to all vehicles during wet conditions.

Hole-in-the-Rock Road: Covering a distance of 62 miles, most of this road traverses Grand Staircase-Escalante National Monument. The final 5 miles extend into Glen Canyon National Recreation Area, concluding at the Hole-in-the-Rock formation on the western shore of Lake Powell. While a high-clearance two-wheel-drive vehicle can navigate most of the route, the last few miles may require walking, bicycling, or transferring to a four-wheel-drive vehicle.

Camping along Lake Powell in undeveloped areas is permitted at no cost, provided you have a portable toilet. Free camping is also available in five locations along the Colorado River. If you prefer established campgrounds with designated sites, the Glen Canyon National Recreation Area oversees four campgrounds, while concessionaires manage an additional four.

Wahweap Campground & RV Park: Situated at the Wahweap Marina, this campground stands as the largest in the recreation area, featuring 112 dry campsites (without hook-ups), 90 full hook-up sites, and six group camping sites. It offers amenities such as restrooms, laundry facilities, a store, a dump station, and potable water.

Bullfrog RV & Campground: Also managed by Aramark, this campground, like Wahweap, is located near the Bullfrog Marina in Utah. It consists of 78 sites and an RV park with 24 full hook-up sites. Amenities include restrooms, showers, laundry facilities, and a store.

Halls Crossing RV & Campground: A ferry ride away from Bullfrog Marina, Halls Crossing provides 31 RV sites and 41 tent sites, complemented by facilities like restrooms, showers, and a store.

Hite Outpost Adventure Center: Operated by Ticaboo Lodge, this campground includes 14 RV sites and 21 tent sites.

Lees Ferry Campground: Just minutes from Lees Ferry, this campground offers 54 sites, restrooms, potable water, and a launch ramp located 2 miles away. Although there are no hookups, open fires are not permitted.

Lone Rock Beach Primitive Camping Area: This primitive campground offers a mix of flush and vault toilets, outdoor showers, a dump station, and potable water. It lacks designated sites, but campfires are allowed.

Aramark oversees the management of two properties within the Glen Canyon National Recreation Area, namely Lake Powell Resort and Defiance House Lodge. Beyond the park boundaries, the city of Page provides a plethora of options, with virtually every major hotel chain having a presence. In more secluded areas, such as Marble Canyon near Lees Ferry, smaller motels can be found.

Lake Powell Resort: Situated adjacent to Wahweap Marina, Lake Powell Resort offers 348 rooms ranging from 300-square-foot accommodations to a lakeview suite with double the space. The property includes an on-site restaurant, two swimming pools, and direct access to the marina.

Defiance House Lodge: While smaller in scale with only 48 rooms, Defiance House Lodge offers breathtaking views of the Bullfrog Marina area. Guests enjoy convenient access to both the marina and nearby hiking trails.

Best Western View of Lake Powell: Among the highly favored hotels in Page, this Best Western property provides an elevated perspective overlooking Lake Powell in the distance, coupled with a complimentary breakfast for guests.

Glen Canyon National Recreation Area offers access through six entrances: Wahweap, Antelope Point, and Lees Ferry in Arizona, and Lone Rock Beach, Bullfrog, and Halls Crossing in Utah. The most frequently used entrance is Wahweap, located near Page. To reach Wahweap from I-40, take exit 201 and follow the signs to Highway 89. Turn right and proceed approximately 125 miles to reach Page.

For those traveling from Las Vegas, head north on I-15 for 125 miles. At exit 16, follow UT 9 east to UT 59 and continue until you cross into Arizona, where the road becomes AZ 389. Turn left onto Highway 89A, follow it into Kanab, and then make a right turn onto Highway 89, leading you into Page.

Tips:

1) If you intend to explore Lake Powell on houseboats or powerboats, particularly during the summer or holidays, it's advisable to make reservations well in advance. Additionally, securing hotel rooms or reserving campground sites early is recommended.

2) Weather conditions on Lake Powell are known to change rapidly. Stay vigilant and monitor the sky, adhering to guidelines provided by the National Weather Service to ensure a safe experience.

3) While pets are generally allowed in most areas of Glen Canyon National Recreation Area, there are exceptions. They are not permitted in archaeological sites and specific locations such as marinas, docks, and launch ramps, unless directly going to or from a vessel. Additionally, certain areas like Orange Cliffs, parts of Cathedral Wash, and other designated zones prohibit pets. Familiarize yourself with the specific regulations to ensure a smooth and enjoyable visit.

GRAND CANYON CAVERNS AND GROTTO

COUNTY: MOHAVE　　　　　　　　　　　　　　　　　　　CITY: PEACH SPRINGS

DATE VISITED:　　　　　　　　　WHO I WENT WITH:

RATING: ☆ ☆ ☆ ☆ ☆　　　　　　　WILL I RETURN?　YES / NO

The Grand Canyon Caverns, the largest dry cavern in the United States, is a natural limestone cavern situated 210 feet beneath the Earth's surface.

Discovered in 1927 by Walter Peck, the caverns came to light when he nearly stumbled into a large, funnel-shaped hole while en route to play poker with friends. The following morning, Peck and his companions explored the hole, revealing glimmers of what seemed like gold color on the tunnel walls when illuminated by a coal oil lantern. Misinterpreting the findings as gold, Peck purchased 800 acres to commence mining operations. To his dismay, the "gold" turned out to be iron oxide (rust). However, displaying entrepreneurial spirit, he constructed a rudimentary manual elevator and started charging visitors $0.25 for entry into the caverns.

During the Great Depression in late 1935, the Civilian Conservation Corps (CCC) struck a deal with Walter Peck. He provided the materials, and the CCC constructed a new entrance to the caverns. Following completion, the entry fee was raised to $0.50 per person, and the old entrance was sealed.

In 1962, amid the Cuban Missile Crisis, the U.S. government stored sufficient food and water rations to sustain 2,000 people for up to two weeks within the caverns. These supplies, intended for emergency use, remain in place and can be observed by visitors exploring the caverns.

Presently, the Grand Canyon Caverns and the adjacent land are under private ownership, where ongoing exploration by workers reveals new caves. The caverns receive air through a network of 60 miles of limestone caves and crevasses that extend from the Grand Canyon.

Upon taking a tour, visitors descend 21 stories underground via an elevator to explore the expansive caverns. Knowledgeable guides lead guests through numerous chambers, providing insights into the caverns' vast expanse. Due to the substantial depth underground, the temperature remains a constant 56°F with zero humidity. Walking trails are equipped with handrails, and benches are strategically placed for resting.

The site offers four distinct tours, including the recently introduced Wild Tour that explores newly discovered caves. The Explorer Tour caters to the more adventurous, venturing off the conventional path, while a Ghost Walk Tour is available for those interested in paranormal activity.

During the tours, visitors have the opportunity to witness the Crystal Room, showcasing stunning formations of selenite crystals. The Chapel of the Ages cavern and the Snowball Palace, accessible through a 160-foot tunnel, are also part of the itinerary. Notable attractions include a mummified bobcat that fell into the cavern over 150 years ago and the remains of a prehistoric ground sloth. Specialized tours are provided for individuals with physical limitations or time constraints.

Cavern Grotto, situated in the Route 66 town of Peach Springs, offers a distinctive dining experience that requires both a reservation and a descent 210 feet below ground level.

In contrast to typical American comfort food establishments, this eatery, located within the Grand Canyon Caverns attraction, beckons patrons to take an elevator journey 21 feet down into a cave system that has existed for 345 million years, encompassing the largest dry caverns in the United States.

What sets Cavern Grotto apart is not only its subterranean setting but also its exclusivity, boasting only four tables for diners. The restaurant's uniqueness recently earned it the No. 6 spot on Time Out's list of the best secret restaurants in the U.S., making it the sole representative from Arizona on a list dominated by concealed, often challenging-to-reach establishments in major cities such as New York, Chicago, Miami, and Los Angeles.

Meals are cooked in a kitchen at ground level, transported down to the cavern via elevator, hoisted 25 feet up to the dining area using a pulley, and then served to the table by a server. The restaurant offers unobstructed 360-degree views of the caves, with no sound interference except for the conversations of fellow diners, as mentioned by Grand Canyon Caverns.

The cost of dining at Cavern Grotto is $49.95 per person, plus tax, and the experience, usually available during lunch hours from noon to 4:45 p.m., includes a lunch entree and side, two drinks from the menu (including beer or wine), and all-you-can-eat dessert. Additionally, the cost covers a tour of the cavern. Food for Cavern Grotto is prepared at the above-ground Caverns Grill Restaurant, featuring items like burgers, a pulled pork sandwich, a fried chicken sandwich, and salads.

GRAND CANYON DESERT VIEW WATCHTOWER

COUNTY: COCONINO   CITY: FLAGSTAFF   *n.c.*

DATE VISITED: WHO I WENT WITH:

RATING: ☆ ☆ ☆ ☆ ☆   WILL I RETURN?   YES / NO

Desert View stands as the easternmost developed area along the South Rim of the Grand Canyon National Park. Commencing from the primary parking area, a brief 0.25-mile (0.4 km) stroll leads past amenities such as restrooms, the general store/market, and the trading post. Beyond these, the Watchtower comes into clear sight.

Regarded as a National Historic Landmark, the Watchtower was erected in 1932. Designed by architect Mary Colter, its architectural influences draw from the Ancestral Puebloan people of the Colorado Plateau. Specifically, this tower mirrors structures found at Hovenweep and the Round Tower of Mesa Verde. Colter emphasized that it was not a direct replica of any particular tower but rather an amalgamation of various influences she had encountered.

The vantage point from the Watchtower offers a distinctive outlook on the eastern segment of the Grand Canyon. Facing northeast, visitors can catch a distant glimpse of the Colorado River as it transitions from the relatively narrow Marble Canyon to the north, expanding into the broader expanse of the Grand Canyon.

The View Room, situated on the lower floor of the Watchtower, is designed in the likeness of a traditional Native American kiva. Throughout most of the year, cultural handicraft demonstrations take place in this space, which also houses a Grand Canyon Conservancy Park Store.

Within the Watchtower View Room, the canyon views are augmented by the use of reflectoscopes—viewing instruments employing polished black glass mirrors. These mirrors effectively cut through the haze and glare of bright sunlight, providing a clearer and more vivid depiction of the Grand Canyon's multicolored layers.

Originally utilized as retail space, the View Room was restored in 2015 to its intended open area, following Mary Colter's design, as it was initially conceived as a rest area. In the 1930s, visitors to the canyon could sit comfortably in this space and enjoy exceptional views. Notably, the fireplace in the room is designed in a way that does not obstruct the view for visitors. By peering into one of the reflectoscopes, visitors can gain a different perspective of the Grand Canyon.

With meticulous attention to detail, Mary Colter orchestrated the placement of every rock and architectural element in the construction of the Desert View Watchtower. Employing primarily locally sourced rocks and repurposed timber, the tower seems to organically emerge from the rim of the canyon, seamlessly blending with the natural surroundings. This design pays homage to the techniques and styles of local tribes while incorporating modern equipment and materials to reinforce the internal structure.

Approaching the building, observers may marvel at its seamless integration into the environment, making it challenging to distinguish where the canyon walls end and the tower begins. Colter expressed her primary objective as designing a building that becomes an integral part of its surroundings, harmonizing with the weathered walls of the promontory.

Colter insisted that the rocks be left in their natural state without cutting or alteration to preserve the essential weathered surfaces that contribute to the blend with the canyon walls. Notable design elements include intricate patterns such as the fading white decorative stones near the top, inspired by a pattern she observed at Chaco Canyon, aimed at breaking the monotony of the Watchtower. The deliberately designed built-in cracks and petroglyphs on some stones draw inspiration from ancient towers she had encountered.

The internal steel framework of the Watchtower was crafted and supervised by the bridge builders of the Santa Fe Railway company. Each exterior stone was then meticulously selected and placed on this framework to achieve the precise aesthetic envisioned by Mary Colter.

Park shuttles are not available for transportation to Desert View. Visitors must either drive their vehicles or opt for a commercial bus tour originating from Grand Canyon Village. The approximately 23-mile (37 km) journey east of Grand Canyon Village on Arizona Highway 64 is considered worthwhile. Desert View Drive provides breathtaking views of the canyon, featuring:

1) Six developed canyon viewpoints
2) Four picnic areas
3) Five unmarked pullouts
4) Accessibility for private vehicles
5) Tusayan Pueblo Site and Museum (closed for winter)
6) Desert View does not offer lodging facilities, but there is a seasonal campground managed by the National Park Service, operational from mid-April to mid-October.

GRAND CANYON NATIONAL PARK

COUNTY: COCONINO, MOHAVE   CITY: FLAGSTAFF *n.c.*

DATE VISITED: WHO I WENT WITH:

RATING: ☆ ☆ ☆ ☆ ☆   WILL I RETURN?   YES / NO

Grand Canyon National Park, a crown jewel of the American Southwest, stretches for 277 miles through northern Arizona, showcasing one of the most stunning natural wonders globally. The canyon, reaching a depth of a mile in most areas, was sculpted over millions of years by the Colorado River, flowing at its base and creating a geographical separation between the North Rim and the South Rim.

Despite the relatively short distance of about 10 miles between the rims in most areas, there is no bridge connecting them, resulting in a roughly five-hour drive from one rim to the other. The South Rim, situated closer to Phoenix and Interstate 40, attracts the vast majority of visitors, while accessing the North Rim requires a journey through southern Utah, making it a more remote and less-visited destination.

The experience of standing in awe of the Grand Canyon itself is remarkable. While the South Rim draws crowds, exploring the Visitor's Center and traversing Grand Canyon Village is recommended. Venturing away from the main tourist hubs allows for more solitude, offering a chance to absorb the canyon's majestic beauty.

For those seeking adventure at the Grand Canyon, a plethora of activities awaits, including camping, hiking, biking, and rafting. From helicopter tours to mule rides, the options are diverse, ensuring visitors never get bored. However, it's crucial to plan activities on the same side of the rim to avoid logistical challenges. Renting bikes on the South Rim for routes like The Hermit Road, a car-free 7-mile scenic ride from March to November, or the longer 42-mile Yaki Point Road, is a popular and picturesque option.

If hiking is your preferred outdoor activity, there's nothing quite like trekking in the Grand Canyon. Hiking trails are available on both the North Rim and South Rim. However, if your goal is to hike down to the river, you should allocate at least two days for the round trip. While there are options for day hikes without an overnight stay, it's essential to be well-informed before embarking on your journey. If you plan to camp in the park outside of designated campgrounds, securing a backcountry permit is necessary.

Bright Angel Trail: This trail is perfect for first-time visitors seeking a manageable yet impressive day hike. Well-maintained with shaded rest stops, it's ideal for summer days when temperatures soar. The full trail from the rim to the base is 9.5 miles one-way, but day hikers can turn back at any point or stay in the campground at the bottom.

Thunder River Trail: Regarded as a backpacking adventure of legend, this challenging journey involves switchbacks down the canyon, leading to a small oasis with waterfalls and lush vegetation amid the desert surroundings. The hike can commence from different trailheads, with a one-way distance ranging between 8 and 15 miles depending on the starting point.

Rim Trail: For those not inclined to descend into the canyon and climb back up, the Rim Trail offers an alternative. Starting at the South Rim Visitor Center, this trail features minimal elevation change. It provides one of the easier Grand Canyon adventures, allowing hikers to walk along the rim, stopping at various viewpoints to enjoy a bird's eye view of the park.

To gain a completely different perspective of the Grand Canyon, trade in your hiking poles for oars and embark on a journey from the bottom. Rafting through the Grand Canyon is an extraordinary adventure, ranging from tranquil floating to navigating through rapid white waters. Rafting options can be as short as half a day or as long as three weeks, but the most popular choice involves spending a few days boating down the river and camping along the way. You can either join a trip organized by a tour operator to handle the details, or apply for a permit to raft on your own.

Grand Canyon National Park features four campgrounds—three on the South Rim and one on the North Rim. Due to high demand, it's advisable to start looking for reservations early, as they tend to fill up months in advance (reservations typically open six months ahead for most campgrounds). With the exception of Trailer Village, none of the campgrounds within the park offer RV hookups.

If you plan to camp in the backcountry, securing a backcountry permit is necessary before your journey begins.

Mather Campground: The sole tent campground open year-round, Mather is situated on the South Rim in Grand Canyon Village. Despite its busy atmosphere with over 300 campsites, it's conveniently located near the entrance.

Desert View Campground: Located approximately 23 miles east of Grand Canyon Village on the South Rim, Desert View operates seasonally and has only 50 campsites, filling up quickly. Its serene setting makes it a preferred choice for campers seeking a quiet nature retreat.

Trailer Village: Exclusive for RV campers, Trailer Village is the only campground in the park with full hookups. It does not offer sites for tent camping and is located on the South Rim, open year-round.

North Rim Campground: The sole option within the park for campers who wish to stay on the remote North Rim.

The sole accommodation available at the base of the Grand Canyon, below the rim, aside from backcountry camping, is Phantom Ranch. Accessible by hiking down, riding a mule, or rafting, its unparalleled location makes it highly sought after, and securing a reservation in one of the cabins or dormitories requires entering a lottery.

Across the park, various lodging options are available, ranging from rustic cabins to resorts. It's crucial to pay attention to the location of your choice, ensuring it aligns with the desired rim to avoid being too far away. Flagstaff, Arizona, serves as the nearest major city to the South Rim, often referred to as the Gateway to the Grand Canyon, and is a common base for visitors.

El Tovar Hotel: This historic hotel, operating since 1905, stands out as the most elegant lodging option within the park. A stay at El Tovar offers a glimpse into frontier days, but due to its high demand, it's advisable to book well in advance.

Little America Flagstaff: With spacious rooms exceeding 420 square feet, Little America is an excellent choice for families or groups. Nestled in the picturesque Ponderosa Pine Forest, it's just an hour and a half by car to the South Rim entrance.

Grand Canyon Lodge: For those seeking to experience the Grand Canyon away from the bustling crowds, the North Rim is an alternative. The Grand Canyon Lodge, located adjacent to the North Rim visitor center for convenience, operates seasonally (usually from mid-May to mid-October).

If you plan to visit the North Rim, your best option is to fly into Las Vegas and then drive from there. Renting a car at McCarran International Airport is convenient, but keep in mind that it's an additional four and a half-hour drive to reach the Grand Canyon. It's advisable to fly in early, make the drive, rest at your hotel, and then start exploring.

For those heading to the South Rim, the recommended airports are Phoenix or Flagstaff. While Flagstaff is the closest, it's a smaller airport with limited flights. Most visitors opt for Phoenix International Airport and commence their journey from there. The drive from Phoenix to the Grand Canyon takes about three and a half hours, so be sure to account for travel time in your plans.

While all shuttle buses within the park are wheelchair accessible for navigating the rim, the trails descending into the canyon are steep, rocky, and narrow. Many historical buildings in the park are not accessible to visitors with mobility challenges. However, there is a Scenic Drive Accessibility Permit available, allowing individuals with disabilities to access park roads typically restricted to tourists.

Visitors with permanent disabilities can also apply for an Access Pass, granting free lifetime admission to over 2,000 recreation areas throughout the U.S., including all national parks.

Tips:

1) Take advantage of free admission on specific days, such as Martin Luther King Jr. Day, Veterans Day, and National Park Week in April.

2) Unless you're exploring the rim or the visitor center, most activities within the canyon require a permit. Ensure you obtain the necessary permissions before your arrival.

3) The summer months are the park's busiest period, but be mindful that Arizona experiences triple-digit temperatures. Prepare for both crowds and intense heat, and make sure to bring ample water.

4) To avoid crowds, consider visiting during the winter, when the desert landscape is blanketed in snow, offering a particularly picturesque experience. Keep in mind that only the South Rim is open during the winter months.

5) Monsoon season, from July to September, brings daily afternoon thunderstorms. Even if the morning seems clear, it's wise to pack a rain jacket.

6) Don't miss the opportunity to witness the breathtaking sunset, especially against the canyon's rusty colors. Hermit's Rest on the South Rim provides particularly scenic views at dusk.

7) The Grand Canyon Skywalk, a man-made walkway hanging over the canyon, may be familiar from photos. However, it's not located within the national park but in an area called Grand Canyon West on the Hualapai Indian Reservation. It's closer to Las Vegas than to the North Rim or South Rim.

HAVASU FALLS

COUNTY: MOHAVE   CITY: PEACH SPRINGS   *n.c.*

DATE VISITED: WHO I WENT WITH:

RATING: ☆ ☆ ☆ ☆ ☆   WILL I RETURN?   YES / NO

Havasu Falls holds immense fame, situated at the bottom of the Grand Canyon in Arizona. While many are aware of its location, the details often remain unknown. Numerous individuals express a desire to visit this natural wonder each year but find themselves unsure of how to plan the trip. It's crucial to understand that Havasu Falls is not within Grand Canyon National Park but rather on an Havasupai Indian Reservation adjacent to the National Park. Consequently, adding a spontaneous visit to the falls during your trip is not feasible; meticulous planning is essential.

The Havasupai waterfalls boast breathtaking beauty, as echoed by countless visitors in numerous social media posts dedicated to this Grand Canyon marvel. The turquoise allure of Havasupai Falls attracts hikers of varying skill levels, from avid backpackers to those who consider a hotel stay camping if it offers fewer than 20 TV channels.

However, it's vital for everyone to recognize that accessing Havasupai involves an 8-mile hike to the village of Supai, followed by an additional 2 miles to reach the campground, and another 3 miles to reach the farthest waterfall. This journey entails a considerable amount of hiking with substantial gear on your back. While it's possible to take a helicopter for transportation, there are reasons not to, which will be discussed later.

Whether your trip is already in progress, you secured reservations promptly, or you acquired spots relinquished by others opting for destinations where compost toilets aren't considered a remarkable upgrade, the Havasu waterfalls hike may be on your horizon.

Hualapai Hilltop, the starting point of your adventure, is a five-hour drive from Phoenix. To avoid the heat on the mostly shadeless trail, an early start is advisable. Since camping is not permitted at the trailhead, it's recommended to book a room the night before in Seligman (two hours from the hilltop) or Peach Springs (90 minutes away).

Indian Road 18, a smoothly paved two-lane road, guides you from Historic Route 66 to Hualapai Hilltop. While there are areas along the winding road where passing is permissible, exercising impatience that poses a risk of serious injury is strongly discouraged. After traversing much of the nearly empty Indian Road 18, encountering a car and a folding table on the shoulder, along with a sign requesting you to stop, may be surprising.

At this point, you'll likely encounter one or two members of a private security firm tasked with monitoring entry. They will ask for your names to confirm reservations and inquire about the presence of weapons, alcohol, or coolers. Weapons and alcohol are prohibited on tribal land, and you'll be reminded that coolers are not allowed in the canyon. Even if your response is negative, you might be requested to open the trunk for a brief inspection. Assuming you've answered truthfully and there's no apparent evidence to the contrary, you'll be on your way shortly.

As you approach the parking lot situated atop Hualapai Hilltop, you'll notice numerous cars squeezed along the roadside. It's essential to resist the temptation to pull into the first available space, as doing so could add an extra half-mile to your hike. While it might not be an issue at the moment, you'll regret the decision when you return to the top, realizing you still have a considerable distance to cover. Instead, drive directly to the parking lot and take the first available space.

While mathematics dictates that a mile consists of 5,280 feet, those calculations have never hiked to Supai. For inexperienced hikers, take note: Each mile on the way to the campground feels, in technical terms, interminable. There are no mile markers to gauge your progress or estimate how much remains (a daunting and spirit-draining amount). If your previous hiking experience involves carrying nothing more than a water bottle from the parking lot to a picnic area, be prepared for a significant difference. Carrying a backpack loaded with a shelter, bed, cookware, and supplies for four days can feel like it weighs roughly 3,000 pounds more. This is especially true for those unaccustomed to trips without hotel accommodations or similar conveniences.

On the descent to Supai Village, smaller trails diverge from the main path, creating a network of paths without any signage. Each Y-shaped intersection poses a choose-your-own-adventure scenario, leaving hikers uncertain about the right direction and wary of venturing into the wilderness, potentially becoming a headline as a missing hiker. Fortunately, these divergent trails eventually converge, ensuring you stay on the correct route. While some of the narrower paths may serve as shortcuts, the lack of signs on any trail doesn't indicate a risk of getting lost—they all lead to Supai. To avoid any discomfort or uncertainty, it's recommended to stick to the main trail.

Upon reaching the small community of Supai, check-in is required at the office. Contrary to expectations, the first building you see is not the office but a small convenience store housed in what appears to be a private home.

Upon reaching Supai, take a moment to relieve yourself of your backpack and experience the almost ethereal lightness of being. Some describe a sensation of almost floating away, while others may feel an invisible hand gently pushing them forward.

Havasupai's sole motel boasts impressive amenities, including beds and plumbing. However, there are two notable drawbacks. Firstly, securing reservations is a formidable challenge, as they are exclusively available via phone and are swiftly booked within hours of their release on June 1 for the following year. Secondly, the lodge is located in the village, situated 2 miles from Havasu Falls, 3 miles from Mooney Falls, and 6 miles from Beaver Falls.

Beyond Supai but preceding the campground, Havasu Falls comes into view. Although the temptation to stop may be strong, it's advisable to resist for a few reasons. At this juncture, it's more practical to use your time locating a campsite, setting up, and taking a short rest to alleviate fatigue. The falls will present a more appealing sight a bit later when sweat is no longer on your brow, and the weight on your back feels less burdensome.

The campground, stretching for a mile, lacks assigned campsites, leaving you to decide based on personal preferences and tolerance for proximity to other campers. Tables are scattered across the campground, but demand often exceeds supply. Considering the remoteness from the nearest plumbing, the composting toilets prove to be bearable. A mild, and not excessively odorous, breeze emanates from below. Overall, the system functions well, though lines may form during peak hours, typically around 7-8 a.m.

Along the trail between the village and the campground, three huts offer fry bread for purchase. One hut even provides fry bread wrapped around hot dogs. The prices are reasonable, the operating hours sporadic, and the fry bread is heavenly.About a third of the way into the campground, a spring provides clean water through a plastic spigot protruding from the base of a cliff.

Durable, water-resistant footwear stands out as the essential accessory for your hike around and exploration near the waterfalls. The pools and waterways are naturally lined with mud, sand, and pebbles, and the abundance of rocks makes barefoot walking uncomfortable. Opting for water shoes is ideal, as they snugly mold to your feet, preventing the entry of sand and mud. Mesh shoes are acceptable, but it's crucial to take them off after each water crossing to clean off the accumulated muck and sand.

Crowds are a common sight throughout the year, except during the less popular months of February and November. Beaver Falls, with its series of cascading, swim-friendly pools, tends to draw more visitors. However, on the trails, a sense of wilderness prevails, a feature that is expected when undertaking a mandatory 10-mile hike, unless one opts for a helicopter ride.

Some visitors may arrive before dawn at the helicopter pads at the trailhead or Supai, hoping to secure a seat for a quick journey covering the distance in minutes. However, it operates on a first-come, first-served basis, with priority given to residents and any necessary supplies being flown in or out. Individuals at the bottom may start queuing as early as 5 a.m. for a chance at a seat. Despite the allure of a swift helicopter ride, experiencing this landscape on foot at least once is deemed more fitting.

The use of pack animals for transporting hikers' gear in and out of the canyon sparks controversy. Accusations of mistreatment and substandard care have circulated, often through social media. Tribal officials claim to monitor the animals' health and express a willingness to investigate any complaints filed with the Animal Control Office in Supai. Ultimately, each hiker must make an informed decision regarding the use of pack animals based on their own judgment.

HEARD MUSEUM

COUNTY: MARICOPA   **CITY:** PHOENIX

DATE VISITED: **WHO I WENT WITH:**

RATING: ☆ ☆ ☆ ☆ ☆   **WILL I RETURN?** YES / NO

Established in 1929 by Dwight and Maie Heard in what is now central Phoenix, this institution was created to house their personal collection of art and artifacts. Today, the Heard Museum has a dual focus on traditional and contemporary Native American art, boasting a permanent collection of over 35,000 artifacts showcased in 10 exhibit galleries.

Some of the recurring exhibits you can explore during each visit include:

History and Collections of the Heard Museum: This exhibit, located in the Sandra Day O'Connor Gallery, chronicles the museum's history spanning over seven decades.

We Are! Arizona's First People: An interactive exhibit providing insights into Arizona's 21 federally recognized tribal communities.

Remembering Our Indian School Days: The Boarding School Experience: Featuring historic photographs, memorabilia, artwork, and first-person oral histories, this exhibit sheds light on the assimilation and Americanization of Native American children.

Every Picture Tells a Story: An interactive exhibit with over 200 cultural and fine art works demonstrating how designs narrate stories based on life experiences related to the environment, nature, animal life, family life, and community. It offers hands-on activities suitable for all ages.

HOME: Native People of the Southwest: Showcasing the Heard Museum's most cherished masterpieces, this exhibit presents sweeping landscapes, poetry, and personal recollections depicting the Native People of the Southwest.

The Heard Museum not only serves as a captivating destination to explore and appreciate Native art and cultures but also goes beyond that by actively committing to the accurate and sensitive interpretation of Native cultures and art. The museum provides various opportunities such as special lectures, school group tours, and a Speaker's Bureau. Additionally, it is renowned for its research facility, The Billie Jane Baguley Library and Archives.

For the public, the Heard Museum offers Guided Tours three times a day, each lasting approximately 45 minutes and complimentary with paid admission. The museum hosts frequent special events, programs, and festivals, showcasing Native art and culture at signature events like the Heard Museum Spanish Market, the annual Indian Fair & Market, and the World Championship Hoop Dance Contest. In addition to these major community events, the museum organizes a diverse range of programs, including artist demonstrations, performances, book signings, gallery talks, public tours, lectures, and workshops.

Unique exhibits at the Heard Museum encompass extensive collections of Native southwest jewelry and about 1,200 kachina dolls donated by the late Senator Barry M. Goldwater and the Fred Harvey Company.

The museum offers beautiful rooms and courtyards suitable for entertaining varying guest sizes, ranging from 20 to several hundred. With Spanish Colonial-style architecture, arched walkways, spacious galleries, outdoor bricked patios, fountains, and lush desert landscapes, the Heard Museum provides a charming environment for special occasions.

Visitors can also explore the museum's gift shop and bookstore, featuring a diverse selection. The gourmet café, open daily from 11 a.m. to 3 p.m., offers a refined dining experience. Notably, both the café and the gift shop can be accessed without paying the museum's entrance fee. The Heard Museum operates every day, with exceptions on New Year's Day, Easter, Memorial Day, Independence Day, Labor Day, Thanksgiving, and Christmas.

HOLE IN THE ROCK

COUNTY: MARICOPA   CITY: PHOENIX

DATE VISITED: WHO I WENT WITH:

RATING: ☆ ☆ ☆ ☆ ☆   WILL I RETURN?   YES / NO

The Hole in the Rock stands out as a well-known free attraction nestled in Phoenix's Papago Park. This site boasts a brief hiking trail leading to a rock formation with a distinctive hole, offering a captivating panoramic view of Phoenix. The hike is conveniently located near the parking lot and typically takes around 10 to 15 minutes to ascend. The trail encompasses some steep sections and occasional steps, but with a leisurely pace, it proves to be relatively easy. The attraction is open daily from 5 am to 7 pm throughout the entire year.

The initial portion of this trail, covering about a third of a mile, is mostly flat and easily manageable. However, as you progress, the trail becomes more challenging due to steeper inclines and slippery, rocky areas. Approaching the rock formation involves negotiating some steps, which, though uneven, are manageable with good balance and careful attention to footing. Visitors are advised to postpone their visit during rainy or wet conditions, as the trail can become slippery. Fortunately, such weather conditions are rare in the Valley of the Sun. According to the City of Phoenix website, the trail is categorized as a "blue path," indicating elevation changes, some uneven surfaces, and obstacles or ruts of about 8 inches or less. Using a wheelchair or stroller on this path is not recommended due to its challenging nature.

The park is dog-friendly, but dogs must be kept on a leash at all times. The trailhead is easily accessible from the sizable parking lot. Optimal visiting times are on weekdays during early mornings or afternoons to avoid crowds. Weekends, particularly between 5 pm and 7 pm, tend to be busier. Late mornings and early afternoons on weekends are moderately crowded, while Tuesday and Wednesday nights are the least busy for evening visits. For late spring, summer, and early fall, comfortable attire like shorts and a T-shirt is recommended. In winter, it's advisable to wear pants, a long-sleeved shirt, or a hoodie. Regardless of the season, it is crucial to bring an ample supply of water for the hike.

The proximity of the Hole in the Rock to the Phoenix Zoo makes it a convenient location for visitors. There is nearby parking, and finding a spot is usually straightforward, with the added benefit of free parking.

For those opting to drive:

If coming from downtown Phoenix, the most straightforward route involves heading directly east on West Van Buren Street for approximately 7 miles.
Turn left at North Galvin Parkway and drive about a quarter mile before reaching the parking lot.

Public transportation is also a viable option, considering the close proximity of both the zoo and the Hole:

Transit Option 1 - #3 Bus:

Take the #3 bus from Van Buren Street and Central Avenue station towards the Phoenix Zoo. Exit in front of the zoo and proceed north to the trailhead for the Hole.

Transit Option 2 - Light Rail + #56 Bus:

Begin by taking the eastbound light rail from Gilbert Road and Main Street Station. Alight at Priest Drive and Washington Street station. Board the #56 Botanical Garden bus heading towards the Botanical Gardens (located along N. Priest Drive just north of Washington Street). Disembark at the Galvin Parkway & Van Buren Street Station, then exit near the zoo.

Transit Option 3 - Light Rail + Walking:

Commence the journey at Van Buren Street and Central Avenue Station heading East. Get off at Priest Drive and Washington Street station. Walk approximately a mile to reach the Zoo and the Hole. It's recommended to take N. Priest Drive and then follow the trail into Papago Park, starting at the northeast corner of N. Galvin Pkwy. and E. Van Buren Street. This walk covers about a mile.

Several attractions are in close proximity to the Hole in the Rock:

1) Phoenix Zoo: Located directly south of the rock, the zoo houses more than 3,000 animals within its expansive 120 acres of land. A visit to the zoo can easily take 2 to 5 hours, with various restaurants and bathrooms available for convenience.

2) Hunt's Tomb: Constructed in 1931, this small white pyramid was built by Arizona's first governor, George W.P. Hunt, as a burial site for his wife. The site features informative signs about the governor and his wife. Notably, Governor Hunt held office when women were granted the right to vote in Arizona, eight years ahead of the U.S. government. The area is typically serene, offering stunning views.

3) Desert Botanical Garden: A mere 5-minute drive from the Hole, this remarkable 55-acre garden boasts five trails, thousands of plants, and a variety of wildlife (safely observed). The garden is suitable for all ages, including young children, and features restaurants and bathrooms. Importantly, one of the trails provides a view of the Hole in the Rock.

HOOVER DAM

COUNTY: MOHAVE CITY: KINGMAN *n.c.*

DATE VISITED: WHO I WENT WITH:

RATING: ☆ ☆ ☆ ☆ ☆ WILL I RETURN? YES / NO

The Hoover Dam, initially named the Boulder Dam, is situated on the Arizona-Nevada border along Highway 93. Positioned 30 miles southeast of Las Vegas, it serves as a significant structure, harnessing the powerful Colorado River to create Lake Mead. This iconic dam has become a renowned tourist attraction, attracting nearly 1 million visitors annually for the Bureau of Reclamation tour. Since the 1930s, the bureau has guided visitors through the dam and power plant, offering a captivating experience that remains impressive to this day.

The construction of the Hoover Dam involved the impoundment of the Colorado River, leading to the creation of Lake Mead. Completed within a span of five years, the contractors had a seven-year allowance from April 20, 1931. However, concrete placement in the dam concluded on May 29, 1935, and all features were finalized by March 1, 1936. Boulder City, established in 1931, served as the residence for the dam workers and is unique in Nevada as the only city where gambling is prohibited. Visitors to this city can enjoy activities such as antique shopping and dining in various restaurants.

For those interested in visiting the Hoover Dam, the visitor center is the ideal starting point. It provides information on reservations, opening hours, special events, and more. Accessing the dam is free, with ample free parking available. Walking across the dam offers excellent photo opportunities and informative displays. Additionally, one can witness the impressive construction of a massive bridge downstream from the Hoover Dam, known as the Hoover Dam Bypass.

Restrooms are conveniently located in the visitor center, parking garage, near the Old Exhibit Building, and in the downstream face towers on top of the dam. A gift shop on the lower floor of the parking garage offers souvenir shopping, and there is also a food concession at the dam.

Before crossing the Hoover Dam, it's crucial to be aware of warning signs and vehicle restrictions. Not all types of vehicles are permitted to cross, and it's advisable to research this information beforehand. RVs and rental trucks can cross but may undergo inspection.

While it may be tempting to stop and take photos or absorb the scenery, designated pullouts are available for safe halts. Stopping on the street is discouraged.

The visitors center is situated on the Nevada side and may experience more significant crowds, but it provides another parking option. Covered or premium parking spots are available for a fee. Oversized vehicles, trailers, and RVs cannot park in the garage closest to the visitors center; instead, they must use a lot on the Arizona side. Budget-conscious visitors can find free parking lots on the Arizona side, a bit further up the canyon, with a closer paid lot available as well.

Tours of the Hoover Dam are offered at the visitors center on a first-come, first-served basis for individuals aged 8 and older. (Children younger than 8 are not permitted on the tour.) For those interested in exploring the Power Plant as well, tickets can be reserved online or at the visitors center, and all age groups are welcome on the Power Plant tour. It's important to note that neither tour is accessible for individuals in wheelchairs or with limited mobility.

The Hoover Dam is approximately a 45-minute drive from the Las Vegas Strip, though specific travel times may vary based on traffic conditions. There are no direct public transportation options to the dam. As the Hoover Dam lacks an exact address, it is advisable to set your GPS to the Hoover Dam Visitors Center.

The nearest cities to the Hoover Dam include Boulder City, Nevada, Henderson, Nevada, and Winchester, Nevada. Accommodation options in the vicinity include the Hoover Dam Lodge & Casino, the Boulder Dam Hotel, and the Best Western Hoover Dam. For more mid-range choices, Lake Las Vegas, with options like The Westin Lake Las Vegas Resort & Spa and the Hilton Lake Las Vegas Resort & Spa, is a convenient location.

Tips:

1) Visit during the slower months of January and February to avoid crowds at the Hoover Dam. The least crowded tour times are typically between 9 a.m. and 10:30 a.m. and from 3 p.m. to 4:45 p.m.
2) Keep in mind the desert climate, as it can get hot at the Hoover Dam due to its significant concrete structures. Dress appropriately and bring an adequate water supply.
3) Take a moment to appreciate the Hoover Dam Bypass when at the site. The bridge over the Colorado River is visible from the dam and offers a stunning and somewhat daunting sight. This 900-foot-high concrete arch bridge is the world's highest of its kind and the second-highest in the United States, following the Royal Gorge Bridge in Colorado.
4) The main segment of the bypass, designed to reduce sharp turns on the highway, is named the Mike O'Callaghan–Pat Tillman Memorial Bridge, and it officially opened in 2010.

HUBBELL TRADING POST NATIONAL HISTORIC SITE

COUNTY: APACHE   CITY: HOLBROOK *n.c.*

DATE VISITED: WHO I WENT WITH:

RATING: ☆ ☆ ☆ ☆ ☆   WILL I RETURN? YES / NO

Explore the Hubbell Trading Post National Historic Site, the oldest continuously operating trading post in the Navajo Nation. Since its establishment in 1878, this trading post has been serving the community of Ganado, providing a diverse range of goods such as groceries, grain, hardware, horse tack, coffee, and Native American art. Upon entering the trading post, visitors will be surrounded by a variety of goods, and as their eyes adjust to the dim lighting, they will be captivated by the rich history within.

Designated as a National Historic Site in 1965, the Hubbell Trading Post has a unique status – it remains in operation as a working trading post. The trading post, initiated in the 1870s, continues to serve the community today. Managed by the National Park Service within the Navajo Nation, the site offers visitors the opportunity to immerse themselves in the history and culture of the region. Take the time to explore the visitor center, trading post, and the surrounding grounds, which include historical structures like the blacksmith shop, chicken coop, bunkhouse, corrals, and kitchen garden. It's a chance to step back in time and discover the legacy of the American Southwest's oldest trading post.

Hubbell Trading Post National Historic Park offers a compelling visit for several reasons. It provides a glimpse into the past through its historic structures and artifacts, once instrumental in the trading activities with the Navajo Indians. The park also serves as an educational platform, offering insights into Native American culture and showcasing well-preserved artwork and architecture from that historical period.

The site itself preserves the legacy of the oldest operational trading post in Navajo territory, established in 1878 by John Lorenzo Hubbell. Serving as a vital trade hub for the Navajo Nation, the Hubbell Trading Post played a crucial role in supporting the community. Its inception followed the Navajo Nation's return to Arizona after the 'Long Walk,' a forced removal from their ancestral homeland to a reservation in Fort Sumner, New Mexico. For the returning Navajo, the trading post became a lifeline, facilitating the exchange of their traditional goods for European products. The Hubbell family's impact extended further, establishing a network of trading posts throughout Arizona.

In 1864, the Navajo Nation was compelled to leave their ancestral land in Arizona and undertake a journey to the reservation located in New Mexico, where they were to be resettled. This forced displacement occurred following a particularly tumultuous period marked by violence between the Navajo Nation and the U.S Army. The Navajo endured significant hardships before, during, and after the Long Walk. Upon reaching New Mexico, the Navajo took residence in the Bosque Redondo Reservation at Fort Sumner. Throughout their time there, the Navajo engaged in trade with settlers as a means of survival. It was during this period that the Navajo were introduced to essential items that later became integral to their way of life, including flour, sugar, coffee, and baking powder.

After spending four years in internment at Fort Sumner, the Navajo were eventually allowed to return to a portion of their ancestral land in Arizona. However, upon their return, they discovered that their way of life had been decimated. The violent clashes with the United States Army during and after the conflict had resulted in the destruction of Navajo livestock, irrigated farmlands, and homes. Faced with the task of rebuilding their lives, the Navajo sought to supplement the food and items they could produce themselves with traditionally European goods. Trade became a crucial means for achieving this, with establishments like the Hubbell Trading Post and others playing a significant role in the survival of the Navajo.

John Lorenzo Hubbell was born in 1853 at his family residence, the Gutiérrez Hubbell House in New Mexico. Engaging in trade at various posts in New Mexico and Arizona, Hubbell eventually settled in Ganado, Arizona, in 1876. In 1878, he purchased a cluster of buildings and transformed them into the Hubbell Trading Post, solidifying his position as the most prominent Navajo trader.

Upon acquiring the trading post, Hubbell initiated the construction of additional structures, including guesthouses and corrals for traded livestock. In 1897, he began building a barn for the trading post, crafted in the traditional Anasazi style using sandstone, mud, and cornstalks. The supplementary buildings were designed in the Navajo Hogan style, traditionally made from logs with the entrance facing east. Recognizing the influx of Navajo visitors, Hubbell provided accommodations at the post.

Originally named Pueblo Colorado, the guesthouse was later renamed Grando in honor of Ganado Mucho, a notable Navajo chief and close friend to the Hubbell family. Ganado Mucho's son, Many Horses, found his final resting place in the Hubbell family graveyard. Navajo individuals traveled from distant locations to exchange wool, rugs, jewelry, sheep, baskets, and pottery at the Hubbell Trading Post. In return, they received essential items like flour, sugar, and other staples to supplement their locally grown produce.

Hubbell not only established a prosperous trading post but also homesteaded 160 acres around it. As the Navajo Reservation expanded, the Hubbell homestead became incorporated into it. Hubbell secured congressional approval to retain his land, which would be encompassed by the expanding reservation.

Hubbell and his sons were involved in the acquisition and construction of twenty-four trading posts, establishing an empire that utilized both the railroad and stagecoaches. This strategic expansion solidified the Hubbell family's position as the most influential Navajo traders of the 19th Century. Hubbell's impact extended to the traditional skills of

Navajo rug weaving and silversmithing, shaped by his stringent standards for the quality of traded items at the Hubbell Trading Post.

Operating the trading post until his death in 1930, Hubbell's youngest son, Roman, assumed leadership thereafter. Roman continued to run and manage the post until his passing in 1957. Following Roman's demise, his wife carried on the tradition, overseeing the post until 1967 when the grounds were transferred to the National Parks Service. Remarkably, the trading post remains active, preserving the original structures and furniture from the Hubbell home.

Entrance to the park is free, with the park pass covering all individuals in a car for per-vehicle sites and up to 4 adults for per-person sites. The Navajo Nation observes Mountain Daylight Saving Time from March to November, differing from the rest of Arizona, which observes Mountain Standard Time. Pets must be restrained or leashed (not exceeding 6 feet) at all times, wearing a collar with current tags.

GPS and cell phone services may not always be reliable in the Navajo Nation. The park operates daily during the summer from 8:30 AM to 4:30 PM (mid-May to mid-October), and winter hours depend on weather conditions and staffing (mid-October to mid-May). The park is closed on Thanksgiving, Christmas, and New Year's Day.

Public Wi-Fi is not available, so visitors should be prepared. Using insect repellent is advisable, especially around water bodies. It's recommended to bring your water bottle, as plastic water bottles are not sold in the park. Limited parking is available in front of the Trading Post and the Visitor Center. There are no on-site restaurants. National Park Passport stamps can be obtained in the visitor center. For electric vehicle users, there are at least 2 EV charging stations in Gallup, Mexico, which is 50 miles away from the park.

Hubbell Trading Post National Historic Site is situated at milepost 446.3 on AZ State Route 264. For those traveling on I-40, they can take U.S. Highway 191 North to Ganado and proceed west on Hwy. 264.

From Gallup, New Mexico, travelers can take U.S. Highway 491 North to U.S. Highway 264 west towards Ganado, passing through Window Rock, Arizona. If coming from Chinle, Arizona, driving south on Hwy. 191 requires turning east when reaching Hwy. 264.

The optimal time to visit Hubbell Trading Post National Historic Site is from early summer to early fall, specifically from mid-June to early September. During this period, visitors can enjoy the beauty and culture of this historic site, benefiting from warm, rain-free days and dry, comfortable air - ideal for outdoor activities.

In Ganado, summers are warm, dry, and mostly clear, while winters are cold, snowy, and partly cloudy. The hot season is from May 30 to September 14, with an average daily high temperature above 78 degrees. The cold season is from November 22 to February 25, with an average daily high temperature below 51 degrees. The snowiest season is from December 24 to February 13, with at least 1 inch of snow in a month, with January receiving the most snow, averaging 1.1 inches.

The visitor center serves as an excellent starting point for exploring Hubbell Trading Post NHS, offering interpretive panels, trading post exhibits, a bookstore, and Navajo rug weaving demonstrations.

The closest motels are found in Chinle (40 minutes), Window Rock (30 minutes), and Holbrook, AZ (1.5 hours). Examples include Thunderbird Lodge in Chinle, Best Western Canyon de Chelly Inn, and Holiday Inn Canyon De Chelly in Holbrook.

Campgrounds are approximately 40 minutes away at Canyon de Chelly National Monument near Chinle, AZ. Additional campgrounds can be found in Chinle, AZ; Window Rock, AZ; Holbrook, AZ; or Gallup, NM.

JEROME

COUNTY: YAVAPAI   **CITY:** JEROME

DATE VISITED: _____   **WHO I WENT WITH:** _____

RATING: ☆ ☆ ☆ ☆ ☆   **WILL I RETURN?** YES / NO

Perched on Cleopatra Hill and boasting the title of "America's Most Vertical City," this destination offers more than just breathtaking views of Verde Valley. Its popularity as a getaway stems from the opportunity to delve into art galleries and distinctive stores such as Nellie Bly Kaleidoscopes. Visitors also indulge in the local wines available at Jerome's tasting rooms. For those with a penchant for history, Jerome State Historic Park is a must-visit, providing insights into the community's mining heritage. With various bed and breakfasts, independently-operated hotels, and top-notch restaurants, Jerome ensures a fulfilling weekend stay for every visitor.

Jerome was established on Cleopatra Hill, situated above an extensive copper deposit. Initially, prehistoric Native Americans mined the area for colored stones. Subsequently, the Spanish arrived in search of gold but discovered copper instead. In 1876, Anglos laid the first claims, and by 1883, United Verde mining operations began, including the Little Daisy claim. The town of Jerome swiftly evolved from a tent city into a prosperous company town, mirroring the fluctuating fortunes of the mines. The mines, the workforce, and those drawn by its wealth collectively shaped Jerome's vibrant history. The mining camp became a melting pot of Americans, Mexicans, Croatians, Irish, Spaniards, Italians, and Chinese, contributing to its diverse and lively atmosphere.

During its heyday, Jerome garnered attention as a booming town, attracting promoters and investors. Financiers played a crucial role in nurturing and exploiting the mines, extracting billions of dollars worth of copper, gold, and silver. Over time, the transportation landscape transformed from pack burros, mule-drawn freight wagons, and horses to steam engines, automobiles, and trucks. Despite challenges such as fires and landslides, Jerome consistently rebuilt itself. However, the closure of the mines in 1953, influenced by fluctuating copper prices, labor unrest, economic depressions, and wars, marked the end of an era.

Following the departure of "King Copper" in 1953, Jerome's population plummeted from its 1920s peak of 15,000 to a mere 50 people. The Jerome Historical Society safeguarded the structures against vandalism, the Douglas Mansion became a State Park in 1965, and Jerome attained National Historic Landmark status in 1976. During the counterculture era of the 60s and 70s, Jerome became a refuge for artists. Newcomers and longtime residents collaborated to revive Jerome.

Today, Jerome thrives with a community comprising writers, artists, artisans, musicians, historians, and families. This lively and harmonious community is rooted in a deep foundation of history and folklore.

To commence your exploration of Jerome, the ideal starting point is the Jerome State Historic Park, housed within the historic Douglas Mansion. Positioned on the opposite side of the town, the museum offers breathtaking views of the city and the remarkable Verde Valley. Inside, you'll receive a comprehensive introduction to what awaits you in the city, serving as an invaluable historical resource dedicated to preserving Jerome's legacy.

Constructed in 1916 by James S. Douglas, the mansion sits atop the hill adjacent to the Little Daisy Mine, which Douglas owned. From the mansion viewpoint, you can still catch a glimpse of the old mine. Following Douglas's passing, the house transformed into a National Museum, showcasing photographs, mining artifacts, minerals, a video presentation, and a 3-D model depicting the town in the 1900s, along with an underground mines model. Adjacent to the mansion is the Audrey Headframe Park, accessible from 8 am to 5 pm, allowing visitors to stand on a glass floor above a 1,900-foot shaft that miners descended daily for their duties in 1918.

The Museum interior provides one of the finest vantage points for observing the city and Cleopatra Hill. The courtyard's lookout point offers panoramic views of Verde Valley and the entire city. Armed with a map and an infographic detailing all the buildings (past and present), visitors gain a comprehensive understanding of the cityscape.

After immersing yourself in history, it's time to return to your car and venture into the city. Main Street is the ideal location for parking, and if you plan to stay overnight, your hotel may offer parking facilities. Alternatively, there are convenient spots across from the Bartlett Hotel. Once parked, cross the street and explore the plaque dedicated to the Bartlett Hotel.

The original structure erected at this location was known as the Grandview Hotel, established in 1895. Serving as a dancehall, dining room, and an upscale social club, it contributed to the high-society scene. Unfortunately, in 1898, a devastating fire swept through the city, resulting in the destruction of the hotel. The Bartlett Hotel emerged from the ashes in 1901, reconstructed with bricks in the hope of better fire resistance. It stood as a luxurious establishment, with each room uniquely decorated to provide guests with a distinctive experience.

For two decades, the Bartlett Hotel housed the offices of The New Jerome's Times, the longest-running newspaper in the area. However, due to declining readership, the newspaper eventually closed its doors. The building also served various purposes over the years, functioning as a bank, drug store, and hosting four different offices and shops on the ground floor. By the late 1940s, structural instability led to the abandonment of the building, leaving only the framing behind. Presently, the Jerome Historical Society has placed wooden ghost apparitions for tourists to toss pennies into, generating funds for future restoration and preservation efforts throughout the city.

After exploring the Bartlett Hotel, continue down the street until you reach the Jerome Historical Society Mine Museum. It offers a deeper understanding of the miners' lives during the boom times in Jerome, presenting their stories from their perspectives. Discover why Jerome earned the moniker "Wickedest Town in The West" and learn about the miners' pursuits in the "billion-dollar mining camp." The museum houses an extensive collection of over 11,000 maps, newspapers, and documents. By visiting, you contribute to the Historical Society's mission of protecting and preserving the town for future generations, making your entry fee an investment in the preservation of this historic city.

If you head northeast along Main Street, you'll encounter the Hotel Connor and the Spirit Room. Make sure to take a break here and enjoy a drink during your journey, especially considering the desert heat that can leave any traveler quite thirsty. This renowned stop for ghost sightings is a must-see structure on your tour.

Constructed in 1898 by David Connor, the Connor Hotel stood as one of Jerome's precious historical gems. Initially boasting over twenty rooms on the second floor, it accommodated various traveling miners, businessmen, and contractors who flocked from all over the West to capitalize on the natural resources of Verde Valley. Despite the affordable room rates of $1.00, a considerable sum in those days, the Connor Hotel lived up to expectations. The first floor featured a bar, card room, and billiard tables, mirroring the amenities of the Bartlett Hotel down the street. Unfortunately, like the Bartlett, the Connor Hotel fell victim to the flames during the great fires of 1898.

However, unlike some other businesses, Connor had insurance and swiftly initiated the construction of his new hotel. He implemented lavish improvements, making it one of the first hotels in Jerome with electricity and telephone lines. Remarkably, its telephone number was simply "8," as there were only a few places with telephones, each assigned a single-digit number.

Regarded as the top-of-the-line hotel in the West and well-known throughout Arizona, the Connor Hotel eventually faced financial struggles as the mines dwindled, and miners returned home. By 1931, the hotel closed its doors, seemingly for the last time. Attempts were made to lease the first floor to different shops to generate income, but the second floor remained inactive until the late 60s when a tourist boom revived the city.

Following a significant renovation to meet modern safety codes and health standards, the hotel now welcomes travelers to experience a piece of history. For day trippers seeking a glimpse of this treasure, the Spirit Room offers a chance to step inside and enjoy a drink at the bar. Adorned with artifacts from the original hotel, the Spirit Room exudes character, resembling a saloon from an old Western movie where one might expect a cowboy to walk through the door at any moment.

By this point, you're likely feeling quite hungry. When it comes to ghost towns, there are often cheesy restaurants with "ghostly" menu items and random western decor plastered all over the walls. However, Bobby D's BBQ Pit offers straightforward, delicious food at reasonable prices. In touristy areas, finding good, affordable food can be a challenge, but this hidden gem is an exception. Conveniently located around the corner from both the Connor Hotel and the Historical Society, it's the perfect spot to grab a meal before continuing your tour. The drinks are served in charming western mason jar glasses, adding to the welcoming, down-home atmosphere. Explore their selection of local craft beers or iced teas. Notable menu items include the brisket and ribs tips, Mac 'n Cheese, Jalapeño Cheddar Cornbread, and Pulled Pork – all smoked in-house. The aroma of BBQ permeates the entire town, making it difficult to resist. Bobby D's is undoubtedly a delectable choice for a satisfying western luncheon.

Once you've indulged in BBQ goodness, it's time to unwind and savor some of Verde Valley's finest wines. Perched atop Cleopatra Hill along the main street, you'll find Caduceus Tasting Room and Espresso Bar. Here, you can leisurely sip on your chosen wine, guided by a friendly and knowledgeable staff. The venue offers ample seating to enjoy one of their incredible charcuterie platters. If wine isn't your preference, the establishment also boasts a selection of exceptional espressos to give you a boost for the remainder of the day.

As you savor your final sip of wine, take a lingering glance at the breathtaking view before heading out the door. Head back along historic Main Street, where local artisans and souvenir store owners have established a presence over the years. This bustling strip offers an array of unique and intriguing delights, from chocolate fudge to vintage dresses, kaleidoscopes, and hand-painted art. There's something to cater to every taste along this vibrant avenue. Amidst the diverse shops, you'll also encounter old, rundown houses that have remained abandoned for years, creating an intriguing juxtaposition of the old and the new. Despite new tenants occupying these buildings, the facades and structures have retained much of their original charm, if not all.

Continue your stroll along Clark Street toward the fork in the road where Clark meets Hill Street. At this juncture, veer off the path and begin ascending Hill Street. Before embarking on the uphill journey, you'll pass by the picturesque Surgeon's House, erected in 1916 for Jerome's Chief Surgeon and utilized throughout the heyday of Jerome's mining boom as the nurse's residence. With mining being a perilous profession, this house served as a medical hub, and rumors persist that ghosts still haunt its halls today.

As you ascend Hill Street, you'll encounter the Award-Winning Asylum Restaurant, situated at the Jerome Grand Hotel. Open for lunch and dinner every day, the restaurant boasts a panoramic view of the entire Verde Valley, providing diners with a truly mesmerizing experience. Despite its somewhat whimsical name, the interior features beautiful art deco decor from the period when the building was constructed. The menu offers classic dishes expertly prepared by some of the best chefs in the Valley. Notable menu selections include the Julienne Pastrami Salad, Char-Broiled Chilean Grilled

Salmon, and Mesquite Bacon Wrapped Filet Mignon, ensuring a delightful culinary experience with a breathtaking backdrop.

Whether you choose to spend the night or make this the final stop on your tour, concluding the day at the Grand Hotel offers a breathtaking view of the city and adds a historical touch to your experience. The current appearance of the Grand Hotel differs significantly from its original form. Initially built in 1926, it served as the Verde County Hospital, becoming one of Arizona's most modern and well-equipped hospitals by 1920, thanks to mining finances supporting top-notch services. However, with the decline of mining in the 1950s, the hospital ceased operations. Left unused for 44 years, the Altherr family renovated it in 1994, transforming it into a hotel for tourists. They took great care to make minimal changes to the building, preserving its historical significance while making it a functional attraction.

The original hospital was constructed in the mission revival style of architecture and stood as one of the last major buildings erected in Jerome. Its location away from the city center spared it from many downtown fires, preserving its architectural integrity. Additionally, as a hospital housing expensive medical equipment, it was designed to be fireproof and capable of withstanding dynamite blasts of up to 260,000 pounds. If you're adventurous enough to stay overnight, be prepared for some chilling surprises. Numerous reported hauntings include mysterious smells in unoccupied rooms, such as cigar smoke and whiskey. Visitors have also witnessed televisions turning on and off inexplicably. On occasion, two apparitions have been seen—one in a white hospital gown and the other in a nurse's outfit—adding an extra layer of intrigue to the Grand Hotel's storied history.

JUAN BAUTISTA DE ANZA NATIONAL HISTORIC TRAIL

COUNTY: PIMA, PINAL, SANTA CRUZ	CITY: NOGALES

DATE VISITED:	WHO I WENT WITH:

RATING: ☆ ☆ ☆ ☆ ☆	WILL I RETURN? YES / NO

The Juan Bautista de Anza National Historic Trail spans 1,210 miles, tracing a historic route from Nogales, Arizona, to San Francisco, California. This trail serves as a commemoration of the 1775-1776 Spanish Expedition, during which approximately 30 families embarked on an overland journey to Alta California. The expedition led to the founding and establishment of significant locations, including the Mission and Presidio of San Francisco, the Mission in Santa Clara, and the Pueblo of San José. The majority of expedition members chose to settle in the present-day San Francisco Bay Area.

In October 1775, amid the burgeoning separation of the nascent United States from Great Britain on the East Coast, Juan Bautista de Anza and approximately 240 Spanish colonists embarked on a 1,200-mile expedition through present-day Mexico, Arizona, and California. Their goal was to establish what would eventually become San Francisco, marking Spain's initial civilian presence in Alta California and establishing the first land route to the territory. The Anza Party navigated rivers, crossed deserts, and often relied on the assistance of American Indian tribes whose lands they traversed. Anza's route not only opened up the interior of Arizona to European settlement but also had a lasting impact on the tribal cultures existing in the region, shaping the cities we recognize today.

Modern travelers can retrace the Anza expedition through Arizona using the Juan Bautista de Anza National Historic Trail provided by the National Park Service. Commencing in Nogales, the route initially follows Interstate 19 north, joins Interstate 10 south of Tucson, continues near Casa Grande along Interstate 8, and finally crosses the Colorado River into California at Yuma.

Along the route, interpretive roadside signs designate numerous Anza Party campsites, including Las Lagunas de Anza wetland near Nogales in Santa Cruz County, where over 200 bird species can be observed. Further north, Tubac Presidio State Historic Park served as Anza's home and Spain's northernmost outpost in Arizona in 1775. Hiking trails from Tubac connect with Tumacácori National Historical Park, 6 miles to the south, preserving three Spanish missions.

In Pima County, visitors can explore the Pascua Yaqui Tribe and the Tohono O'odham Nation at the Yoemem Tekia Cultural Center and Museum and the Himdag Ki: Tohono O'odham Nation Cultural Center and Museum. A visit to Mission San Xavier del Bac is also recommended, where the Anza Party stayed, and three couples from the expedition were married. The party camped in today's Saguaro National Park, safeguarding 143 square miles of the Sonoran Desert and its iconic saguaro cacti.

Upon entering present-day Pinal County, the expedition set up camp in the vicinity of what is now Picacho Peak State Park. Anza took a detour to explore the ruins at the current Casa Grande Ruins National Monument. This monumental Hohokam compound, abandoned around three centuries prior to Anza's arrival, continues to captivate visitors today. The expedition also spent time in Pima villages, with expedition diarist Pedro Font describing the residents as "gentle and of good heart." For a deeper understanding of Pima culture's past and present, a visit to the Gila River Indian Community's Huhugam Heritage Center is recommended.

Continuing west along the Gila River in today's I-8 corridor, the Anza Party camped with the ancestors of the present-day Salt River Pima-Maricopa Indian Community. Anza had initially met this community during his scouting journey in 1774. The Painted Rock Petroglyph Site features interpretive signs detailing the 1775 Anza Party's passage through this area.

Anza fostered positive relationships with the various tribes encountered, and the expedition's success was greatly indebted to the support of these communities. On November 30, 1775, with the assistance of the ancestors of the present-day Fort Yuma-Quechan Tribe, the Anza Party crossed the Colorado River. The term "Yuma" originates from "humo," the Spanish word for "smoke," which collectively referred to the Quechan, Cocopah, and Maricopa people due to the numerous campfires. The Yuma Crossing National Heritage Area, spanning 21 square miles, safeguards wetlands along the Colorado River. A few years later, in 1781, the Yuma Revolt saw the Quechans drive the Spanish out of this crucial river crossing in response to the impacts of colonization.

KARTCHNER CAVERNS STATE PARK

COUNTY: COCHISE   CITY: BENSON *n.c.*

DATE VISITED: WHO I WENT WITH:

RATING: ☆ ☆ ☆ ☆ ☆   WILL I RETURN?   YES / NO

In November 1974, Gary Tenen and Randy Tufts embarked on an exploration of the limestone hills at the eastern base of the Whetstone Mountains with the goal of discovering a previously unknown cave. Their quest led them to an incredible find, and for three years, they kept their discovery a secret. In February 1978, they revealed their findings to the property owners, James and Lois Kartchner. Recognizing the potential threat of unregulated use on unprotected caves, Tenen and Tufts decided to take measures to protect this significant discovery. Over the next few years, they explored the possibility of developing the cave themselves.

Some members of the Kartchner family residing in Tucson were impressed by the successful development and operation of Catalina State Park by Arizona State Parks. With the aim of preserving this extraordinary resource, they approached State Parks to gauge interest in acquiring the cave.

The Discovery Center is situated at the northeast end of the primary parking lot. Visitors are advised to arrive an hour before the scheduled tour to acquire tickets and engage in Discovery Center activities. The facility comprises the front desk, a theater offering a 15-minute video presentation played twice hourly, a museum featuring exhibits on cave formations, cave life, hydrology, and history, a gift shop with cave-related and southwestern-themed souvenirs, and an amphitheater for interpretive programs, weddings, or special events. The front desk provides park information, reservation tickets, and walk-up tickets (availability may vary, and reservations are recommended). Additionally, there is a Discovery Center Scavenger Hunt designed for kids to enhance their experience.

Explorers of Kartchner Caverns quickly realize that the Discovery Center lives up to its name. Caves, being mysterious and unfamiliar to humans, evoke curiosity and prompt us to seek answers to numerous questions. The museum's numerous interactive displays offer visitors the opportunity to personally uncover these answers.

Initial panels in the geology exhibits provide insights into how caves form, the reasons behind the appearance of formations, and the locations of other caves. Specific displays focus on Kartchner Caverns, one of the most extensively studied public caves globally, ranking among the top ten for its unique mineralogy. Visitors can touch local rock types, explore a cut-away view of the cave hill highlighting major features and tour routes, and take a virtual tour of the cave's prominent formations at the Underground Journey exhibit. The hands-on hydrology display allows guests to trace water underground, typically concealed from view, illustrating why water is vital to maintaining the cavern as a "living" cave.

The Discovery Center proudly showcases original 86,000-year-old sloth bones and a 36,000-year-old horse skull. Additionally, small bones from a bear, extinct antelope, bobcat, ringtail cat, and rabbit are on display.

Arizona State Parks collaborated with cave experts before development, resulting in a display highlighting the challenges faced by public caves and stressing the importance of their preservation.

Gift Shop - Operating hours are 10:00 a.m. to 3:00 p.m. (summer) and 9:00 a.m. to 5:00 p.m. (winter). The store can be reached at (520) 586-4167. The gift shop offers tasteful, unique gifts with a southwestern flair. A diverse range of Kartchner Caverns State Park souvenirs, including apparel and collectibles, is available for both adults and kids. The selection also features Native American jewelry, postcards, magnets, and rocks, with an emphasis on products made in America, especially locally crafted items. Book enthusiasts can explore an eclectic collection covering topics such as the cavern, nature, desert animals and birds, Arizona, Native American history, and southwest cookbooks. The Children's section includes educational toys, puzzles, plush animals, and puppets to complement children's storybooks. The shop boasts a variety of worldly and colorful rocks, crystals, minerals, and fossils for those interested in earth sciences.

The Bat Cave Cafe operates daily from 11 a.m. to 2 p.m., with the possibility of extended hours depending on guest participation. Group catering services are also available, and interested parties are encouraged to call in advance for more information at (520) 586-4167. The Cafe offers a menu featuring freshly made salads, sandwiches, wraps, quesadillas, and individual pizzas. Additionally, a variety of beverages and Blue Bunny Ice Cream treats are available to complement your meal. Guests have the opportunity to enjoy their meals in a serene patio atmosphere surrounded by the Hummingbird Garden. For catering arrangements, individuals should coordinate with the park concessionaire, Aramark. It is advised to contact Aramark at 520-586-4166 to discuss catering options or seek permission if arranging catering independently.

The campground loop at Kartchner Caverns provides picturesque views of Whetstone Mountain from all 60 campsites. Each campsite within the loop is equipped with a table, fire ring, hose bib, and power post, ensuring convenience in a clean, flat space. Positioned near trailheads leading to the Sky Island mountain range and in close proximity to the cave, discovery center, and clean restroom and shower facilities, these campsites offer a comfortable stay. All campsites feature electric hookups and water, and the camping fee includes access to shower/restroom facilities, water, electricity, and the dump station.

Back-in sites have a 110-volt AC power post with a 30-amp RV connection and a 20-amp receptacle. Pull-through sites feature a 220-volt 50-amp AC and a 110-volt 30-amp AC RV connection, along with a 20-amp GFI receptacle. Site lengths vary from 35' for the shortest back-in sites to 60' for the pull-through sites, all of which are single width. Side areas of the sites provide ample space for pull-out units, and shared-use group areas in the campground have grills/charcoal BBQs available.

The campground includes three handicapped-designated sites (one being a pull-through site), 12 pull-through sites, and 43 other sites of varying sizes. Handicapped-designated sites feature paved access to the site and adjacent restroom, a paved pad, and a wheelchair-accessible table.

Waste bins and shower/restroom facilities are situated on the upper west end of each campground, and restroom buildings include bottled water vending machines and dishwashing sinks on the rear east side.

It's important to note that the entrance gate is closed nightly at 10 p.m., and the two-loop campground is located off the main road past the Discovery Center on the southwest end of the park. Camping fees, payable with cash, Visa, or Mastercard, can be settled at the Contact Station on the day of arrival or at the Discovery Center the following day. Fees must be paid daily or in advance, with a maximum 14-day stay limit.

Campers arriving before 12 noon on the day of arrival will be charged the park entrance fee. Check-in time is 2 p.m., and while arriving earlier doesn't guarantee site availability, check-out time is at 12 noon on the scheduled departure date. Campground Hosts manage access card keys for after-hours entry into the park.

Indulge in awe-inspiring mountain views by choosing one of the four cabins facing west. Each cabin accommodates up to six individuals, featuring one queen-sized bed and two sets of bunk beds. Equipped with air conditioning, a table with four chairs, and a mini-fridge, these cabins offer a comfortable and relaxing stay. Cabin guests are responsible for bringing their own linens, as the "dry" cabins lack plumbing. However, conveniently located clean restrooms and showers are nearby. Guests staying in the cabins must bring their own linens or opt for sleeping bags and pillows. Pets are permitted in cabins 3 and 4.

The primary parking lot for the Discovery Center is found at the third right turn after leaving the contact station. General parking is available throughout the lot, featuring 13 handicapped-accessible parking spaces and two van-accessible sites in the northeast section. Additionally, 16 oversized RV parking spaces are situated in the southeastern section. A designated section for eight school or tour buses is located at the second right turn after leaving the contact station. Another lot with 23 spaces is present at the Guindani trailhead, situated at the far southwest end of the park, marking the end of the main road.

The park is equipped with modern restrooms at the Discovery Center, Campground, and Trail Head. Handicap-accessible and family facilities, complete with baby changing stations, are available at the Discovery Center and Campground. Restrooms are conveniently located near rental cabins and campgrounds. Basic, non-handicap accessible facilities can be found at the Trail Head. Users are urged not to dispose of stored wastewater in the restroom; instead, the Dump Station should be utilized for this purpose.

Showers are provided in the campground restroom buildings at the upper west end of each campground loop. The use of showers is included in the camping permit fee, with no separate charges for their use. All showers are designed to be handicapped accessible. The restroom building also houses flush toilets and sinks with handicapped accessibility. Each of the men's and women's restrooms features two showers, and a single shower is available in the family restroom.

The Dump Station is situated along the main road on the south end of the park, adjacent to the campground entrance. It comprises two 110-foot lanes, two pumps, a waste receptacle, and a non-potable water source. Users can access the lanes from either end in any direction. A paid camping permit is required to utilize the dump station, and visitors are encouraged to leave the area clean for the next user.

The group day use area is situated in the northwest corner of the main parking lot and comprises three covered ramadas, eighteen picnic tables (including one handicapped accessible table), water faucets, drinking fountains, 110 electrical outlets with lighting, waste receptacles, and a designated area for band performances and dancing. An optional large covered gas grill and built-in counter are available for an extra fee. All fees must be paid in advance when making a reservation, and payments can be made with cash, Visa, or Mastercard at the Discovery Center's front desk. Personal checks are not accepted. Reservation fees apply specifically to the rental of the group day use area, and additional charges apply to per-vehicle day use, camping, and tour fees. The covered group ramada can accommodate 200-250 persons, with the potential for an additional 50-100 if utilizing the uncovered gravel area on the north side, at no extra cost.

Covered picnic tables are strategically placed around the main parking lot and near the food concession area outside the Discovery Center. Seven single table sites are positioned on pads beneath a shaded ramada, equipped with a water source on the west and south ends of the main parking lot. Two handicapped accessible sites, featuring a wheelchair-accessible table and adjacent parking, are centrally located on the west side. All perimeter tables are easily accessible via developed sidewalks and pads.

Three uncovered tables on pads are situated in the southeast section of the main parking lot, with only one table accessible via a paved sidewalk.

To prevent the spread of White Nose Syndrome, a fungal disease affecting bats, Kartchner Caverns adheres to established nationwide protocols. Visitors who have been in another cave or mine since 2005 are requested not to wear or bring the same clothes or shoes used on those trips. If arriving in shoes from another cave, visitors will be directed to a White Nose Syndrome Decontamination Station, where their shoes will be sprayed with rubbing alcohol to eliminate the fungus.

Pets are permitted in all outdoor areas but must be leashed. However, they are not allowed inside buildings or on cave tours, except for service animals. Pets should not be left unattended in vehicles or outdoors in the parking lot. Access to water for pets should be ensured, and they should be confined to trails and developed areas due to potential hazards from desert plants and cacti. Unrestrained pets may face risks from wildlife and other animals in the area.

On March 3, 2011, Alamo Lake State Park (in collaboration with the Astronomers of Verde Valley, AstroVerde.org) and Kartchner Caverns State Park (in partnership with the Huachuca Astronomy Club of Southeast Arizona, HACAstronomy.com) achieved the distinction of being the first state parks in the United States to receive the "One Star at a Time" award, officially joining the Global Star Park Network. This accolade recognizes the public stargazing events hosted at both parks, aimed at raising awareness about astronomy and safeguarding dark skies for future generations. The awards were bestowed by the StarLight Initiative, the One Star at a Time organization, and Astronomers Without Borders. The Global Star Park Network is committed to preserving nocturnal environments, educating the public, and enhancing the quality of human habitats.

The origin of Kartchner Caverns dates back 330 million years when a shallow inland sea covered the area, depositing sediment layers that eventually solidified into limestone. Over time, uplift and geological processes formed the Whetstone Mountains, with a particular type of limestone, the Escabrosa limestone, experiencing a significant downward shift due to a seismic event or fault.

The formation of the caverns began with rainwater, slightly acidic from absorbing carbon dioxide, gradually dissolving passages in the down-dropped limestone block. As groundwater levels lowered, extensive air-filled rooms were left behind. Kartchner Caverns' diverse speleothems, or cave decorations, took shape drop by drop over the course of the next 200,000 years.

Surface water, carrying dissolved minerals from the limestone, seeped into the cave. Upon reaching the cave, the release of trapped carbon dioxide caused the water to deposit its mineral load, primarily calcite. Over time, these minerals contributed to the creation of the stunning speleothems and the array of colors seen in the cave. Notably, Kartchner Caverns is a "living" cave, with formations still actively growing.

Annually, from May to October, the Big Room tours at Kartchner Caverns are temporarily suspended to allow the resident bats to tend to their offspring and prepare for their winter migration. The predominant bat species in Kartchner Caverns is the common cave bat or Myotis velifer, although there are also small populations of other bat species present. The efforts focus on safeguarding these bats that return each year to nest. This involves continuous monitoring of their overall health, tagging bats for movement tracking, and noting the presence of at least one bat returning annually since 2009.

A selected group of bats is captured approximately once a month for thorough examination. This examination includes checking for parasites, assessing the condition of their teeth and wings, measuring their weight and size, and determining their reproductive status. After collecting the necessary measurements and data, the bats are released back into the night sky. This careful approach aims to ensure the well-being of the bat population and contributes to our understanding of their habits and health.

During the summer months, Kartchner Caverns' Big Room transforms into a maternity roost for over 1,000 female cave myotis bats (Myotis velifer). Around late April, pregnant females return to Kartchner Caverns, giving birth to a single pup in late June or early July. The newborns stay in the roost each evening while their mothers venture outside the cave to forage for insects. Over their 5-6 month residency, the bat colony consumes approximately half a ton of insects, including moths, flying ants, beetles, mosquitoes, and termites. The mothers and their offspring depart in mid-September to commence their migration to a winter hibernation roost.

The presence of bats in Kartchner Caverns plays a vital role in supplying fresh nutrients to the cave ecosystem every summer. Upon returning to the roost, the bats excrete waste, forming substantial guano piles. Many other organisms in the cave rely on these guano piles as a food source. Fungi and bacteria are the first to consume the guano, followed by nematodes, mites, isopods, amphipods, and book lice. Subsequently, spiders, scorpions, mites, millipedes, and centipedes feed on these organisms. Scavengers like crickets and beetle larvae complete the cleanup process. The energy generated from bat guano sustains this intricate food chain.

Various Arizona wildlife species commonly found in the Arizonan deserts can be observed in and around the park. It is crucial to approach wildlife with a practical amount of respect and maintain a suitable distance for both their well-being and our safety. It is imperative not to disrupt their lives as we enter their habitat and to avoid creating opportunities for interference by introducing exotic food sources or shelter that may attract them.

The park's close proximity to the canyons, arroyos of the Whetstone Mountains, Sonoran and Chihuahuan Desert terrain, and the riparian areas of the San Pedro River offers a unique opportunity to encounter species from each of these habitats. The park frequently hosts the large, dark raven, which can become a nuisance if food is left unattended in picnic or camping areas. Southeastern Arizona attracts hummingbirds from various regions during their migratory travels, and many can be observed year-round in the Hummingbird Garden.

Lizards are a common sight, scurrying among rocks or up tree trunks. Gila monsters, tortoises, and coach whips may be observed in season. It's important to exercise caution in warm months to avoid disturbing the various species of rattlesnakes present. To ensure safety, maintaining a respectful distance, staying on trails, avoiding overgrown areas, using a light to check warm roadways after dark, and keeping pets restrained are recommended to prevent contact with these important but potentially dangerous desert dwellers.

The Hummingbird Garden provides an opportunity to observe colorful butterflies and intricately patterned moths during blooms. Assassin bugs, horse lubber grasshoppers, and walking sticks offer a fascinating entomological experience. Caution is advised for scorpions, with a display in the Discovery Center highlighting cave-dwelling insects in dark cavern environments.

Mountain lions roam the Whetstone Mountains, and precautions should be taken in camps or on trails. Coyotes or gray foxes represent the canine species in the park. While these animals are seldom seen, pets should not be left unattended outdoors, especially at night, due to their predatory nature. Skunks, raccoons, coatimundi, and ringtail cats may pose a nighttime nuisance if food is left unsecured in camp areas. Jackrabbits, cottontails, squirrels, javelina, and Coues whitetail deer may be spotted wandering through the park or using the trails. Additionally, bats play a significant role in the cave and park habitat, with various species like common cave bats, pallid bats, Mexican free-tailed bats, and long-nosed bats contributing to the ecosystem.

Kartchner Caverns State Park offers more than just underground wonders – it features a network of hiking trails designed for both leisurely walks and more challenging hikes. Whether you want to delve deep into the Whetstone Mountains or stay close to camp, the choice is yours.

The Ocotillo Trail, extends 1.7 miles and complements the existing Foothills Loop trail. The combined loop covers approximately 3.2 miles, and please note that motorized vehicles or bicycles are not allowed on this trail. Access to the Ocotillo Trail can be achieved from two points on the Foothills Loop. To the north, start from the group ramada, head north on the Foothills Loop (counterclockwise), and turn right onto the Ocotillo Trail after about 1/2 mile. To the south, begin at the group ramada, head south on the Foothills Loop (clockwise), and proceed straight onto the Ocotillo Trail after about 1 mile. The trail involves a gentle but continuous elevation gain until reaching the saddle, marking the midway point. Be aware of several wash crossings, especially during summer monsoon storms. While benches are scattered along the route, shade is limited for most of the trail. The northern segment of the trail winds through gentle hills, wash crossings, and encircles the northern side of a large limestone hill. Periodically, you'll be treated to expansive views of the San Pedro River Valley and the Dragoon Mountains to the east. The saddle provides an excellent vantage point to appreciate the renowned "sky island" mountain ranges, including the Huachuca Mountains to the south, the Whetstones to the south and west, and the Rincon and Winchester ranges to the north. The southern part of the trail traverses a steep hillside overlooking a shallow drainage. Throughout your hike, numerous ocotillo plants, fittingly named, can be observed. In spring, enjoy the reddish-orange blossoms adorning the tops of these spiky desert plants, attracting hummingbirds. Ocotillo only produce their bright green leaves when there is sufficient moisture, shedding and regrowing them multiple times a year to conserve moisture during drought periods. Other plant life includes prickly pear, cholla, barrel cactus, mesquite, whitethorn, catclaw acacia (wait-a-minute bush), brittlebush, ephedra (Mormon tea), century plants, shin dagger agave, desert spoon, beargrass, and yucca.

The Guindani Trail, situated on the eastern flank of the Whetstone Mountains within the Coronado National Forest, spans a length of 4.2 miles. The trail difficulty varies, with the initial mile being an easy walk, the subsequent two-thirds classified as moderate, and the final section marked as strenuous. This shared-use, non-motorized trail is well-marked with directional signs. Elevations along the Guindani Trail range from 4750' at the park trailhead to over 5620' at its highest point. The summits along the crest of the Whetstone Mountains surpass 7000' in elevation. The lower elevations feature mesquite-invaded Chihuahuan semi-desert grassland, while the higher slopes exhibit an open oak-juniper woodland. The trail entrance is on the west side of Kartchner Caverns State Park campgrounds, marked by a kiosk.

The Foothills Loop Trail covers approximately 2.5 miles and is rated as moderate to difficult. There are four access points, including one at the northwest end of the Discovery Center parking lot, near the group use ramada. The trail is solely for hiking, prohibiting bicycles or motorized vehicles. It ascends the limestone hill north of the cave and descends into the wash along the fault between the Whetstone Block and the San Pedro Block. A short spur trail leads to the scenic Mountain Viewpoint. Informational signs along the Foothills Loop Trail highlight trail features, such as foothills, scenic views, riparian areas, bedrock mortar, and the Native American history of the area. Vegetation on the hike includes ocotillo, creosote bush, mesquite, desert broom, acacia, wait-a-minute bush, scrub oak, barrel cactus, prickly pear, buckhorn cholla, and hackberry.

The Hummingbird Garden Walk, situated on the southwest side of the Discovery Center, is adorned with various local vegetation. Some varieties include catclaw acacia, velvet honeysuckle, beargrass, yellow bells, black spine prickly pear, autumn sage, agave, desert bird of paradise, desert spoon, fairy duster, chaparosa, and hesperaloe. Hikers are advised to wear comfortable clothing and durable shoes, carry plenty of water, especially in the summer, and use hats and sunscreen to prevent exhaustion and heat-related injuries. Staying on developed trails is recommended to prevent erosion, damage to vegetation, and personal injury.

PARK HISTORY

In November 1974, Gary Tenen and Randy Tufts embarked on an exploration of the limestone hills at the eastern base of the Whetstone Mountains. Their objective was to discover a cave that had remained unknown to others, and they succeeded in finding one. Recognizing the potential environmental threat posed by unregulated use of unprotected caves, Tenen and Tufts decided to keep the discovery a secret until

February 1978. It was then that they revealed their remarkable find to the property owners, James and Lois Kartchner.

Understanding the importance of safeguarding the cave, Tenen and Tufts spent several years exploring the possibility of developing it themselves. Some members of the Kartchner family, impressed by the successful development and operation of Catalina State Park by Arizona State Parks, proposed the idea of approaching the agency to consider acquiring this exceptional resource.

In late 1984, Randy Tufts met with Charles R. Eatherly, the Special Projects Coordinator for the Arizona State Parks Board, at their office in Phoenix. Eatherly was involved in working with citizen committees across the state to identify potential sites for future State Parks. During their meeting, Tufts, seeking guidance on how a site becomes a State Park, requested privacy by closing the door. Once the door was closed, Tufts, still maintaining secrecy about the resource, expressed his interest in the acquisition process.

Despite being unable to disclose the nature or location of the resource, Tufts and Eatherly discussed the necessary steps involved in the acquisition of property for a State Park. Eatherly emphasized that the process was lengthy, spanning two to five years, with no guaranteed success. Additionally, each step of the process would be open to public scrutiny.

Tufts was insistent that Eatherly needed to witness the cave site firsthand. A meeting was scheduled for January 1985, and Eatherly met with Tufts and Tenen at the San Pedro Motel in Benson. The discoverers requested Eatherly to sign a secrecy oath, but he explained that, as a State employee, he couldn't comply with such a request.

Under the cover of darkness, outside the motel room, Eatherly was blindfolded. The car, with Eatherly still blindfolded, was driven around town in different directions and then out to the highway. Subsequently, the car ventured off the paved road through a gate that needed unlocking, navigating a rough road. The blindfold was removed after a while, and introductions were made to the Kartchner family. Tufts hinted at what awaited them, mentioning a "living cave with rooms filled with beautiful formations."

Equipped with flashlights, the group traversed a flat area, descended through a dry wash, and climbed a steep hillside to the edge of a large sinkhole. Dropping down about ten feet to the bottom, they waited for Tufts and Tenen to clear the entrance. Crawling through a small hole, the group slowly descended through chambers and tight holes toward the Blowhole, a vent for escaping air or gas. Before entering the Blowhole, the group discussed what lay ahead.

As the group crawled through the Blowhole, Eatherly found himself unable to move at one point due to the confined space. After some struggle, he managed to free himself and return to a more open area. The decision was made to return to the motel, where they spent the evening discussing the cave, examining pictures and slides showcasing its beautiful colored formations. Tufts and Tenen once again urged Eatherly to sign a secrecy pledge, but he maintained he could only discuss the matter with State Parks staff.

Tufts mentioned that Dr. Ed McCullough from the University of Arizona would tour the cave the next day. In response, Eatherly proposed a slide presentation for State Parks staff in Phoenix. Tufts and Tenen agreed to give the presentation, emphasizing the need for secrecy to protect this remarkable resource.

Upon Eatherly's return to the State Parks office, he briefed Director Mike Ramnes and Deputy Director Roland Sharer about the potential State Park. A meeting was scheduled for February 6, 1985, where ASP staff, including Ramnes, Sharer, Mike Pastika, Tim Brand, Jim Neidigh, Tanna Thornburg, Paul Malmberg, John Schreiber, and Charles Eatherly, viewed the slide presentation of the cave, referred to as "Xanadu" by Tufts and Tenen. The staff expressed great excitement about the prospect of acquiring the cave for a new State Park, with the main concern being securing the necessary appropriation for the purchase and completing the required developments. The cave was temporarily named Secret Cave, and Tufts and Tenen agreed to provide the agency with a copy of the slide presentation and other cave information to pursue acquisition by the State.

Director Ramnes brought the remarkable Secret Cave to the attention of Governor Bruce Babbitt. After learning about the cave, Governor Babbitt, who holds a geology degree, went on a cave tour guided by Tufts and Tenen. Given the limited state finances at the time, State Parks staff collaborated with Governor Babbitt, exploring the potential of a State land exchange as one option. The Nature Conservancy was also enlisted to assist in acquiring this valuable resource for the State. Despite ongoing efforts, various acquisition options did not prove feasible during that period.

Ken Travous assumed the role of Arizona State Parks Executive Director in 1987 and expressed a strong interest in acquiring Secret Cave, making it a high priority. However, when Governor Babbitt left office in 1987, the cave lost one of its key supporters. Director Travous proposed using revenue from park fees to purchase the cave, seeking input from staff on this idea. With strong support, Travous engaged in discussions with legislators and determined that using park fees for the acquisition would be an acceptable approach, avoiding the need for an appropriation from the General Fund. Special legislation was required to authorize the acquisition, utilizing a Certificate of Participation (COP) as the means to make monthly payments for the property. State Parks collaborated with two appraisers, Sanders K. Solot and Associates for the ranch land and H.C. Cannon for the cave. Working alongside The Nature Conservancy, the agency aimed to acquire and safeguard this natural resource.

In January 1988, Eatherly, serving as the legislative liaison for Arizona State Parks, assisted Travous in navigating discussions with legislators to determine the most feasible approach for passing the necessary legislation. At the time, Joe Lane served as Speaker of the House, representing the district containing the cave. John Hays, Chairman of the

Senate Natural Resources Committee, proved instrumental, having toured the cave with Governor Babbitt in 1985. Representative Larry Hawk, Chairman of the House Natural Resources Committee, aided the agency in passing a bill through the House before Governor Evan Mecham's impeachment proceedings began. The bill granted State Parks the authority to acquire the property and established the State Park Acquisition and Development Fund, where park fees and concession revenues would be deposited. These deposits would cover the monthly payments for the Certificate of Participation (COP), with the remaining funds allocated for park developments.

To illustrate the potential State Park resource to the Legislature while maintaining secrecy, staff sought assistance from Delbert Lewis, owner of Channel 3 TV. Lewis, previously involved in the development of McFarland State Historic Park, agreed to send his staff to photograph the cave and create a video presentation for the agency.

Steve Bodinet, a special reporter from Channel 3 TV, accompanied Parks Director Travous into the cave for photography. Bodinet provided narration, and together with other Channel 3 staff, created an impressive video showcasing the cave for State Parks. This video presentation played a crucial role in closed caucus meetings within both the House and Senate, where legislators could witness the proposed acquisition resource. The closed nature of these meetings helped maintain confidentiality about the cave and its location.

Given that 1988 was the year of Governor Evan Mecham's impeachment, legislators welcomed the opportunity to focus on a positive bill. To ensure the passage of the State Parks' bill authorizing the cave property's acquisition, both the Senate and House convened simultaneously. As soon as one body completed its work on the amended bill, the other followed suit. This efficient process took place in a single afternoon, and the bill was promptly sent to Governor Rose Mofford's office for her signature. This bill possibly holds the record for the shortest time taken for any legislation to pass through the legislature and receive approval.

On April 27, 1988, members of the Kartchner family, along with Randy Tufts and Gary Tenen, were introduced in both the Senate and House. Later that afternoon, they joined Arizona State Parks Board members and staff in the Governor's office to witness Governor Rose Mofford signing the bill.

State Parks leased the property on April 29, 1988, and obtained the Option to Purchase from The Nature Conservancy in July 1988. The acquisition of the Kartchner property was completed on September 16, 1988, with Jeff Dexter appointed as the first Park Manager.

Overcoming more than 10 years of challenges in research, planning, construction, legislative hurdles, mining concerns, and legal issues, the upper caverns were ready to open to the public. The total cost of developments up to this point exceeded $28 million. The Conservation Celebration of Kartchner Caverns State Park took place on November 5, 1999, with a ribbon-cutting ceremony initiated by Governor Jane D. Hull. The event included the participation of legislators, past and present Parks Board members, Joe Lane (Assistant to the Governor), Ken Travous (Executive Director), and members of the Kartchner family. The lower caverns opened to the public four years later on November 11, 2003, with Governor Janet Napolitano leading the celebration.

Attractions in the Area

Southern Arizona is rich in cultural, historical, and natural treasures, offering numerous opportunities for half or full-day side trips in the surrounding region. Step into the Old West by visiting the OK Corral where the Earp brothers once stood, immerse yourself in the history of mining boomtowns on Brewery Gulch, or explore the remnants of old forts and Native American hideouts. Take a hike in the lush riparian areas of the San Pedro River or enhance your wildlife observation experiences at nearby locations. For visitors staying at the park campgrounds or cabins, there are additional exploration options in the nearby attractions.

Benson:
The city of Benson, located ten miles north of the park, is a short ten to fifteen-minute drive away. It offers restaurants, lodging, fuel stations, banks, a library with Wi-Fi access, groceries, laundry facilities, a golf course, and parks. Visit the Benson Visitor Center at 249 E. 4th Street, Benson, AZ 85602, or call (520) 586-4293.

Sierra Vista:
Situated 20 miles southeast of the park, Sierra Vista is a 45–60 minute drive away. It provides a variety of amenities, including restaurants, lodging, fuel stations, banks, libraries, groceries, laundry services, theaters, shopping centers, golf courses, and parks. For information, contact the Sierra Vista Convention and Visitors Bureau at 1011 N. Coronado Dr., Sierra Vista, AZ 85635, or call (520) 417-6960 or toll-free at (800) 288-3861.

Fort Huachuca:
An active military base established in 1877, Fort Huachuca is located 20 miles away, adjacent to Sierra Vista. It requires a 45–60 minute drive, and visitors need a driver's license and vehicle information to register at the front gate. Explore early military history at the Fort Huachuca Museum by calling (520) 533-3638.

Tombstone:
Known as the "Town too Tough to Die," Tombstone is home to the OK Corral and Boot Hill Cemetery, located 30 miles from the park and accessible by a 45–60 minute drive. Enjoy shops along the main walkways, gunfight re-enactments, stagecoach rides, and other amusements. The Tombstone Courthouse State Historic Park, dating back to 1882, holds artifacts from Tombstone's history. Contact the Tombstone Chamber of Commerce at P. O. Box 995, 4th and Allen, Tombstone, AZ 85638, or call (520) 457-9317 or toll-free (888) 457-3929.

Bisbee:
Situated 50 miles southeast of the park, Bisbee requires a one and a half-hour drive. The city is a blend of the old and the new, with a historic downtown recalling its mining town past and newer areas functioning as a modern municipality. Explore the Lavender Pit or take the Copper Queen underground mine tour. For information, contact the Bisbee Visitor Center at #2 Copper Queen Plaza and Convention Center, Bisbee, AZ 85603, or call (520) 432-3554 or toll-free (866)-2BISBEE.

Cochise Stronghold:
Cochise Stronghold, named after the legendary Apache chief who skillfully evaded U.S. troops in the rugged hills and canyons of the Dragoon Mountains, is situated approximately 45 miles from the park. The drive takes 60–90 minutes. Visitors can immerse themselves in the history of this scenic "hideaway" with hiking trails and picnic opportunities. For more information, contact by phone at (520) 364-3468 or (520) 364-6800.

Amerind Foundation:
Hidden among the Dells of Texas Canyon in the Dragoon Mountains, the Amerind Foundation is located 26 miles east of the park, just off I-10, requiring about a half-hour drive. This site features a museum showcasing Native American artifacts and artwork, serving as an archaeological research center. To learn more, contact them at (520) 586-3666.

San Pedro River Riparian Natural Area:
Spanning a 37-mile-long vegetated strip in the center of the San Pedro River valley, this natural area offers hiking and nature viewing opportunities. The San Pedro House serves as the visitor center and trailhead and is managed by the Bureau of Land Management. Located 30 miles southeast, it entails a 1-hour and 15-minute drive. For inquiries, call (520) 439-6400.

Patagonia:
Once a mining town, Patagonia, situated 40 miles from the park, is now a hub for hiking and wildlife viewing. It takes an hour to drive, and the town offers restaurants and shops featuring unique artworks and antiques. The Nature Conservancy's riparian area along Sonoita Creek, south of town, provides additional exploration opportunities. Further south, off Highway 82, lies Patagonia Lake State Park and Sonoita Creek State Natural Area, offering aquatic recreation, birding, and hiking trails. For more details and contact information, visit the respective park's sites.

Nogales:
Approximately 60 miles south of the park, Nogales serves as the primary border entry point into Mexico from southeastern Arizona. The journey takes about an hour and a half. Nogales, comprising two towns on either side of the border, is known for shopping and entertainment. Visitors can haggle for bargains, but due to changing laws regarding crossing documents, it's advisable to call U.S. Customs in advance for updated

information. Contact U.S. Customs at (520) 287-1410 or (520) 885-0694. For more general information, reach out to the Nogales-SCC Chamber of Commerce Office at 123 W. Kino Park Way, Nogales, AZ 85621, or call (520) 287-3685.

KOFA NATIONAL WILDLIFE REFUGE

COUNTY: LA PAZ, YUMA   CITY: YUMA *n.c.*

DATE VISITED: WHO I WENT WITH:

RATING: ☆ ☆ ☆ ☆ ☆   WILL I RETURN? YES / NO

Covering an expansive 665,400 acres in the remote desert region between Quartzsite and Yuma in the southwest corner of Arizona, Kofa National Wildlife Refuge is renowned for its rugged terrain. While it predominantly draws wildlife enthusiasts, hikers, and photographers, during the day, rockhounds explore the Crystal Hill Area in search of quartz. As night falls, stargazers shift their focus skyward to appreciate the celestial wonders.

Prior to Charles E. Eichelberger's gold discovery in 1896, the region that eventually became the Kofa National Wildlife Refuge saw limited human activity. Although Eichelberger's King of Arizona mine didn't achieve the same success as some other mines in the state, it yielded sufficient gold and silver during its peak, leading to the emergence of a town supporting it with a population of around 300. The town adopted the name Kofa, derived from the stamped initials "K of A" marking mine property.

Mining activities thrived in the area for the following two decades. However, as returns dwindled, the mines, including the King of Arizona, shut down, ceasing operations in 1939. Around the same time, the local desert bighorn sheep population began declining, capturing the attention of conservationists.

Major Frederick R. Burnham, serving as the honorary President of the Arizona Boy Scouts, initiated a "Save the Bighorns" campaign, organizing a poster contest, delivering talks at school assemblies, and promoting radio dramatizations. This successful effort led to the designation of land for a wildlife refuge in 1939.

During World War II, conservation efforts were temporarily halted as the area became a training ground for tanks and infantry under General George S. Patton, Jr. Despite subsequent clean-up efforts, remnants such as unexploded ordinances, mineshafts, and other mine-related hazards still exist in the Kofa National Wildlife Refuge.

Take advantage of the picturesque landscapes provided by Kofa National Wildlife Refuge's Castle Dome and Kofa mountain ranges. While these ranges offer captivating subjects for photographers, the breathtaking beauty can be appreciated without a camera. Explore any of the five well-maintained dirt roads leading into the wildlife refuge from US Highway 95. Pipeline Road (mile marker 95) spans the entire width of the refuge, and King Valley Road (mile marker 76) leads to the mining district, featuring attractions like the King of Arizona Mine and abandoned buildings. Numerous unmaintained dirt roads extend further into the refuge, but a 4-wheel drive is necessary for navigation.

Despite the rugged terrain and challenging climate, Kofa National Wildlife Refuge is teeming with wildlife, offering a unique opportunity to observe desert creatures in their natural habitat. Common sightings include jack rabbits, lizards, rattlesnakes, and desert bighorn sheep. Additionally, one may encounter mountain lions, coyotes, bats, or desert tortoises. The refuge stands out as one of the few places globally where free-ranging Sonoran pronghorns can be observed.

For bird enthusiasts, the refuge provides an opportunity to spot up to 193 documented species. Keep an eye out for white-winged doves, Gambel's quails, golden eagles, and canyon wrens. Birdwatching hotspots include watering holes, dry washes, narrow canyons, and the vicinity of stock tanks like Charco 4 and Cholla Tank.

Hiking remains a popular activity in Kofa National Wildlife Refuge, even though it officially offers just one designated trail—Palm Canyon Trail. This challenging and rocky trail initiates at the terminus of Palm Canyon Road, extending half a mile into the canyon. The trail offers views of California fan palms, the sole native palm species in Arizona. The round trip for the hike takes about an hour, but allocate an extra 30 to 45 minutes if you plan to ascend to the actual palms before retracing your steps. To access the trailhead, turn onto Palm Canyon Road (mile marker 85) and proceed 7.1 miles to reach the parking lot. While Palm Canyon Trail stands as the sole officially designated trail in the refuge, visitors are allowed to hike anywhere within the wildlife refuge, ensuring they avoid mines or any areas marked as closed.

While the era of mining for gold and silver that attracted miners to the region over a century ago has concluded, recreational rockhounding is permitted in the 1.5-square-mile Crystal Hill Area, situated off Pipeline Road. Rockhounds primarily search for quartz crystals in the area's washes and on the rocky slopes of Crystal Hill. Regardless of the findings, there is a limit of 10 specimens or 10 pounds (whichever comes first) within a 12-month period.

Kofa National Wildlife Refuge is situated 18 miles south of the point where Interstate 10 intersects Quartzsite and 40 miles north of Yuma. To reach the wildlife refuge from Interstate 10, travel south on US Highway 95 towards Yuma and make a left turn onto one of the maintained dirt roads at mile markers 85, 92, 85, 76, or 55. Each of these five roads provides access into the wildlife refuge. Conversely, if traveling from Yuma, head north on US Highway 95 towards Quartzsite and enter at the same mile markers.

Maps and brochures can be obtained from 8 a.m. to 4:30 p.m., Monday through Friday, at the Visitor Center in Yuma. The wildlife refuge remains open throughout the year, and no entrance fee is required.

Tips:

1) Ensure you are well-prepared before entering the wildlife refuge, as no services are available within. Maintain a full tank of gas, carry ample water, snacks, and a map. Be

aware that cell phone service may be limited or unavailable.

2) Certain areas within the refuge are off-limits to safeguard wildlife, including desert bighorn sheep and Sonoran pronghorn. Mines are also designated as restricted areas, so heed warning signs.

3) Due to military training during World War II, unexploded ordinances may be present. If encountered, refrain from handling and promptly report to refuge authorities.

4) For the best wildlife viewing experience, plan your visits during sunrise and sunset. Avoid summer afternoons and windy days. Bring binoculars and maintain a safe distance from wildlife.

5) Camping is permitted for up to 14 days within a 12-month period. While you can choose your campsite anywhere in the refuge, vehicles must stay within 100 feet of the road. Two cabins are available on a first-come, first-served basis without reservations or fees.

6) Campfires are allowed in Kofa National Wildlife Refuge, but only dead wood found on-site can be used. To ensure sufficient firewood, it is recommended to bring your own.

7) Hunting is allowed for desert bighorn sheep, mule deer, cottontail rabbit, quail, fox, and coyote in designated areas within the wildlife refuge, provided proper licenses and permits are obtained.

LAKE HAVASU STATE PARK

COUNTY: MOHAVE   **CITY:** LAKE HAVASU CITY

DATE VISITED: **WHO I WENT WITH:**

RATING: ☆ ☆ ☆ ☆ ☆   **WILL I RETURN?**   YES / NO

Lake Havasu State Park boasts a picturesque shoreline, making it an ideal destination for those seeking beautiful beaches, nature trails, boat ramps, and convenient campsites. Positioned near the iconic London Bridge of Lake Havasu City, this park serves as a haven for water sports enthusiasts. It features four boat ramps, 54 campsites, 13 beachside cabins, a special events area (excluding holiday weekends), a picnic area, and a beach area. The Mohave Sunset Trail, stretching 1.75 miles, winds through the lowland desert and along the shoreline, while the Arroyo-Camino Interpretive Garden showcases the diverse desert life, including birds, lizards, and desert cottontails.

Visitors can seek guidance from knowledgeable rangers at the park's visitor center, which also houses a store with limited supplies and a gift shop offering memorable souvenirs. Despite being within Lake Havasu City limits, the park provides an escape from the city hustle. Camping along Lake Havasu allows for an extended stay, facilitating the enjoyment of various outdoor activities. With campsites near the lake shore, visitors can easily transition from lake activities to camp life, enjoying burgers, beverages, and quality time with friends or family.

Campground reservations offer access to shower/restroom facilities, water, dump stations, and day-use facilities. Each site includes a picnic table and a fire ring, with many offering shade armadas. Most sites accommodate both RVs/motorhomes and tents, allowing a maximum stay of 14 nights with a total occupancy of 10 individuals and a maximum of six adults per campsite. Check-in time is 2 p.m., and check-out time is 12 noon.

For those not inclined towards camping, 13 new cabins, air-conditioned and located lakeside, provide a comfortable alternative. Positioned to offer stunning Lake Havasu sunsets, these cabins also feature modern restrooms and showers nearby, ensuring a cozy camping experience.

The day-use beach area provides a picnic area with tables, shade ramadas, grills, potable water, and restrooms. It's an excellent spot to witness lake activity and appreciate the natural beauty of the historic area while enjoying a picnic.

The park offers handicap-accessible restrooms, located in Lots 1, 2, and 4, with additional restroom buildings in the campground. Showers are exclusive to registered campers, and a dump station is available. The park operates year-round.

Mohave Sunset Trail, spanning 1.75 miles with an easy rating, meanders through the lowland desert and along the shoreline within Lake Havasu State Park. The trail is designated for pedestrian traffic only, excluding bicycles. Pets are permitted but must be kept on leashes.

The Arroyo-Camino Interpretive Garden serves as an educational space highlighting the rich variety of life within the park and the surrounding desert. Common sightings include birds, lizards, and desert cottontails.

Lake Havasu City weather is generally predictable, with sunny days and a gentle breeze. Fall, winter, and spring are optimal for hiking park trails and observing wildlife and birds. Lake Havasu City winters feature warm days and cool nights, ideal for enjoying campfires. Winter rains, occasional and mild, prepare for the spring wildflower season, with great blooms during years of above-average precipitation. Lake Havasu weather varies by season, providing visitors with diverse experiences. During the average summer, hot days and warm nights prevail. Lake Havasu State Park offers an excellent retreat for cooling off by the lake, featuring white sand beaches for easy water access. Monsoon season (June – September) brings sporadic afternoon thunderstorms with heavy winds and rain.

Lake Havasu State Park welcomes all watercraft users to experience the Colorado River, emphasizing responsible usage. This entails ensuring that your watercraft adheres to the regulations set for both motorized and non-motorized vessels in your home state. Since the Colorado River falls under the jurisdiction of both Arizona and California, boaters must be acquainted with the watercraft regulations applicable in both states. Additionally, visitors have the option to rent motorized watercraft from Wet Monkey Powersport Rentals, the onsite concessionaire. For more details, you can visit wetmonkeyrentals.com or contact them at (928) 855-2022. Havasu Riviera Marina, operating as a concession of Lake Havasu State Park, provides services such as boat ramps, dry docks, storage, and more.

Lake Havasu State Park features four boat ramps, each accessible through wayfinding signs: 1) The personal watercraft and jet ramp, located in Lot 1 at the north end of the park, strictly prohibits watercraft with propellers. 2) North Ramp and South Ramp, situated in Lot 2 directly east of the contact station (known as Windsor launch ramps). 3) Windsor Ramp 3, positioned toward the south end of the park past the campground area, forming part of Lot 3.

All boat ramps are available for the launch of non-motorized watercraft.

Lake Havasu State Park provides a generously sized designated swimming area at the day-use beach, adorned with beautiful white sand. While swimming is permitted along the shoreline, safety remains a top priority. The white sand beaches are generally soft, but rocky conditions may be present in the water. It's advisable to wear comfortable foot cover and bring a light mat to place under your towel if you plan to swim beyond the designated area. Refrain from swimming near boat ramps or docks for safety reasons. The temperature of the water in the Colorado River can vary, ranging from temperate in the shallows to near-freezing in open water. If you are concerned about temperature drops, consider wearing an insulated swimming outfit, such as a thermal swimming suit. In all situations, swimmers should exercise caution, as there is no lifeguard on duty. Swimming is undertaken at your own risk. The park features several beaches, providing a serene setting for leisure in Lake Havasu City. For detailed beach guidelines, refer to the signage at each beach.

Lake Havasu has consistently yielded impressive catch rates of larger-than-average bass, making it a prime destination for anglers. The success of this lake in terms of fishing can be attributed to a collaborative effort among multiple agencies. The installation of fish habitat, including "fish condos" and various plastic and natural planted structures, on the initially barren lake bottom has fostered a thriving food chain. This expansive 19,000-acre impoundment on the Colorado River boasts abundant fish, with common limits and frequent visits from the tournament circuit, attracted by optimal conditions, delightful weather, and the welcoming atmosphere of the greater Lake Havasu area.

The current fishing scene at Lake Havasu for both largemouth and smallmouth bass is experiencing a peak period. A habitat improvement initiative launched in the 1990s has led to a substantial increase in the population of these sought-after species. Inexperienced anglers often find success, while seasoned ones consistently report outstanding fishing opportunities. Alongside the added habitat, Lake Havasu presents various options, such as tules, boat docks, canyon areas, and rocky shorelines, each requiring a slightly different approach for bass fishing success.

Lake Havasu is known for the possibility of hooking into double-digit bass, but the clarity of the water presents a challenge. Anglers often resort to smaller lures and lighter lines for a natural presentation, with spinnerbaits, crankbaits, and other reaction-type lures retrieved quickly to induce strikes before the bass can react. The clear water also allows for sight fishing during the spring spawn, providing a unique experience for anglers equipped with polarized sunglasses.

To sustain the bass population, catch and release are encouraged during the spawn, ensuring the fish can resume their activities after a quick release. Lake Havasu stands out for its exceptional smallmouth bass fishing, offering a variety of habitats like rocky shorelines and submerged rockpiles. Anglers employ artificial lures and plastic baits, adjusting their tactics based on factors like water clarity and weather conditions.

During winter, when the Arizona desert cools off, smallmouth fishing at Lake Havasu intensifies. Focus on windswept banks with swift drop-offs, using brightly colored crankbaits or suspended jerkbaits. The lake's clear water demands a stealthy yet aggressive approach, with light line and realistic lures being effective. Spawning smallmouth readily take soft plastics, and practicing catch and release, especially during the spawn, contributes to the sustainability of the fishery.

Lake Havasu is also renowned for its giant striped bass, offering excellent striper fishing year-round. Covering plenty of water and using a quality fish finder are key to locating active schools. Fishing at night is popular, with anchovies and live shad as preferred baits. Striped bass become particularly active in the mornings and evenings, providing exciting topwater or boil fishing experiences. The lake's catfish angling is equally impressive, hosting both channel and flathead catfish. Bait collection is easy, with bluegill and redear sunfish abundantly available. Standard catfish baits like raw shrimp, anchovies, chicken liver, and "stink" baits are effective for channel catfish, while flathead anglers can make use of the readily available bluegill and redear sunfish. Practicing catch and release contributes to the overall health of the catfish population.

Lake Havasu State Park serves as a habitat for a variety of wildlife. The mammalian inhabitants encompass different bat species (Myotis and others), kit and gray fox (Vulpes macrotis and Urocyon cinereoargenteus), mountain lion (Puma concolor), and bobcat (Lynx rufus), although sightings of the latter two are infrequent. Additionally, two skunk species (Mephitis mephitis and Spilogale gracilis) reside in the area. Various species of squirrels, mice, and rats also call this park home. The park provides habitat for diverse snakes and lizards, including the protected desert tortoise (Gopherus agassizii) in California and managed populations in Arizona. Frequently observed avian species include Gambel's quail, roadrunner, great blue heron, red-tailed hawk, American kestrel, killdeer, great horned owl, hummingbirds, and turkey vultures.

The plant life within Lake Havasu State Park exhibits a diverse range, featuring cottonwood (Populus spp.) and willow (Salix spp.) along the riverbanks, while mesquite (Prosopis spp.) and various cacti thrive in the drier regions. The park hosts an array of flowering plants in spring, including Aster spp., lilies (from the Liliaceae family), Agave spp., daisies (Eriophyllum spp.), primroses (Oenothera spp.), and poppies (Argemone spp. and Eschscholzia spp.). Following a wet winter, the park may showcase a spectacular wildflower display. Additionally, there are several rare buckwheat (Eriogonum spp.) and penstemon spp. in Mohave County.

PARK HISTORY

During the fourth meeting of the State Parks Board on August 12, 1957, Alvin O. Hurst, Chief of the Lower Colorado River Survey at the National Parks Service, presented the potential for recreation development along the Colorado River from Yuma to Davis Dam. The Parks Board, impressed with the presentation, expressed interest in becoming a future partner in developing recreational facilities for certain sites along the river. While the Board hesitated to make a definitive commitment at that time, they instructed the Director to continue working with Mr. Hurst for future park development.

In early 1961, the Parks Board authorized a staff evaluation of the Lower Colorado River and its adjacent land for potential State Parks. In December 1961, areas deemed of State Park caliber and statewide significance were identified as study areas. Subsequent evaluations and studies were conducted in collaboration with the U.S. Department of the Interior's Lower Colorado River Land Use Office planning staff, involving Arizona agencies. By April 1962, the Parks staff proposed adopting areas meeting State Park criteria with a flexible priority program, pending legislative and budgetary authorization. The Parks Board approved this program, including the sites that eventually became Buckskin Mountain State Park, Lake Havasu State Park, and Cattail Cove State Park.

The Parks' study, referred to as a "prospectus," underwent review and evaluation by the Advisory Committee of the Lower Colorado River Land Use Plan and the Lower Colorado Land Use Office. The final general program, encompassing Lake Havasu and adjacent land areas administered by Arizona State Parks, was included in the Lower Colorado Land Use Plan. The Secretary of Interior, Stewart Udall, approved the plan on January 13, 1964.

The U.S. Department of the Interior, Bureau of Reclamation, leased the lands within Lake Havasu State Park and Cattail Cove State Park to the State Land Department on January 14, 1965, through Contract Number 14-06-300-1533. The State of Arizona then subleased these properties to State Parks on February 1, 1965, for park and recreation purposes. Additionally, the lease document included the cancellation of the concession contract with McCulloch Properties Incorporated, which was replaced by a new concession contract on 1200 acres, mainly on Pittsburg Point, between MPI and the State of Arizona for the 50-year term of the lease.

In 1965, the concession lease area included the Lake Havasu Travel Trailer Park and the Cove Campground, later renamed Crazyhorse Campground. Over the next three years, MPI (McCulloch Properties Incorporated) expanded with additions like Lake Havasu Airport, Nautical Inn, State Beach, and Lake Havasu Marina. The Park's headquarters was situated within the concession area, with Woodrow Seney serving as the first Park Manager. The focus of the staff was on developing and maintaining boat-in campsites along the Park shoreline. They also worked on safeguarding resources and removing submerged cottonwood trees that posed a navigational hazard for boaters.

During this period, Cattail Cove saw initial development, with Glen Cross becoming its first Park Manager. Between 1969 and 1971, the reconstruction of the London Bridge and the creation of the London Bridge Channel altered the concession lands, turning Pittsburg Point into an island. MPI acquired the London Bridge, disassembled it into numbered pieces, and shipped it to Lake Havasu City. The addition of this historic attraction led to a significant increase in visitors to the area and the Park. Another contributing factor was the completion of Highway 95 between Parker and Lake Havasu City. Within the Park, two units were formed: Cattail Cove, already developed and open to visitors, and Windsor Beach, which was being planned for camping and day use developments.

In the 1970s, substantial recreational improvements were made at Windsor Beach, a concession operation was introduced at Cattail Cove, and enhancements were implemented for the 250+ boat-in campsites along the shoreline. These improvements included shade ramadas, picnic tables, and fire grills for individual sites, along with new restroom facilities. A headquarters building was constructed at the original office location on Pittsburg Point. Funding for improvements during the 1970s and 1980s came from the State Lake Improvement Fund (SLIF) and the Land and Water Conservation, matched by State Funds. In 1979, Site Six, the former McCulloch outboard motor test facility, was purchased and renovated to create a First Aid and Safety Center for Lake Havasu. Campground and boat ramp improvements were made at both Cattail Cove and Windsor Beach.

In 1986, a land exchange between the Federal Government and the Arizona State Land Department led to a boundary change for the Park. This exchange was prompted by the Bureau of Reclamation's acquisition of State Trust lands for the Central Arizona Project (CAP). The Federal Government compensated the State Trust with federal land, with Pittsburgh Point in Lake Havasu City being the most valuable, offsetting a significant portion of the Federal Government's land debt to the State.

The State Parks Board agreed to modify the Park boundaries, making the lands available for transfer to the State Land Department. Pittsburg Point, including its concession operations, was transferred, along with the northern section of the Windsor Beach Unit and the land west of Highway 95 from Mudshark Beach to Contact Point. Lake Havasu City received a land patent for Rotary Beach, 4 acres of Windsor Beach for a police station, and the Site-Six building and property. State Parks obtained a land patent for the remaining 331 acres of the Windsor Beach Unit and a patent for 286 acres of land along Oak Creek (Red Rock State Park) southwest of Sedona. This exchange reduced Lake Havasu State Park's acreage to 10,866 acres.

Shortly after the 1986 land exchange, the Park was split into two units for administrative purposes. The Upper Lake Unit covered the area from Standard Wash north to Contact Point and Windsor Beach, while the Lower Lake Unit, operating from Cattail Cove, covered the area from Standard Wash south to one mile past the Larned Landing area. In January 1987, the Lower Lake Unit became a separate Park known as Cattail Cove State Park, located 15 miles south of Lake Havasu City off AZ 95.

The Lake Havasu State Park headquarters moved to the new Water Safety Center at Contact Point in 1993, replacing the facilities at Site-Six and the old office on Pittsburg Point.

In 1995, the Park boundary changed again. The Parks Board relinquished its lease in return for patents and long-term leases on the lands it had developed along the shore of Lake Havasu. At Lake Havasu State Park, Contact Point Unit, the agency received a patent, deed, and lease on 591.94 acres. At Cattail Cove State Park, the agency received a patent and lease on 2374.70 acres. Since 1995, the agency has patented 5 acres and purchased 1.258 acres added to the Windsor Beach Unit. The total acreage of Lake Havasu State Park is now 928.076 acres.

Lake Havasu State Park offers water-oriented recreation opportunities year-round. The mild winters attract visitors from cooler regions, while the hot summers draw a younger, boating-oriented crowd mainly from southern California and Arizona.

Cattail Cove State Park serves as a recreational hub for accessing Lake Havasu. Visitors can engage in activities like hiking, picnicking, camping, swimming, fishing, water skiing, or boating on the lake. The park is a preferred access point for utilizing boat-in campsites along the shoreline.

Explore Nearby Attractions: 1) Buckskin Mountain State Park (27 miles). 2) River Island Unit (25 miles). 3) Cattail Cove State Park (15 miles). 4) Yuma Territorial Prison State Historic Park - This park, operating as a prison from 1876 to 1909, showcases original cellblocks, a dining hall, cemetery, and features a reconstructed guard tower along with a modern Visitor Center (152 miles).

Other Points of Interest: 1) London Bridge - Explore the "world's largest antique," conveniently located two miles from the park entrance. 2) Lake Havasu Museum of History - Discover the area's rich history by visiting this museum. 3) Bill Williams National Wildlife Refuge - Experience the riparian-desert interface, perfect for birdwatching and hiking. 4) Havasu National Wildlife Refuge - Check out the refuge's informative website for species lists and additional details.

LAKE MEAD NATIONAL RECREATION AREA

COUNTY: MOHAVE   CITY: KINGMAN *n.c.*

DATE VISITED: WHO I WENT WITH:

RATING: ☆ ☆ ☆ ☆ ☆   WILL I RETURN? YES / NO

The proximity of Las Vegas to both glamorous entertainment and the untamed beauty of nature is truly remarkable. One prime illustration of this duality is the aquatic paradise known as the Lake Mead National Recreation Area, which happens to be the first and largest of its kind in America. Spanning the Nevada-Arizona border, this area encompasses 1.5 million acres of land, featuring both Lake Mead and the interconnected Lake Mohave. The convenience of a short, 40-minute drive has made this locale, offering camping, boating, fishing, swimming, and hiking opportunities, a cherished destination for locals and an easily accessible trip for visitors. Despite hosting 7.5 million annual visitors, the vast expanse ensures that the area is not overcrowded.

In the United States, only 40 areas have received the designation of a national recreation area (NRA), established by Congress to safeguard locations with scenic and natural resources. The inaugural NRA was the Boulder Dam Recreation Area, established in 1936 through a collaboration between the US Bureau of Reclamation (creators of Hoover Dam) and the National Park Service (NPS). Given that the construction of the dam and reservoir had disrupted the environment, this new designation provided a means for the National Park Service to conserve the land while allowing outdoor enthusiasts to appreciate it. As the Bureau of Reclamation constructed more dams in proximity to urban areas, the NRA system expanded.

The creation of the Boulder Dam, now known as Hoover Dam, resulted in the formation of the 115-mile-long Lake Mead. Subsequently, in 1953, the Davis Dam was built to create Lake Mohave, serving both hydroelectric power and water supply purposes for Arizona, Nevada, and California. In 1964, both lakes and the surrounding wilderness areas were collectively designated as the Lake Mead National Recreation Area. This diverse landscape encompasses the ecosystems of the Mojave Desert, the Great Basin Desert, and the Sonoran Desert, all safeguarded by the National Parks Service. The majority of visitors are avid water enthusiasts, drawn to activities like jet skiing, leisurely houseboat days, and kayak exploration of the lakes' numerous inlets and 500 miles of shoreline.

If you have an ample amount of time in the Lake Mead area, whether you're spending a few days on a houseboat, camping, or staying in Boulder City, it's worth considering various experiences around Lake Mead.

Hoover Dam: If you haven't visited before, dedicating at least half a day to Hoover Dam is a must. Take a tour, marvel at the dizzying drop from the top of the dam, and appreciate the view from the Mike O'Callaghan-Pat Tillman Memorial Bridge, which now overlooks the entire dam.

Kayaking/Canoeing: For those who enjoy exploring from the water, consider taking a tour that includes Hoover Dam and Black Canyon from Willow Springs Marina. Here, you can sign up for rafting tours launching below the dam and concluding at Willow Beach. Renting a canoe or kayak at the marina and taking a shuttle to the dam is also an option. One particularly enchanting experience is kayaking Emerald Cave, located 2 miles upstream from Willow Beach in Arizona, where the cave glows emerald green in the afternoon light. Various outfitters offer kayak rentals and tours; Kayak Lake Mead provides trips in the Black Canyon, to the Crane's Nest Rapids, into Arizona Hot Springs, and a 22-mile round-trip in the Black Canyon to Hoover Dam for experienced paddlers.

Boat Rentals: If you have your own boat or wish to rent one, multiple marinas, including Boulder Basin, East Lake Mead, Overton Arm, and Lake Mohave, offer motorboats, fishing boats, houseboats, jet skis, and other watercraft. Notable marinas include Boating Lake Mead, Callville Bay Marina, and Willow Beach Marina, which provide information on rates, rentals, and requirements.

Hiking: The park offers numerous hiking opportunities within its 185,000 acres. The Mojave Desert ecosystem dominates the park, hosting 900 plant species and 500 animal species. Hiking trails showcase rainbow-colored rock formations, and you might encounter unique wildlife such as Desert bighorn sheep and the famed desert tortoise, Nevada's state reptile. Popular hikes include the Historic Railroad Trail, a 7.5-mile round trip through old railroad tunnels, and the River Mountain Loop Trail, a 35-mile paved trail connecting River Mountain, Lake Mead NRA, Hoover Dam, Boulder City, and the Las Vegas Valley. The park also features equestrian trails for horse enthusiasts.

Fishing: Anglers can pursue largemouth and striped bass, with carp being a common sight around marina docks. Check the licensing requirements for the respective state you're fishing in, as the lakes span the Arizona and Nevada state lines. The NPS website provides information on these requirements. The area also offers excellent campsites and surprisingly good beaches, including Cottonwood Cove Beach in the Lake Mohave section.

Lake Mead National Recreation Area is accessible year-round, 24/7. The Lake Mead Visitor Center, situated in Boulder City, operates from 9 a.m. to 4:30 p.m. every day, excluding Thanksgiving, Christmas, and New Year's Day. Entrance and lake use fees apply, and payment can be made online or at the entrance stations.

To familiarize yourself with this extensive recreation area, a visit to the visitor center is highly recommended. Rangers can provide guidance, assist with additional planning, and engage kids in the junior ranger program. Don't overlook the exhibit featuring a relief map of the park, information about its resident animals, and the park's film detailing desert life.

The Lake Mead National Recreation Area has nine main access points, and reaching the Lake Mead Visitor Center is straightforward. Follow US-93, located 4 miles southeast of

Boulder City. The drive typically takes less than 45 minutes from the Las Vegas Strip. For a unique experience, the Desert Princess, a Mississippi-style riverboat, offers cruises on Lake Mead. The National Park Express operates a round-trip shuttle to the cruise area. While public transportation directly to Lake Mead is unavailable, many tour operators offer shuttles from resorts on the Las Vegas Strip.

Tips:

1) Check and adhere to all fees for motorized boats, especially if you bring your own, as they need to be licensed. Fishing licenses vary based on the state you're fishing in, given that the area spans the Arizona/Nevada state line.

2) Hikers should stick to protected trails marked with yellow signs emphasizing exploration by "human power only." Despite its recreational appeal, the NRA is a protected area with delicate natural habitats.

3) Summer weather in this region of Nevada and Arizona can be extreme, reaching up to 120 degrees F (49 degrees C) in the shade. Spring and fall are the optimal times for hiking. For hiking inquiries or ranger-led hikes, contacting the visitor center in advance is advisable. Ranger-guided hikes are conducted in the evenings during the hot months.

LAKE POWELL

COUNTY: COCONINO   CITY: PAGE n.c.

DATE VISITED: WHO I WENT WITH:

RATING: ☆ ☆ ☆ ☆ ☆   WILL I RETURN?   YES / NO

Page, Arizona, boasts Lake Powell, the second-largest man-made lake in the United States, attracting nearly three million visitors annually.

Stretching 186 miles with 1,960 miles of shoreline—longer than the entire west coast of the continental United States—Lake Powell offers exploration opportunities in its 96 major canyons. Access to many canyons is limited, necessitating watercraft due to the scarcity of roads.

Page and four marinas—Wahweap, Bull Frog, Dangling Rope, and Rainbow Bridge—provide boat and personal watercraft rentals. Tour boat cruises, ranging from one to seven hours, operate year-round at Wahweap and Bull Frog marinas. Dangling Rope Marina is only reachable by boat and is located 3/4 of the distance between Wahweap Marina and Rainbow Bridge National Monument.

The lake offers various activities such as swimming, fishing, scuba diving, snorkeling, water skiing, hiking, and sightseeing, along with abundant photographic opportunities. Scenic flights by plane or helicopter offer a bird's-eye view of the extensive canyons extending from the main channel.

Lake Powell's waters warm around early June and remain so until October, boasting unmatched clarity. Classified as a "high desert" area due to its 3,700 ft. elevation, Lake Powell experiences an arid climate with humidity generally below 40%. Winter sees significant cooling of water temperatures, rising into the high 70s during summer. Snowfall at Lake Powell enhances its beauty, creating striking contrasts against red-rock cliffs and azure blue waters.

Glen Canyon National Recreation Area, established in 1972, encompasses Lake Powell. Encompassing 1.25 million acres, with the lake occupying only 13%, or 161,390 acres, the area invites exploration by four-wheel drive or on foot. Several miles from any marina, a boat journey transports visitors to a world free from signs of civilization.

Named after Civil War veteran Major John Wesley Powell, Lake Powell's creation resulted from Glen Canyon Dam, extending nearly one-third of a mile across the canyon. Powell, who explored the Green and Colorado rivers in 1869, passed through the dam site. Lake Powell, partly in Arizona and mostly in Utah, reaches depths of over 500 feet. Arizona lays claim to the dam, filled over 17 years from March 13, 1963, to June 22, 1980, reaching a planned level of 3,700 feet above sea level. Lake levels fluctuate based on spring runoff and electricity production needs from the dam's eight generators. Tributaries, including the Escalante and San Juan rivers, contribute to the lake's diverse fishing opportunities. Striped bass, large and smallmouth bass, crappie, catfish, and carp populate the lake.

Lake Powell's fishing patterns undergo seasonal changes, offering year-round opportunities due to its moderate water temperatures ranging from 45°F to 85°F, preventing freezing. The lake, never fully frozen, allows for fishing even in winter. The most productive days often occur during the off-season when the lake is calm and resembles a mirror.

Constant factors in fishing include locating bait fish like shad and crawfish, which follow consistent seasonal patterns. Game fish such as large and smallmouth bass, striped bass, walleye, crappie, catfish, and carp can be found where the bait fish are abundant.

Spring marks the most active fishing season when warming water triggers the spawn phenomenon. Pre-spawn fish move from canyons to sandy and gravel-covered points. Popular baits during this time include hula-grubs and spinner baits. During the spawn, brightly colored plastic worms or hula-grubs pitched into well-defined beds yield frequent strikes. Post-spawn, fish move to deeper areas, and soft plastics and spinner baits become effective. Additionally, topwater bites are observed during early or late hours.

Summer brings increased boat activity, especially houseboats, jet skiers, and water skiers. Early and late hours are optimal for topwater fishing with a split-shot rig. Midday, fish move towards the main channel and bays, making deep fishing more productive.

Fall is considered the most pleasant time on Lake Powell by anglers. Fish move to shallow waters, head towards canyon backs, and may engage in feeding frenzies. Topwater baits, spinner baits, and soft plastic jerk baits prove effective. Adjusting to warmer and cooler periods by fishing slower and deeper enhances productivity.

Contrary to winter being seen as a time to store equipment, fishing in winter can be highly productive. Even in December, successful guided trips for largemouth bass have been reported, emphasizing the year-round appeal of Lake Powell for fishing enthusiasts.

Every year, Lake Powell transforms into a focal point for celebrations and traditions, featuring various local events and festivals that showcase the rich culture of the region. From arts and crafts fairs to music and dance festivals, each event provides insight into the local way of life. The annual Lake Powell Festival, a fantastic cultural showcase, brings together artisans and performers.

Lake Powell and its surroundings host numerous cultural and heritage sites with significant historical importance. Antelope Canyon, known for its mesmerizing natural beauty, holds historical significance for the Navajo people. Additionally, the awe-inspiring Rainbow Bridge National Monument is revered by Native American tribes.

Immersing yourself in the local culture is possible through hands-on experiences. Culinary workshops offer the opportunity to learn traditional Navajo dishes, guided tours allow engagement with local customs, and native dance performances provide thrilling experiences. Exploring local crafts further highlights the artistic heritage of the region.

As a water enthusiast's paradise in the desert, Lake Powell offers a myriad of activities. Jet skiing and wakeboarding provide excitement against the backdrop of red-rock canyons. Boat rentals and houseboat vacations offer a unique way to appreciate the vastness of the lake, with places like Wahweap Marina serving as starting points for water journeys.

Glen Canyon National Recreation Area, encompassing Lake Powell, invites hikers of all levels. Trails such as Navajo Canyon or those surrounding Bullfrog Marina offer breathtaking views and a deep connection to nature, with AllTrails helping you find the perfect path.

For adrenaline seekers, Lake Powell's surroundings provide opportunities for heart-pumping adventures. Rock climbing the rugged canyons or ziplining across them offers novel ways to engage with the landscape. Land-based rental companies, often near marinas, equip you with gear for ATV or biking escapades, ensuring you won't miss a beat.

Adventure awaits with ATV rides on dusty trails, rock climbing adventures for all experience levels, and unique aerial views through paragliding and ziplining. Lake Powell's diverse offerings cater to a wide range of interests and provide unforgettable experiences in the heart of the desert landscape.

If you're searching for ways to unwind and relax at Lake Powell, the wellness centers offer a haven for stress relief. With therapeutic massages and rejuvenating facials, your vacation can be both relaxing and exciting.

Lake Powell's beaches beckon you to soak in the sun and enjoy the calm waters. Swimming and lounging by the water provide a great way to spend the day, with options for those who prefer pool privacy or the natural beauty of the lake's sandy shores. Bask in the sun, swim freely, and let the area's beauty help you find tranquility.

Garden strolls and picnics in the surrounding parks offer unrivaled peaceful settings. Whether seeking a solitary moment amidst greenery or a family outing, these areas provide a refuge from the hustle and bustle. Explore various trails to enjoy local flora and fauna, creating a perfect opportunity for relaxation and reconnection with nature.

Lake Powell offers more than just scenic landscapes; culinary activities add another highlight to your trip. From sampling local cuisine reflecting unique flavors to hands-on cooking classes with regional dishes, there's plenty to satisfy culinary curiosity. Lake Powell's culinary scene showcases southwestern influences and fresh, locally-sourced ingredients. Dive into regional staples like fish tacos, known for their zest, or indulge your sweet tooth with frybread and honey—a delicate balance of crispy and sweet. Embark on a culinary journey with local cooking classes, where chefs guide you through southwestern-inspired dishes. Capture the essence of Lake Powell's food scene and bring home recipes to impress friends and family.

Local markets boast fresh produce and handcrafted goods embodying Lake Powell's spirit. Here, you can gather fresh ingredients for culinary adventures or find unique local crafts, ideal for souvenirs. Indulge in local delicacies from homemade jams to artisanal cheeses.

For a fun evening near Lake Powell, explore lively shows or serene evening cruises. Dive into local culture at venues like Grand Canyon Brewing & Distillery, offering local brews and live entertainment. Evening cruises under the night sky provide a magical experience as the sunset transitions into starry nights.

When exploring Lake Powell, the shopping experience is as remarkable as the breathtaking landscape itself. From the local artisan shops with handcrafted jewelry capturing the desert spirit to pottery reflecting the lake's mesmerizing hues, you'll discover unique finds that serve as perfect memorabilia. Local artisan shops offer a chance to purchase handcrafted souvenirs, each with its own story. Artists often share insights into their craft, creating an interactive and personal shopping experience. As you explore Lake Powell's bustling shopping districts, you'll encounter diverse stores, from markets with locally-produced snacks to chic boutiques featuring the latest fashion. It's not just about shopping; it's about the vibrant atmosphere each district brings. For a variety of options, this is the place to be.

Lake Powell provides numerous family-friendly activities to engage everyone, from the youngest travelers to adults. Enjoy a day filled with educational fun, picturesque play areas, and hands-on workshops designed for memorable family moments.

Imagine a sun-soaked afternoon at one of Lake Powell's lush parks or play areas, ideal for a family picnic or letting kids play in safe, well-maintained environments. Whether tossing a frisbee or exploring park trails, these spaces are perfect for family activities promoting togetherness.

Interactive workshops, from learning about the lake's ecosystem to craft sessions using natural materials, are popular with families seeking educational and entertaining experiences.

When planning your Lake Powell adventure, understanding local customs and managing expenses can enhance your experience without overspending. Respect for local etiquette is crucial, considering the area's significance to Native American tribes. Stay on designated paths to avoid environmental damage and show respect to cultural sites. A friendly greeting and a smile go a long way in connecting with the local community.

Remember the principle of "leave no trace" by keeping the lake clean, disposing of rubbish properly, and taking it with you.

Lake Powell isn't just a destination; it's an immersive experience. Whether gliding across the water at dawn or enjoying the quiet of a desert sunset, each moment adds to the unforgettable narrative of Lake Powell.

LOWELL OBSERVATORY

COUNTY: COCONINO   **CITY:** FLAGSTAFF

DATE VISITED: **WHO I WENT WITH:**

RATING: ☆ ☆ ☆ ☆ ☆   **WILL I RETURN?** YES / NO

Percival Lowell, a prominent member of the Lowell family in Boston during the early 20th century, gained recognition as an astronomer who promoted the idea that Mars harbored an advanced and highly technological civilization. Despite being a wealthy amateur scientist involved in various pursuits like business, writing, mathematics, and a strong interest in Japan, Lowell shifted his focus to astronomy in 1894. Using his wealth, he established an observatory named after him.

Lowell's fascination with astronomy and the possibility of extraterrestrial life grew after encountering two influential works: "The Planet Mars and Its Conditions of Habitability" (1892) by French Spiritualist Camille Flammarion and "Life on Mars" (1893) by Italian astronomer Giovanni Schiaparelli. Schiaparelli's book featured hand-drawn maps of Mars, illustrating a complex system of "canali" (Italian for "channels"), mistranslated as "canals" in English. This misinterpretation suggested artificial construction, leading Lowell to dedicate the next 15 years to studying Mars at his observatory in Flagstaff, Arizona.

Flagstaff was chosen as the location for Lowell's observatory due to its high altitude (over 7,000 feet), minimal cloudy nights, and distance from city lights. These criteria, now considered crucial for optimal observing conditions, were introduced by Lowell. From Arizona, he published his findings and illustrations of Mars' surface features in three books: "Mars" (1895), "Mars and Its Canals" (1906), and "Mars As the Abode of Life" (1908). In these works, Lowell proposed that the canals were evidence of a technologically advanced society attempting to extract water from the polar ice caps of their drying planet.

Despite generating public excitement, Lowell and his observatory faced skepticism and ostracization from the scientific community. Lowell's observations of Mars weren't the only inaccuracies; he also drew maps of Venus with spoke-like features from a central dark spot. As Venus' atmosphere is now known to be opaque, it was suggested that Lowell might have been observing an image of the blood vessels in his own eye.

Nevertheless, Lowell made significant contributions to astronomy, and craters on the Moon and Mars are named in his honor. His pursuit also led to the discovery of Pluto. To explain discrepancies in the orbits of Uranus and Neptune, Lowell proposed the Planet X hypothesis, suggesting an unseen ninth planet perturbing outer planets' orbits. While Pluto's influence on Uranus and Neptune is negligible, Lowell's idea of another body beyond Neptune was accurate. In 1930, using the 13-inch astrograph, Clyde Tombaugh discovered Pluto. Pluto's name and symbol were influenced by Percival Lowell's initials, PL.

The 24-inch Alvan Clark telescope, used by Lowell for his observations, is now employed for educational purposes. Housed in a dome designed by local bicycle mechanics, the Sykes brothers, it features an "inverted bucket" shape constructed from local Ponderosa pine, with a rotating roof set on a track. The dome was swiftly completed in ten days and has remained in good condition, except for the roof's rotation mechanism. When the original metal wheels malfunctioned, the observatory staff attempted to rotate the wooden roof by floating it in a ring-shaped trough of saltwater. However, this method was abandoned due to the saltwater's threat to the instruments. Today, the dome lid is supported by numerous 1954 Ford pickup tires. Inside the dome, Mrs. Lowell's frying pan serves as a makeshift lens cap for the guide telescope mounted on the side of the Clark refractor.

Being one of the oldest observatories in the U.S., the site has a rich history of significant astronomical discoveries, a tradition that persists. Research conducted at the observatory includes Vesto Slipher's 1912 observations of redshifted galaxies, supporting the expanding universe theory, and recent determinations of the orbits for Pluto's moons, Nix and Hydra. It's fitting that Percival Lowell's final resting place is atop Mars Hill, overlooking his beloved observatory. Mrs. Lowell commissioned an extravagant mausoleum in honor of her husband at this location.

General Admission provides all-day access to Lowell Observatory, allowing you to explore 127 years of astronomical discoveries. You can walk in the footsteps of Clyde Tombaugh, the discoverer of Pluto in 1930, and marvel at the still-operational 24-inch Clark Refractor, a 125-year-old telescope. During the night, you can use the six state-of-the-art telescopes at the Giovale Open Deck Observatory to observe planets, distant gas clouds, and galaxies under Flagstaff's famously dark skies. General Admission also includes access to various talks and tours offered throughout the day.

When visiting Lowell Observatory, it's recommended to do some research beforehand due to the numerous programs, buildings, telescopes, historical artifacts, and events available. The Giovale Open Deck Observatory, a new public observing plaza with six advanced telescopes, offers a unique celestial viewing experience. A tour of the Clark Telescope, the oldest building at the observatory, is another highlight, as it played a crucial role in uncovering evidence of the expanding universe.

Notable features of Lowell Observatory include an impressive children's program and the operation of the Lowell Discovery Telescope (LDT) in Happy Jack, Arizona. The LDT is one of the world's most powerful telescopes, weighing 6700 pounds and costing $53 million USD.

MATHER POINT

COUNTY: COCONINO   **CITY:** FLAGSTAFF *n.c.*

DATE VISITED: **WHO I WENT WITH:**

         RATING: ☆ ☆ ☆ ☆ ☆   **WILL I RETURN?** YES / NO

Mather Point stands out as the Grand Canyon's most crowded and well-liked observation point, primarily because of its convenient location near the visitor center complex and primary parking areas.

For many South Rim visitors, Mather Point serves as the initial introduction to the marvel of the Grand Canyon. Situated a brief walk from the Grand Canyon Visitor Center and parking lots 1-4, Mather Point provides a panoramic perspective of the canyon. On a clear day, the view extends over 30 miles (48 km) to the east and 60 miles (96 km) to the west. Peering into the canyon, one can observe snippets of the Colorado River, Phantom Ranch at the canyon's base, and a network of trails crisscrossing the terrain.

Although there is no parking directly at Mather Point, the parking lots near the Grand Canyon Visitor Center are a short walk away, and the free Kaibab/Rim Route (orange) shuttle bus also stops here.

Due to its expansive view and the striking formations visible from the location, Mather Point is a favored spot for both sunrise and sunset enthusiasts throughout the year. It's advisable to arrive early to witness the captivating color transformations as the sun ascends and descends.

This scenic spot is dedicated to Stephen Tyng Mather, the inaugural director of the National Park Service. Originally a prosperous businessman from Chicago, Mather was not only a fervent conservationist but also a strong advocate for public lands. In 1915, he relocated to Washington D.C. to play a pivotal role in the establishment of the National Park Service, eventually becoming its first director in 1917. Throughout his tenure until 1929, Mather tirelessly promoted access to parks, their development, and their responsible utilization.

Mather firmly believed that the breathtaking scenery should be the primary consideration in designating a national park. He actively worked to secure the establishment of new parks before the lands could be developed for alternative purposes. Mather's vision centered on garnering support from enthusiastic park users, who would then convey their endorsement to elected representatives. Under his leadership, the Park Service expanded to include renowned sites such as Grand Canyon, Shenandoah, Great Smoky Mountains, Mammoth Cave National Parks, and numerous others.

Stephen Tyng Mather laid the groundwork for the National Park Service, delineating and implementing policies to ensure the development and conservation of these areas, preserving them unimpaired for the benefit of future generations.

49 MCCORMICK-STILLMAN RAILROAD PARK

COUNTY: MARICOPA   **CITY:** SCOTTSDALE

DATE VISITED: _____   **WHO I WENT WITH:** _____

RATING: ☆ ☆ ☆ ☆ ☆   **WILL I RETURN?**   YES / NO

The McCormick-Stillman Railroad Park is managed by the Parks & Recreation Department of the city of Scottsdale. Situated in the heart of Scottsdale, Arizona, this 30-acre park stands out as the most distinctive of its kind in the country. Visitors can enjoy a ride on the Paradise & Pacific Railroad and the vintage 1950 Allan Herschell carousel. The park also offers a range of shops and museums, unique playgrounds, and play areas, providing a serene environment for relaxation amid the lush greenery.

Entrance to the McCormick-Stillman Railroad Park is free of charge. However, there is a $3.00 fee for tickets to ride the train and carousel, with children aged two and under riding for free. Access to the Scottsdale Railroad Museum and Model Railroad Building comes at no cost. The park welcomes visitors 363 days a year, weather permitting, with closures only on Thanksgiving and Christmas Day. Attraction hours may vary depending on the season.

You can find the McCormick-Stillman Railroad Park at the southeast corner of Scottsdale Road and Indian Bend Road, approximately 1.7 miles west of the Loop 101, at the exit for Indian Bend Road/Talking Stick Way.

Between 1942 and 1954, Anne and Fowler McCormick, the grandson of John D. Rockefeller, embarked on the ambitious task of acquiring the expansive McCormick Ranch tracts of land. By the time Anne passed away in 1969, the ranch spanned nearly seven square miles. Among its 4,236 acres were over 640 acres of irrigated land, complete with water tanks for both livestock and wildlife. Additionally, the ranch served as a breeding ground for top-quality purebred Arabian horses and Angus cattle. The McCormick Ranch's horse operations were situated at Scottsdale Road and Northern Ave., marking the present-day main entrance to the McCormick Ranch housing development.

MCDOWELL SONORAN PRESERVE

COUNTY: MARICOPA   CITY: SCOTTSDALE

DATE VISITED: WHO I WENT WITH:

RATING: ☆ ☆ ☆ ☆ ☆   WILL I RETURN?   YES / NO

Immersing oneself in the diverse wonders of the Sonoran Desert becomes effortlessly achievable by stepping away from paved surfaces and entering the Scottsdale McDowell Sonoran Preserve.

Boasting over 200 miles of nonmotorized trails, this preserve in the northeast Valley serves as a significant attraction for hikers, bikers, and equestrians of all skill levels.

During the bustling winter visitor season, having a reliable selection of short and easy treks becomes prudent to showcase the remarkable beauty and variety of local trails.

The Latigo-Sidewinder loop stands out as an accessible and enlightening option, offering a brief journey filled with botanical, geological, and scenic marvels. This quick exploration of a family-friendly section within the preserve is ideal for entertaining guests or simply indulging in the local flora and fauna without much complexity. The trail begins at the new Pima-Dynamite trailhead, where welcoming amenities such as restrooms, shaded seating areas, and interpretive signs are available.

Embarking on an easy half-mile walk along the wide, sandy Latigo Trail takes you into the preserve's far west edge, passing beneath powerlines that intriguingly mimic the long, slender stalks of native ocotillo cactus. Along this initial stretch, a veritable botanical garden unfolds, featuring blooming native plants like sulfur-yellow desert marigolds and brittlebush, red chuparosa shrubs, fairy dusters, delicately fragrant desert lavender, and the golden desert rock pea.

Fruit-bearing thornbushes, wolfberries, and the invasive mistletoe serve as enticing attractions for various bird species, including cactus wrens, phainopeplas, mockingbirds, and doves. Meanwhile, the landscape is animated by the lively movements of rabbits, squirrels, and lizards darting among jojoba bushes and numerous species of cholla cactus.

Upon reaching the Sidewinder Trail junction, take a right turn and follow the signs leading to the main botanical highlight—a splendid crested saguaro. A sign adjacent to this rare specimen presents theories on the formation of the contorted, fan-like crests found on these intriguing desert plants. Just beyond the crested saguaro, the trail meanders through a boulder-lined corridor, offering an optional brief detour to the Sidewinder Overlook. Here, a platform of granite shelves provides a vantage point for viewing mountain ranges.

Newcomers often find themselves captivated by the abundance and diversity of desert plant and animal life, as well as the juxtaposition of the low, arid environment with a backdrop of mountain peaks, which may be snow-capped in winter.

Returning from the overlook, follow the signs back to the Latigo Trail, completing the loop to the trailhead for a satisfying 2.7-mile journey.

51 METEOR CRATER NATIONAL LANDMARK

COUNTY: COCONINO **CITY:** FLAGSTAFF *n.c.*

DATE VISITED: **WHO I WENT WITH:**

RATING: ☆ ☆ ☆ ☆ ☆ **WILL I RETURN?** YES / NO

Meteor Crater is not just a colossal indentation in the Earth; it stands as a tangible testament to an ancient collision with a massive meteor, hence its name. This geological wonder has become a noteworthy attraction for road trippers and visitors exploring Arizona.

Situated in the high desert near Flagstaff, Meteor Crater is characterized by its astonishing size and scale, which may seem almost unbelievable when witnessed in person. Standing on the crater's edge, one can gaze across and observe boulders resembling houses in size. There are only a handful of intact craters globally, and Meteor Crater is among the most impressive.

Found in northern Arizona, this expansive, bowl-shaped crater originated approximately 50,000 years ago when a meteorite collided with the Colorado Plateau. Also known as The Barringer Crater, it spans about ¾ of a mile from rim to rim. Interestingly, the impacting meteorite, officially named the Canyon Diablo Meteorite, was a comparatively modest 160 feet wide.

Upon impact, the Canyon Diablo Meteorite ejected rocks and debris up to 2 kilometers in all directions, displacing a significant amount of earth and carving out the cavernous hole we see in the Arizona landscape today. The dry conditions of the region have contributed to the crater's exceptional preservation since its formation.

Composed of extremely dense nickel-iron, the meteorite's weight was disproportionately heavy for its size. Fragments of the original meteorite were discovered both inside and around Meteor Crater, with most pieces being as small as pebbles.

To grasp the crater's depth from rim to bottom (approximately 600 feet/180 meters), envision the Statue of Liberty in New York City; you could stack two statues on top of each other within the crater. With a width of about ¾ of a mile (1.2 km) from rim to rim, standing on the edge can evoke a sense of dizziness due to the vast emptiness below.

Meteor Crater is located on the Colorado Plateau, positioned between Flagstaff and Winslow just a few miles south of Interstate I-40. If traveling from Flagstaff, the route involves heading east on I-40 for 35 miles to exit 233, Meteor Crater Road. Following this road for a mere 5.7 miles leads to the visitors center, conveniently close to the main highway.

For those coming from Winslow, the journey is a relatively short 18 miles on I-40. Summers at Meteor Crater can be hot and consistently sunny. At an elevation of 5,700 feet, the sun's rays are more intense, and the higher elevation also brings the potential for fairly chilly winter months. While it's not a common occurrence, snowfall at Meteor Crater is not unheard of.

It's worth noting that the crater and the surrounding land are privately owned by the Barringer family, who informally refer to it as Barringer Crater. However, in 1967, Meteor Crater received the designation of a National Natural Landmark, and its official name became Meteor Crater.

This National Natural Landmark status ensures perpetual protection from mining and other industrial activities. Even if the Barringers were to sell the land and the crater, the Meteor Crater would retain its protected status.

The Discovery Center and Space Museum serves as an excellent starting point for your visit (after you've had an initial look at the crater, of course). Here, you can delve into the details of the meteorite impact through hands-on exhibits and interactive displays. One highlight is the opportunity to view the largest remaining piece of the meteorite, a massive 1,400 lbs object that measures only about two feet across.

Exiting the Discovery Center, head to one of the observation decks. From this vantage point, you can survey the expansive Meteor Crater landscape and attempt to fathom the colossal force behind the impact that created such a vast, gaping hole in the ground.

On the observation deck, telescopes are available to provide a closer look at the rim located ¾ of a mile away. These telescopes are strategically positioned and labeled with the specific points of interest they highlight. Some are directed toward the crater's bottom, revealing an old abandoned mining camp and research buildings. Remarkably, astronauts have undergone training in the crater's depths, emphasizing the truly otherworldly nature of this location.

For those seeking a guided experience, there is a rim tour that not only educates but also involves a 30-40 minute hike along the rim. Local guides and experts share insights about the ancient impact and various intriguing facts about Meteor Crater, pointing out notable features in and around the crater.

Accessibility is a priority, with all features in the Discovery Center and the main observation decks wheelchair accessible. The theater rooms are also accessible, and the Collision!4D film offers an interactive experience, particularly enjoyable for kids. With such inclusive features, Meteor Crater promises an enjoyable visit for the entire family.

Pets are not permitted inside the Discovery Center, on the trails, or on the observation decks. However, there is a recently constructed outdoor pet ramada with kennels, providing a covered space to keep your pets secure while you explore Meteor Crater. For safety considerations, visitors are not allowed to hike down to the bottom of the crater. Ongoing year-round research takes place in that area, and the trail leading down is rugged, unmaintained, and exposed to the elements. It is advised to appreciate the crater's view safely from the rim.

The allure of Meteor Crater bears a resemblance to the attraction of the Grand Canyon, albeit on a smaller scale. Gazing at the vast expanse of emptiness before you is truly awe-inspiring and can almost feel surreal unless witnessed in person.

Try to envision the exact moment of impact, when trillions of tons of dirt, rocks, and debris were catapulted into the sky and scattered across the surrounding area. The sheer scale of such an event is challenging to grasp.

Meteor Crater serves as a noteworthy addition to any road trip or can even stand as a destination on its own, particularly appealing to those intrigued by space or geology.

Despite its seemingly remote location, a journey to Meteor Crater can transform into a memorable day for any family.

COUNTY: PIMA   CITY: TUCSON *n.c.*

DATE VISITED: WHO I WENT WITH:

RATING: ☆ ☆ ☆ ☆ ☆   WILL I RETURN?   YES / NO

San Xavier del Bac is a stunning mission church situated just south of Tucson in the Sonoran Desert, renowned as the "White Dove of the Desert" and designated as a National Historic Landmark. Resembling a European artifact, San Xavier stands as a masterpiece of mission architecture. Positioned in serene grandeur on an Indian reservation, it has served as an architectural landmark and spiritual hub for the Papago Indians since its establishment in 1797.

The mission, partly restored, stands as the preeminent example of Spanish Colonial and Mexican Baroque architecture within the United States, presenting an unexpected sight in this country. Stepping inside reveals a wealth of features, including vibrant frescoes, sculptures, an intricate retable (a devotional panel), and various chapels. The initial glimpse of the church is truly striking. While driving south on I-19 from Tucson and entering the San Xavier Indian reservation, the mission emerges as a gleaming white monolith against the backdrop of the tan landscape. Its stark whiteness creates a vivid contrast with the desert hues of pinks, beiges, and greens. The twin-towered church, adorned with a massive carved entrance portal, stands prominently alone on the plain.

During the 1700s, Spanish colonists extended their presence northward from Mexico into what is now Arizona, expanding the territories claimed for New Spain. Jesuit missionaries played a significant role in this expansion, establishing a series of missions along the Santa Cruz River in the Sonoran Desert. The San Xavier del Bac Mission, recognized today as a National Historic Landmark, was established in 1700 by Father Eusebio Kino, a Jesuit missionary dedicated to spreading Christianity in New Spain. The Tohono O'Odham, along with subsequent Franciscan missionaries, erected a mission at this location, a site that continues to captivate the imaginations of visitors.

Constructed between 1783 and 1797, the iconic white stucco church stands on the spot chosen by Father Kino and has evolved into a cherished component of the community's history. Over generations, it has been meticulously restored and cared for. Reverently referred to as the "white dove of the desert," the mission is situated in the San Xavier Reservation, which is part of the Tohono O'odham Nation located southwest of Tucson, Arizona.

In historical terms, the O'odham people inhabited a vast region in the Southwest, encompassing areas extending from Sonora, Mexico, in the south to Central Arizona (just north of Phoenix, Arizona) in the north, west to the Gulf of California, and east to the San Pedro River. While the Spanish referred to this land as the Papaguería and the Pimería Alta, it had served as the O'odham's home for thousands of years. Their way of life involved hunting rabbit and deer, gathering agave, cholla, saguaro fruit, prickly pear cactus, and other wild foods, as well as practicing irrigation farming to cultivate corn, beans, and squash. The settlement of San Xavier del Bac, located near the Santa Cruz River, represented a Tohono O'odham town known as Wa:k, a term in the native language denoting water. The mission's name reflects the fusion of Spanish Catholic and O'odham desert cultures, symbolizing the unique and continuous availability of water. The feasibility of irrigation farming in the intermittently flowing Santa Cruz River at San Xavier del Bac was facilitated by volcanic outcrops, which directed the underground flow of water upward, ensuring a year-round flow of the river at the site.

Father Eusebio Kino, a dynamic Jesuit missionary, played a pivotal role in establishing a chain of missions across present-day Sonora and Southern Arizona. His first interaction with the O'odham community of Wa:k (Bac) occurred in 1692. Father Kino aimed to Christianize and Hispanicize native communities by introducing European technologies. However, despite his efforts, minimal changes were observed, and traditional subsistence activities persisted, with the addition of the Old World crop, winter wheat, filling a crucial gap in the O'odham agricultural cycle. Cattle, horses, and sheep were integrated with traditional foods and agriculture during Father Kino's time.

In 1700, Father Kino reportedly began the construction of a church near Wa:k, although it appeared to be a temporary structure. When Jesuit Father Visitor Jacobo Sedelmayer visited the settlement in 1751, no church was found.

The first permanent church at San Xavier, a small flat-roofed, hall-shaped adobe building, was initiated by Jesuit missionary Father Alonso Espinosa in 1756 and became operational by 1763. Father Francisco Garcés inherited this adobe church upon his arrival in 1768 as the first Franciscan minister after the expulsion of the Jesuits in 1767. By 1772, the mission, now under Franciscan control, reported planting wheat, corn, and other crops and had a population of 270 people.

The Franciscans completed the mission church that still stands at San Xavier del Bac around the time when the Spanish Empire in North America was diminishing. Father Juan Bautista Velderrain commenced construction in 1783, securing a loan of 7,000 pesos. Mexico gained independence in 1821 after 11 years of revolution, leading to the secularization of missions and requiring Franciscan allegiance to the Mexican government. In 1828, San Xavier del Bac's resident priest, Father Rafael Diaz, refused to align with the new regime and left the mission, resulting in a 36-year period without a priest at San Xavier.

The mid-19th century marked a period of instability for San Xavier del Bac. In 1853, the Gadsden Purchase land treaty transferred ownership of the mission to the United States from Mexico. Subsequently, in 1859, the Catholic Church placed the parish under the jurisdiction of the Santa Fe diocese. Under the leadership of Bishop Lamy, the diocese undertook repairs on the church's exposed adobe brick, and in 1864, Jesuit Father Carolus Evasius Messea resided there for eight months. During Father Messea's tenure, he established the first public school in Arizona at San Xavier del Bac. However, due to a lack of local community interest and limited funding, the parish faced closure. In 1874, the U.S. government established the San Xavier Reservation.

In the early 20th century, Bishop Henry Granjon initiated renovations and new construction on the church. He oversaw repairs to the church façade and mortuary wall, which had been damaged in an earthquake in 1887. In 1913, the church welcomed its first priest since Father Messea, namely Father Ferdinand Ortíz, a Franciscan and Tucson native. Since Father Ortíz's arrival, California Franciscans have managed the church and served the San Xavier Reservation. In 1947, they founded a school for local O'odham children. Subsequently, in 1949, renovations were conducted, including the installation of new floors, repairs to the roof and walls, and improvements to living conditions within the convento.

Constructed by O'odham laborers, the main structure is crafted from fired adobe bricks assembled with lime mortar, with its exterior walls adorned in white stucco. The primary building takes the form of a Latin cross, featuring two octagonal towers crowned with belfries at its front. A large dome spans the transept crossing, accompanied by smaller domes to the north and south. The mission property encompasses the main church, mortuary chapel, dormitory, patio, garden, and convento.

Inside the chapel, a meticulously restored interior, overseen by Vatican conservators in the 1990s, unveils detailed paintings and vibrant geometric designs. The interior is adorned with intricately painted and carved religious imagery covering the walls and vaulted ceilings. Wooden statues of San Xavier and the Virgin are positioned against a molded background behind the altar, while carved wooden statues of saints grace various areas of the church. Additionally, visitors have the opportunity to ascend the volcano outcropping and witness the green fields cultivated for centuries in the Santa Cruz River Valley.

Under the stewardship of the parish and a local non-profit organization, the splendid Spanish colonial church at San Xavier del Bac endures. Designated as a National Historic Landmark by the Secretary of the Interior in 1960, the church remains a vital center serving the residents of the San Xavier Reservation. The church welcomes visitors daily, excluding special services. Free tours are offered regularly, and the public is invited to join the San Xavier community for regular masses.

COUNTY: YAVAPAI   CITY: CAMP VERDE *n.c.*

DATE VISITED: WHO I WENT WITH:

RATING: ☆ ☆ ☆ ☆ ☆   WILL I RETURN? YES / NO

Approximately one and a half hours north of Phoenix, two national monuments offer an enriching day trip from the Phoenix area: Montezuma Castle National Monument and Tuzigoot National Monument. These sites showcase the ancient dwellings of the Sinagua people, Native Americans who inhabited Arizona centuries before Christopher Columbus arrived in the Americas.

Montezuma Castle National Monument is situated within a sheer limestone cliff recess, approximately 100 feet above the Verde Valley in Camp Verde, Arizona. Constructed and utilized by the Sinagua people—ancestors of the Hohokam and other indigenous groups of the southwestern United States—the dwellings date back to around 1100 AD to 1425 AD. The primary structure comprises five stories and 20 rooms, totaling about 4,000 square feet of living space, developed over three centuries.

Facing the adjacent Beaver Creek, Montezuma Castle overlooks fertile fields where Sinagua farmers cultivated corn, beans, squash, and cotton. The nearby creek served as a reliable water source. The elevated construction of this dwelling suggests a deliberate choice to avoid the annual flooding of Beaver Creek during the summer monsoon season, providing protection against invaders and erosion.

Montezuma Castle stands as one of the best-preserved ancient structures in North America, showcasing remarkable architectural resilience. A short distance west of the main ruin, Castle B, a less well-preserved complex with rudimentary rooms on several levels, can be found. Since 1951, visitors have been prohibited from climbing up to the ruins due to their unstable condition, but a 1/3-mile loop trail allows for a scenic walk and photography.

About 11 miles away (a 20-minute drive) lies Montezuma Well, another facet of the Montezuma Castle monument. This well is a submerged limestone sinkhole, approximately 55 feet deep, formed by the collapse of a large underground cavern. Along the 1/3-mile path to the well, visitors can explore well-preserved stone cliff dwelling ruins and the remnants of a pithouse. The well's waters were utilized by the inhabitants of the era for crop irrigation.

The name "Montezuma Castle" is inaccurately attributed to the monument. When European-Americans encountered the ruins in the 1860s, already abandoned for an extended period, they erroneously named them after the renowned Aztec ruler Montezuma, incorrectly linking him to their construction. In reality, the dwelling had been deserted over 40 years before Montezuma's birth, and it did not serve as a "castle" for royalty but rather functioned more like a multi-story apartment complex for numerous residents.

Tuzigoot National Monument preserves the remnants of a Sinaguan village established over 1,000 years ago above the Verde Valley. The term "Tuzigoot," originating from Apache, translates to "crooked water." Positioned atop a limestone and sandstone ridge just east of Clarkdale, Arizona, 120 feet above the floodplain of the Verde River, Tuzigoot is a two- to three-story pueblo ruin. The monument encompasses 110 stone masonry rooms.

It is believed that the population at Tuzigoot, and the subsequent construction of additional rooms, consisted of farmers seeking refuge from drought in surrounding regions. Visitors are encouraged to explore the interior and surroundings of Tuzigoot, attempting to envision the daily life of the Sinagua people who engaged in farming, hunting, pottery crafting, and artwork in this area centuries ago.

Both Montezuma Castle and Tuzigoot fall under the management of the National Park Service. While the museum at Montezuma Castle offers informative content, it could benefit from some refurbishment. On the other hand, the Visitor Center at Tuzigoot is exceptionally well-executed.

Both monuments hold significant interest, but Tuzigoot tends to be more popular among the younger crowd, as visitors can walk up, around, and inside the structure. Allocate a few hours to explore the museum, reopened in June 2011 at the Tuzigoot Visitor Center. Afterwards, traverse the trail through the Tuzigoot pueblo and Tavasci Marsh, covering a distance of about 1/3 mile. Engage with a ranger to delve into the history of the Sinagua people and their lives in the Verde Valley.

No food is available at these locations, so it's advisable to bring your own food and beverages. Montezuma Castle has a designated picnic area.

For visits during the spring and summer, ensure you have a hat and sunscreen, as there is limited protection from the sun.

Both Montezuma Castle and Tuzigoot have entrance fees.

MONUMENT VALLEY NAVAJO TRIBAL PARK

COUNTY: NAVAJO   CITY: PAGE *n.c.*

DATE VISITED: WHO I WENT WITH:

RATING: ☆ ☆ ☆ ☆ ☆   WILL I RETURN?   YES / NO

Situated on the border between Arizona and Utah, Monument Valley stands out as one of the most iconic landscapes in the United States, gaining recognition from its appearances in classic Westerns and films like "Forrest Gump" (where Forrest decides to halt his run against the backdrop of Monument Valley's distinctive buttes). However, it deviates from the typical national park setup. Contrary to being a national park, Monument Valley is located on Navajo lands and functions as a tribal park managed by the Navajo people, who hold it in high regard as a sacred site.

Due to its sacred nature, access within the park is restricted. While visitors can independently drive through a 17-mile section, any further exploration requires the assistance of a Navajo guide. This unique aspect contributes to the distinctiveness of Monument Valley, providing an opportunity to learn about Navajo history, culture, and traditions directly from the tribal members who welcome you to their lands. To fully experience the beauty of the rock formations, it's advisable to stay overnight at the park's hotel, The View, allowing you to witness the sunrise, sunset, or both against the stunning backdrop of Monument Valley.

If you're pressed for time, take a self-guided tour by driving along the challenging 17-mile dirt road, passing the Mittens and Totem Pole formations. For those with more time, consider booking a tour with a Navajo guide either online or at the park's visitor center. These tours vary from 90 minutes to full-day adventures, and some guides may even offer traditional meals, entertainment, and the option for overnight stays in a Hogan.

However, the range of activities within the park is limited. There are no ranger-led programs, helicopter rides, or hot air balloon rides available. Additionally, activities such as mountain biking, off-roading, riding your own horse, or attempting to climb the monuments are strictly prohibited.

The Wildcat Trail is the sole trail that can be hiked without an escort in Monument Valley. If you wish to engage in any other activities, hiring a Navajo guide is necessary. It's advisable to book a hiking tour in advance, as there's no guarantee that a guide at the visitor center will be available or prepared to take you on a hike upon your arrival.

The Wildcat Trail, a 3.2-mile path starting at the campground next to The View Hotel, forms a loop around the Left Mitten before returning. Opt for a sunrise hike for a cooler experience, and enjoy the soft light that bathes the valley in ever-changing colors.

While the majority of visitors opt for a 4x4 tour to explore Monument Valley, there are alternative experiences available, such as horseback rides and photography tours.

Different Navajo guides or companies provide slightly varied tours, but the following are common options within the park:

Basic Scenic Tour: These tours, lasting approximately 90 minutes, follow the 17-mile route that visitors could navigate independently. Despite the ability to drive on their own, many individuals choose to pay the $65 to $75 per person fee for a guided tour. This is often due to a reluctance to subject their vehicles to the challenging road. Navajo guides not only spare your vehicle but also provide insights into the formation origins, identify filming locations, and share cultural knowledge.

Cultural Tour: Scheduled in the late afternoon, this tour builds upon the full valley tours, incorporating a cultural experience such as a weaving demonstration or live music. As the sun sets, the tour continues with a Navajo dinner, typically featuring puffy fry bread topped with meat and beans, followed by traditional dancing and music.

Time of Day Tour: Since light significantly impacts the color of the rock formations, several tours are centered around specific times of the day. While many prefer sunrise, others find sunset equally impressive, and some tours even take place during a night with a full moon. These tours are often led by photographers who understand how light affects the landscape.

Photography Tours: Conducted by Navajo photographers, these tours cater to various skill levels and camera types, including cell phones. However, it's advisable to check with the guide or company regarding equipment compatibility before committing.

Overnight Tours: For those seeking a nighttime experience, several companies offer the option to stay overnight in a Hogan, a traditional Navajo structure. These tours typically include dinner and breakfast.

A comprehensive list of guided tour operators can be found on the Navajo Nation Parks and Recreation website. It's not uncommon for individuals and smaller guide companies to temporarily suspend tour offerings, only to resume later, sometimes under a different company name. However, there are established companies in Monument Valley that consistently provide quality experiences for their guests, often with experienced guides.

Roy Black's Guided Tours, founded by a Navajo individual who grew up in Monument Valley, specializes in sharing Navajo culture. Their tours encompass 4x4 adventures and overnight stays in Hogans. Notably, Roy Black's Guided Tours stands out as one of the few companies in Monument Valley offering guided horseback tours ranging from 30 minutes to six hours.

Monument Valley Simpson's Trailhandler Tours boasts guides who possess an unparalleled knowledge of the valley, having been born and raised there. This company offers an extensive array of tours, including Hogan stays, cultural experiences, sunrise/sunset outings, and guided hikes.

Goulding's Lodge Tours, operating from Goulding's Lodge located 5 miles from the park's entrance, conducts partial and full-day tours of the valley. Their offerings also include sunrise, sunset, and full moon tours, along with tours of the areas surrounding Monument Valley Tribal Park.

Camping options are available both inside and near Monument Valley, providing diverse choices for visitors.

The View Campground: Positioned within the park, this campground offers dry RV and tent camping, providing unobstructed views of the Mittens. It's worth noting that the RV sites here do not come with hookups. Restrooms and showers are accessible for all campers.

Goulding's RV & Campgrounds: Situated five miles outside the park, close to Goulding's Lodge, this campground provides RV sites equipped with full hookups along with tent camping spaces. In addition to standard amenities such as restrooms and grills, the campground offers Wi-Fi access and the convenience of a laundromat, a store, and access to the indoor pool at the lodge.

Monument Valley KOA: Roughly 1.5 miles north of the park entrance, Monument Valley KOA offers full hookup RV and tent sites. Campsite amenities include a dog park, basic Wi-Fi, and the option to purchase firewood.

Accommodations within Monument Valley offer unique experiences, and staying inside the park at The View, aptly named for its balconies providing scenic views, is an option. However, this privilege comes at an additional cost, and dining choices are limited. Another nearby option is Goulding's Lodge, which also has limited food options. For a broader selection, Kayenta, located 25 miles south of the park's entrance, offers chain hotels and several decent restaurants, some featuring Navajo specialties.

The View Hotel: As the sole hotel within the park, The View Hotel, operated by the Navajo tribe, stands out for its remarkable Southwest views. With 96 rooms, each featuring a private balcony, guests can enjoy breathtaking scenery. The hotel's restaurant offers a taste of Navajo cuisine, and on-site amenities include a gift shop and the park's visitor center.

Goulding's Lodge: Initially a trading post and a hub for director John Ford and his crew during Monument Valley filming, Goulding's Lodge boasts 152 rooms, Wi-Fi, and cable TV. The lodge features a restaurant, indoor swimming pool, museum, theater, laundromat, and convenience store. If you plan on a guided tour through Monument Valley, Goulding's has its own tour company departing from the property.

Monument Valley is quite isolated, with the nearest major cities being Phoenix and Albuquerque, both approximately 320 miles away.

If you are traveling from Phoenix, you can take I-17 north to I-40, heading east towards the outskirts of Flagstaff. Follow the signs to connect with US-89 north, and drive around 70 miles before turning onto US-160, heading east towards Tuba City. Continue on this route to Kayenta, then turn north on US-163 and travel 25 miles to reach the entrance of the park.

For those coming from Albuquerque, take I-40 west to Gallup. From Gallup, head north on US-491. Just before leaving Gallup, take a left onto SR 264, heading west to Burnside. Once in Burnside, take US 191 north, driving 40 miles until you reach Indian Route 59. At the intersection of IR-59 and US-160, make a left turn. Proceed for 8 miles, then turn right onto US-163. Continue north for 25 miles to arrive at the park's entrance.

Tips:

1) The admission fee for the park is $20 per vehicle, accommodating up to four people. It's essential to note that this is not a national park, so America the Beautiful and other passes are not valid here.
2) Navajo Nation follows daylight saving time, unlike the rest of Arizona. When scheduling a tour, be sure to confirm whether daylight saving time is in effect and adjust your plans accordingly.
3) Drones, weapons, and alcohol are strictly prohibited on Navajo land. Visitors should adhere to these guidelines to ensure a respectful and safe experience.
4) Due to the sacred nature of the monuments, climbing on them is strictly prohibited. Visitors are expected to show reverence for these landmarks and refrain from engaging in any activities that could be considered disrespectful.

MT. LEMMON SCENIC BYWAY

COUNTY: PIMA CITY: TUCSON *n.c.*

DATE VISITED: WHO I WENT WITH:

RATING: ☆ ☆ ☆ ☆ ☆ WILL I RETURN? YES / NO

The Mount Lemmon Scenic Byway, known as the Catalina Highway or the Sky Islands Scenic Byway, begins at the northeast edge of Tucson and ascends 27 miles to the summit of Mount Lemmon, standing at an elevation of 9,157 feet. This journey involves a vertical ascent of over 6,000 feet, akin to traveling from the Sonoran desert floor to the coniferous forests of Canada, traversing various ecosystems en route. The majority of the route passes through the Coronado National Forest, offering numerous campgrounds and trailheads, providing opportunities for additional adventures in diverse climate zones. Towards the top, you'll encounter Mount Lemmon Ski Valley, the southernmost ski area in the country, and the charming town of Summerhaven, home to the famed Cookie Cabin and its noteworthy dinner-plate-sized cookies.

Commencing at Tanque Verde Road in Tucson, the Catalina Highway swiftly climbs through the high Sonoran desert, surrounded by increasing numbers of "hoodoos" – tall, thin spires of weathered rock. Each turn unfolds more majestic views and vibrant rock formations. Windy Point, located approximately halfway, stands out as a highlight with its expansive parking area, restrooms, diverse trail options, and panoramic views of valleys and mountains. While Windy Point may draw crowds, the plethora of vantage points ensures solitude and ample photo opportunities. Continuing the ascent, the vegetation transforms, eventually resembling a mixed conifer forest more commonly associated with the Pacific Northwest than Arizona. A Forest Service ranger station along the route provides helpful recommendations for trails and camping.

The byway concludes in the shadow of Mount Lemmon at the Marshall Gulch picnic area, also serving as a trailhead for hiking enthusiasts. It's recommended to time the descent to catch the sunset at Windy Point, offering a picturesque view, followed by the city lights of Tucson at the last few turnouts before returning to the valley floor. This adventure caters to a range of interests, from geology and photography to mountain biking or hiking.

MUSICAL INSTRUMENT MUSEUM

COUNTY: MARICOPA   CITY: PHOENIX

DATE VISITED: WHO I WENT WITH:

RATING: ☆ ☆ ☆ ☆ ☆   WILL I RETURN? YES / NO

One of the premier music-related museums globally and a top-notch museum nationally, this affiliate of the Smithsonian is a must-visit when in Phoenix. Featuring a collection of 7,000 to 8,000 musical instruments from 200 countries and territories worldwide, the Musical Instrument Museum (MIM) stands out for more than just its extensive exhibits. At MIM, visitors not only observe musical instruments but also listen to them being played through wireless headsets near each exhibit. Additionally, videos showcase artisans crafting the instruments and musicians demonstrating their use.

Exploring the two-story, 200,000-square-foot building typically takes three to four hours for most visitors. Apart from the galleries, MIM offers amenities such as an onsite restaurant, a 300-seat theater, and a STEM Gallery delving into the intersections of music, science, technology, and mathematics. The museum also hosts various family-friendly events throughout the year, including Experience India and Celebrate Bluegrass.

Established in April 2010, MIM was initiated by Robert J. Ulrich, the former CEO and chairman emeritus of Target Corporation. Ulrich, an art and museum enthusiast, initially contemplated opening an art museum close to his residence in the Valley. However, after visiting the Musical Instruments Museum in Brussels, Belgium, he reconsidered. Recognizing that most musical instrument museums primarily focused on classical Western instruments, he abandoned his plans for an art museum and instead opted for one dedicated to everyday musical instruments.

A team of five curators collaborated with ethnomusicologists, organologists, and other field experts to curate the museum's collection of 13,600 instruments based on their historical, artistic, and cultural significance, with over half of them displayed for visitors. The exhibited instruments may vary over time, and curators continually augment the collection, particularly with folk and tribal instruments.

Considerable thought went into the architecture and design of the building. Its sandstone walls are designed to evoke the topography of the Southwest, with raised shapes resembling musical notes. The windows, when viewed from a distance, resemble piano keys, and the rotunda's curve inside mimics the lines of a grand piano. Observing the inlaid world map in the rotunda is worthwhile— the stones used are sourced from the regions they represent.

Music enthusiasts could easily lose themselves in the Geographic Galleries for hours, but restricting your visit to just the collections means missing out on some of the museum's most outstanding exhibits. It's advisable to manage your time wisely to ensure you get the full experience during your visit.

Geographic Galleries: Serving as the nucleus of the museum, these five galleries individually spotlight major world regions—Africa and the Middle East, Asia and Oceana, Europe, Latin America and the Caribbean, and the United States and Canada. Noteworthy attractions include the world's largest playable sousaphone, traditional attire from the regions, and special displays featuring iconic American musical instrument manufacturers like Martin, Steinway, and locally-based Fender.

Experience Gallery: This interactive space allows visitors to play instruments similar to those on display, such as the West African djembe drum and Peruvian harp. There's even a chance to strike a massive gong. While kids are particularly drawn to this area, adults are also encouraged to try their hand at playing.

Artist Gallery: Witness the instruments employed by your favorite musicians. Although exhibits change regularly, past showcases have featured instruments used by Johnny Cash, Carlos Santana, Taylor Swift, Maroon 5, John Lennon, and Toby Keith.

Mechanical Music Gallery: Home to musical instruments that "play themselves," this gallery includes player pianos, mechanical zithers, and cylinder music boxes.

Collier STEM Gallery: Delve into the intersections of music, science, technology, engineering, and mathematics through exhibits covering topics like how sound is produced, the human ear, and related subjects.

Conservation Lab: A sizable viewing window provides a glimpse into how experts undertake the repair, maintenance, and preservation of the collection.

Target Gallery: Serving as an exhibition space, this gallery hosts traveling shows and special engagements. Please note that there is an additional charge for entry to the Target Gallery.

MIM provides various tour options, including group tours, and occasionally offers packages.

Free Orientation Tour: This complimentary tour, lasting 30 to 45 minutes, gives an overview of three Geographic Galleries. Reservations are not required for groups of fewer than 10 people. Simply arrive on Monday or Friday at 2 p.m., or on every Saturday or Sunday at 11 a.m. or 2 p.m.

VIP Tour Add-On: This exclusive behind-the-scenes tour offers insights into exhibit creation, behind-the-scenes activities at the MIM Music Theater, and more. Reservations must be made in advance, and there is an additional charge of $7 per person on top of the general admission fee. Tours are limited to three to five people.

Balloons and Tunes Package: This package begins early with a hot air balloon ride over the Sonoran Desert and continues with a visit to MIM.

MIM organizes concerts in its Music Theater, hosts various special events throughout the year, and provides classes suitable for all age groups.

MIM Music Theater: This cozy venue, accommodating 300 seats, showcases around 200 artists annually, with many making their debut performances in Arizona. Concert tickets can be purchased either online or at the box office situated in the museum's main lobby.

Signature Events: These weekend-long programs, designed for families, celebrate diverse cultures, music genres, and musical icons. They feature live music, dance performances, hands-on activities, curator talks, and more. Admission to signature events is complimentary with a paid museum admission. Typically, MIM hosts one signature event per month.

Programs: MIM offers several programs tailored for children. "Mini Music Makers" introduces the youngest, aged 0 to 5, to music through songs, dance, and playing instruments. "Musical Adventures," designed for kids aged 6 to 10, explores various cultures. "Junior Museum Guides" is a program that prepares students in grades 6 through 12 to become museum guides.

The museum operates daily from 9 a.m. to 5 p.m., with the exception of Thanksgiving. On Christmas Day, it opens an hour later at 10 a.m. Tickets can be purchased in advance online or at guest services upon arrival, and admission to special exhibitions and concerts requires separate ticket purchases.

MIM tends to experience its peak attendance on weekday mornings during the school year when students visit on field trips. However, weekends, especially during holidays or special events, can also be bustling. It is advisable to plan your visit accordingly.

While cameras are allowed, backpacks, food, and beverages are not permitted inside. However, you can purchase food and drinks at Café Allegro.

Situated in North Phoenix just off the Loop 101, MIM is easily accessible. If driving from downtown Phoenix, take the Piestewa Freeway (SR 51) north to the Loop 101, then head east to Tatum Boulevard. Turn right on Tatum and proceed one block to East Mayo Boulevard. MIM is located at the corner of Tatum and East Mayo boulevards, offering ample free parking.

For visitors from the East Valley, head to US 60 and travel north on the Loop 101 to Tatum Boulevard. From the West Valley, take the I-10 to the Loop 101, and head north to Tatum Boulevard.

Public transportation is also an option. The most direct route is likely taking the Valley

Metro Light Rail to the 44th Street station and then boarding Bus 44. Although the journey from the station to MIM takes about an hour and includes 53 stops, the bus conveniently stops at the corner of Tatum and East Mayo boulevards where the museum is located.

MYSTERY CASTLE

COUNTY: MARICOPA   CITY: PHOENIX

DATE VISITED:	WHO I WENT WITH:

RATING: ☆ ☆ ☆ ☆ ☆   WILL I RETURN? YES / NO

Mystery Castle stands as a notable Point Of Pride in Phoenix, acknowledged by the Phoenix Pride Commission. The castle was constructed by Boyce Luther Gulley, who, around 1927, left his wife and daughter in Seattle upon discovering he had tuberculosis. Upon arriving in Phoenix, he commenced the construction of a "castle" that he had once promised to his young daughter during their moments of building sand castles on a beach. Mary Lou Gulley was just a toddler when her father departed abruptly and never returned.

Boyce Gulley outlived his initial expectations, devoting 15 years to constructing his envisioned residence. Intriguingly, he did not succumb to tuberculosis as anticipated. Before his passing, Boyce Gulley left specific instructions for his wife and daughter, who inherited the Phoenix house, emphasizing that a trap door within the dwelling should remain unopened for two years following his demise. Complying with his wishes, his wife and daughter refrained from opening the trap door for the designated period. Positioned in a room whimsically labeled "purgatory" (nestled between the chapel and the bar), the trap door's contents remained a mystery until 1948 when LIFE Magazine visited the Gulley home for a feature on Mystery Castle. The unveiling of the trap door's secrets is part of the tour experience.

While the tour welcomes children, and there are minimal restrictions on touching various items (which abound in the house), youngsters might not find as much fascination in the eccentrically constructed home as adults do. During visits, it was observed that children seemed more inclined to engage in activities like throwing rocks in the yard rather than exploring the interior of the house.

For numerous years, Boyce Gulley's daughter, Mary Lou, personally greeted tour participants within the primary section of the Mystery Castle. While her bedroom remained off-limits, visitors could explore her kitchen and other rooms in the main living area. Although the architectural wonder of Mystery Castle captivated many, conversing with Mary Lou often emerged as the tour's most captivating aspect. As Mary Lou's health declined, tours persisted with her remaining in the background.

Mary Lou Gulley's mother passed away in 1970. In November 2010, Mary Lou Gulley passed away, yet the foundation responsible for overseeing the historical property continues to conduct tours. Mystery Castle holds a place on the Phoenix Historic Property Register, ensuring its preservation even in the absence of Mary Lou Gulley. The property stands as a remarkable testament to the ingenuity of its architect and builder, who crafted an 8,000 square foot home on 40 acres using discarded items, remnants, personal belongings, donations, and whatever else he could acquire or negotiate for.

Today, the property spans just over 7 acres, nestled at the base of South Mountain.

Mystery Castle is situated on the northern side of South Mountain, near the location of the former town dump. Boyce Gulley utilized salvaged materials, auto parts, junk, and various artifacts sourced from the Southwest and Mexico to construct his home. The house boasts a total of 13 fireplaces, each with distinctive features such as special bricks on the exterior.

In the mid-2000s, Mystery Castle was a sought-after venue for weddings, but Mary Lou Gulley, in charge at the time, decided to discontinue hosting weddings on the premises. The chapel room, featuring a wedding altar, stands as a reminder of its past popularity for such events.

Following Boyce Gulley's passing, his wife and daughter were informed about the house by a Phoenix-based attorney and subsequently relocated to Phoenix to inhabit it. At that time, Mary Lou Gulley was a teenager.

The castle comprises 18 rooms, featuring items associated with well-known names such as original Frank Lloyd Wright furniture, John Wayne memorabilia in the bar, and furniture donated by Barry Goldwater for the project.

Upon exploring the house, visitors will encounter an eclectic array of items, including Navajo baskets, pet rocks, dolls, cat statues, paintings, antiques, and more. Much of this collection was amassed by Mary Lou during her years of residence. While some items hold significant value, others may not, and the exposure to numerous tours over the years has contributed to a worn appearance in the decor.

To visit the house, there is an admission fee, which is imposed to support the maintenance of both the property and the house.

The guided tour typically lasts about an hour, but once it concludes, visitors are free to explore the house at their own pace. The story behind Mystery Castle is extensive and captivating.

The size of tour groups varies, ranging from a single person to around 40 individuals. Larger tours can pose challenges for movement, and since reservations are not accepted, the composition of each group is unpredictable. Those who prefer a less crowded experience may find weekdays more suitable than weekends.

A crucial note is that the parking lot is unpaved, rocky, and uneven. The house and surrounding walkways present similar conditions, featuring steep, uneven steps and surfaces that lack levelness. Unfortunately, Mystery Castle is not wheelchair accessible, and individuals with walking difficulties or balance issues may find the terrain uncomfortable.

Furthermore, it's important to be aware that the only restroom available is a porta-potty located in the parking lot, and there are no provisions for water or any other food or beverages on-site. Visitors are welcome to bring their own water.

Mystery Castle operates from early October to the end of May. However, contacting them by phone to confirm its current status is advised. It's worth noting that while calling, it may be unlikely for someone to answer or return your call if a message is left.

For those seeking directions to Mystery Castle, travel south on 7th Street. Approximately two miles south of Baseline Rd., you'll encounter a roundabout. Navigate around it to head east (left) on Mineral Rd. The road leads directly to the parking lot, as it is a dead end.

NORTH KAIBAB TRAIL

COUNTY: COCONINO   CITY: JACOB LAKE *n.c.*

DATE VISITED: WHO I WENT WITH:

RATING: ☆ ☆ ☆ ☆ ☆   WILL I RETURN?   YES / NO

The North Kaibab Trail, situated in the Grand Canyon National Park, is the least frequented yet the most demanding among the three established trails. With its trailhead almost a thousand feet higher than the South Rim trails, hikers on the North Kaibab Trail traverse through various ecosystems spanning the distance between Canada and Mexico. As they start their descent, the rim offers a glimpse of the expansive Bright Angel Canyon, framed by fir trees, aspen, ferns, and wildflowers. The trail is ingeniously carved into the Redwall Limestone cliffs, resembling half-tunnel sections cut directly from solid rock.

Further down the trail, the ecology evolves, presenting hikers with views of the canyon walls surrounded by a mix of riparian and desert vegetation. Noteworthy side trips along the way include Roaring Springs and Ribbon Falls, providing a refreshing contrast to the often hot conditions on the main trail. Constructed during the 1920s to match the quality and slope of the South Kaibab Trail, the present-day North Kaibab Trail replaced an older route notorious for crossing Bright Angel Creek 94 times (the current trail only crosses it 6 times). Despite its masterful construction and maintenance, the North Kaibab Trail poses challenges from start to finish, and hikers should not be misled by its apparent ease and convenience.

Drinkable water is accessible at various points along the trail, including the trailhead, Supai Tunnel, Roaring Springs, the Manzanita Rest Area, Cottonwood Campground, and Bright Angel Campground. However, it's important to note that all these water sources, except for Bright Angel Campground, are available seasonally and are turned off in the fall. The specific dates vary, and the shutdown of each station depends on temperature conditions; typically, the rim and Supai Tunnel are the first to be turned off. It's crucial to be aware that pipeline breaks due to erosion can occur randomly, so the availability of potable water should be considered a bonus rather than a guarantee. Before descending, check the trailhead signage, and always carry an alternative and lightweight water treatment method.

Camping freely along the North Kaibab Trail is not allowed. Visitors are required to camp in designated campgrounds: Cottonwood Campground (CCG), located approximately 7 miles from the North Kaibab trailhead near the trail's midpoint, or Bright Angel Campground (CBG), situated right next to the Colorado River at the bottom of the canyon and 14 miles from the North Kaibab trailhead.

The trailhead for the North Kaibab Trail is situated 41 miles south of Jacob Lake on Highway 67, specifically 1.5 miles north of Grand Canyon Lodge. There is a small parking area available, but spaces are limited. For transportation, individuals can opt for the

Grand Canyon Lodge shuttle service, which operates twice each morning (details regarding times and fares can be obtained at the lodge). Alternatively, if staying at North Rim Campground, the trailhead is just a half-mile walk away.

Hikers embarking on a rim-to-rim hike with only one vehicle often rely on the private Trans-Canyon Shuttle (928-638-2820). This shuttle service operates daily from May 15 to October 15, departing from the North Rim around 6 a.m. and departing from the South Rim around 1 p.m. It's worth noting that North Rim park facilities, including the lodge, store, and gas station, close on October 15. However, Highway 67 remains open to vehicle traffic until winter conditions make access impossible. While road closure can happen anytime after October 15, the highway often stays open into November. Once closed, Highway 67 remains inaccessible until May 15, and reaching the trailhead by vehicle before that date is not possible.

Similar to the Bright Angel Trail rather than the South Kaibab Trail, the North Kaibab Trail initiates its descent steeply down the head of a valley using numerous switchbacks. After passing through lush greenery and enjoying breathtaking views from the trailhead, hikers reach the distinctive Supai Tunnel. At this location, hikers can find potable water (available from mid-May to mid-October) and pit toilets, although there is no emergency phone. The trail continues with switchbacks leading to the massive cliffs of Redwall Limestone, where, in many sections, the trail is carved into the cliff like a half tunnel. The Redwall section is truly awe-inspiring, combining fantastic exposure and views with a sense of the era when engineering marvels were a commonplace occurrence.

As the trail's descent brings hikers to the flatter bottom of Bright Angel Canyon, a recommended side trip is Roaring Springs. This location features water gushing directly out of the cliffs, cascading over moss and fern to create Bright Angel Creek, which accompanies hikers all the way to the Colorado River. Roaring Springs serves as a significant water source, supplying drinking water to every visitor and resident within Grand Canyon National Park. The water is transported to the South Rim through a pipeline buried beneath the North Kaibab Trail, installed between 1965 and 1970. An intriguing sight is the pipeline stretching across the Colorado River on the underside of the Bright Angel Trail's Silver Bridge.

Around mile 5.4, an unexpected dwelling comes into sight, formerly known as the Pumphouse Residence or the Aiken Residence. For decades, this house was inhabited by the artist and park employee Bruce Aiken, who lived, painted, and worked there. In earlier years, fortunate hikers could enjoy a refreshing cup of lemonade from one of the Aiken kids, raised at the bottom of the Grand Canyon. The Pumphouse has now been automated, transforming the renowned house into a ranger station. Close to the house, hikers can access the Manzanita Rest Area, offering amenities such as access to Bright Angel Creek, a toilet, drinking water, and shaded benches.

Passing the old Aiken Residence is a welcome indication for descending backpackers, as it signifies the approach to Cottonwood Campground. Those lucky enough to spend the night at Cottonwood Campground will have the opportunity to explore a picturesque oasis located 1.6 miles downstream: Ribbon Falls, a hidden gem of the North Kaibab Trail. Situated in a grotto on the west side of Bright Angel Creek, reaching Ribbon Falls is a short but highly rewarding side trip. Hikers caught in the midday heat might consider taking a break here from 10 a.m. to 4 p.m.

Between Cottonwood Campground and Bright Angel Campground, the trail enters the Inner Gorge, a narrow canyon within the canyon. Here, the trail is enclosed on both sides by 1.7 billion-year-old Vishnu Schist. The contact between the top of the Vishnu Schist and the overlying Tapeats Sandstone marks the Great Unconformity, representing a geological gap of over 1 billion years. Although the trail in this section is not challenging in terms of elevation, it's crucial to note that it becomes particularly perilous during the summer months. Due to the entire 7.2-mile stretch being at a low elevation, temperatures soar from early morning to late afternoon. The black rock gorge through which the trail passes turns into an oven-like environment, comparable to walking through a parking lot in Phoenix or Las Vegas during summertime. It is advisable to plan to reach Bright Angel Campground before ten in the morning to avoid the intense heat.

The Grand Canyon is, first and foremost, a place characterized by extremes. Adapting precautions based on seasonal changes in trail conditions is essential. In the deep winter months, the upper part of the trail in Roaring Springs Canyon may be covered in ice and consistently snowbound. Hikers on the North Rim must be ready for severe winter weather conditions. As for the warmer months, which can commence as early as May and extend through September, it is crucial for hikers to exercise discipline by starting their hike well before dawn or after 3 p.m. The key to success and enjoyment largely relies on thorough planning and preparation, emphasizing the principles of "Plan Ahead and Prepare" (Leave No Trace). Ensuring success in the summer may be as straightforward as avoiding the trail and staying out of the sun between 10 a.m. and 4 p.m. Attempting to hike the entire North Kaibab Trail in a single day is not advisable, especially during summer, as it becomes nearly impossible to avoid the intense heat during the day.

O.K. CORRAL

COUNTY: COCHISE   CITY: TOMBSTONE

DATE VISITED: _____   WHO I WENT WITH: _____

RATING: ☆ ☆ ☆ ☆ ☆   WILL I RETURN?   YES / NO

Explore the renowned site of the legendary Gunfight at the O.K. Corral in the historic town of Tombstone. Witness daily reenactments of the thrilling showdown featuring Wyatt Earp, Doc Holliday, Virgil and Morgan Earp, as well as the Clantons and McLaurys. Stand at the very spot where the Gunfight unfolded and marvel at life-sized animated figures of the gunfighters strategically placed according to Wyatt Earp's map. Discover Doc Holliday's room and delve into five historical museum displays. Immerse yourself in over 100 captivating photos capturing the essence of 1880s Tombstone and Apache Geronimo, taken by Tombstone photographer C.S. Fly. Observe the 1880s blacksmith at work in the Corral. Open daily from 9 a.m. to 5 p.m. (Closed on Christmas Day and Thanksgiving). Admission fee applies, with free entry for kids under 6.

The origin of this tale can be traced back to Ed Schieffelin, a tall, bearded prospector facing tough times, who arrived at Camp Huachuca in Arizona in 1877. Despite warnings that he would only find his tombstone in the hills across the San Pedro Valley, Schieffelin persisted in his search for ore. After several months, he discovered silver ledges and named his first claim Tombstone, a retort in today's terms.

By 1881, Tombstone, Arizona, had burgeoned into the largest city between St. Louis and San Francisco. Despite its seemingly cosmopolitan amenities like a bowling alley and ice cream parlor, the town was entrenched in a violent era. The body count was so high that it was famously quipped, "Tombstone had a man for breakfast every morning."

On October 26, 1881, the town witnessed a significant event as a longstanding feud erupted in a narrow vacant lot near the O.K. Corral. When the dust settled, three men lay dead, and three more were wounded.

On that snowy October day, Tombstone City Marshal Virgil Earp designated his brothers, Wyatt and Morgan Earp, along with Doc Holliday, as deputy city marshals. Draped in black frock coats, with Holliday concealing a sawed-off shotgun beneath, they confidently traversed the streets to confront a group of ranchers and rustlers, including Ike and Billy Clanton, Frank and Tom McLaury, and Billy Claiborne. Ostensibly, the lawmen's mission was to disarm members of the Cowboys, a loose federation of outlaws, as firearms were prohibited in town. Tensions had been escalating between the two factions for months.

The confrontation unfolded in a vacant lot approximately 100 feet west of the back entrance to the O.K. Corral. Verbal exchanges took place, and the debate still rages on about who fired the first shot. Ike Clanton and Billy Claiborne hastily fled as the fight erupted. The violence quickly spilled into Fremont Street, now State Route 80. When the smoke cleared, the McLaury brothers and Billy Clanton lay dead, while Virgil, Morgan, and Holliday sustained injuries. Remarkably, Wyatt emerged unharmed. The iconic shootout of the American West, known as the Gunfight at the O.K. Corral, concluded in a mere 30 seconds.

Just four days following the infamous gunfight, Ike Clanton brought forth murder charges against the Earps and Holliday. Justice of the Peace Wells Spicer organized a preliminary hearing to assess whether there was sufficient evidence for a trial. Despite a month of testimonies and a lineup of witnesses, Justice Spicer determined that no laws had been violated.

However, this resolution did little to quell the ongoing conflict. Two months later, Virgil fell victim to an ambush, suffering serious injuries. Shortly thereafter, Morgan met his demise with a shot to the back. With no one held accountable for these crimes, Wyatt Earp decided to take matters into his own hands. Alongside a few companions, he embarked on a vengeful journey known as the Vendetta Ride, relentlessly pursuing and eliminating those he believed were responsible. Following this bloody pursuit, Wyatt departed the Arizona Territory.

A visit to Tombstone today wouldn't be complete without a stop at the O.K. Corral. The property has been expanded to include the exact location where the famous gunfight unfolded. Make sure to allocate enough time for exploring the blacksmith shop, stables, and C.S. Fly's Photo Gallery. The re-enactment of the shootout occurs daily at 11 a.m., noon, 2 p.m., and 3:30 p.m., with each show lasting 30 minutes—an intriguing skit that concludes with a well-staged spectacle of chaos. Following the performance, the gunfighters are more than willing to pose for photographs.

To reach the O.K. Corral from central Phoenix, head east on Interstate 10, passing Tucson, until you reach Benson. Then, go south on State Route 80 (at Exit 303) to reach Tombstone. You'll find the O.K. Corral at 326 E. Allen St.

OAK CREEK CANYON

COUNTY: YAVAPAI   CITY: SEDONA   *n.c.*

DATE VISITED: WHO I WENT WITH:

RATING: ☆ ☆ ☆ ☆ ☆   WILL I RETURN?   YES / NO

Oak Creek Canyon stands as a breathtaking gorge etched into the periphery of the Mogollon Rim on the Colorado Plateau, tracing the path of the Oak Creek Fault. The geological narrative of this region unfolds vividly as tectonic forces maneuvered the land on either side of the fault, and subsequent erosion by Oak Creek sculpted a remarkable canyon.

Stretching approximately 12 miles, the Canyon is a testament to the perpetual flow of Oak Creek, sustaining plant life and wildlife, and offering opportunities for fishing and swimming. As Oak Creek continues its journey, it winds through Sedona, Arizona, ultimately joining forces with the Verde River southeast of Cottonwood, Arizona.

The Canyon's depth varies from 800 to 2000 feet, featuring trails that facilitate exploration from the Canyon's floor up to the 6500-foot eastern rim and 7200-foot western rim. Some of these trails trace the historic routes used by early settlers of Oak Creek Canyon to access the plateau's summit in the days predating the construction of roads. On the western side, trails lead into the Red Rock-Secret Mountain Wilderness, adding another dimension to the natural beauty of the area.

The lush, green Oak Creek Canyon, adorned with a perennially flowing stream, creates a striking juxtaposition against the iconic red rocks of Sedona and the canyon's breathtaking, multicolored cliffs that tower above the forested landscape. In the fall, the vibrant red foliage adds a stunning touch to the scenery. A well-established network of trails, ranging from easy to challenging, offers access to the pristine wilderness areas. The natural water chutes at Slide Rock State Park have captivated generations of families, while the leisurely stroll along the West Fork of Oak Creek is a must-see for everyone.

Around 65 million years ago, amid a significant period of mountain-building activity, the movement along the Oak Creek Fault led to an uplift of the east side of what we now know as Oak Creek Canyon by approximately 600 feet. The exposed upper rock layers gradually eroded until a balance was restored, aligning the eastern and western sides of the fault.

Over the course of several million more years, a canyon took shape. Streams, initially carrying gravel and later lava, entered the canyon from the north. About six million years ago, the fault reactivated, and the contemporary Oak Creek Canyon began to take form. This time, the fault played a role in causing the eastern rim of the Canyon to descend by roughly 700 feet compared to the western rim.

For a comprehensive view of the Canyon's captivating geological evolution, Oak Creek Vista stands out as one of the prime locations. Positioned at the top of the Canyon, the Vista offers a panoramic perspective where the noticeable drop on the eastern side can be easily observed.

To reach Oak Creek Canyon, travelers can take Highway AZ-89a, heading north from Sedona and traversing the entire 16-mile canyon. The highway then navigates through switchbacks, leading out of the canyon and eventually reaching Flagstaff. Oak Creek Vista, situated at the top of the switchbacks, provides unparalleled views into the canyon. The North Gateway Visitor Center, located at the vista turnout, serves as a convenient starting point for those entering from Flagstaff.

Oak Creek Canyon falls within the boundaries of Coconino National Forest, and parking within the canyon requires a Red Rock Pass, available at any visitor center. Additional fees are applicable for camping. Oak Creek is home to trout, making fishing a popular activity in the canyon.

Visitor Centers:

1) South Gateway Visitor Center: Situated in the Village of Oak Creek, south of Sedona along AZ-179. Contact: 928-284-5324.
2) Sedona Oak Creek Chamber of Commerce: Located in uptown Sedona near the junction of AZ-179 and AZ-89a. Address: 331 Forest Rd., Sedona, AZ 86336.
3) North Gateway Visitor Center: Found at the northern end of Oak Creek Canyon, on AZ-89a near Flagstaff. Positioned within the Oak Creek Vista (the overlook at the top of the switch-backs entering the canyon).
4) Additionally, there is the Oak Creek Watershed Council, serving as a public service task force that combines valuable visitor information with a focus on environmental issues.

OATMAN GHOST TOWN

COUNTY: MOHAVE   CITY: OATMAN

DATE VISITED: _____   WHO I WENT WITH: _____

RATING: ☆ ☆ ☆ ☆ ☆   WILL I RETURN? YES / NO

Oatman stands as a boom town with roots dating back to the 1860s. The discovery of a lucrative ore body in 1915 triggered a gold rush that spanned a decade. During this period, the town attracted miners and prospectors from various regions, flourishing with a population of over 3,500 residents. However, in 1924, the primary mine in the town ceased operations, leading to a decline in activity. Although some mining persisted until 1944, the last mines eventually closed.

In the present day, Oatman thrives as a tourist destination centered around the allure of wild west nostalgia and burros. Visitors can relish in the ambiance of a wild west experience, complete with roaming donkeys, wooden sidewalks, staged gunfights, distinctive souvenir shops, and engaging annual events. Conveniently located within an easy drive from Laughlin, Nevada, or Bullhead City, Arizona, Oatman Ghost Town offers a delightful destination for a day of enjoyment.

Upon entering Oatman Ghost Town, the ubiquitous presence of wild burros captures your attention. Descendants of pack animals used by prospectors in the 1800s, these wild burros have found a home in Oatman, Arizona. While most of them are amicable, feeding them is discouraged, and caution is advised as they have been known to nip.

Oatman Ghost Town, renowned for its wild west ambiance, offers a unique experience with staged shootouts right in the middle of the street. Scheduled at noon and 3:30 pm on most days, these entertaining cowboy gunfights are a highlight not to be missed. Although the shows are free, the actors collect donations for local charities. Be cautious and avoid getting in the way of these dedicated cowboys who take their roles seriously.

Along Main Street, the Glory Hole Museum stands as a treasure trove of antiques, memorabilia, and artifacts from Oatman's rich history. The exhibits include a bed from the ghost town's red-light district, desks from the Oatman School, bottles, and mining equipment. Originally built in 1915, the museum building served as the town's drugstore.

During the bustling boomtown era, Oatman's streets were adorned with saloons. Today, the town boasts quirky souvenir stores, each with peculiar and amusing names such as Jackass Junction, Outlaw Willies, The Classy Ass, Oatman General Store, Yellow Hammers Place, Bucktooth Burro, Jack Ass Treasures, Fast Fannys, and Saving Your Ass. Every store is stocked with souvenir T-shirts, and an insider tip suggests that the shirts become more affordable the further up the main street you venture.

One of Oatman's notable attractions is the historic 1902 Oatman Hotel. Apart from offering delicious buffalo burgers, the hotel is famous for hosting the honeymoon of renowned actors Clark Gable and Carole Lombard in 1939, elevating the hotel's status. The honeymoon suite, located on the second floor, is accessible for viewing through a window in the door. Additionally, there's a sizable gift shop on the upper level. Visitors are encouraged to leave their mark by signing a dollar bill and affixing it to the bar's ceiling.

For a memorable experience, the "Making Memories" photo studio allows visitors to dress up as cowboys or cowgirls. With a selection of Western outfits and backgrounds, you can obtain an Old Time Photo from this studio. Adding a unique touch, if you ever find yourself in sudden need of getting married, the owners are licensed ministers and can officiate your union. The studio is located at 88 Main Street, Oatman, AZ.

The primary thoroughfare in the town is Oatman Road, which traces the historic Route 66. This two-lane highway spans a 42-mile stretch, ascending Sitgreaves Pass at 3,550 feet and meandering through the stunning Arizona desert. An essential stop along Route 66 is Cool Springs Station, once a service station and now repurposed into a Route 66 museum. Constructed in the 1920s, the site originally featured a gas station, cabins, and a restaurant.

For those with a hankering for southwestern comfort cuisine, Oatman provides a selection of eateries to satisfy your cravings. The Olive Oatman Restaurant is a great choice for delicious chili and peach fry bread. If you have a sweet tooth, the Oatman Candy Shop is the place to be for prickly pear candy. For a laid-back drink visit, Judy's Saloon and the Oatman Hotel serve breakfast and lunch.

Situated on historic Route 66, Oatman Ghost Town is conveniently located 25 miles from Needles, California, 30 miles from Laughlin, Nevada, and 28 miles from Kingman, Arizona.

COUNTY: APACHE, COCONINO, MOHAVE, NAVAJO	CITY: PAGE *n.c.*

DATE VISITED:	WHO I WENT WITH:

RATING: ☆ ☆ ☆ ☆ ☆	WILL I RETURN? YES / NO

The Old Spanish National Historic Trail, often referred to as the "longest, most winding, and challenging pack mule route in American history," traverses the states of New Mexico, Colorado, Arizona, Utah, Nevada, and California. This trail, which served as a crucial land route in 19th-century Mexico connecting Tierra Adentro (New Mexico) to California, unfolds a historical narrative of New Mexican traders. Encompassing diverse landscapes such as deserts, mountains, and lakes, the Old Spanish National Historic Trail spans across six Western states.

Embark on a journey through the Southwest along the Old Spanish National Historic Trail, extending from Santa Fe to Los Angeles, to immerse yourself in a rich tapestry of history, culture, and breathtaking scenery. The economic prospects of transporting New Mexico serapes and woolen goods to Los Angeles, along with managing California-bred horses and mules back to Santa Fe, motivated traders. The challenge lay in finding a practical overland route through the remote deserts and mountains of Mexico's northern frontier. Antonio Armijo, a visionary Mexican trader, displayed the courage to lead the inaugural commercial caravan from Abiqui, New Mexico, to Los Angeles in 1829.

Over the subsequent two decades, both Mexican and American traders followed variations of Armijo's route, engaging in trade with indigenous tribes along the way. The Old Spanish Trail emerged as a network, blending indigenous footpaths, early trade and exploration routes, and horse and mule paths. Santa Fe became the focal point of the continental trade network connecting Mexican and U.S. markets. This network comprised not only the Old Spanish Trail but also the Santa Fe Trail and El Camino Real de Tierra Adentro. With the United States gaining control of the Southwest in 1848, alternative routes to California surfaced, leading to a sharp decline in the use of the Old Spanish Trail.

Apart from the Old Spanish Trail, there were two additional trails that converged in Santa Fe. El Camino Real de Tierra Adentro, known as the Royal Road to the Interior Lands, served as a wagon road connecting Mexico City to Santa Fe. The Santa Fe Trail, on the other hand, was a wagon route cutting across the plains, establishing a link between Santa Fe and Missouri.

However, by 1869, a railway route had been established, connecting the Midwest plains to San Francisco Bay. Parts of the Old Spanish Trail transformed into wagon roads for local travel, marking the conclusion of the era of cross-country mule caravans on the Old Spanish Trail.

The administration of the trail is a collaborative effort between the Bureau of Land

Management and the National Park Service, both aiming to promote preservation and public use. These federal agencies closely cooperate with the Old Spanish Trail Association, American Indian tribes, state, county, and municipal governmental bodies, private landowners, nonprofit organizations, and various other stakeholders.

Identifying remnants of the trail in today's landscape proves challenging. The majority of the Old Spanish Trail routes have succumbed to the forces of nature or undergone alterations due to subsequent human activities. Nevertheless, a few of the landmarks that once served as guides for trail travelers are still visible today.

63 ORGAN PIPE CACTUS NATIONAL MONUMENT

COUNTY: PIMA   CITY: AJO *n.c.*

DATE VISITED: WHO I WENT WITH:

RATING: ☆ ☆ ☆ ☆ ☆   WILL I RETURN?   YES / NO

Organ Pipe Cactus National Monument serves as a showcase for the breathtaking Sonoran Desert. The monument highlights a diverse range of plant and animal life, a rich cultural history, a delightful assortment of hiking trails, and opportunities to explore the rugged beauty of this captivating region in the United States. Approximately 150,000 visitors from across the globe visit this national monument each year. Located in southwestern Arizona near the Mexican border, the nearest major city is Tucson, approximately 2 hours east of the park. Encompassing over 330,000 acres of desert and mountain landscapes, Organ Pipe Cactus National Monument remains open 24 hours a day, 365 days a year. While the park itself is accessible at all times, the visitor center operates from 9 a.m. to 5 p.m., with closures on Thanksgiving and Christmas.

There are two primary airport choices commonly utilized by travelers heading to this park. However, neither option is as close as some might prefer, as both airports necessitate a minimum 2.5-hour drive.

Phoenix Sky Harbor International Airport (PHX) is situated approximately 130 miles from this national monument. The journey from this airport to the park typically takes around 2 hours and 30 minutes. PHX Airport provides a range of nonstop and connecting flights to various destinations worldwide, including Calgary, Dallas, Las Vegas, Nashville, and Seattle. Airlines operating at this airport include American, Frontier, Southwest, and Spirit. Upon arrival, numerous car rental kiosks are conveniently available to help you arrange the final leg of your trip to Organ Pipe Cactus National Monument.

Tucson International Airport (TUS) is also roughly 2 hours and 30 minutes away from the park. This airport handles up to 60 flights daily and offers both nonstop and connecting flights to over 600 destinations globally, serviced by airlines such as Alaska, American, Delta, Southwest, Sun Country, and United. The drive to the park is scenic, offering beautiful spots to stop, stretch, and explore along the way. Rental agencies at the airport can assist you in securing a vehicle for your journey to the destination.

The most effective mode of transportation within this national monument is by private vehicles. The park features numerous scenic drives that meander through the desert and ascend into the mountains, offering ample opportunities to park and explore along the way. The recommended route for driving to this national monument is via Arizona Highway 85, known for being the quickest and most straightforward road. Another option is entering via Darby Well Road, but this choice requires a high-clearance, 4-wheel drive vehicle.

Visitors to this national monument can indulge in a plethora of delightful sights and activities. Whether one's preference is birdwatching, hiking, engaging in ranger programs, or embarking on a leisurely tour along a scenic drive, the park caters to a diverse range of interests.

Birding stands out as a popular activity within this national monument, boasting a habitat for over 270 bird species throughout the year. Key locations for birdwatching include the Kris Eggle Visitor Center, Twin Peaks Campground, Ajo Mountain Drive, and Alamo Canyon. Resident bird species encompass the roadrunner, verdin, cactus wrens, and phainopeplas.

Organ Pipe Cactus National Monument provides excellent hiking opportunities, with over 28 miles of established trails awaiting exploration. The trails vary in length and difficulty, accommodating hikers of all ages and skill levels. Notable trails include the Desert View Trail, Dripping Springs Mine, Arch Canyon, and the Palo Verde Trail. Visitors who complete a 5-mile hike during their stay can receive a Hike for Health pin from the rangers at the visitor center. It is crucial to come prepared for the park's extreme heat and intense sunshine.

For enthusiasts of astronomy or those simply seeking to marvel at the night sky, this park proves to be an ideal destination. The skies here boast exceptional darkness and are devoid of light pollution, creating an optimal environment for observing celestial wonders. From December to mid-April, the park offers a range of ranger-led programs dedicated to the night sky. During these programs, visitors have the opportunity to witness and learn about the captivating celestial displays from knowledgeable park rangers or guest speakers. Prime locations for stargazing include the Twin Peaks Campground Amphitheater and Pinkley Peak Picnic areas, equipped with telescope viewing pads. Additionally, the Alamo Canyon Campground and Ajo Mountain Drive Areas provide excellent opportunities for astrophotography.

Participating in ranger-led programs emerges as one of the most effective ways to delve into the natural and cultural history of the monument. These programs are available daily from December to mid-April, coinciding with the park's peak season. A diverse array of programs, ranging from night sky sessions and guided hikes to wildlife talks, are offered. Typically, these events take place at the Twin Peaks Campground Amphitheater or on the back patio of the Kris Eggle Visitor Center.

To fully appreciate the numerous highlights of Organ Pipe Cactus National Monument, the most recommended approach is to embark on one of the scenic drives within the park. While there are several scenic routes available, the most popular among them is the Ajo Mountain Drive. Stretching across 21 miles of gravel and asphalt, this road guides visitors through desert washes and into the Ajo Mountains. The drive unfolds breathtaking views of the cacti that lend their name to the park, as well as picturesque vistas of the desert and mountain landscapes. Other scenic drives within the park include the North and South Puerto Blanco Drives, Alamo Canyon, Bates Well Road, and Pozo Nuevo Road. Each route boasts distinct viewpoints and provides access to various trailheads throughout the park. These scenic roads offer an excellent means of exploring the park by car, and cyclists often find joy in biking along different routes, relishing both the stunning views and a rewarding workout.

The Kris Eggle Visitor Center serves as an excellent starting point for your adventures within this national monument. Manned by park rangers, this facility provides visitors with orientation and answers any queries about the monument. Additionally, the center houses an information desk, an exhibit area, and a bookstore. Operating seven days a week, the facility opens from 9 a.m. to 5 p.m., with closures on Thanksgiving Day and Christmas Day.

While any visit to this national monument ensures an unforgettable experience, choosing the timing can enhance your trip, especially if you have specific events or activities in mind. The summer months can be challenging, with early June considered the most bearable, falling within the dry season but with daytime temperatures exceeding 100 degrees. It is crucial to come prepared for extreme heat and sun during summer visits. For a more serene experience with fewer crowds, November stands out as an ideal month, characterized by lovely weather ranging from the low 50s to mid-70s, with minimal precipitation. March emerges as the best month for weather, with temperatures ranging from the low 50s to mid-70s and typically no rainfall, providing an optimal time for outdoor exploration. September presents an opportunity to save on travel expenses, as the park sees fewer visitors due to the return of school and reduced Labor Day travel. This period often offers lower flight and accommodation rates, allowing travelers to save significantly.

Throughout the year, this national monument consistently offers a diverse array of programs, particularly during the bustling months from December to March. These regular programs encompass evening sessions at the amphitheater, patio talks, and night viewing programs. Annually, either in February or March, the park hosts a Star Party, providing educational opportunities facilitated by astronomy experts and allowing attendees to observe the night sky through high-quality telescopes. While the event has been held over two nights in past years, there are aspirations to extend it to a week in the near future.

Determining where to stay is a crucial initial step in planning any vacation. When visiting this national monument, various options exist for establishing your home base, both within and outside the park boundaries. The sole lodging option within the park is camping, with two developed campgrounds and numerous opportunities for backcountry camping.

The Alamo Canyon Campground, situated at the base of the eastern mountains, offers a primitive camping experience with stunning views of the mountains, desert, and night sky. Locating this campground can be challenging, as there is no road sign along Alamo Canyon Road. Positioned at milepost 65.5 on the eastern side of Highway 85, north of the bridge that crosses the wash, the campground features four campsites equipped with charcoal grills, picnic tables, and pit toilets. These campsites are exclusively designated for tent camping.

For camping enthusiasts seeking the excitement of backcountry camping at this national monument, numerous opportunities await. This option is ideal for visitors eager to promptly immerse themselves in exploring the park's beauty. Designated zones within the park, such as Tillotson Peak West, Sweetwater Pass, Bates Mountains, and Cristobal Wash, permit backcountry camping, each with its specific regulations. Individuals opting for this form of camping must secure a backcountry permit from the Kris Eggle Visitor Center and adhere to the outlined regulations.

The primary campground within this national monument is the Twin Peaks Campground, strategically situated in the Sonoran Desert, merely 1.5 miles from the Kris Eggle Visitor Center. Surrounded by organ pipe cacti and desert flora, this developed campground guarantees breathtaking views of the monument's mountain areas. Comprising 208 sites, including tent-only and RV-only sites without hookups, this campground offers a more primitive camping experience. Amenities include restrooms with running water, solar-heated showers, a dump station, fire rings, and raised grills.

Given its remote location, there are limited towns in close proximity to this national monument. The nearest town, located about 30 minutes away, while other options involve nearly a 2-hour drive. Ajo stands as the closest town to this national monument, situated approximately 30 minutes north of the park. This small town provides accommodation options, including a hotel, motel, a few bed and breakfasts, and private vacation rentals. With various dining choices, including authentic Southwestern restaurants, cafes, bars, and grills, Ajo caters to diverse tastes. The Mexican restaurants, popular among both locals and tourists, add to the culinary options. For recreation, Ajo boasts beautiful places to explore, such as historic churches, wildlife refuges, and history museums.

Oasis Coffee stands out as a highly regarded restaurant in close proximity to Organ Pipe Cactus National Monument. Operating from Monday to Saturday, this establishment serves breakfast, lunch, and late afternoon snacks. The menu features a variety of items, including gourmet coffee and tea drinks, panini sandwiches, cookies, and pastries. Customers particularly praise the caramel macchiato, mocha frappe, and lemon cream cheese cookies. For those seeking a place to refuel before, during, or after park excursions, Oasis Coffee is a recommended choice.

Situated within a small-town marketplace, Olsens Patio Café offers a quaint dining option. Open every day of the week for breakfast, lunch, and early dinners, the menu includes made-to-order hamburgers, french fries, onion rings, and breakfast sandwiches. Patrons highly recommend the Ruben sandwich, homemade ice cream, carne asada, and the green chili burger with pepperjack cheese. Make sure to visit Olsens Patio Café during your trip to Organ Pipe Cactus National Monument, where you can enjoy excellent meals and cap off your day with a delightful ice cream dessert.

Organ Pipe Cactus National Monument Facts

1) On April 13, 1937, President Franklin D. Roosevelt formally established Organ Pipe Cactus National Monument.

2) The ancient Hohokam people were the original inhabitants of the Arizona region where the park is located. Numerous artifacts supporting this historical connection, such as ancient petroglyphs, seashell jewelry, and pottery, have been unearthed in the area.

3) In 1976, Organ Pipe Cactus National Monument received the prestigious designation of an International Biosphere Reserve. This recognition signifies the park's exemplary representation of the Sonoran Desert ecosystem.

4) The organ pipe cactus, prominently featured in the park, boasts an impressive lifespan of over 150 years. These slow-growing plants typically bloom for the first time around the age of 35.

5) Organ Pipe Cactus National Monument has a sister park in Mexico known as El Pinacate y Gran Desierto de Altar. This selection was made due to the striking similarities between the two parks, encompassing wildlife, plant life, and desert landscapes.

OUT OF AFRICA WILDLIFE PARK

COUNTY: YAVAPAI   **CITY:** CAMP VERDE

DATE VISITED: **WHO I WENT WITH:**

RATING: ☆ ☆ ☆ ☆ ☆   **WILL I RETURN?**   YES / NO

Situated approximately two hours from most points in Phoenix, the Out of Africa Wildlife Park occupies over 100 wilderness acres at the foothills of the Mingus Mountain range in Camp Verde, Arizona. The climate and terrain closely resemble the Masai Mara region of Kenya and the Serengeti of Tanzania, creating a suitable environment for its diverse inhabitants, including bears, tigers, leopards, giraffes, zebras, wolves, deer, and more. The primary goal of the park is to offer these animals a natural habitat while allowing visitors to appreciate and enjoy them. Owned and operated by Dean and Prayeri Harrison, the park distinguishes itself from traditional zoos, functioning more as a wildlife refuge. Here, individuals have the opportunity to witness the beauty of hundreds of creatures not commonly found in the Arizona desert.

Approximately half of the animals at Out of Africa Wildlife Park are rescues, and their individual habitats vary in size from about half an acre to 6-1/2 acres. The emphasis is on providing a setting that mimics the natural environment of these animals, fostering their well-being while offering an educational and enjoyable experience for human visitors.

Exploring Out of Africa Wildlife Park can easily occupy 4 or 5 hours, particularly if you wish to participate in all the available tours and shows on a given day. It's essential to note that not all shows are offered daily, so checking the schedule beforehand is advisable.

The Tiger Splash show, the park's most popular attraction, took a few years to reintroduce after the move to Camp Verde. This show stands out because the animals are not trained, adding an element of unpredictability to the tiger's actions. The Tiger Splash Arena has ample seating, with only a few rows in the back featuring benches with backs. Most seats resemble concrete steps, and the majority of the area is covered. Due to the expansive habitats provided for the animals, offering them space to move freely, play, find shade, and hide, there may be times when certain animals are not visible. Visitors are encouraged to be patient or return later in the day for another chance.

Out of Africa, although situated about 2,000 feet higher in elevation than Phoenix and relatively cooler, experiences hot temperatures in the summer, requiring visitors to take precautions. The park caters to all age groups, but it does not have a traditional petting zoo. Hands-on activities include opportunities to feed a tiger (additional charge), feed a giraffe or camel, or touch a snake. The terrain consists of dirt paths and uneven surfaces, requiring preparedness for walking.

While the African Bush Safari is a ride-only experience, the wildlife preserve allows visitors to either walk, ride, or combine both modes of exploration. The Wildlife

Preserve, featuring big cats, hyenas, bears, and more, is particularly enjoyable. Snack bars near the Tiger Splash Arena offer reasonably priced refreshments. It is advisable to postpone visiting the gift shop until the end of the visit to minimize the items to carry. Out of Africa maintains a rustic atmosphere, lacking the features of a theme park. Tour vehicles may not be overly glamorous, except for those on the VIP tour, and the park does not feature carnival-type rides, only trams and tour buses.

The Unimog Tour at Out of Africa Wildlife Park is crafted for smaller groups, requiring participants to be at least 5 years old. This one-hour personalized tour traverses the park, encompassing the African Bush Safari, where animals approach the vehicle. The park further offers exclusive experiences such as the Behind the Scenes VIP Tour and a Zipline Tour. Various packages are available, with reservations being mandatory, and pricing varying for each experience.

The Zipline Tour is not the typical zipline adventure; it spans a full 2-1/2 hours, featuring five lines starting from a 75' high platform overlooking the wildlife park. Participants must be at least 8 years old, weigh between 60 and 250 pounds, and be in good health. Phones and cameras are not allowed during the tour. Admission to the park is not included in the zipline price, necessitating separate tickets for ground-level experiences at Out of Africa Wildlife Park. No prior zipline experience is required, and both daytime and nighttime zipline tours are offered. For pricing, additional information, and reservations, visitors can check Predator Zip Line online.

Out of Africa operates seven days a week, 363 days a year, from 9:30 a.m. to 5 p.m., with no ticket sales after 4 p.m. The park remains open on holidays, excluding Thanksgiving and Christmas.

Originally situated just outside Fountain Hills, Out of Africa relocated to Camp Verde in 2005, approximately 90 minutes north of Phoenix.

PAINTED DESERT

COUNTY: NAVAJO   **CITY:** HOLBROOK *n.c.*

DATE VISITED: **WHO I WENT WITH:**

RATING: ☆ ☆ ☆ ☆ ☆   **WILL I RETURN?** YES / NO

The Painted Desert, spanning more than 93,500 acres and extending over 160 miles, starts approximately 30 miles north of Cameron, Arizona, near the southeastern rim of the Grand Canyon and continues to the Petrified Forest, about 26 miles east of Holbrook, AZ. Along its course, it brushes against the Wupatki National Monument Indian Ruins. This unique landscape earned its name due to its diverse color palette, ranging from lavenders to various shades of gray, accompanied by vibrant hues of red, orange, and pink. The Painted Desert, characterized by its extensive badland hills and buttes, may appear barren and austere, yet it captivates with its stunning array of colors, resembling a rainbow on the earth's canvas.

Nature, in a process spanning millions of years, has meticulously crafted this natural masterpiece, often likened to a multi-colored layered cake. The Painted Desert tells a story of the Earth's dynamic history, marked by shifts in the crust caused by volcanic activity and earthquakes, as well as the influence of both fresh and sea waters. The area showcases colorful sediments, including bentonite clay and sandstone, arranged in graceful layers that interact with the Arizona sun, creating an ever-changing exhibition of vibrant splendor.

The most frequented segment of the Painted Desert lies at its eastern end, approximately 115 miles east of Flagstaff, Arizona. Both the Painted Desert and the Petrified Forest are situated about 26 miles east of Holbrook on Interstate 40, where the Painted Desert Visitor's Center is located. To access the western end of the Painted Desert from Flagstaff AZ, one can travel north on US 89, passing through Cameron and reaching Tuba City. Travelers have the opportunity to spend several hours leisurely exploring these routes, enjoying scenic views, pausing for photo opportunities, and exploring trading posts and gift shops along the way.

While the Painted Desert offers a mesmerizing experience, a comprehensive exploration of its wonders is incomplete without a visit to the Petrified Forest National Park, which is also located about 25 miles east of Holbrook, Arizona, adjacent to the Painted Desert. Shaped by erosion, water, and silica, the remnants of a once majestic pine forest have resurfaced over millions of years, gleaming like diamonds. Once a habitat for dinosaurs and other prehistoric inhabitants, the Petrified Forest continually unveils the traces of its tumultuous history. As the repository of the largest known concentration of solar calendars, this National Park allows visitors to delve into the lives of ancient Indian tribes who roamed and settled in this region. Notable sites like Puerco Pueblo and Agate House stand as enduring monuments to the resourcefulness of these ancient tribes.

While life continued among the vibrant peaks of the Painted Desert, the awareness of its existence in the annals of modern civilization did not dawn until the 16th century. Spanish explorers passing through are believed to have bestowed the name "El Desierto Pintado" upon it when confronted with its colorful horizon. Subsequently, with the disappearance of the ancestral inhabitants, diverse groups of people traversed the region. In the 1800s, military personnel, ranchers, and tourists explored the scene. In 1906, after years of depleting the finite petrified wood supply, specific areas were designated as the original Petrified Forest National Monument. Over time, additional acreage was acquired and safeguarded under both the Petrified Forest and Painted Desert designations. Present-day civilians have access to an array of artifacts collected and preserved at the Petrified Forest National Park museum. National Heritage Areas have been established to promote conservation and education about the seemingly endless history of this fragment of the planet. Alongside the historical and educational aspects, numerous tourist-oriented sites have been developed over the past century.

One noteworthy location is the Painted Desert Inn, constructed in 1924 by Herbert Lore. Initially intended for lodging and various tourist services such as meals and shopping, the inn was acquired by the National Monument in 1936. After a brief closure during World War II, the Fred Harvey Company assumed management in 1947. Not long after, the renowned architect Mary Colter, responsible for many Grand Canyon attractions, including the Desert View Watchtower and Hopi House, was enlisted to redesign portions of the Inn. Progress brought about destruction as the Inn closed when I-40 replaced Route 66. Abandoned and decaying for 27 years, this desert oasis faced imminent demise twice before earning a spot on the National Register of Historic Places in 1975. Presently, the Painted Desert Inn has been restored and serves as a tourist point with a gift shop and bookstore but no longer offers lodging facilities.

Today, the Painted Desert and Petrified Forest stand as protected lands, weaving a rich history of various ancient peoples, presenting breathtaking views, and offering a glimpse into a life known only to dinosaurs.

PETRIFIED FOREST NATIONAL PARK

COUNTY: NAVAJO   CITY: HOLBROOK   *n.c.*

DATE VISITED: WHO I WENT WITH:

RATING: ☆ ☆ ☆ ☆ ☆   WILL I RETURN?   YES / NO

Located in northeastern Arizona, Petrified Forest National Park boasts one of the world's largest concentrations of petrified logs. These logs were carried into an ancient river system over 200 million years ago and became trapped in sediment and debris, limiting oxygen and slowing decay. Over ensuing centuries, minerals permeated the wood, replacing organic material with quartz.

Encompassing 221,390 acres, the park features over 800 archaeological and historic sites, including two Puebloan structures, petroglyphs, and a segment of the historic Route 66. Nomadic individuals traversed this area over 13,000 years ago, eventually leading to settled communities that farmed the grasslands. In 1100 A.D., the Puebloans erected Agate House, which still stands today. A century later, they built Puerco Pueblo, abandoned for unknown reasons in the late 1300s.

While many visitors explore the vibrant landscape by car, pausing at scenic overlooks and trekking maintained trails, the park is also popular among backcountry hikers and campers.

Petrified Forest National Park offers two visitor centers positioned at each end of the 28-mile main park road. Many visitors commence their journey with the 18-minute orientation film at the Painted Desert Visitor Center, conveniently located just off I-40 at exit 311. At the southern entrance, the Rainbow Forest Museum serves as another visitor center, housing paleontological exhibits, including prehistoric animal skeletons. While most visitors opt for a car exploration, the park also accommodates cycling along its 28 paved miles or horseback exploration in the backcountry. To engage in horseback riding, visitors need to bring their own horse and obtain a free permit from one of the visitor centers.

Numerous trails originate from the Rainbow Forest Museum parking lot, with most being under 2 miles in length. A shelter is available at the intersection of the trails, and visitors can combine both trails for a 2.6-mile hike.

Giant Logs Loop: A 0.4-mile loop showcasing Old Faithful—a 10-foot-wide petrified log—and other sizable, tree-shaped blocks of quartz.

Long Logs: A 1.6-mile loop through one of the park's highest concentrations of fossilized logs.

Agate House Trail: A two-mile trail leading to an eight-room pueblo constructed of petrified wood atop a small hill.

Blue Mesa Trail: A mile-long loop through the badlands, exhibiting shades of blue, purple, and gray due to bentonite clay, on a paved and gravel trail.

Puerco Pueblo: A 0.3-mile, paved trail allowing visitors to stretch their legs while observing the knee-high remains of the pueblo's 100-plus rooms.

The majority of visitors explore Petrified Forest National Park by car, traversing a 28-mile route that spans the entire park. North of I-40, eight overlooks offer panoramic views of the park's vibrant badlands, mesas, and buttes. The Painted Desert Inn, now a National Historic Landmark and museum, showcases exhibits on recent human history. A notable landmark on this route is a rusty 1932 Studebaker, marking the location where Route 66 once passed through the park.

Heading south of I-40, drivers encounter Puerco Pueblo's ruins before reaching Newspaper Rock, where an overlook provides a glimpse of over 600 petroglyphs, some dating back 2,000 years. If time permits, The Tepees overlook offers an opportunity to capture photos of tepee-shaped rock formations before proceeding to Blue Mesa. While this section is best explored on foot through a one-mile trail amidst the rock formations, a 3.5-mile loop road is also available for a drive with four overlooks. Continuing the journey, visitors can stop at Agate Bridge, a 110-foot petrified log spanning a gully, and the Jasper Forest overlook, offering a panoramic view of glittering fossils.

There are no established campgrounds within Petrified Forest National Park; however, backcountry camping is permitted with the issuance of a free permit, which can be obtained at the visitors center on the day of your visit. Backcountry camping groups are limited to eight individuals, and the lighting of fires is prohibited. For information on designated backcountry camping areas in the Painted Desert, Zone 5, and the Rainbow Forest, refer to the official park website.

The town closest to Petrified Forest National Park is Holbrook, situated 20 miles west of the park along I-40. Holbrook offers several motels for accommodation, primarily basic roadside hotels. While the Painted Desert Inn may appear on the map, it currently operates solely as a museum. Two standout motel options in Holbrook include:

Best Western Arizonian Inn: This smoke-free property provides cozy and recently renovated rooms, including complimentary breakfast.

La Quinta Inn & Suites by Wyndham Holbrook Petrified Forest: A newly refurbished hotel with a modern feel, offering amenities such as free breakfast, a fitness center, and an indoor pool.

Exploring Petrified Forest National Park requires a personal vehicle, as there is no public transportation or shuttle service within the park. The park features a single main road, and depending on the entry point, you can cover the entire 28-mile stretch. If you enter from I-40, your journey concludes at the Rainbow Forest Museum near Highway 180.

Alternatively, if you enter from Highway 180, your route concludes in the vicinity of I-40. The drive from the Rainbow Forest Museum back to Heber and I-40 takes approximately 25 minutes.

For those traveling from Phoenix, take I-17 north to Flagstaff, and proceed east on I-40, watching for exit 311. If starting from the East Valley in the Greater Phoenix area, opt for Highway 87 north to Payson, turn right onto Highway 260 towards Heber, and then take 377 towards Holbrook. Just before reaching Holbrook, make a right turn onto Highway 180. If coming from Albuquerque, take I-40 west to exit 311.

Petrified Forest National Park is largely accessible by car, and its trails, while short and mostly paved, can be suitable for people with disabilities. The park offers accessibility features, making it inclusive for various visitors. Puerco Pueblo trail is recommended for wheelchair users as it leads to the remains of a hundred-room pueblo and is wheelchair-friendly. The Agate House trail is partially paved, but some parts may have a rough surface. The Long Logs Trail, despite its paved first half, may not be suitable for some wheelchair users due to narrow turns and steep gradients.

Accessible restrooms are available at key locations like the Painted Desert Visitor Center, Chinde Point picnic area, and Rainbow Forest Museum. Both visitor centers offer educational films with closed captions and feature touch tables for interactive exploration of fossils.

Tips:

1) Cell service is generally available throughout the park, including the backcountry.
2) The park hosts Native American cultural demonstrations and displays artwork from its artist-in-residence program. It is also an International Dark Sky Park, organizing astronomy events.
3) Taking petrified wood from the park is illegal, and folklore suggests it brings a curse. The Rainbow Forest Museum has an exhibit documenting unfortunate experiences of those who took wood.
4) Participate in the dog-friendly BARK Ranger program, offering perks like treats and park-specific dog tags.
5) For a deeper understanding, consider enrolling in classes offered by the Petrified Forest Field Institute.
6) Wildflowers bloom from March to October, with May, July, and August being optimal months for viewing.

PHOENIX

DATE VISITED: **WHO I WENT WITH:**

RATING: ☆ ☆ ☆ ☆ ☆   **WILL I RETURN?** YES / NO

Phoenix, the fifth-largest city in the nation, has served as a retreat for the affluent, celebrities, and those seeking refuge from winter ever since The Wigwam and the Arizona Biltmore debuted in 1929. While these resorts and similar establishments continue to attract guests with expansive pools and top-notch golf courses, Phoenix and the broader Greater Phoenix area, collectively referred to as the Valley of the Sun, provide a multitude of other attractions.

Ranging from breathtaking hikes in the Sonoran Desert to UNESCO World Heritage sites, Phoenix stands out as a unique and unparalleled destination.

To make the most of the Valley's sunny weather and mild temperatures, it's advisable to schedule your visit between November and March. Keep in mind that January through March is considered the high season, and securing last-minute accommodations during the Cactus League spring training might be challenging. However, if you can tolerate triple-digit temperatures, you'll find excellent deals on resort stays from Memorial Day through Labor Day.

Public transportation in the Valley is somewhat limited. The Valley Metro Light Rail operates from northwest Phoenix through downtown Phoenix and into the East Valley. Buses cover various areas, but they may not always reach points of interest, limiting your options for travel. Given that the metropolitan area spans nearly 15,000 square miles, most visitors opt to rent a car or rely on ride-hailing services like Uber.

Due to its central location, Phoenix serves as an excellent hub for exploring the state of Arizona. Consider allocating time for day trips to the Grand Canyon, Sedona, Tucson, or Tombstone.

Phoenix is renowned for its stunning Sonoran Desert surroundings, but there's more to experience than striking a pose with a saguaro or basking in the sun by the pool. The Valley offers a plethora of activities, including exploring world-class museums (including one exclusively dedicated to musical instruments) and visiting remarkable attractions like architect Frank Lloyd Wright's winter residence. History enthusiasts can delve into the stories of the native people and early settlers who laid the foundation for the present-day city, while sports fans can passionately support their favorite professional teams. The Valley boasts an abundance of activities, making it impossible to fit everything into a single vacation. Here are some key highlights to kickstart your exploration:

Discover the Sonoran Desert: Embark on a hike up the popular Camelback Mountain or explore South Mountain Park, one of the world's largest municipal parks. For those seeking a more leisurely experience, jeep tours and horseback rides offer a less physically demanding option, with guides sharing insights into the region's flora, fauna, and history. To independently explore the plant life of the Sonoran Desert, a visit to the Desert Botanical Garden is a must.

Check Out a Museum: The Musical Instrument Museum, ranked among the top 20 museums in the nation, showcases over 8,000 instruments from 200 countries and territories. Art enthusiasts will appreciate the Heard Museum's renowned collection of 44,000 Native American pieces, while the Pueblo Grande Museum Archeological Park features a prehistoric ball court, replica dwellings, and a museum dedicated to the Hohokam people, the area's earliest settlers.

Visit Frank Lloyd Wright's Winter Home: Pay homage to Frank Lloyd Wright by touring Taliesin West, now a UNESCO World Heritage Site. The 90-minute tour provides a glimpse into the famous architect's home, drafting room, and music pavilion. For those interested in more of Wright's work, tours of the Arizona Biltmore (where he served as a consultant) or the Price House (by appointment only) are available.

Attend a Sports Game: From late February until opening day, 15 Major League Baseball teams engage in Cactus League spring training games at 10 ballparks across the Valley. In January, Phoenix hosts the highly attended Waste Management Phoenix Open, one of the premier golf tournaments of the year.

Celebrate the Latinx Culture and Art in Arizona: Embrace the richness of Latinx culture by visiting the Arizona Latino Arts & Cultural Center in downtown Phoenix on E. Adams Street. This cultural hub showcases a diverse array of works and collections that depict scenes from Latin American, Mexican, and Indigenous life and history. The center also hosts insightful exhibitions on cultural heritage and traditions, all open to the public free of charge, aiming to foster education and understanding within the community.

Explore Papago Park: Located approximately 20 minutes from downtown Phoenix between Scottsdale and Tempe, Papago Park offers a wonderful escape to the outdoors. The park is home to attractions such as the Papago Golf Course, the Phoenix Zoo, and the Desert Botanical Garden. With a history ranging from being an Indigenous reservation to a POW camp during WWII, a VA hospital, and a Great Depression-era fish hatchery, Papago Park boasts intriguing trails suitable for hikers of all ages. Whether you opt for a 2.3-mile loop around the park to admire its buttes and rock formations or prefer the 0.3-mile (short and steep) Hole-In-The-Rock trail for Instagram-worthy views, the park has something for everyone.

Phoenix is renowned for its steak offerings and Mexican cuisine. Indulge in high-quality cuts at The Stockyards, situated on the site of what was once the world's largest cattle feedlot, or at Durant's, a popular spot among celebrities and local politicians. Several upscale resorts also feature top-notch steakhouses. For exceptional Mexican fare, head to Barrio Café, or savor a cheese crisp (a tortilla toasted and covered in gooey cheddar cheese) at Macayo's, which also claims to be the birthplace of the chimichanga, created when its founder accidentally dropped a burrito into the fryer.

Take a Day Trip to Nearby National Monuments: Utilize the six days each year when national park sites offer free admission to explore prehistoric sites and ruins around Phoenix. Examples include Montezuma Castle National Monument and Tuzigoot National Monument, both constructed by the Sinagua people between 1100 and 1425 AD. Nestled into sheer limestone cliffs, these ruins are remarkable and are within a 90-minute drive of Phoenix, making them excellent day trip options. Even on non-free days, the $10 entry fee grants access to both sites for up to seven days.

Beat the Heat at a Public Pool: Throughout the metro Phoenix area, splash pads and splash parks have become increasingly prevalent. With a summer season lasting five months, it's no surprise that these water play areas are among the most sought-after amenities at Parks and Recreation Departments across the Valley of the Sun. If you're seeking some pool time, the city's public swimming pools typically have affordable entry fees, and some even offer family-friendly features such as wave pools and slides.

Embark on a Scenic Drive Along the Apache Trail: The Apache Trail, also recognized as Route 88, presents one of the most breathtaking drives in the vicinity of Phoenix, showcasing 40 miles of canyons, geological formations, desert flora and fauna, desert and lake vistas, and seasonal wildflowers that bloom at specific times of the year. It's advisable to avoid this drive during rainy or very windy conditions, as well as on the hottest days of the year—unless you have utmost confidence in your car's maintenance and are prepared for scenic stops in extreme heat.

Conquer Camelback Mountain: Hiking is an immensely popular activity in Phoenix, and numerous free hiking spots are available. Nestled in the heart of the city amidst freeways, neighborhoods, and resorts, Camelback Mountain stands out as a prime location, featuring a trail to the summit that spans just over three miles of steep hiking round-trip. For a less challenging option with a rewarding conclusion, consider the Waterfall Trail in the nearby White Tank Regional Park.

Explore Local Art Scenes in Phoenix and Nearby Scottsdale: Engage with Phoenix's vibrant art scene by participating in open studio tours, providing an excellent opportunity to connect with local artists. On the first Friday evening of each month, you can embark on a free, self-guided tour of galleries, studios, and art spaces scattered throughout downtown Phoenix. This event is particularly enjoyable in the fall and winter months when temperatures are more moderate. Approximately a 20-minute drive away, downtown Scottsdale hosts the Scottsdale ArtWalk every Thursday night since 1975. This event allows art enthusiasts and observers to visit art galleries, making it a delightful way to spend an evening—whether you're window shopping, seeking artistic souvenirs, or searching for a standout piece to adorn your home.

Ascend South Mountain on Foot, Bike, or Drive: South Mountain Park and Preserve, recognized as the largest city park globally, spans nearly 17,000 acres. Contrary to traditional parks with grassy areas and playgrounds, South Mountain Park is a desert mountain preserve. If you enjoy walking, hiking, or biking, consider exploring this scenic outdoor space when the temperatures are more bearable, especially during the cooler hours of the morning in the summer months.

Discover a Riparian Habitat: Riparian areas, ecosystems thriving along river banks, play a crucial role in maintaining ecological balance in Phoenix. These areas also offer an excellent opportunity to learn about the local environment through native wildlife and plants. Whether at a riverside park like Water Ranch in Gilbert or the Rio Salado Habitat Restoration Project in Phoenix, you can engage in activities such as running, bird watching, picnicking, and overall enjoyment of nature in these free and publicly accessible locations.

Explore Goldfield Ghost Town: Located near Apache Junction, this 1890s mining town was on track to surpass Mesa in population before a vein fault disrupted its growth, leading to the scattering of its residents. Presently, Goldfield serves as an ideal day trip for those seeking to immerse themselves in the Old West experience. Admission is free to wander around and witness the weekend gunfights held from October through May. However, certain attractions, such as the mine tour and narrow gauge railroad, come with admission fees. If you're interested in horseback rides and jeep tours departing from Goldfield, it's advisable to book them in advance.

Experience the Sonoran Desert from a Hot Air Balloon: Soaring above the rugged mountains and cacti-filled landscapes in a hot air balloon provides a unique perspective of the Sonoran Desert. Apart from enjoying a bird's-eye view of the Valley, you may also spot animals that are not visible from the ground. Tour operators like Hot Air Expeditions offer post-ride gourmet breakfasts or hors d'oeuvres—with champagne, of course. For those with a fear of heights, alternative ways to explore the Sonoran Desert include guided horseback rides or booking a 4x4 tour.

Explore Hohokam Ruins at the Pueblo Grande Museum: Situated on the remnants of a 1,500-year-old Hohokam village, this museum delves into various aspects of Hohokam life, including agriculture, canal building, crafts, trade, and astronomy. The outdoor area features an excavated ball court, a replica adobe compound, and other structures along the Ruin Trail. With hands-on activities for children, this museum is a family-friendly option for delving into Phoenix's history.

Discover the Hall of Flame Museum of Firefighting: Recognized as the world's largest historical firefighting museum, it showcases over 130 wheeled pieces, including horse-drawn and steam engines, along with 10,000 artifacts ranging from helmets and badges to fire extinguishers. The National Firefighting Hall of Heroes honors firefighters who made significant sacrifices. Conveniently located near the Phoenix Zoo, Desert Botanical Garden, and Papago Park, the Hall of Flame is an accessible stop before venturing to nearby attractions.

Visit the Phoenix Zoo: As the nation's largest privately-owned, nonprofit zoo, it houses over 3,000 animals, including zebras, sloths, Asian elephants, giraffes, and Komodo dragons. The zoo's four main trails (Africa, Arizona, Tropics, and Children's) provide glimpses of most animals, some of which are part of the zoo's conservation program, aimed at releasing them into the wild later. Allocate at least three hours to observe the animals, or longer to enjoy rides and attractions like the Red Barn, where children can interact with sheep and goats and explore farm tractors. During the summer, arriving early is recommended, as many animals seek shade and hide during the heat of the day. The zoo operates every day except December 25.

While the culinary landscape in the Valley was historically dominated by steaks and Mexican dishes, it has evolved to include a diverse array of cuisines, ranging from Thai to Ethiopian. Notably, the area is home to what some consider the finest pizzeria in the nation, Pizzeria Bianco.

Phoenix has also emerged as a noteworthy destination for cocktails, earning national acclaim. Establishments like Bitter & Twisted, Century Grand, and Little Rituals have received recognition at the Tales of the Cocktail Spirited Awards, which is the cocktail world's equivalent of the James Beard Awards.

The Valley boasts an impressive craft beer scene, with breweries predominantly situated in downtown Phoenix, Scottsdale, Tempe, and the East Valley. If you have a taste for sours, be sure to visit Arizona Wilderness Brewing Co., named the best new brewery in the world upon its opening in 2013.

Whether you desire the opulence of the highest thread counts in luxurious sheets within a Five-Diamond resort, the ambiance of an eclectic lounge in a boutique hotel, or a more budget-conscious approach in a conveniently located hotel room, the Valley offers a plethora of choices.

The resorts surrounding Phoenix and Scottsdale, adorned with stunning swimming pools, traditional and desert golf courses, and exquisite dining options, rank among the finest in the nation. The legendary Arizona Biltmore, known as the "Jewel of the Desert," has hosted every sitting president from Herbert Hoover through George W. Bush. (It's also the birthplace of the Tequila Sunrise cocktail and where Irving Berlin penned "White Christmas" poolside.) A newer luxury option is the Andaz Scottsdale Resort & Spa, offering breathtaking views of Camelback Mountain.

Old Town Scottsdale is home to many of the Valley's premier boutique hotels. Hotel Valley Ho, constructed in 1956, is a boutique retreat blending mid-century modern architecture with a chic, contemporary atmosphere. Alternatively, consider booking a room at Bespoke Inn Scottsdale, a boutique inn featuring a 43-foot long infinity lap pool and a James Beard Foundation-nominated restaurant, Virtù. In downtown Phoenix, boutique options include the Kimpton Hotel Palomar and the art-centric Found:Re.

For a budget-friendly experience in downtown, the Hilton Garden Inn Phoenix Downtown is worth considering. Housed in a building originally erected in 1932, it showcases an original Art Deco design and a grand lobby with restored columns and marble accents.

The most convenient way to reach Phoenix is by flying directly into Phoenix Sky Harbor International Airport (PHX). An alternative option in the East Valley is Phoenix-Mesa Gateway Airport (AZA), although it offers fewer commercial flights. Regardless of your choice, renting a car is advisable for exploring both the city and its surroundings.

Tips for saving money:

1) During the summer, many resorts and hotels offer significant discounts on their rooms. Additionally, if you visit in the summer, you can make substantial savings on your car rental, and certain restaurants may even have special summer deals.
2) Several of the smaller museums in the Valley offer free admission, while others have designated free days. On First Fridays, both the Heard Museum and Phoenix Art Museum offer free entry.
3) City parks throughout the Valley are free to access. Whether you choose to hike South Mountain or Papago Park, take a leisurely stroll around Tempe Town Lake, or explore Sahuaro Ranch Park, these outdoor spaces provide cost-free recreational opportunities.

PHOENIX ART MUSEUM

COUNTY: MARICOPA   CITY: PHOENIX

DATE VISITED: WHO I WENT WITH:

RATING: ☆ ☆ ☆ ☆ ☆   WILL I RETURN?   YES / NO

Boasting a collection exceeding 20,000 objects, the Phoenix Art Museum stands as the largest visual arts museum between Denver and Los Angeles. Its diverse array includes American, Western American, Latin American, Asian, European, modern, and contemporary art. Notably, the museum houses an outstanding photography collection and an extensive assortment of nearly 6,000 fashion pieces spanning five centuries. A visit to the Phoenix Art Museum can seamlessly be combined with exploration of the nearby Heard Museum, renowned for its Native American art. Convenient access to other downtown museums, such as the Arizona Science Center, is facilitated by the light rail.

While officially inaugurated in November 1959, the museum's collection traces its roots back to Arizona's early days, when the Phoenix Women's Club committed to acquiring one artwork annually to foster art and culture in the city. This collection expanded alongside Phoenix's growth, prompting the need for a dedicated museum in the mid-1950s. Construction commenced in January 1959, and by November of the same year, the museum opened its doors, featuring artworks from the late-14th century to the contemporary era. Over the years, the museum has continually augmented its collections, with a particular focus on Western art and fashion design.

The museum's permanent gallery encompasses nine distinct collecting areas: American art, Western American art, Latin American art, Asian art, European art, modern art, contemporary art, fashion design, and photography. Many visitors initiate their exploration on the second floor, commencing with the European collection and progressing through the American and Western American collections. However, it is essential not to overlook the remarkable Asian collection on the first floor, boasting over 2,700 works from countries such as China, Japan, Korea, India, Iran, Nepal, and others.

A notable attraction within the museum is the Thorne Rooms, located adjacent to the European collection on the second floor. These miniature replicas meticulously recreate the architecture and interior design of 20 American and European rooms on a 1:12 scale. In the Katz Wing on the second floor, the fashion design collection is showcased, featuring historic attire and accessories, along with pieces from renowned designers like Chanel and Christian Dior.

Venturing to the third floor is worthwhile to witness the permanent installation titled "You Who Are Getting Obliterated in the Dancing Swarm of Fireflies." Created by Yayoi Kusama, this mixed media installation employs LED lights to craft an infinite experience. While on the third floor, visitors can explore the contemporary art and photography collections.

For a comprehensive overview of the permanent collection's highlights, visitors can opt for a one-hour, docent-led tour, available once or twice daily. Alternatively, there is a self-guided audio tour, provided in both English and Spanish.

The Phoenix Art Museum presents a comprehensive calendar of special events and programs, encompassing movies, concerts, lectures, open gallery talks, and art classes. Additionally, the museum offers yoga sessions and mindfulness classes that explore prominent artworks. Advance registration is typically required for most special events, programs, and workshops, so it's advisable to check the calendar before your visit. Some activities may involve an additional fee.

Operating from Wednesday to Sunday, the museum experiences quieter periods on weekday afternoons and early evenings. Weekday mornings can be busier due to school tours or groups from children's summer programs. Local visitors often frequent the museum on Saturdays and Sundays, often combining their visit with brunch at Palette, the museum's café.

Tickets can be conveniently purchased online through the museum's website or at Visitor Services in the Greenbaum Lobby. In-person transactions may necessitate a debit or credit card for completion (verify the current status of this policy on the website before departing).

Plan to allocate at least two hours for your museum visit, and longer if you intend to explore a special exhibit. Phoenix visitors looking to maximize their attractions can easily pair a visit to the Phoenix Art Museum with a trip to the nearby Heard Museum. Alternatively, taking the light rail to Heritage Square provides access to tour the Arizona Science Center or Children's Museum of Phoenix.

The Phoenix Art Museum is situated in downtown Phoenix, just north of the I-10. Parking is free, and visitors usually encounter little difficulty finding a space in the spacious lot shared with the Phoenix Theatre.

For those approaching from the south: Travel west on I-10 towards Phoenix, take the 7th Street exit, and keep to the right at the fork in the exit ramp. Subsequently, turn right (north) onto 7th Street. At the following intersection, make a left (west) onto McDowell Road, followed by a right (north) onto Central Ave.

If coming from the west: Head east on I-10 toward Tucson, and take the 7th Avenue exit. Keep left at the fork in the exit ramp, turn left (north) onto 7th Avenue, and proceed to McDowell. Make a right (east) onto McDowell, and at Alvarado Street, just past Central, make a left (north).

For those coming from the north: Take I-17 and exit at McDowell Rd. Turn left (east) on McDowell Rd. At Alvarado Street, just past Central, make a left (north).

The Phoenix Art Museum is also accessible by light rail, with the Central/McDowell station being the designated stop.

Tips:

1) Avail yourself of free admission on the first Friday of each month from 3 p.m. to 7 p.m., just preceding the initiation of First Friday festivities in downtown Phoenix. Visit the museum for live music, dance performances, art-making activities, and more.
2) Make the most of Pay-What-You-Wish Wednesday occurring every week between 3 p.m. to 7 p.m. During this time, pay an amount that suits your budget for museum entry.
3) For those visiting with children, obtain a family guide at Visitor Services. This comprehensive guide includes a map, details about museum highlights, engaging art-based activities, and even themed scavenger hunts for an interactive experience.
4) Capture memories with still photography (without flash) permitted for personal, non-commercial use. However, please be aware that works on loan (not part of the permanent collection) may have restrictions on photography.
5) Browse through the offerings at the Museum Shop, featuring art books, stylish décor, art supplies, children's gifts, locally-made items, and more. Even if time is limited for a full museum tour, consider a visit to the gift shop for souvenir shopping.
6) Indulge in the culinary offerings at the Phoenix Art Museum's café, Palette. The menu includes salads, sandwiches, simple entrees for lunch and dinner, as well as a delightful Sunday brunch. Enjoy your meal indoors or on the patio, offering scenic views of the Dorrance Sculpture Garden, accompanied by Arizona wine, local beer, or premium cocktails.

PIMA AIR AND SPACE MUSEUM

COUNTY: PIMA   CITY: TUCSON

DATE VISITED: WHO I WENT WITH:

RATING: ☆ ☆ ☆ ☆ ☆   WILL I RETURN?   YES / NO

The Pima Air & Space Museum, situated in Tucson, Arizona, stands as the largest nonprofit aerospace museum in the United States. Its inception in 1976 aimed at the preservation of historic aircraft, and over the years, it has evolved into a globally renowned attraction. The museum boasts an extensive collection of approximately 400 aircraft, spanning commercial, civil, military, and experimental categories. Covering 125,000 square feet across 6 hangars and an additional 80 acres of outdoor space, visitors have endless opportunities for exploration.

Located conveniently off I-10 at exit 267, the museum's address is 6000 E. Valencia Road. The admission fee grants access to various exhibits, including the Main Hangar, three WWII Hangars, the Dorothy Finley Space Gallery, the Arizona Aviation Hall of Fame, the 390th Memorial Museum, and the entire 80-acre outdoor area with around 200 planes. Free parking is available, accommodating RVs as well, although overnight parking is not allowed. The museum store and the restaurant are the only climate-controlled areas, so it's advisable to dress appropriately for the weather. Visitors are encouraged to bring water, sunglasses, and sunscreen. Depending on the group size and interests, a visit typically requires 2-4 hours.

Despite its size, the museum seldom experiences overcrowding, with summer being the slower season due to higher temperatures deterring some tourists. Weekends, particularly Fridays and Mondays, tend to be busier, while Tuesdays, Wednesdays, and Thursdays are quieter. Black Friday stands out as the busiest day of the year, and the week between Christmas Day and New Year's Day sees heightened activity.

Guests should note that outside food and drinks, except for water, are not allowed at the Pima Air & Space Museum. However, there are two picnic tables available for use, with one located in the RV parking lot under a ramada and the other near the Administrative Hangar close to Valencia Road. Limited dining options are available in the immediate vicinity, making it advisable to plan meals outside regular times or dine at the on-site casual eatery, Flight Grill.

Positioning itself as a multi-generational attraction, the museum prides itself on providing a enjoyable experience for the entire family. Catering to all age groups, from infants to grandparents, the museum offers a captivating encounter with history, fostering a lifelong passion for aviation. Special features include a playground, hands-on activities, and simulators designed for young visitors. While older children (ages 8 and up) and those deeply interested in aviation will find the museum particularly appealing, younger children will also be fascinated by the abundance of airplanes and the opportunity to explore cockpits and control towers.

COUNTY: MOHAVE   CITY: FREDONIA *n.c.*

DATE VISITED: WHO I WENT WITH:

RATING: ☆ ☆ ☆ ☆ ☆   WILL I RETURN?   YES / NO

Situated in Northern Arizona, Pipe Springs National Monument unfolds the historical narrative of the Anasazi Ancestral Puebloan people, the Kaibab Paiute Indians, and the Mormon Pioneers of the Church of Jesus Christ of Latter-day Saints. Within this dry and arid landscape, the water of Pipe Spring has served as a vital oasis.

For over a thousand years, the Kaibab Paiute Indians cultivated crops, engaged in hunting, and gathered grass seeds in this region. In the 1860s, Mormon Pioneers entered the area, establishing a fort known as Winsor Castle. These pioneers initiated a significant cattle ranching operation and constructed Winsor Castle directly above the mainspring in 1872. In 1907, the Kaibab Paiute Indian Reservation was designated, encompassing the Pipe Spring Ranch. Subsequently, the United States government acquired Pipe Spring Ranch in 1923, designating it as a National Monument under the management of the National Park Service. Pipe Springs National Monument narrowly avoided being listed among the Least Visited US National Parks, with 25,179 visitors recorded in 2018. The list cutoff was set at 25,000 visitors and below, allowing Pipe Springs National Monument to just surpass this threshold.

Pipe Spring National Monument is situated in northern Arizona, encompassed by the Kaibab Indian Reservation. Historically, the Pipe Springs area was inhabited by the native Paiute Indians until the arrival of members of the Church of Jesus Christ of Latter-day Saints in the 1850s. Archeological evidence suggests that over a thousand years ago, the Pueblan Anasazi, semi-nomadic hunters and gatherers, resided in the region. However, a severe drought between 1000 and 1250 AD likely made it unsustainable for such a large Anasazi tribe. Following this period, around 1300 AD, the semi-nomadic Kaibab Paiutes settled in the area, demonstrating a better understanding of utilizing local resources. They engaged in farming, cultivating maize and beans near flowing springs, and practiced a mobile lifestyle, tracking game such as deer, rabbits, and pronghorn. Additionally, they gathered nuts, roots, and cactus fruit.

By the 1870s, the Kaibab Paiutes saw a drastic decline in their population, plummeting from nearly 5,000 to 200 individuals due to Navajo raids and diseases introduced by European settlers. The first Europeans known to have traversed Pipe Springs were Catholic Fathers Francisco Dominguez and Silvestre Veliz de Escalante during their 1776 expedition through New Mexico, Arizona, and Utah. The native Paiutes played a crucial role in aiding the priests, providing them with food and guiding them along safe routes.

In the late 1850s, prompted by the Mormon Church's call to expand and settle in southern Utah, some members of the Church migrated further, reaching Arizona. Soon, Mormons took control of the land and the springs previously inhabited by the Paiutes. In

1863, James Whitmore became the first white settler to introduce livestock to the area. Whitmore established corrals, planted orchards, and witnessed a growth in his livestock numbers.

In the 1860s, the tension between the Mormon settlers and Navajo tribes escalated, marked by Navajo raids on livestock corrals, including one that resulted in the death of James Whitmore, the original settler. This conflict led to reciprocal attacks. In response to these challenges, a stone building was constructed in 1868 to serve as a stronghold against Navajo attacks. The establishment of a large ranch at Pipe Springs was the brainchild of Brigham Young, the second leader of the Mormon Church, following the founder, Joseph Smith.

The Mormon tradition of tithing, contributing ten percent of income to church officials, often involved offering livestock. Brigham Young saw the Pipe Springs area as a lucrative investment and purchased the land from James Whitmore's widow. Anson Perry Winsor was appointed as the ranch manager, and together with Young, they constructed courtyards surrounded by gates to secure the numerous springs in the area. A room with cold springs was maintained to store dairy products and make butter, with the temperature maintained around 48 degrees. Gun port windows were added for defense against potential native attacks, although they were never utilized. Telegraph lines connecting Pipe Springs to Salt Lake City, Utah, were also installed.

During the 1870s, Pipe Springs experienced consistent growth, earning the nickname "The Honeymoon Trail" among Mormons, as couples often stopped there during or after their marriage ceremonies in the Mormon temple at St. George, Utah. The ranch expanded to include dairy cattle and served as a hideout for polygamists in the 1880s and 1890s when polygamy faced increased scrutiny. This period also witnessed conflicts over water rights between the Mormons and the Paiute nation.

In 1907, federal concerns for the Paiute natives led to the establishment of the Kaibab Paiute Reservation, encompassing a portion of their ancestral lands, with the Mormon ranch situated at its center. The ranch was sold in 1923, and President Warren G. Harding created Pipe Springs National Monument two months before his death. The monument aims to showcase pioneer life, tools, and techniques employed on the ranch for livestock and dairy production. The National Park Service presents the ranch to visitors, providing a glimpse into its 19th-century appearance and offering demonstrations of pioneer activities.

Pets must be kept on a leash at all times and confined to sidewalks. Cell service is unreliable or nonexistent at the visitor center. The Visitor Center, Museum, and Monument operate from 8:30 AM to 4:30 PM, seven days a week, with closures on Thanksgiving, Christmas, and New Year's Day. The park lacks Wi-Fi connectivity. It's advisable to use insect repellent, particularly when in outdoor areas, especially around bodies of water. Visitors should bring their water bottles, as plastic water bottles are not available for purchase in the park. There's a spacious parking lot adjacent to the visitor center. The park does not house any restaurants. Visitors can obtain National Park Passport stamps at the visitor center.

COUNTY: YAVAPAI   **CITY:** PRESCOTT

DATE VISITED: **WHO I WENT WITH:**

                RATING: ☆ ☆ ☆ ☆ ☆   **WILL I RETURN?**   YES / NO

Prescott, Arizona, established as Arizona's inaugural territorial capital, emerged in the wake of the 1863 gold rush. Boasting over 500 structures listed on the National Register of Historic Places, Prescott encapsulates a rich history. The city offers insights into figures like Teddy Roosevelt and the Rough Riders, Tom Mix, Doc Holliday, the Goldwater family's history, the origins of the rodeo, the culture of the Yavapai people, and more. Positioned within a 2 to 2.5-hour drive from most Phoenix locations, Prescott serves as an ideal day trip for both adults and children, offering a plethora of activities.

Upon arriving in downtown Prescott, it is recommended to find parking in close proximity to Courthouse Square. Gurley Street serves as the well-known east/west main street in the downtown area. Courthouse Square is delineated by Gurley, Montezuma Street (Whiskey Row), Goodwin, and Cortez. Optimal parking, found about a block away, can be located in the municipal lot on Cortez, just south of Courthouse Square. A visit to the Chamber Of Commerce Visitor's Center, situated in the vicinity, is highly recommended for obtaining useful maps, brochures, and information about the area. Notably, public restrooms are conveniently located at the base of the Courthouse, on the Whiskey Row side, merely across the street and less than half a block from the Chamber of Commerce building.

Upon reaching this area, visitors are greeted with their first view of Whiskey Row. Over a century ago, this locale served as a hub where miners and residents dined, consumed liquor (as the water was deemed unsafe), secured haircuts, sought job opportunities, exercised their voting rights, and enjoyed entertainment. Notably, the second level hosted brothels. While the number of bars on Whiskey Row has diminished over the years, recent additions include art galleries, ice cream shops, and gift stores, diversifying the offerings. Whiskey Row attracts visitors from across the state, especially on the 4th of July during the Frontier Days celebrations, featuring the World's Oldest Rodeo.

While on Whiskey Row, a must-stop is the Palace Restaurant and Saloon, known for its excellent burgers. Having been in operation since 1877, it holds the distinction of being Arizona's oldest frontier saloon. Stepping into the back room unveils large paintings on the walls, including one commemorating the filming of Steve McQueen's Junior Bonner at the location. The original Palace Bar faced destruction in the Whiskey Row fire of 1900; however, it was salvaged and reinstated when the saloon was reconstructed in 1901. Tragically, in May 2012, a fire destroyed the Bird Cage Saloon, another local landmark on Whiskey Row, along with its contents. The blaze also claimed Larry & Hy's Bare Bones BBQ and the Prescott Food Store.

The Yavapai County Courthouse stands at the heart of downtown activity. A visit around the front allows you to observe the Rough Rider statue.

The Courthouse Plaza is a bustling hub on most weekends, hosting craft fairs and community events. Checking the City of Prescott event calendar is advisable to stay informed about ongoing activities.

For further exploration, consider visiting the Smoki Museum, Fort Whipple, and the Citizens Cemetery. A leisurely drive through the historic neighborhoods of downtown Prescott unveils beautifully restored Victorian homes and historic hotels.

The Sharlot Hall Museum, the largest museum in central Arizona's territory, has a rich history. In 1909, Sharlot Hall became the Territorial Historian, making her the first woman to hold territorial office. She initiated the museum in 1928, housing her collection of artifacts and historical documents in the Governor's Mansion, which is preserved on the museum grounds and open for visitation. The museum features both permanent and special exhibits, living history programs, and outdoor theater performances. Annual festivals, such as the popular Arizona Cowboy Poets Gathering, take place at the museum. Additionally, on the property, visitors can explore the one-room schoolhouse, the Ranch House, Fort Misery, the Governor's Mansion, and the print shop.

If you have additional time, or if you plan to stay for the weekend, there are various other attractions to explore.

The Smoki Museum is dedicated to showcasing American Indian art and culture. It's essential to note that the Smoki, pronounced smoke'-eye, were residents of Prescott, not native peoples, and were committed to preserving the knowledge of American Indian culture.

On your way out of town toward Sedona on Highway 89A, you'll find the Phippen Museum of Western Art.

The Heritage Park Zoo is a non-profit facility with a focus on the conservation and protection of both indigenous and exotic animals.

For outdoor enthusiasts, Prescott offers 1,600 acres of parks and numerous hiking trails. Watson Lake, located just a few miles from downtown Prescott, allows overnight camping and provides opportunities for boating.

Directions to Prescott: Take I-17 North, then head Northwest on State Route 69 into Prescott. From most locations in the Phoenix area, you should reach Prescott in approximately 2 to 2-1/2 hours.

Prescott, Arizona, sits at an elevation of about 5,300 feet, offering a cooler climate compared to the Valley of the Sun. During winter, Prescott undergoes a charming transformation into "Arizona's Christmas City."

RED ROCK SCENIC BYWAY

COUNTY: COCONINO, YAVAPAI   CITY: SEDONA *n.c.*

DATE VISITED: _____   WHO I WENT WITH: _____

RATING: ☆ ☆ ☆ ☆ ☆   WILL I RETURN?   YES / NO

The Red Rock Scenic Byway, officially designated as State Route 179, is a picturesque roadway situated just south of Sedona, Arizona. Despite its relatively short length of 15 miles, connecting Sedona to the Interstate 17 interchange, this route is celebrated for its breathtaking natural beauty. Winding through the iconic iron-infused rock formations and desert landscapes of Sedona and the Coconino National Forest, the byway offers an enchanting journey.

As the byway unfolds, travelers are treated to spectacular views of towering red sandstone cliffs, rugged canyons, and distinctive red rock formations such as Cathedral Rock, Bell Rock, and Courthouse Butte. These formations mark the southwestern edge of the Colorado Plateau. Various viewpoints and pullouts along the route invite visitors to pause and marvel at the striking scenery, where vibrant red rocks contrast against a backdrop of lush green foliage. The region also hosts several hiking trails, allowing adventurers to delve into the heart of the red rock formations and immerse themselves in the unique desert environment.

Recognized as one of the most scenic drives in Arizona, the Red Rock Scenic Byway holds the prestigious designation of an All-American Road, the highest accolade bestowed by the National Scenic Byways Program.

The Red Rock Scenic Byway commences in Sedona, where Highway 179 terminates at the junction with Highway 89A (34.866068, -111.763487). Winding its way along Highway 179, the byway extends until it reaches Interstate 17, covering a distance of 15 miles. The entire drive takes approximately 20 minutes. Despite its brevity, this scenic route manages to showcase a plethora of attractions. One of the most renowned spots is the Chapel of the Holy Cross, located about 3 miles into the journey. This architectural marvel is nestled into the hillside, offering breathtaking views from its elevated circling walkway. While the hike up to the chapel is short but steep, it is well-rewarded with stunning vistas.

Continuing on AZ-179, several exceptional hiking opportunities present themselves. The Little Horse Trail, a moderate 4.3-mile out-and-back trail, provides an up-close encounter with the rock formations flanking the byway. Slightly farther down, the Bell Rock Pathway Trail spans 2.8 miles out and back, featuring views of Bell Rock and Courthouse Butte. Although mostly easy, the trail includes a few steeper climbs near the Bell Rock summit. Keep in mind that a Red Rock Pass or a National Park America the Beautiful Pass is required for parking at these trails and others in the area.

For those who bypassed the Bell Rock Trail, the Bell Rock Vista offers an opportunity to observe this iconic rock formation up close. This is the endpoint of the trail, providing ample parking and access to additional trailheads such as the Phone Trail (10 miles, 1,377 ft elevation change, Out & Back) and the Courthouse Butte Loop Trail. This stretch is characterized by wide-open spaces devoid of man-made structures.

After the vista, the scenic byway passes through the Village of Oak Creek, a small town with an array of shops, restaurants, cafés, and a few hotels.

Approaching the conclusion of the scenic byway, the last noteworthy stop is the trailhead for the challenging Kel Fox Trail (7 miles, 1,325 ft elevation change, Out & Back). Shortly after this point, AZ-179 concludes, providing the option to merge onto I-17 or proceed forward onto a Forestry Service Road leading to the Montezuma Castle National Monument.

RED ROCK STATE PARK

COUNTY: YAVAPAI   **CITY:** SEDONA *n.c.*

DATE VISITED: **WHO I WENT WITH:**

RATING: ☆ ☆ ☆ ☆ ☆   **WILL I RETURN?** YES / NO

Red Rock State Park, spanning 286 acres, stands as both a nature preserve and an environmental education center, boasting breathtaking scenery. The park's trails wind their way through the landscape, adorned with manzanita and juniper, leading visitors to the lush banks of Oak Creek. Native vegetation and red rock hills frame green meadows, while the meandering creek shapes a diverse riparian habitat teeming with plant life and wildlife. This habitat serves as the backdrop for the park's environmental education focus.

The park offers an array of specialized programs catering to school groups and private parties. Various daily and weekly events enhance the visitor experience. Red Rock features essential amenities such as a visitor center, classroom, theater, park store, ramada, and hiking trails.

The Miller Visitor Center at Red Rock houses exhibits and a park store. Families with children aged 4–12 can participate in the Junior Ranger program. The theater continuously screens movies like "The natural wonders of Sedona" and "Oak Creek Loved to Death," providing comprehensive insights into Sedona's history, wildlife, and captivating aerial views of the red rocks. While movie presentations may occasionally yield to special events, visitors can confirm the schedule with park staff upon arrival. Educational opportunities abound at the Miller Visitor Center, featuring hands-on exhibits centered around localized biotic communities to help visitors grasp the essence of the area before exploration. Interpretive panels in the exhibit area vividly bring the park's various habitats to life, offering insights into the region's early human inhabitants and showcasing wildlife through roving displays.

Within the Visitor Center, a gift shop awaits, offering a diverse selection of souvenirs, including t-shirts, magnets, walking sticks, books, maps, and postcards spotlighting Sedona. Beverages and snacks are also available for purchase.

All group areas within the park are open to the public on a first-come, first-served basis when not previously reserved. Reservations are accepted up to six months in advance, except for wedding reservations, which can be secured up to 12 months ahead. To reserve a day use area, individuals should contact park manager via email. A non-refundable reservation fee is applicable, and payment must be received at least 30 days in advance to confirm the reservation; these fees are non-refundable. Additionally, per person entry fees remain in effect.

Picnic tables and shelters are conveniently situated in all group day use areas and can be reserved by reaching out to the park. When not reserved, these areas are open to the public on a first-come, first-served basis. Throughout the Twin Cypress area, various uncovered picnic tables and barbecues are scattered in open regions, accessible for use even when the ramada areas are reserved.

The park features modern and accessible restrooms at both the Visitor Center and the Twin Cypress group use area, ensuring convenience for visitors.

Red Rock State Park offers a variety of events throughout the year, aiming to highlight the unique beauty of the Sedona area in an educational and entertaining manner. Among the most popular events are the full moon hikes and bird walks, which are held consistently throughout the year. Led by experienced rangers and knowledgeable volunteers familiar with the park's points of interest, these guided experiences provide participants with a firsthand exploration of the diverse and captivating landscape in one of Arizona's most stunning locations.

The trail system at Red Rock State Park spans 5 miles and features interconnected loops that guide visitors through the vibrant Oak Creek greenery and the renowned red rocks of Sedona. Specifically designed with families in mind, these Sedona hiking trails are well-marked for safety and enjoyment. Two primary loops, Eagle's Nest Loop and Apache Fire Loop, are linked by the Coyote Ridge Trail, creating an excellent trail network for family activities. Eagle's Nest, the park's highest point with a 300-foot elevation gain, provides breathtaking views of Sedona's iconic red rock formations, contributing to its status as a global destination. These major loops are connected through the Kisva Trail along the riparian corridor, extending to the shorter loop of the Yavapai Ridge Trail. The Javelina Trail leads through pinyon/juniper woodlands, completing the connection with other loops. Visitors are encouraged to obtain detailed trail information from the visitor center before embarking on their hiking adventures. Bikes and horses are permitted only on designated routes.

Red Rock State Park offers limited equestrian trails within the park, but it facilitates access to various Forest Service trails in close proximity. Notably, the Lime Kiln Trail near the park entrance and the Turkey Creek trail at the park's east gate provide opportunities for equestrian activities. Horses are advised to follow the painted horse tracks on paved roads, and a hitching post is conveniently located near the Visitor Center.

While most park trails are not open to bicycles, there is access to popular Forest Service trails from within the park. The Lime Kiln Trail, just outside the park entrance, and various trails near the east gate offer biking opportunities. A common biking route is the 6.2-mile Cathedral Bike Loop, leading bikers out of the park through the east gate, along Verde Valley School Road, crossing Oak Creek (without a bridge), and returning to the park entrance via the Upper Loop Road.

Completed in 2006, the Lime Kiln Trail offers a picturesque hiking experience in the Sedona area, connecting Dead Horse Ranch State Park in Cottonwood to Red Rock State

Park in Sedona. Spanning a 15-mile section of Arizona's high desert, this trail is designated for shared use and is exclusively non-motorized. The Lime Kiln leg of the trail traces a segment of the historic Lime Kiln Wagon Road, originally constructed to provide access to a kiln built in the 1800s. This kiln served the purpose of burning limestone to produce lime, a crucial component in mortar for constructing fireplaces and chimneys. Following the kiln's construction, the road was extended, becoming a route connecting Sedona and Jerome. Along the trail, hikers can still observe the remnants of the kiln, offering a glimpse into the historical significance of the area.

The park is home to a rich diversity of wildlife, and sightings are frequent, providing ample wildlife viewing opportunities at Red Rock State Park. Visitors commonly encounter mule deer, javelina, coyotes, and bobcats throughout the year. Additionally, a wide variety of birds populate the area. During the warmer months, sightings of blacktail rattlesnakes, tarantulas, and various lizard species are not uncommon. Lucky visitors may even catch a glimpse of one of the resident river otters in Oak Creek, especially when crossing Kingfisher Bridge.

Mule deer are permanent residents of Red Rock State Park and are frequently spotted along roads or on the various trails. Despite their generally elusive nature, these deer have become somewhat accustomed to human presence, often allowing for quick photo opportunities before retreating into the dense riparian areas for cover. While capturing photos, it's crucial to maintain a safe distance to ensure the well-being of both visitors and deer. To increase chances of encountering mule deer, arriving early or staying late is recommended, as they are most active during sunrise and sunset. Hikers should minimize noise, stay vigilant for subtle movements in the vegetation, and consider using small binoculars to spot these majestic creatures.

Javelinas, known for their entertaining behavior, are also part of the park's wildlife. As herd animals, encountering one javelina often means others are nearby. Visitors can use their senses, including a skunk-like odor emitted by javelinas, to detect their presence. Maintaining a respectful distance from these animals is essential, and visitors should avoid disturbing them. Javelinas are relatively nearsighted, so providing ample space and calmly alerting them to your presence is recommended for a safe observation.

Coyotes are regularly seen in the park, although they tend to be more elusive. As primarily nocturnal creatures, their activities increase during the night when the park is closed. However, daylight sightings can occur, especially during hunting forays near sunrise or sunset. Visitors lucky enough to witness coyotes during the day should enjoy the experience from a safe distance. It's important to remember that these are wild animals, and visitors are encouraged to take photos and observe without interfering with their natural behavior.

Red Rock State Park organizes bird walks throughout the year, allowing visitors to appreciate the diverse avian population. The timing of these walks varies with the seasons. To make the most of the experience, visitors should stay hydrated, wear comfortable hiking shoes, and dress appropriately for the weather. The park boasts a rich variety of resident and migratory birds, and a pair of binoculars can aid in identifying different species or observing birds among the vegetation.

Red Rock State Park, situated in the distinctive geological landscape of north-central Arizona near Sedona, encompasses one to two river miles along perennial Oak Creek. This unique location provides a mix of riparian and upland environments that support diverse plant and animal species. Designated as part of the Lower Oak Creek Important Bird Area, the park is a habitat for rare avian species like the Common Black Hawk, Wood Duck, and Common Merganser.

Botanically, the riparian areas feature Fremont cottonwood (Populus fremontii), sycamore (Platanus wrightii), velvet ash (Fraxinus velutina), and Arizona alder (Alnus oblongifolia). The upland areas are home to velvet mesquite (Prosopis velutina), netleaf hackberry (Celtis reticulata), juniper (Juniperus osteosperma and deppeana), and various smaller bushes and wildflowers.

The presence of Oak Creek contributes to the park's role as habitat for several frog species and rare native fish. Additionally, the Sonoran mud turtle, recognized as a Sensitive Species by the U.S. Forest Service, resides in the park. Various snakes, lizards, and small mammals populate Red Rock State Park, while larger mammals like mountain lion, coyote, mule deer, javelina, and otter also call the park home.

Similar to many regions in Arizona, Red Rock State Park faces the presence of non-native plants and animals. These species enter the area through accidental or intentional human activities. Non-native plants include giant reed, tamarisk, Johnson grass, and tumbleweed. Non-native fish species are also present in the park.

PARK HISTORY

In the autumn of 1980, Governor Bruce Babbitt and his friends were hiking along Oak Creek, southwest of Sedona, when they encountered a property owner who informed them they were on private land and asked them to leave. This incident raised concerns for Governor Babbitt about the increasing closure of public access to areas along waterways like Oak Creek.

The specific property in question was part of the Smoke Trail Ranch, situated along lower Oak Creek southwest of Sedona. Acquired by Helen and Jack Frye in 1941, the ranch served as a retreat for Jack Frye, who was the president of Trans World Airlines. The property boasted panoramic views of the Sedona red rock formations and was traversed by a 1.4-mile stretch of Oak Creek surrounded by lush riparian habitat.

The existing park boundaries encompass at least five documented homesteads from the late 1800s to the early 1900s, according to the National Forest Service records. Richard Huckaby, granted a homestead patent in 1900 for 80 acres, appears to have been the first Anglo settler in the park's current vicinity. Juan Armijo and his son Ambrosio were granted three homesteads in 1913, 1927, and 1939, initiating use of the western part of the park. Another 20-acre parcel was utilized by Henry Schuerman, Sr. in the 1890s, who later sold it to Fritz Schuerman, and a frame house known as the Willow House was built in 1931.

In the early 1970s, a developer acquired the remaining 330+ acres of the Smoke Trail Ranch from Helen Frye with plans to build a resort complex. Financial constraints led to the developer losing the property. In 1976, the religious group Eckankar, of which Helen Frye was a member, became the owner of the property. Eckankar was developing it as a religious retreat, and it was their decision to evict Governor Babbitt's hiking group from the premises.

Following research on the property's ownership and recognizing its recreational potential, Governor Bruce Babbitt approached the State Parks to explore the possibility of establishing a new state park. To achieve this, the Governor proposed working with Eckankar, Anamax Mining Company, and the State Land Department to negotiate a land exchange that would transfer the property into state ownership. However, the Governor required the support of the State Parks Board to pass legislation enabling the exchange of land across county boundaries and to confirm the Parks Board's acceptance of the property as a state park.

The negotiation involved a three-way exchange, with Anamax Mining Company purchasing the 286 acres along lower Oak Creek in Yavapai County from Eckankar. Subsequently, Anamax would exchange this property with the State Land Department for state land that Anamax had been leasing for the Twin Buttes Mine in Pima County. While discussions with Eckankar began, finalization was contingent on the Legislature passing a bill authorizing the exchange of State Trust lands across county boundaries.

State Parks collaborated closely with the Governor to garner support for the necessary legislation during the 1981 session. The original bill for the land exchange introduced in the Senate did not pass within the required timeframe. Therefore, the House selected Senate Bill 1184 and executed a "strike everything" amendment, incorporating the essential language for the land exchange across county lines. This bill successfully passed the Legislature, and Governor Babbitt signed it into law as Chapter 274 of the 1981 Legislature on April 27, 1981.

The legislation mandated that the Oak Creek land received by the State Land Department in the exchange be considered for use as a State park. Furthermore, it specified that State Parks must formulate a proposal and a plan addressing the utilization of the lower Oak Creek site as a State Park. The master plan and report, covering all aspects of establishing the park, including funding, management, operations, and any additional legislation required, had to be completed by the end of December 1981.

To streamline the master planning process, a 12-member Ad Hoc Advisory Committee was established. The committee comprised individuals from various sectors, including Robert Lopez from Cup of Gold Estates, Robert Gillies from the Sedona Ranger District, US Forest Service, Kerry Baldwin, President of the Arizona Association for Learning in and about the Environment, Dr. Eugene MacFarlane from Keep Sedona Beautiful, Gene Palmer from the Sedona-Oak Creek Chamber of Commerce, Howard Craig from Sedona Red Rock Taxpayers Association, Edgar Lindfors, a homeowner on Red Rock Loop Road, Sam Fitzpatrick from Coconino Taxpayers Association, Wallace Leininger from Cup of Gold Estates, Ed Rabovits, Headmaster of Verde Valley School, Jean Strong from Eckankar, and Dave Maggard, Director of the Yavapai County Planning and Zoning Department. The committee played a crucial role in facilitating communication and acting as a liaison between State Parks, the private sector, and the business community.

The Ad Hoc Advisory Committee engaged in activities such as touring the site, visiting Dead Horse Ranch State Park to understand the operational aspects of a state park, and reviewing and providing recommendations on the proposed Lower Oak Creek State Park Master Plan. On October 1, 1981, the committee reviewed and approved the proposed Master Plan. This plan was subsequently presented to the Parks Board on October 16, 1981, for consideration. Following a staff presentation and detailed discussions, the Board provided conceptual approval for the Park Master Plan.

In compliance with legislative requirements, a presentation of the Master Plan was delivered to the Yavapai County Board of Supervisors on November 2, 1981. During the presentation, there was an extensive discussion regarding the improvement and paving of the Red Rock Loop Road. At one point, a committee member emphasized the importance of not jeopardizing the proposed State Park. The Board of Supervisors, in a supportive move, sent a letter to the President of the Senate endorsing the plan for the Park.

A public presentation of the proposed Lower Oak Creek State Park Master Plan was conducted at the Sedona Elks Lodge on the evening of November 19, 1981. The plan outlined day-use areas for picnicking and recreational activities.

The Master Plan for the Lower Oak Creek State Park outlined the utilization of existing structures where feasible. Specific structures were designated for purposes such as a visitor center, providing scenic views of Oak Creek and the Red Rocks, and another for an environmental education center. Paving of interior roads and parking areas was included in the plan. The development aimed to incorporate numerous paved hiking trails, emphasizing the interpretation of natural and historical features. Limited overnight camping facilities were proposed for groups participating in environmental education programs. The public presentation of the Park Master Plan in Sedona garnered support from over 125 attendees.

During the Parks Board meeting on December 4, 1981, the final Master Plan and the Report for a Potential State Park on Lower Oak Creek were reviewed and approved. Copies of the Report and Plan were subsequently printed and distributed to the

Governor, President of the Senate, Speaker of the House, and the State Land Commissioner by the December 31, 1981, deadline.

Discussions between representatives of Eckankar, Anamax Mining Company, and the State Land Department had been ongoing before the necessary legislation was passed to enable the land exchange. After the passage of Senate Bill 1184 in April 1981, which authorized the exchange, all parties were prepared to expedite the acquisition and exchange processes.

Following the completion of appraisals and land surveys, Anamax Mining Company acquired the 286-acre parcel of land, the primary remaining portion of the Smoke Trail Ranch, on July 22, 1981, for $5,148,000. Anamax Mining Company had already filed the application for the exchange with the State Land Department, and the majority of legal requirements for processing the land exchange had been fulfilled. With the established acquisition cost for the Sedona lands, the acreage of State land of equivalent value in Pima County could be determined, and the exchange was publicly advertised for review. The land exchange was successfully concluded in the fall of 1981 when Anamax Mining Company obtained title to the 3,947 acres of State Land in Pima County.

After the State Land Department acquired the 286-acre parcel, the State Parks Board obtained a Special Land Use Permit for the protection and security of the property. During the initial years, public access to the site was restricted, but various groups used the facilities for special meetings. These groups included the Department of Administration Budget Office, Governor's Commission on the Environment, Arizona Game and Fish Project Wild Workshop, Natural Areas Advisory Committee, State Land Department, Inter-Tribal Council, Arizona Chapter of the American Planning Association, and State Parks for seminars, workshops, and park manager meetings.

Administrative responsibility for the site was initially managed by Mike Sipes, Jon Clow, and Duane Hinshaw until John Schreiber assumed the role of permanent manager. Despite submitting budget requests to the Legislature each year in an effort to secure funding for park development, the Parks Board faced challenges during the legislative sessions of 1982 and 1983, experiencing a reduction of 15 positions and over $500,000 in operating budget reductions. Consequently, the initial appropriation recommended for the Lower Oak Creek site was not addressed for several years.

In September 1983, six members of the Arizona Chapter of the American Planning Association (APA) volunteered their time for the Lower Oak Creek Charrette. The APA members—Betty Drake, John Sather, Dave Zlotshewer, Bruce Lindquist, Jack Bestall, and John Tandy—reassessed and explored development potentials for the Lower Oak Creek site. This collaborative effort involved the design team, the State Land Department, the Governor's Office, and the State Parks Board. Their conceptual plans included an outdoor classroom center with dormitories for overnight stays, a restaurant, and cabins on the hill south of the Creek. The team presented their concept plan to Governor Babbitt, guests, and staff, emphasizing the integration of facilities and programs that could generate revenue to cover the annual State Land lease fee. In collaboration with local citizens and agency staff, an alternate planning document was prepared for consideration by the State Land Department and State Parks Board. This effort earned the Arizona Chapter a National Award at APA's Annual Meeting in 1984.

The State Parks Board faced concerns regarding the State Land lease payments for the Lower Oak Creek site after its development and public opening. In 1985, an opportunity arose for the Parks Board to potentially obtain a Recreation and Public Purposes Patent for the 286-acre parcel. This involved a complex land exchange between the State Land Department and the Federal Government. To proceed with this exchange, the Parks Board had to relinquish a part of its Federal lease on lands within Lake Havasu State Park, including Pittsburg Point (a concession area) and a section of the adjacent shoreline. These lands were highly valuable to the Federal Government in their dealings with the State of Arizona, serving as compensation for State lands taken for the Central Arizona Project. As an incentive, the 286-acre Lower Oak Creek site was included in the agreement to become property of the Federal Government.

A Memorandum of Agreement outlining the disposal of Federal Lands at Lake Havasu City was signed by the BLM, State Land, State Parks, and Lake Havasu City in November 1985. However, during the progression of this intricate exchange in June 1986, the National Wildlife Federation filed a lawsuit, resulting in a preliminary injunction against the BLM's Land Withdrawal Program. This legal action temporarily halted BLM's involvement in the land exchange, requiring resolution before proceeding. Eventually, the lawsuit was settled, and the land exchange was successfully completed. On November 7, 1986, State Parks acquired the 286-acre parcel from the Federal Government through a Recreation and Public Purposes Patent.

After acquiring the Lower Oak Creek site, the Parks Board officially designated the area as Red Rock State Park. Early printed materials may still refer to the park as Lower Oak Creek State Park or Smoke Trail Ranch State Park. In 1987, operating and development funds were allocated, leading to the initiation of the design for the park entrance road (along the alignment of the Lower Red Rock Loop Road) by the Arizona Department of Transportation. State Parks enlisted a private consultant for the design and construction of the park's visitor center.

The dedication and opening ceremony of Red Rock State Park occurred on October 19, 1991. Executive Director Ken Travous extended a warm welcome to guests and introduced Billie Axline Gentry, a member of the Parks Board, as the Master of Ceremonies. Mrs. Gentry introduced Representative John Wettaw of Flagstaff, expressing gratitude for his assistance in securing the necessary legislation and appropriations for the Park. Representative Wettaw provided insight into the Park's development history. Subsequently, Mrs. Gentry introduced Duane Miller, a Parks Board member for 25 years, along with his wife Beverly and their family. The Miller Visitor Center was named in their honor, recognizing their significant years of service to Arizona State Parks.

AREA ATTRACTIONS

Sedona is renowned for its appeal to outdoor enthusiasts, offering an abundance of hiking trails, diverse plant and wildlife, and the iconic red rock vistas. The region is a treasure trove for adventure seekers, provided they know where to explore. Various tour options, including horseback, jeep, bicycle, raft, helicopter, biplane, and hot air balloon tours, are available. Additionally, one can delve into the area's rich history by visiting ancient cultural sites. While Red Rock State Park prohibits swimming, Slide Rock State Park, just north of Sedona, boasts Arizona's premier natural water slide.

A substantial portion of Sedona can be experienced by car. Driving along Highway 179 provides close-up views of breathtaking red rock formations like Bell Rock and Courthouse Butte. Further red rock sights can be witnessed from Dry Creek and Boynton Pass Roads, but these routes may involve unpaved roads where vehicles with higher clearance are recommended. Heading north on 89A toward Flagstaff leads through Oak Creek Canyon, offering one of Arizona's most picturesque scenic drives.

However, Sedona is not only celebrated for its natural beauty; it also attracts visitors with its world-class shopping and dining establishments, creating a holistic Sedona experience. Uptown Sedona is a hub for numerous shops and galleries featuring distinctive southwest art and souvenirs. The area is also home to a variety of restaurants, hotels, and resorts, enhancing the overall allure of Sedona.

Oak Creek Canyon, renowned for its vibrant rocks, expansive vistas, and distinctive formations, is a globally acclaimed destination for its breathtaking scenery. Beyond its scenic beauty, this high-country haven is also recognized for blue ribbon trout fishing and offers diverse opportunities for wildlife viewing.

Coconino National Forest stands out as one of the most diverse National Forests nationwide, showcasing landscapes that range from Sedona's iconic Red Rocks to Ponderosa Pine Forests and alpine tundra. Exploring mountains, canyons, fishing in forest lakes, and leisurely wading in creeks and streams are some of the diverse experiences this forest offers.

Prescott National Forest, spanning approximately 1.25 million acres, borders three other National Forests in Arizona. Its territory extends west of Prescott, covering areas like Juniper, Santa Maria, Sierra Prieta, and Bradshaw Mountains. The eastern part of the forest encompasses Black Hills, Mingus Mountain, Black Mesa, and the Verde River headwaters.

Montezuma's Castle National Monument provides a glimpse into the past with one of the best-preserved cliff dwellings in North America. Nestled into a towering limestone cliff, this 20-room high-rise apartment narrates a thousand-year-old tale of ingenuity and survival in a challenging desert landscape.

Boynton Canyon Trail stands out among the picturesque box canyons of Arizona's Red Rock Country. Known for its scenic beauty, this trail is easily accessible from nearby towns via well-paved roads.

Tuzigoot National Monument showcases an ancient village or pueblo built by the Sinagua culture. With 110 rooms, including second and third-story structures, it offers a window into the rich history of the region.

COUNTY: COCONINO   CITY: FLAGSTAFF *n.c.*

DATE VISITED: WHO I WENT WITH:

RATING: ☆ ☆ ☆ ☆ ☆   WILL I RETURN?   YES / NO

For those who may be hesitant or unable to venture below the rim of the Grand Canyon, there's a delightful trail that peacefully winds along 13 miles of the South Rim, offering spectacular views. This mostly paved trail is wheelchair-friendly and suitable for those who prefer a more level path. Starting at the South Kaibab trailhead, the easternmost shuttle stop, the trail gently extends to its endpoint at Hermits Rest.

The trail provides an opportunity to explore the extensive geologic history of the Canyon, with the Trail of Time acting as a guide. This 1.3-mile section, established in 2010, features interpretive elements, age markers, and samples from each layer, offering informative and intriguing insights. At the eastern end, don't miss the Yavapai Museum of Geology. Heading west from the Bright Angel trailhead, you can observe the fossil record at your feet. If you have bicycles, you can ride along the western access road, enjoying a 7-mile journey to Hermits Rest with the freedom to make stops at your leisure.

Accessing the Rim Trail is possible anywhere between the South Kaibab trailhead and The Village. For convenience, starting at the shuttle stop just west of the Bright Angel trailhead is recommended.

Key Trail Details:

Length: 13 miles from start to finish
Elevation Loss/Gain: Negligible, overall about 200 feet; wheelchair-accessible for almost all sections
Camping: None
Water: Despite the seemingly easy trail, it's crucial to carry water. Water or filling stations are available at the South Kaibab trailhead, Geology museum, Hermits Rest, and Grand Canyon Village.

The Rim Trail features nine distinct scenic overlooks, each offering a unique perspective of the canyon. Here's a summary of each lookout:

Trail View Overlook: Located 0.5 miles west of the Village Route Transfer stop, providing a fantastic view of Bright Angel Canyon.

Maricopa Point: Positioned 1.1 miles west of the Village Route Transfer Stop, it offers a 180-degree unobstructed view of the Grand Canyon, including Orphan Mine.

Powell Point: Found 1.8 miles west of the Village Route Transfer Stop, showcasing the

Powell Memorial. Visitors can climb stairs for a closer look at the monument and enjoy impressive canyon views.

Hopi Point: Situated 2.1 miles west of the Village Route Transfer Stop, featuring vault toilets and offering views of the Colorado River.

Mohave Point: Located 3.1 miles west of the Village Route Transfer Stop, providing additional views of the Colorado River.

The Abyss: Positioned 4.2 miles west of the Village Route Transfer Stop, offering insights into the role of gravity in shaping the Grand Canyon.

Monument Creek Vista: Found 5.2 miles west of the Village Route Transfer Stop, showcasing Monument Creek and Granite Rapid of the Colorado River.

Pima Point: Situated 6.7 miles west of the Village Route Transfer Stop, offering views of the Cataract Plains.

Hermit's Rest: Located 7.8 miles west of the Village Route Transfer Stop, this stop provides restrooms, running water, and a gift shop with a snack counter. It serves as the access point for the Hermit Trail if you wish to embark on a hike.

Here are some essential details to keep in mind for your Grand Canyon Rim Trail experience:

Safety Caution: Certain parts of the Rim Trail approach the edges of cliffs without guardrails. Exercise caution, especially with children.

Scenic and Less Crowded: The section between Hermits Rest and Bright Angel Trailhead offers some of the finest views with fewer crowds. Utilize the red route to access these viewpoints.

Shuttle Stops: The red bus makes nine stops on its way to Hermits Rest but only three on the return journey (Pima Point, Mohave Point, and Powell Point). Plan your hike accordingly.

Water Availability: There is no water source along the trail. Ensure you have an adequate water supply. Water is accessible at Hermits Rest, Bright Angel Trailhead, within Grand Canyon Village, and the South Kaibab Trailhead.

Shuttle Schedule: Shuttle buses commence operations one hour before sunrise and continue for an hour after sunset, approximately every 15 minutes.

ROUTE 66

DATE VISITED: **WHO I WENT WITH:**

RATING: ☆ ☆ ☆ ☆ ☆   **WILL I RETURN?** YES / NO

Established on November 11, 1926, Route 66, affectionately known as the Mother Road, stands as one of the most iconic highways in the United States. Boasting a remarkable inventory of over 250 bridges, buildings, and other sites officially listed on the National Register of Historic Places, the route encapsulates a multifaceted history that transcends mere tales of the road itself.

Along Route 66, there exist dozens, if not hundreds, of landmarks, locations, and scenic landscapes. Rather than rushing through, travelers are encouraged to seize the opportunity to revel in the breathtaking beauty that the road has to offer.

While generally considered safe, Route 66 is susceptible to unexpected weather conditions. It is advisable to consistently check the weather forecast before embarking on your journey, and keeping a weather news source open on the radio can help you stay updated.

To make the most of your journey, meticulous planning is essential. Delve into the major cities dotted along the Mother Road and invest time in crafting an itinerary that aligns with your travel preferences.

For enthusiasts of hiking, Route 66 in Arizona presents some outstanding spots, including the Petrified Forest National Park in northeastern Arizona, Badger Trail in Kingman, and Lenox Crater Trail in Flagstaff. These trails offer a chance to explore the natural beauty and diverse landscapes along the historic route.

Stretching from east to west, Route 66 commences its epic journey in Chicago, meandering through the states of Illinois and Missouri before extending westward through Oklahoma, Texas, New Mexico, and Arizona, ultimately culminating in California. The total length of Route 66 is approximately 2,450 miles, although variations can occur based on the chosen route. Opting for the interstate and adhering closely to the road may result in a slightly shorter drive.

Renowned as the most picturesque route from Chicago to Los Angeles, the Mother Road has ingrained itself as a symbol of freedom, mobility, and the relentless pursuit of the American Dream. It epitomizes the quintessential American road trip, offering a captivating experience for those seeking to make the drive an indelible and memorable part of their journey.

Route 66 has left an indelible mark in popular culture, featuring prominently in numerous movies, TV shows, books, and works of art that chronicle the evolution of the

American road. Recognizable appearances include films like "Easy Rider," "Bagdad Cafe," "No Country for Old Men," "Little Miss Sunshine," and the animated feature "Cars." These portrayals contribute to capturing the allure of the expansive and often desolate landscapes encountered during the iconic road trip along Route 66.

Route 66 encompasses some of the most mesmerizing drivable segments of the historic highway, featuring extensive stretches adorned with breathtaking landscapes and renowned attractions. Here are notable destinations to explore along Route 66, from iconic landmarks to world-famous museums.

The Painted Desert, situated approximately 50 miles from the New Mexico border in northeastern Arizona, extends from the eastern edge of Grand Canyon National Park to the southeast into Petrified Forest National Park. This expansive and striated badland spans over 160 miles (260 km). Characterized by picturesque hills rising from a flat desert terrain, the Painted Desert serves as a compelling illustration of the ongoing processes of weathering, erosion, and deposition.

During sunrise, the Painted Desert reveals its enchanting palette, showcasing vivid colors such as oxide red, ochre yellow, and burnt sienna, complemented by subtle lavenders. This geological marvel offers a visual spectacle that surpasses even the most lifelike paintings. To fully appreciate this natural wonder, it's advisable to pause and immerse yourself in the panoramic views as you traverse through.

Petrified Forest National Park, an integral part of the Painted Desert, is renowned for its extensive deposits of petrified wood. Covering an area of 346 square miles (900 sq. km), this park extends beyond its archaeological significance. Although seemingly desolate, closer examination unveils an ongoing geological experiment that spans an impressive 200 million years, providing a rare and unique experience for fortunate observers.

As you navigate through this surreal landscape, you'll encounter wide ravines, blue-striped badlands, and an expanse of petrified tree skeletons, resembling an ancient forest frozen in time. The Petrified Forest National Park offers a glimpse into the intricate processes that have shaped the Earth over millions of years.

Continuing south on Route 66, you'll come across the Barringer Crater, also known as the Meteor Crater. Formed over 50,000 years ago, this crater, named after geologist Daniel Barringer, is the first proven meteorite impact site on Earth. With a diameter of nearly one mile (1.6 km), a circumference of 2.4 miles (3.8 km), and a depth exceeding 550 feet (167 m), it's comparable to the size of approximately 20 football fields combined. While descending into the crater is strictly prohibited due to preservation efforts, visitors are welcome to capture photographs and explore various exhibitions. The Barringer Crater is a captivating destination for aspiring geologists, meteorologists, and space enthusiasts alike.

Situated a 30-minute drive from the Meteor Crater, Walnut Canyon National Monument is located approximately 10 miles (16 km) southeast of downtown Flagstaff. Renowned for its impressive rock formations and ancient cliff dwellings, the monument stands as a unique historical landmark narrating the story of ancient inhabitants. Along the trails, visitors can easily envision the bygone days of a distant past. The cliff dwellings, constructed by the Sinagua between 1125 and 1250 CE (Common Era), remain remarkably intact, resembling structures designed by modern architects. Overlooking Walnut Creek, these dwellings create a striking cityscape at the base of Mt. Diablo. In addition to the cliff dwellings, the Walnut Canyon Visitor Center offers a glimpse into ancient life through exhibits and murals. The center showcases artifacts and materials collected at the site, including clay pitchers and cloth made from cotton and yucca fibers. Visitors can also explore the pithouses and freestanding pueblos scattered along the canyon rim, while enjoying the scenic views that the national monument has to offer.

The Sunset Crater, also recognized as the Sunset Volcano, is a volcanic crater situated approximately 15 miles (25 km) northeast of Flagstaff, Arizona, and 80 miles from the Grand Canyon along the historic Route 66. As the youngest volcano on the Colorado Plateau, it derives its name from the multicolored, red-splattered cone that gives the appearance of being bathed in the light of the sunset. The Sunset Crater experienced an eruption around 900 years ago, approximately in A.D. 1085. Despite extensive research by numerous scientists, the exact cause of its eruption remains unknown. Fortunately, the volcano is currently dormant, allowing visitors to explore the Bonito Lava Flow and hike the trails in the surrounding area.

Covering approximately 3,000 acres, the Sunset Crater National Volcanic Monument is relatively small compared to other volcanic sites in the region. The Loop Road provides access to the entire area and extends to Wupatki National Monument, an archaeological site with Native American significance. Unfortunately, the trail leading to the summit of Sunset Crater is closed due to deep ruts and erosion caused by the footsteps of thousands of past hikers. However, alternative routes such as the Lenox Crater Trail or the Forest Service Trail allow visitors to ascend to the top of another cinder cone, providing a vantage point to look down into the Sunset Crater.

Route 66 passes directly through Flagstaff, a vibrant town situated on the Colorado Plateau. Unlike other historic sites along Route 66 that have been impacted by the decline of the old road, Flagstaff is encompassed by high mountain wilderness. The city, home to nearly 150,000 residents, exudes energy and takes pride in its historical heritage. Flagstaff offers numerous must-visit attractions, including the Mix Zips, the Museum Club, and the Flagstaff Visitor Center. For those seeking relaxation, downtown Flagstaff boasts a plethora of espresso bars catering to its diverse visitors. Additionally, the city features a variety of ethnic restaurants specializing in German, Thai, Greek, or Indian cuisine, ensuring plenty of dining options. Flagstaff's hiking trails attract enthusiasts worldwide, benefiting from its proximity to the Coconino National Forest. With over 90 trails available, popular choices include West Fork Trail, Boynton Canyon Trail, Courthouse Butte Loop, and Devil's Bridge. Anglers can indulge in fishing at West Clear Creek, Verde River, and the C.C. Cragin (Blue Ridge) Reservoir, targeting species like pike, catfish, and similar fish.

Known as the Gateway to the Grand Canyon, Williams, Arizona, situated along Route 66, is a town brimming with character, charm, and distinctive signage. Despite having a population of only around 3,000 permanent residents, Williams surprises visitors with a plethora of activities. A crucial starting point for newcomers is the Williams Visitor Center, offering insights into the town's history, prominent establishments, and attractions. Knowledgeable staff provide information on various aspects of Williams, ensuring a well-rounded introduction. Post-visit, embark on a train journey from the Grand Canyon Railway Depot for a taste of Old West railroad experiences, or delve into the town's history at the Welcome and History Park. Thrill-seekers can experience the Route 66 Zipline, dangling 110 feet above the ground and spanning 1,400 feet, providing breathtaking views of Grand Canyon Boulevard. Other notable attractions include the Bearizona Wildlife Park and Grand Canyon Deer Farm, catering to wildlife enthusiasts, while the Canyon Coaster Adventure Park and Grand Canyon Go-Karts offer opportunities for lighthearted fun and excitement.

The journey from Sedona to Jerome, and vice versa, spans approximately 45 minutes, offering ample time to explore both locales within a day or two. Sedona stands out as one of Route 66's highly frequented vacation spots, particularly popular among New Age enthusiasts drawn to activities such as psychic channeling and astral travel in the desert town. Sedona invites exploration of concealed caves, canyon hikes, and ascents to some of the region's tallest peaks. During the summer, visitors can relish swimming opportunities in the numerous lakes and rivers dotting Oak Creek Canyon. Heading south on Route 66 leads to Jerome, a desert town once labeled "The Wickedest Town in the West" and now recognized as the largest ghost town in America, boasting fewer than 500 permanent residents. A stroll through Jerome provides a nostalgic journey, immersing visitors in numerous historical sites, buildings, and museums that transport them back in time.

Seligman, famously known as the Birthplace of Historic Route 66, stands out as a popular stop along the Mother Road, offering a nostalgic retreat. The town is teeming with retro shops, motels, and diners, creating an ideal spot to take a break. A notable attraction in Seligman is the Return to the 50s Museum, housed in a former gas station, showcasing vintage motorcycles, cars, Route 66 memorabilia, and items from the 1950s. Notably, characters from Pixar's animated movie "Cars," like Tow Mater, are featured, with the entire film being inspired by the town of Seligman. Visitors can explore specialty gift shops, the Motoporium, and the historic 1860 Arizona Territorial Jail. To cap off the experience, a visit to the famous Roadkill Cafe is a must, where patrons can try specials like Bad-Brake Steak, Deer Delectables, Splatter Platter, Caddie Grilled Patty, and Swirl of Squirrel, among other offerings.

The Grand Canyon Caverns provide a mesmerizing encounter with a natural marvel that began evolving 345 million years ago. Situated 200 to 300 feet below ground, these caverns offer a distinct escape from the urban environment, representing one of the largest dry cavern systems in the United States that remains largely untouched. Exploring the depths, visitors encounter a treasure trove of undersea fossils dating back 3 million years and captivating prehistoric formations. For those with more time, the caverns offer the unique experience of staying overnight in furnished suites, complete with an RV-style bathroom, kitchenette, book library, refrigerator, microwave, and even a TV. Upon resurfacing, visitors can dine in nearby restaurants or cocktail lounges, peruse the gift shop, or embark on hiking trails in the vicinity.

Situated in the northwestern region of Arizona, Kingman, also known as The Heart of Historic Route 66, serves as a vibrant homage to the iconic Mother Road. Within Kingman, visitors can explore prominent attractions such as the Historic Route 66 Museum, the Kingman Railroad Museum, and the Desert Diamond Distillery. For aviation enthusiasts, a visit to the Kingman Airport north of the town is a must. Functioning both as a storage facility for commercial airlines and a significant airplane boneyard, the airport offers a unique experience. With over 100 restaurants, cafes, and diners, along with approximately 35 hotels and motels, Kingman provides a diverse range of accommodations and dining options. Notably, the El Trovatore Motel stands out as one of the few pre-World War II motels still in operation, offering a nostalgic glimpse into the "good old days" of the 1930s, 40s, and 50s.

Oatman, situated between Kingman, Arizona, and Needles, California, is a captivating town perched atop the Mojave Desert. Known for its enigmatic charm, Oatman boasts a unique characteristic – it is home to more donkeys than residents. Numerous donkeys freely roam the streets of Oatman, often approaching inquisitive visitors seeking treats and affectionate head pats. The townspeople hold a special regard for these burros, treating them like part of the community. A testament to this unique bond is the annual Burro Biscuit Toss, a playful competition where both residents and visitors vie to throw a gold-painted burro dropping the farthest. The victor is rewarded with burro-themed merchandise, a bar of soap, and a monetary prize.

Along Route 66, you'll discover a variety of accommodations to choose from. Here are some popular motels and hotels at different locations:

Holbrook: Brad's Desert Inn, The Wigwam Motel
Flagstaff: Super 8 by Wyndham Flagstaff, Little America Hotel
Seligman: Deluxe Inn, Historic Route 66 Motel
Williams: Grand Canyon Hotel, Red Garter Inn, The Lodge, Rodeway Inn & Suites Downtowner
Kingman: Super 8 by Wyndham Kingman, El Trovatore Motel
Winslow: La Posada Hotel & Gardens, Earl's Route 66 Motor Court

----

SABINO CANYON

COUNTY: PIMA   CITY: TUCSON *n.c.*

DATE VISITED: WHO I WENT WITH:

RATING: ☆ ☆ ☆ ☆ ☆   WILL I RETURN? YES / NO

Sabino Canyon stands out as one of the most popular hiking destinations in Tucson. Featuring 14 trails and boundless vistas showcasing desert flora, and picnic tables for relishing a scenic lunch, the canyon also offers a convenient shuttle service to explore the area.

Sabino Canyon is situated on the northeast side of Tucson within the Coronado National Forest, approximately 16 miles away from downtown Tucson. To reach the location, input the following address into your GPS: 5700 N. Sabino Canyon Road, just north of Sunrise Drive. While the Sabino Canyon Recreation Area and its parking lot are open 24 hours a day, the visitor center operates from 8 a.m. to 4:30 p.m. daily, and camping is not permitted.

For day visitors, the entrance fee is $8 per car, and if you plan to stay for the week, the price increases to $10. However, the most cost-effective option, especially for Tucson residents keen on frequenting Sabino Canyon, is the annual pass, available for $40 per car and purchasable at the visitor center. Payment can be made on-site, where a staff member may be present at an entrance booth to collect fees. Alternatively, you can pay for a day or week pass online or at a kiosk near the entrance. Sabino Canyon also welcomes visitors with Coronado passes or valid Interagency Passes, including Senior, Access, and Military passes.

Sabino Canyon provides two parking lots, one being an overflow lot situated north of the main lot, typically open during peak seasons when the primary lot reaches full capacity. Fees are generally waived in the Coronado National Forest on specific days throughout the year, such as Martin Luther King Jr. Day, National Get Outdoors Day in June, and Veteran's Day. Refer to recreation.gov for a comprehensive list of fee-free days.

Two shuttles operate in the area—one serving Sabino Canyon and the other designated for the Bear Canyon trailhead. The Sabino Canyon shuttle covers a more extensive route with additional stops. The Sabino Canyon shuttle, which is emission-free and includes narration, charges $15 per adult and $8 for children aged 3-12. On the other hand, the Bear Canyon shuttle, powered by gas, offers rides at $8 per adult and $5 for children aged 3-12. Operating every 30 minutes, the Sabino Canyon shuttle runs from 9 a.m. to 4 p.m., while the Bear Canyon shuttle operates on the same schedule but starts 15 minutes later, running from 9:15 a.m. to 4:15 p.m. It's advisable to check for seasonal variations in hours ahead of your visit.

The visitor center serves as a combination of a gift shop and a miniature museum. Within the gallery area, which opens on Tuesdays, Thursdays, and Saturdays, visitors can explore small exhibits delving into Sabino Canyon's history, educational materials about local animals, and details about the various plant species you might encounter during your visit. On the other side of the visitor center, a plethora of souvenirs and trinkets awaits, ranging from apparel and seed packets to prickly pear candy, coffee mugs, magnets, bookmarks, and water bottles. Additionally, there's a collection of desert-themed books, covering topics such as hummingbirds, lizards, children's literature like "The Three Little Javelinas," a historical exploration of the Sonoran Desert, and an engaging activity book titled "Who Pooped in the Desert?" Functioning as an information hub, the visitor center provides details about the trails through its TV screens displaying the day's weather and hiking tips, a whiteboard indicating current closures, and knowledgeable staff ready to address any inquiries. Outside the visitor center, giant directories offer an abundance of information, including recommendations on hiking attire, a schedule of guided walks, and maps for exploration.

Adjacent to the east side of the visitor center, positioned just north of the primary parking lot, lies the Bear Canyon trailhead. This trailhead grants access to well-frequented locations like Sabino Dam, Seven Falls, and Blackett's Ridge Trail. On the opposite side of the visitor center, towards the west, the path leads to upper Sabino Canyon. To reach some of the trails in this direction, there is a 3.7-mile walk along a paved roadway. Notable trails and destinations in this westward direction encompass Hutch's Pool, Anderson Dam, and Sabino Canyon Trail.

The Sabino Canyon Recreation Area boasts a diverse collection of 14 trails, each varying in difficulty and length. As you embark on your hiking journey, trail signs, accompanied by their respective distances, guide your way. Noteworthy trails include the Eight-point-four-mile roundtrip Seven Falls, the Two-point-five-mile roundtrip Sabino Dam Trail, and the Five-point-seven-mile Phoneline Trail, extending from the visitor center to the summit of Sabino Canyon Road. Many visitors also find pleasure in traversing the approximately Four-mile one-way paved roadway leading to upper Sabino Canyon.

For those with limited time, the directory in the area offers the following recommendations based on available time:

1) Less than an hour: Take a stroll along the half-mile Bajada Loop Nature Trail near the visitor center.
2) 1-2 hours: Opt for a guided tour on the Sabino Canyon shuttle. For those inclined towards hiking, explore trails like Sabino Dam or the Rattlesnake Trail Loop.
3) 3-4 hours: Utilize a one-way shuttle to delve into either canyon for hiking or a picnic, then make your way back down the road.
4) All day: Embark on an extensive hike to Seven Falls or choose any other trail that captures your interest.

The paved roads, Sabino Canyon Road and Bear Canyon Road, are designed to be accessible for wheelchairs.

Following substantial rainfall in Tucson, there's a possibility of witnessing waterfalls and rainwater coursing through Sabino Creek. While this occurrence isn't guaranteed, it presents a breathtaking spectacle when it does happen. Before embarking on your hike, it's crucial to check the weather conditions and steer clear of the area if heavy rainfall and/or flood risks are forecasted. Flash floods can occur suddenly and pose potential dangers.

For an easy stroll or hike with the potential to witness water, head to Sabino Dam. To reach it, use the Bear Canyon Trailhead and turn right upon reaching the pavement. Follow the roadway, and you'll encounter signs pointing to the dam. (If the dam is flowing, you might also hear the water.) Along the Bear Canyon Trail, there's a chance to glimpse a waterfall at Seven Falls, characterized by several stream crossings and sections with steep inclines. The Bear Canyon Trail is classified as moderate to difficult. Another location where water might be present is Anderson Dam, situated near upper Sabino Canyon and one of the last shuttle stops. Hutch's Pool in upper Sabino Canyon is another spot with year-round water, accessible along the West Fork Trail. A tip: Opting to walk along the roadway to access the trail covers approximately 8 miles roundtrip, essentially doubling the hike. If you prefer to avoid the roadway, take the shuttle and complete the remaining journey to Hutch's Pool on foot.

Show consideration and respect towards any wildlife you may encounter, which can include various species such as snakes, mountain lions, and birds.

Restrooms, water fountains, and vending machines are available in certain locations near the primary parking lot. Additionally, there are grills in specific areas, although their usage may be temporarily halted if there are forest fire restrictions in effect.

The Sabino Canyon Volunteer Naturalists invest their time in "assisting individuals of all ages in developing an appreciation for the natural beauty of Sabino Canyon." They provide educational programs tailored for both children and adults, encompassing group hikes, bird walks, and field trips.

SAGUARO NATIONAL PARK

COUNTY: PIMA   CITY: TUCSON

DATE VISITED: WHO I WENT WITH:

RATING: ☆ ☆ ☆ ☆ ☆   WILL I RETURN?   YES / NO

Situated in southern Arizona, Saguaro National Park is bisected by the city of Tucson. The park comprises two districts: the Rincon Mountain District, spanning 67,476 acres to the east of Tucson, and the Tucson Mountain District, covering 25,391 acres to the west. These districts are dedicated to preserving the saguaro (sa-WAH-row), the largest cactus species in the United States, growing exclusively in the Sonoran Desert and reaching towering heights of up to 50 feet, surpassing the length of an average school bus.

While the park attracts visitors eager to admire the iconic saguaros, hiking stands out as the primary activity, complemented by the allure of scenic drives. However, it is crucial to check the weather conditions before your visit. In the summer, temperatures can surpass 110 degrees Fahrenheit, posing risks of severe dehydration and even fatalities for the unprepared. Winters may bring up to 2 feet of snow within a 48-hour period, and during the monsoon season, canyons and arroyos are susceptible to flooding.

Separated by approximately 30 miles, each district boasts a visitor center and a short, picturesque drive. However, immersing oneself in the saguaro experience is best achieved through hiking. The park boasts a total of 171 miles of designated trails, including some that are multi-use. For mountain biking enthusiasts, the Rincon Mountain District offers options like the 2.5-mile segment of the Cactus Forest Trail and the 2.9-mile Hope Camp Trail. Those inclined toward cycling can enjoy a scenic loop in either district.

Saguaro National Park presents a diverse range of hiking options, catering to various skill levels and preferences. The western Tucson Mountain District, closely located to the Arizona Sonora Desert Museum, is favored by tourists, while the Rincon Mountain District, situated across the city, attracts local adventurers. Both districts offer excellent hiking opportunities.

Apart from following designated trails, the Rincon Mountain District allows backcountry hiking in the Saguaro Wilderness Area.

Highlighted Rincon Mountain District Hikes:

1) Desert Ecology Trail: This quarter-mile trail, open to pets, runs along the Javelina Wash and features signs introducing hikers to the Sonoran Desert inhabitants. It is wheelchair accessible.
2) Freeman Homestead Trail: A 1-mile trail with interpretive signage and children's activities, forming a loop to a homestead site and a grove of large saguaros. Look out for great horned owls in the cliffs above the arroyo.

3) Loma Verde Loop: A 3.8-mile trail providing stunning views of cacti forests. Crossing a seasonally flowing arroyo might be necessary in spring or after heavy rain.

4) Hope Camp Trail: Traversing an old ranch road to two abandoned cowboy camps marked by windmill ruins, this 6.6-mile out-and-back trek offers an overlook of Box Canyon, with waterfalls visible in wetter months.

5) Garwood and Wildhorse Trails: Combining these trails with others forms a 6.4-mile loop. The Garwood Dam Trail leads to a 1950s-era dam, taking hikers through the cactus forest that inspired the park's creation in 1933. The Wildhorse Trail extends to the Little Wildhorse Tank, a key water source in the park.

Tucson Mountain District Hikes:

1) Desert Discovery Nature Trail: Located a short drive from the Red Hills Visitor Center, this interpretive trail spans less than half a mile and is wheelchair accessible.

2) Passey Loop Trail: Situated at the park's northern edge, this 1.6-mile trail offers an easy, flat walk through the desert. The trailhead is off Iron Ridge Drive.

3) Wild Dog Trail: Stretching nearly 2 miles, this trail starts from Hohokam Road, at the Valley View Overlook Trailhead, and leads to the Signal Hill picnic area. For non-hikers, there's an option to drive around the loop.

4) Sendero Esperanza Trail: Begin with the Gould Mine Trail, transition to the Sendero Esperanza Trail, and ascend to the Hugh Norris Trail for expansive desert views. The out-and-back route covers approximately 4 miles. For those seeking a more challenging hike, continue on the Hugh Norris Trail to Wasson Peak, the park's highest point (an 8-plus mile journey).

The Saguaro National Park features only two scenic drives, one in each district. A recommended approach for park visits, especially for families with young children, those seeking accessible trails, or those with limited time, is to take a loop drive with stops at interpretive trails. These accessible trails typically take less than half an hour for most visitors to hike and provide an educational introduction to the park's flora and fauna.

Cactus Forest Loop Drive: Located in the Rincon Mountain District, this 8-mile drive crosses the Javelina Wash multiple times, traverses the mountains, and descends to lower elevations. Noteworthy is the Desert Ecology Trail, offering insights into saguaros and the desert. Visitors might consider a lunch break at the Micah View or Javelina picnic areas.

Bajada Loop Drive: Spanning 6 miles through the Tucson Mountain District's foothills, this gravel road features scenic pullouts, picnic areas, and the brief Desert Discovery Nature Trail with interpretive signage. While a high-clearance vehicle or four-wheel drive is unnecessary, trailers exceeding 35 feet and vehicles wider than 8 feet are restricted from the loop.

Camping within Saguaro National Park is restricted to those willing to hike a minimum of nearly 4.5 miles to access one of six designated campgrounds situated in the Saguaro Wilderness Area. Securing a backcountry permit is necessary for overnight stays, with a fee of $8 per campsite per night.

Manning Camp: Constructed by former Tucson Mayor Levi Manning, this camp stands as the largest in the park, featuring only six sites. Visitors must be prepared for a hike of over 7 miles to reach Manning Camp.

Happy Valley: Positioned approximately 4.5 miles from the trailhead, this camp is situated at an elevation of 6,200 feet, providing remarkable desert views.

You have various accommodation options in Tucson, conveniently located within a half-hour of either entrance to Saguaro National Park. Here are three noteworthy choices:

Tanque Verde Ranch: Situated just 7 miles from the eastern district's entrance, this historic guest ranch provides a range of experiences, including horseback riding, spa services, and upscale dining. Guests can opt for all-inclusive, bed-and-breakfast, or meals-only packages.

Hilton Tucson East: Also located 7 miles from the Rincon Mountain District, this seven-story hotel boasts mountain views and an inviting pool.

JW Marriott Star Pass Resort: Regarded as one of Tucson's premier resorts, JW Marriott Star Pass offers amenities such as a hotel spa, multi-level pool with a lazy river, and desert golf courses designed by Arnold Palmer. Accessing the western Tucson Mountain District from here requires a scenic 20-minute drive through Tucson Mountain Park.

How to Get There

Begin your journey by flying into Tucson International Airport, conveniently situated 8 miles south of downtown. Your transportation to the park will be influenced by your accommodation and the district you plan to visit.

For access to the Rincon Mountain District entrance, follow Broadway Boulevard to Freeman Road. Take a right onto Freeman Road and travel south for 3 miles. Make a left onto Old Spanish Trail, and after a quarter-mile drive, you'll arrive at the park entrance.

To reach the Tucson Mountain District from Tucson's city center, head west on Speedway Boulevard, traversing Gates Pass to Kinney Road. Take a right and continue 4 miles into the park, with the visitor center located 1 mile further north.

For those approaching from the north, utilize I-10 and take exit 242 for Avra Valley Road. Proceed west for 6 miles to Sandario Road. Make a left turn on Sandario Road and cover a distance of 14 miles. Take another left onto Kinney Road and drive 2 miles, with the visitor center situated on your left.

The visitor centers in both districts are fully equipped with accessibility features, including designated parking spaces, accessible restrooms, drinking fountains, paved cactus garden paths, and captioned orientation programs. Throughout the entire park, there are accessible picnic areas.

In the Rincon Mountain District, both the Desert Ecology Trail and a segment of the Mica View Trail are designed to be accessible. Similarly, in the Tucson Mountain District, the Desert Discovery Trail, which spans half a mile and is paved, offers accessibility.

Tips:

1) The visitor centers in both districts observe closures on Tuesday and Wednesday, although the park remains open.
2) Pets are permitted only on paved roads, interpretive trails, and in picnic areas.
3) During the summer, it is advisable to hike early in the day and plan on consuming one liter of water per hour per person. Turn around when half of your water is consumed.
4) While hiking, wear closed-toed hiking shoes, loose-fitting natural-fiber clothing, a wide-brimmed hat, sunglasses, and sunscreen. Avoid wearing sandals.
5) Refrain from putting your hands or feet in holes or under rocks to minimize the risk of bites or stings from poisonous creatures like rattlesnakes and scorpions.

SCOTTSDALE

COUNTY: MARICOPA   CITY: SCOTTSDALE

DATE VISITED: WHO I WENT WITH:

RATING: ☆ ☆ ☆ ☆ ☆   WILL I RETURN?   YES / NO

Scottsdale, Arizona, known as "The West's Most Western Town," has a population exceeding 200,000 and enjoys over 300 days of sunshine annually. With over seven million annual visitors, the city has earned a reputation as an upscale resort destination, drawing the rich and famous for leisure and shopping. However, Scottsdale offers more than just luxurious resorts and fine dining establishments with scenic views. The city is rich in accessible and cost-free museums and attractions, making it an ideal destination for budget-conscious travelers.

Explore the Butterfly Wonderland: Step into the Butterfly Wonderland at OdySea and experience the enchantment of thousands of butterflies within one of the largest atriums in the country. Beforehand, catch the 3D movie "Flight of the Butterflies," ideal for children, offering a close-up look at the lives of these majestic creatures. Explore the Butterfly Emergence Gallery to witness the fascinating process of butterfly metamorphosis. After immersing yourself in the world of winged wonders, head next door with the kids to conquer the OdySea Mirror Maze or visit the OdySea Aquarium for a glimpse beneath the waters of oceans, seas, and rivers.

Swim alongside Dolphins at Dolphinaris Arizona: Scottsdale is also home to Dolphinaris Arizona, providing an opportunity to interact with bottlenose dolphins up close. Various packages are available, including options to enter the water with these extraordinary marine mammals. Alternatively, opt for a land-based experience if you prefer to stay dry. Regardless of your choice, you'll gain insights into dolphins, their ecosystems, and the conservation measures necessary to protect and preserve them in their natural habitat.

Participate in the Barrett-Jackson Classic Car Auction: The Barrett-Jackson Classic Car Auction is a must-see for avid car collectors. Hosted annually in both Scottsdale and Palm Springs, this eight-day event showcases over a thousand cars on the auction block, accompanied by special exhibits and seminars open to the public. It's an opportunity to explore some of the most exclusive vehicles, including those formerly owned by celebrities, and potentially make a purchase.

Engage in Outdoor or Indoor Golf: Scottsdale is a haven for golf enthusiasts, boasting approximately 50 golf courses in the vicinity. Notable championship courses like TPC Scottsdale, which hosts the Waste Management's Phoenix Open, offer diverse and challenging terrains. You don't necessarily have to play at a high-end golf resort for an enjoyable experience; the region provides numerous budget-friendly golfing options. If the weather is too scorching for outdoor play, consider joining locals at Topgolf Scottsdale. This indoor target golf facility employs cutting-edge technology, providing a genuine indoor playing experience rather than just a simulation.

Explore the Fiesta Bowl Museum: Situated within the corporate offices of the Fiesta Bowl in central Scottsdale, the Fiesta Bowl Museum is a fascinating stop for football enthusiasts. Visit on a weekday to discover college football trophies and exhibits detailing the history of the Fiesta Bowl organization, its dedicated volunteers, and the games. Admission to the museum is free, making it an excellent destination for fans eager to see all the teams' helmets gathered in one place.

Cycle along the Indian Bend Wash Greenbelt: The picturesque Indian Bend Wash Greenbelt features 11 miles of biking and walking paths, surrounded by lakes and golf courses. Connecting four parks—Vista Del Camino, Eldorado, Indian School, and Chaparral—this urban greenspace is a popular destination for various recreational activities, including inline skating, jogging, and dog walking. Families who enjoy cycling will particularly appreciate the dedicated paths, separated from the road with clearly marked crossings for enhanced safety.

Attend a Concert at ASU Kerr: ASU Kerr Cultural Center, a part of Arizona State University, was initially constructed as a venue for chamber music performances. While it still hosts chamber music events, the cultural center has expanded its offerings to include jazz, Celtic, and classical concerts. Despite its small size, the theater provides an intimate setting for presentations and serves as a wonderful way to show support for the university's fine arts programs.

Explore Old Town Scottsdale: The winding streets and unique shops and galleries of Old Town Scottsdale offer a delightful way to spend an evening on vacation. Known as the "Fifth Avenue Shops," this vibrant downtown area exudes cultural charm. Depending on the season, visitors can explore modern art, attend the farmer's market, sample fine wines and craft beer, all while enjoying a leisurely walk or bike ride.

Visit the McCormick Stillman Railroad Park: Situated in the heart of Scottsdale, the McCormick Stillman Railroad Park provides distinctive amenities for children, including a charming carousel. Explore their railroad-themed museum exhibits or relax on the grass while your kids play on the unique playground facilities. Don't miss the opportunity to take a ten-minute train ride, offering a scenic tour through the park's arboretum.

Experience the Parada del Sol Rodeo: North Scottsdale becomes the gathering point for professional cowboys from across the country during the Parada del Sol Rodeo. Organized by the Scottsdale Jaycees, this rodeo is the culmination of events that include the Parada del Sol Parade and the Coors Hoedown. Taking place in early March with multiple showings, attendees can purchase tickets in advance to enjoy the entire rodeo event or focus on the thrilling bull riding competitions.

Indulge in Culinary Delights at the Scottsdale Culinary Festival: Beyond the spotlight on fine art, Scottsdale takes center stage each April with a multi-day festival celebrating food, music, and entertainment. Food enthusiasts can savor the burger battle, indulge in chocolate and wine pairings, attend cocktail demonstrations, and experience the highlight of a five-course wine-paired dinner. The proceeds from this popular event contribute to funding art education programs for students in the Valley of the Sun.

Explore the Scottsdale ArtWalk: Every Thursday night throughout the year (excluding Thanksgiving), Scottsdale's art gallery scene comes alive after dinner, with open doors and special showings. Wander through downtown streets to partake in artists' receptions, view show openings, and witness demonstrations. Best of all, it's a free experience, unless, of course, you find a piece you can't resist taking home.

Participate in a Scottsdale Art Show: Two prominent art shows grace Scottsdale each winter, lasting for about six weeks. The Arizona Fine Art Expo and the Celebration of Fine Art attract serious art enthusiasts and casual browsers alike. These events, perfectly timed to escape the winter chill up north, offer demonstrations and workshops across various mediums such as oil, glass, stone, metal, and ceramics. Explore the booths to discover new items for your home decor.

Embark on a Scottsdale Trolley Tour: Hop on a two-hour guided tour aboard the Scottsdale trolley, providing insights into the city's different districts, including Old Town Scottsdale, Craftsman Court, the Civic Center area, and the Scottsdale Arts District. The tour brings the city's history and architecture to life, along with stories about its significant historical figures. Feel free to ask questions of your knowledgeable tour guide, who can assist with recommendations for dining, souvenir shopping, and even suggest nearby hiking spots.

Experience Baseball's Spring Training: Throughout the entire month of March, the valley becomes a hub of excitement for baseball enthusiasts as Major League Baseball's spring training takes center stage. Witness the Cactus League in action, offering an affordable opportunity to see professional teams and players. Scottsdale Stadium is the home for the San Francisco Giants during spring training, while Salt River Fields at Talking Stick, just north of downtown Scottsdale, hosts the Arizona Diamondbacks and the Colorado Rockies.

Explore Scottsdale's Museum of the West: Nestled in the downtown Scottsdale Arts District, at the intersection of Scottsdale Road and Main Street, the Museum of the West stands as one of the city's newest and most captivating destinations. This museum provides a journey through the evolution of the Old West to its contemporary iteration, showcasing the western spirit through paintings, sculptures, films, lectures, and community events.

Visit Taliesen West on a Guided Tour: Situated in the foothills of the McDowell Mountains, surrounded by the Sonoran Desert, is a 600-acre historical landmark designed and constructed by Frank Lloyd Wright and his students. Wright's original winter residence, now housing the Frank Lloyd Wright School of Architecture, is located on the grounds. Embark on a guided tour to explore the unique setting and buildings that seamlessly blend landscape architecture with massive walls, thoughtful structures, and handcrafted furniture.

McDowell Sonoran Preserve: The McDowell Sonoran Preserve, inaugurated in 2009, welcomes the public to immerse themselves in the breathtaking Sonoran Desert. Serving as the largest and most significant entry point to the Preserve, this area is set to cover 36,400 acres of desert upon completion. Visitors can revel in the diverse flora and fauna of the desert, encountering vibrant wildflowers, majestic Saguaro cacti, quails, and other desert creatures. The Gateway Access Area, positioned east of Thompson Peak Parkway and half a mile north of Bell Road, offers amenities such as free shade ramadas, a dog comfort station, an equestrian staging area, and more. Trail maps are available at the parking area to assist visitors in navigating the preserve.

SEDONA

COUNTY: COCONINO, YAVAPAI   **CITY:** SEDONA

DATE VISITED: **WHO I WENT WITH:**

RATING: ☆ ☆ ☆ ☆ ☆   **WILL I RETURN?** YES / NO

Sedona is commonly associated with Jeep tours and outdoor adventures amidst the captivating red rock formations, yet this city of 10,000 residents offers much more. Its main streets are adorned with art galleries, while five-star restaurants attract food enthusiasts, and romantic resorts create an ideal in-state retreat. Although Sedona is a favored destination for Phoenicians seeking respite from the triple-digit heat in the Valley, it also allures several visitors from Hollywood. Notable personalities like Nicholas Cage, Johnny Depp, Oprah Winfrey, and Kristen Bell have been spotted strolling through the Uptown district or exploring the nearby trails. However, you need not be a celebrity to enjoy a top-notch experience in Sedona.

There really isn't a unfavorable time to visit Sedona. While the shoulder months of April, September, and October, with average temperatures ranging from the mid-60s to low 70s, are popular among most visitors, May tends to be similarly pleasant. Due to its elevation of 4,350 feet, the summer months of June, July, and August can see temperatures reaching up to 90 degrees Fahrenheit.

Typically, visitors drive to Sedona, park their vehicles, and explore the area on foot. To navigate local attractions without returning to their cars, visitors can opt for the Sedona Trolley (though it's not a hop-on, hop-off service), use rideshare services, or rent a Jeep, street-legal ATV, or a similar vehicle. The only public transportation available is the Verde Lynx bus, but its limited schedule and route make it an impractical choice for most tourists.

Sedona serves as an excellent home base for exploring other parts of the state. A mere two-hour drive from Sedona leads to the Grand Canyon, one of the Seven Natural Wonders of the world, while the ghost-town-turned-art-community of Jerome is just a 45-minute drive away. Additionally, the city is conveniently located 20 minutes from some of northern Arizona's finest wineries in Cornville.

Sedona is renowned for its outdoor adventures, offering diverse ways to experience the beauty of Red Rock Country. While hiking is the most evident choice, there are alternative options such as mountain biking on many trails or embarking on an off-roading adventure through guided or self-guided tours. For those seeking a more leisurely day, soaking in the healing energy of a vortex, indulging in a spa day, or leisurely strolling through boutique shops and art galleries are also enticing options.

Hiking is a prominent activity, with over 100 trails in the Sedona area, many of which are family-friendly. If you're unsure where to start, the knowledgeable staff at the Hike House can recommend the best trails based on your preferences and physical abilities.

For a particularly Instagram-worthy hike, the Devil's Bridge trail leading to a 50-foot-high natural sandstone arch is a great choice.

Embarking on a Jeep tour is another popular option, with local pioneer Don Pratt introducing Jeep tours in the 1960s. The iconic Broken Arrow Tour by Pink Jeep Tours, traversing boulder-laden trails to scenic vistas, remains a quintessential Sedona experience. Similar guided tours are available through other providers, or you can opt for the adventure of renting a Jeep or ATV for self-guided exploration.

When it comes to shopping, Uptown Sedona and Tlaquepaque Arts & Shopping Village are the primary shopping areas, but boutiques and art galleries also line SR 179 leading into the city. While Tlaquepaque is known for its art galleries and specialty stores, Uptown offers a variety of souvenir shops, including those selling the famous Original Red Rock Dirt Shirts.

Dining in Sedona is not only a culinary experience but also a feast for the eyes, as the scenery often plays a significant role. Throughout most of the year, patrons opt to dine on restaurant patios, while some establishments boast floor-to-ceiling windows that showcase equally impressive views. Given the frequent influx of day trippers from Phoenix, lunch emerges as the busiest mealtime, featuring menus dominated by burgers, sandwiches, and salads in Sedona.

As the evening descends, fine dining establishments like Mariposa Latin Inspired Grill and Elote Café take center stage, offering delectable steaks and dishes influenced by Southwestern flavors. For those seeking a premium wine or craft cocktail, resort restaurants typically provide excellent options, with upscale venues like The Hudson offering both. If you lean more towards beer, Sedona caters to beer enthusiasts with three craft breweries, including the acclaimed Oak Creek Brewing Co.

The most practical means of reaching Sedona is by car. Visitors from out-of-state typically arrive at Phoenix Sky Harbor International Airport or Phoenix Mesa Gateway Airport and opt for car rentals. However, some airlines do fly into Flagstaff Pulliam Airport, a smaller yet closer regional airport. There's also the option of bus and shuttle services from Phoenix to Sedona.

Phoenix Sky Harbor International Airport, being one of the nation's busiest airports, is a common arrival point for twenty airlines. Its Rental Car Center is conveniently located minutes from Interstate 17, the major highway leading north to Sedona.

Phoenix Mesa Gateway Airport, situated in the East Valley, is a smaller airport with fewer flights and rental cars. However, it offers easier access. Since it's approximately 30 miles southeast of Sky Harbor, landing here does add an additional 40 minutes to the drive to Sedona.

Best things to do in Sedona:

Hike to the Devil's Bridge: Explore one of the many trails in the Sedona area, and for a hike with picturesque views suitable for most hikers, Devil's Bridge is an excellent choice. The initial 3/4-mile to the trail's namesake, a 50-foot-high natural arch, is relatively flat, but the steep, natural rock staircase to its top can be exhilarating. The reward includes stunning views of the red rocks and the opportunity to pose on the arch's pinnacle. To avoid the crowded trail, consult the Hike House in Sedona, where the Sedona Trail Finder can suggest hikes based on your preferred distance, elevation changes, difficulty, and time. Alternatively, visit the Sedona Red Rock Trails website for comprehensive information on hiking, mountain biking, and equestrian trails in the region.

Soar Over Sedona's Red Rocks in a Hot Air Balloon: Gain a different perspective by taking to the skies in a hot air balloon. Balloon rides provide a bird's eye view of landmarks like Cathedral Rock, Oak Creek, Bell Rock, and even sights as far north as the San Francisco Peaks. Floating slightly above the ground, you might even spot wildlife like deer that are not usually visible from the ground. Consider booking with Northern Light Balloon Expeditions or Red Rock Balloons, the only two companies permitted to take off in the Sedona area, as others operate near Cottonwood. If an open-air balloon ride is not your preference, a helicopter tour offers a similar breathtaking perspective.

Gaze Into the Night Sky: Sedona, designated as an International Dark Sky Community, attracts stargazers from around the world. Set up telescopes along forest roads outside Sedona to observe planets, stars, and other celestial wonders. Enjoy naked-eye views of the Milky Way or enhance your experience with binoculars at Two Trees Observing Area, Boynton Canyon Trailhead, Merry-Go-Round Rock, and other locations. Alternatively, join a stargazing tour offered by Sedona Stargazing or Sedona UFO Tours to explore the heavens through a telescope.

Experience the Mystical Energy of a Vortex: Technically, the entirety of Sedona is recognized as a vortex—a region of heightened spiritual energy conducive to prayer, meditation, and healing. However, certain sites in the area, such as Bell Rock and Airport Mesa, are believed to possess more concentrated spiritual energy. You can independently explore these vortex sites using a map from the city's visitor center or online resources. Alternatively, you can enhance your experience by hiring a guide who can lead you through meditation, yoga, or healing rituals at these sites.

Indulge in a Spa Day: Sedona boasts some of the finest spas in the state. For an unparalleled spa experience, consider booking a room at Enchantment Resort. While its spa, Mii Amo, is exclusively available to resort guests, the Crystal Grotto's relaxing ambiance is worth the visit after your treatment. Alternatively, indulge in a Native American-inspired treatment at Sedona's New Day Spa. For a more unique experience, The Spa at Sedona Rouge specializes in treatments with a Moroccan-style steam room, while True Rest Float Spa offers an anti-gravity experience as you float in saltwater for an hour.

Ride in an Iconic Pink Jeep: If you've ever taken a Jeep tour during your travels, you likely have Don Pratt to thank. In 1960, Pratt initiated tours of the Sedona area using a Jeep painted pink, and the idea gained popularity. Today, Pink Jeep Tours stands as the premier Jeep tour operator in the region. Book the Broken Arrow Tour for a thrilling ride over rugged terrain, including a steep descent down The Road of No Return. Alternatively, opt for the Ancient Ruins tour to explore 700-year-old cliff dwellings. Pink Jeep also offers vortex, wildlife, and winery tours, along with a roundtrip journey to the Grand Canyon.

Marvel at the Chapel of the Holy Cross: Originally planned for construction in Budapest under the guidance of Frank Lloyd Wright's son, Lloyd Wright, this striking chapel perches on the red rocks just off SR 179, offering a breathtaking view of the valley below. Open every day from 9 a.m. to 5 p.m., visitors can admire the architecture both inside and out. While admission is free, parking in the 45-space lot can be challenging. Many visitors find themselves parking on the road below and walking up the winding drive to the church's entrance, a small effort that's rewarded by the stunning view.

Cool Off at Slide Rock State Park: Situated in Oak Creek Canyon, just north of Sedona, this state park offers an 80-foot-long natural water slide coated with algae and a half-mile-long swimming area—an ideal spot for refreshing splashes on hot summer days. To ensure entry, especially during weekends or school breaks, it's advisable to arrive early and plan for a full day. In between swims, take a leisurely hike on the easy 1/4-mile trail leading to the Pendley Homestead. Here, you can explore the house, apple packing barn, and various farming implements.

Explore Sinagua Ruins and Petroglyphs: The Sinagua people inhabited the Sedona area from approximately 1150 to 1400 A.D., and although their departure remains a mystery, their ruins and petroglyphs dot the landscape. Visit the region's largest cliff dwellings at the Palatki Heritage Site, explore more ruins at the Honanki Heritage Site, and observe petroglyphs at the V Bar V Heritage Site. All three sites, managed by the U.S. Forest Service, require a Red Rock Pass, obtainable from an onsite vending machine. If navigating forest roads feels daunting, several Sedona tour companies offer guided visits to these sites.

Dine With a View: Given Sedona's stunning scenery and top-notch restaurants, enjoying a meal with a picturesque view is a must. For an unforgettable dining experience with a panoramic view, reserve a table at Mariposa Latin Inspired Grill. Whether you choose to dine inside, with floor-to-ceiling windows framing the red rocks, or on the patio, Chef Lisa Dahl delights with a menu featuring fish dishes, perfectly cooked steaks, handmade empanadas, and other Latin American fare. Enhance your meal with a glass of wine from the restaurant's 600-bottle vault.

Stroll Through Sedona's Art Galleries: Art galleries line State Routes 179 and 89A and fill shopping plazas like Tlaquepaque Arts & Crafts Village and The Shops at Hyatt Pinon. These galleries showcase a diverse range of mediums, from watercolors to metalwork and Native American art. On the first Friday of each month, don't miss First Friday in the

Galleries when establishments open their doors after hours, offering drinks, small bites, live music, and the chance to meet artists.

SELIGMAN

COUNTY: YAVAPAI

CITY: SELIGMAN

DATE VISITED: **WHO I WENT WITH:**

RATING: ☆ ☆ ☆ ☆ ☆   **WILL I RETURN?** YES / NO

A quaint, small town situated along a preserved segment of Route 66 encapsulates a lively piece of Americana. Positioned between Flagstaff and Kingman in Northern Arizona, Seligman serves as a guardian of yesteryear's American culture at the commencement of the picturesque drive, representing the longest remaining stretch of Route 66 in the United States.

The current essence of Seligman is greatly indebted to Angel Delgadillo, a barber from Seligman who spearheaded initiatives for the preservation of Route 66. When the town was bypassed by Interstate 40 in 1978, Delgadillo established the Historic Route 66 Association of Arizona. In 1987, Seligman earned the distinction of being the Birthplace of Historic Route 66, as the State of Arizona officially recognized the road stretch from Seligman to Kingman as part of Historic Route 66. This designation reignited interest in the old-fashioned Americana associated with Route 66, and Seligman remains the starting point for the longest surviving section of this iconic American highway, spanning 160 miles to Topock, Arizona.

The town is brimming with nostalgic shops, motels, and diners, making it an ideal spot to pause and unwind. A standout attraction in Seligman is the Return to the 50s Museum, situated in a former gas station, displaying vintage motorcycles, cars, Route 66 memorabilia, and items from the 1950s. Notably, characters from Pixar's animated film "Cars," including Tow Mater, are prominently featured, as the entire movie drew inspiration from the town of Seligman. Visitors can explore specialty gift shops, such as the Motoporium, and visit the historic 1860 Arizona Territorial Jail. To complete the experience, a visit to the renowned Roadkill Cafe is a must, offering specialties like Bad-Brake Steak, Deer Delectables, Splatter Platter, Caddie Grilled Patty, and Swirl of Squirrel, among other unique offerings.

Although Seligman is a small town, it boasts a variety of distinctive gift shops worth exploring. Angel and Vilma Delgadillo's Route 66 Gift Shop, a family-owned and operated business, holds a significant legacy as the first store to introduce "Route 66 themed items." Historic Seligman Sundries, listed on the Register of National Historic Places, not only serves as a visitor's center but also stands as the town's sole coffee bar, featuring a vintage soda fountain. The uniquely adorned Rusty Bolt, adorned with mannequins, offers a distinct and some might say "quirky" shopping experience, providing numerous photo opportunities. Lastly, there's the Route 66 General Store, which, despite prominently featuring Route 66 memorabilia, is truly a general store offering "one-stop shopping" with a range of items, including snacks, hardware, propane, souvenirs, and hunting and fishing supplies.

Adding to the list of must-see attractions in Seligman is the 1860 Arizona Territorial Jail. A sign outside the jail claims it once housed notorious outlaws like Seligman Sam, Three-Finger Jack, James Younger, and many others. In 1866, a group of Navajo Native Americans managed to escape through a tunnel leading to the O.K. Saloon, but their attempt ended in tragedy as they were killed in a gun battle with Marshal Carl 'Curley' Bane. Accounts of the individuals once incarcerated in the jail may vary, creating an intriguing aspect of the town's history.

Another noteworthy spot featuring vintage cars and motorcycles is a Route 66 memorabilia and souvenir shop. This shop offers custom-made T-shirts and artwork, making it a fascinating stop for antique enthusiasts. Additionally, visitors can enjoy a complimentary cup of coffee as part of the Motoporium's hospitality policy or view a life-size Elvis statue.

Continuing the exploration of Seligman, dining at the Roadkill Café is a unique experience. Embracing the roadkill theme with the motto "You kill it, we grill it," the Roadkill Café/O.K. Saloon presents specials like "Deer Delectables, Bad-Brake Steak, Fender Tenders, Caddie Grilled Patty, Splatter Platter, Swirl of Squirrel, Big Bagged Stag, Highway Hash," and their renowned char-broiled burgers. Ordering your food is said to be just as entertaining as savoring the flavors.

The recently renovated Historic Route 66 Motel, situated directly on the iconic Route 66, emphasizes its proximity with just a 2-hour drive to the Grand Canyon. Additionally, it offers convenient access to various Arizona attractions. The rooms are equipped with amenities such as free Wi-Fi, a phone, satellite TV, refrigerator, and a coffee bar. Positioned across the street from the Roadkill Café/O.K. Saloon, it provides a central location for guests.

For a truly unique lodging experience, consider the Grand Canyon Caverns. The Caverns Inn, located 220 feet underground, is accessible by elevator and is recognized as the "largest dry caverns in the country." A favorite among RV enthusiasts, the site also features above-ground amenities like a classic vintage motel, a diner, a gift shop, numerous photo opportunities, and even a rodeo ring hosting cowboy round-ups. Reservations are limited, so quick action is advised. Even if you don't stay overnight, you can still explore the caverns through a guided tour.

While Seligman is renowned for its association with iconic highways and a nostalgic representation of Americana, another intriguing activity is touring Seligman Airport. Open to the public since 1985 and owned by Yavapai County, the airport is just minutes away from restaurants and other Route 66 attractions. If you have an interest in aviation and landscapes, a visit to Seligman Airport is recommended.

Amidst the transient nature of Seligman, where most visitors merely pass through on their road trips or journeys to other destinations, the Black Cat Bar offers a sense of community. Catering to tourists, bikers, truck drivers, and locals seeking social connections, this establishment provides a communal space. After exploring all the other attractions in town, a visit to the Black Cat Bar completes the full Seligman experience.

SLIDE ROCK STATE PARK

COUNTY: COCONINO   CITY: SEDONA *n.c.*

DATE VISITED: WHO I WENT WITH:

RATING: ☆ ☆ ☆ ☆ ☆   WILL I RETURN?   YES / NO

Slide Rock State Park, originally known as the Pendley Homestead, is a 43-acre historical apple farm nestled in Oak Creek Canyon. Frank L. Pendley, who arrived in the canyon in 1907, officially obtained the land through the Homestead Act in 1910. His ingenuity played a crucial role in the park's history, as he successfully implemented a distinctive irrigation system that is still in operation today. This innovation enabled Pendley to establish his initial apple orchard in 1912, marking the beginning of the agricultural legacy that has defined the site since then. In addition to apples, Pendley cultivated garden produce and maintained a small number of livestock.

Being one of the few remaining intact homesteads in the canyon, Slide Rock State Park stands as a notable representation of early agricultural development in Central Arizona. The site also played a significant role in fostering the tourism industry in Oak Creek Canyon. The completion of the canyon road in 1914 and its subsequent paving in 1938 greatly contributed to the promotion of recreational activities in the area. In response to this trend, Pendley built rustic cabins in 1933 to accommodate vacationers and sightseers.

Present-day visitors can still experience the fruits of Pendley's labor. The park showcases historic cabins that provide a glimpse into the past, while the creek offers an exhilarating slide for adventure seekers and a refreshing spot for those seeking respite from the heat.

Nestled within the captivating red rock formations of Oak Creek Canyon just north of Sedona, Arizona, this stunning northern Arizona park offers a plethora of activities amid its scenic surroundings. Whether you're interested in exploring the lush vegetation, meandering through wildlife habitat, engaging in trout fishing upstream of the park, or experiencing the renowned natural slide in Oak Creek, there's something for everyone. The park provides convenient facilities to enhance your visit, including a well-stocked park store offering a diverse range of items and souvenirs, making it a helpful resource for any forgotten essentials.

Open year-round with seasonal hours, the Slide Rock Market is a go-to spot for ice, snacks, water, sunscreen, and other necessities. Additionally, it features Slide Rock State Park memorabilia and souvenirs. Conveniently located on the right side, just off the main paved path through the park, the market is easily accessible for visitors heading down to the sliding area.

Adding to the charm of the park is the historic Pendley Homestead, situated along the main paved trail. Developed by Frank Pendley in the early 1900s, the homestead boasts a still-standing apple orchard established in 1912. A gazebo-style kiosk with eight poster boards provides insightful information about the Pendley Homestead and the park in general. The homestead, showcasing historic farm implements along the Pendley Homestead Trail, offers visitors a captivating glimpse into the past and presents delightful photo opportunities. When exploring this breathtaking area, the reasons behind the Pendleys' decision to build in such a picturesque location become evident.

There are two covered ramadas equipped with electrical outlets and picnic bench seating, each capable of accommodating approximately 50 people. These ramadas can be reserved for a fee. Refunds will not be issued for cancellations made 30 days or less before the reservation date. Charcoal fires are allowed only in designated grills, and wood fires are not permitted in these grills. Propane grills and stoves are acceptable, and smoking is restricted to vehicles only. Ramada reservations are not accepted between the Friday before Memorial Day and Labor Day Monday.

In addition, there are fifteen open-air picnic areas suitable for small groups near the entry station and parking lot, available on a first-come, first-served basis. Similar to the ramadas, charcoal fires are allowed only in designated grills, with no wood fires permitted. Propane grills and stoves are permitted, and smoking is allowed in vehicles only.

The park also provides two modern restroom buildings with ADA accessibility, sinks, and a drinking fountain located above the creek, featuring flush toilets. Additionally, a flush-free, waterless vault toilet is situated near the creek, though it is not ADA accessible.

Slide Rock, measuring 80 feet in length and 2.5 to 4 feet in width, features a gradual seven percent decline from top to bottom. The rocks are covered with algae, enhancing the slipperiness of the ride on this natural water slide. While the entire swimming area extends nearly half a mile, much of the attention is centered around this captivating natural feature.

For those who prefer a more relaxed experience, there's ample space along the creek's shore to lounge and observe other water enthusiasts swimming, jumping, and sliding in the midst of one of Arizona's most picturesque landscapes. Bringing a towel and some shade allows visitors to kick back and enjoy the sounds of fun in this natural playground in northern Arizona.

It's essential to note that there is no lifeguard on duty, and individuals are advised to watch their kids and use the slide and swimming area at their own risk. Visitors are encouraged to bring an adequate supply of drinking water and sunscreen to use during their stay. Wearing shoes is recommended for better grip while navigating the slippery, algae-covered sandstone.

While the water feature garners much attention, Slide Rock is also home to a diverse array of wildlife. Coues whitetail deer are regularly spotted throughout the park, often lounging and feeding in the apple orchards and occasionally approaching the main trails.

Javelina sightings are common in the thick, brushy areas near the main picnic area and parking lot.

The park is also a haven for colorful birds, with Steller's Jays displaying vibrant blues against the backdrop of the red rock escarpments. Numerous hummingbirds add to the lively atmosphere as they zip around the park. Bringing binoculars on your visit can enhance the experience of observing the area's birds and wildlife.

Coues Whitetail Deer, a smaller sub-species of whitetail deer, are frequently spotted in the park, providing visitors with the opportunity to observe these unique deer in their natural habitat. Exclusive to Arizona, New Mexico, and northern Mexico, Coues whitetails are a delightful sight within their restricted range, such as Sedona's Slide Rock State Park. Their graceful movements allow them to navigate the steep, rugged terrain of their typical habitats, and unlike mule deer, which are most active around sunrise and sunset, Coues whitetails can often be seen feeding and active throughout the day. Using small binoculars or a camera zoom helps enjoy these park regulars from a distance, ensuring their comfort within the park and continued enjoyment for all visitors. Look for deer feeding on lush vegetation on the west end of the park, and stay vigilant for their presence in the picnic area.

Arizona's black bear population thrives in prime habitat, with Slide Rock State Park located in the heart of their territory. Black bears exhibit various colors, including brown, blonde, and cinnamon, offering wildlife enthusiasts the chance to witness different color phases in their natural surroundings. Although black bears are naturally secretive, encounters are possible in the park. Visitors are encouraged to maintain a safe distance if they encounter a bear, enjoying the experience while respecting the wild nature of these animals. During the fall months, as bears increase their calorie intake before hibernation, they are more actively feeding throughout the day, presenting the best chance to see them in Oak Creek Canyon country.

Visitors to the park also have the unique opportunity to encounter one of Arizona's native treasures, the Collared Peccary, commonly known as Javelina. These medium-sized mammals are a delightful sight as they go about their daily activities within the park. Javelinas are herd animals, so if one is spotted, others are likely nearby. Watch for movement in the brush or listen for subtle social feeding sounds. Javelinas emit a distinct odor from a gland on their back, making them easily identifiable. Despite their nearsightedness, they offer photographers and wildlife watchers a chance for up-close observations. It's essential to admire these wild animals from a safe distance, as they may not respond well to close proximity. Javelinas often seek the warmth of the sun on chilly days in Oak Creek Canyon, and the far west end of the picnic area is an excellent spot to observe them enjoying the park.

Just in time for summer, Slide Rock State Park has earned a spot on the Travel Channel's "10 Top Swimming Holes in the United States" list. Sedona's iconic red rocks contribute to the creation of the "ultimate water slide" at this renowned destination. The list was compiled for the Travel Channel's new series, "Top Secret Swimming Holes."

Positioned beneath an apple orchard and surrounded by the striking red rocks of Oak Creek in Sedona, Slide Rock features an 80-foot-long and 2.5 to 4 feet wide natural slide with a seven percent decline from top to bottom. The rocks are covered with algae, creating a slippery ride for visitors.

Slide Rock encompasses a 1/2-mile stretch of Oak Creek that is open for swimming, wading, and sliding. The world-famous slide, after which the park is named, is a thrilling 80-foot-long chute worn into the sandstone. Known for inducing smiles, laughter, and creating lasting memories, Slide Rock State Park is a must-visit Arizona wonder nestled at the base of Oak Creek Canyon.

While Slide Rock State Park is primarily known for water recreation, anglers can enjoy excellent trout fishing upstream of the park in one of Arizona's most picturesque locations. The Arizona Game and Fish Department regularly supplements the naturally thriving populations of wild brown and rainbow trout with stocked trout in this stretch of Oak Creek. Trophy fish of both trout species are frequently caught, especially in the more secluded sections of the creek north of Slide Rock and south of the West Fork confluence.

Fishing within the designated swimming areas of Slide Rock is prohibited, but a short hike upstream provides access to expansive pools, undercut banks, and gentle riffles favored by trout. Approach from downstream to go unnoticed, cast beyond hiding spots, and present bait or lures naturally. Both brown and rainbow trout respond to a variety of flies and lures, with the larger brown trout often succumbing to well-placed flies. Nymphs, leeches, and floating flies are effective, and matching your fly to the insects present on the water enhances success.

Inline spinners and small Rapala-type lures are also successful, especially when fished upstream with attention to potential hiding spots like rocks, undercut banks, and submerged branches. Adjust your retrieve speed to match the current for an enticing presentation. Bait fishermen should avoid glass packaging; if using bait packaged in glass, transfer it to plastic to prevent downstream hazards. Nightcrawlers are popular in this stretch, while various dough baits work well on stocked trout. Properly rigging dough bait for trout is essential, and in areas with current, no additional weight is needed. Cast upstream and let your bait drift back to entice a strike from a beautiful Oak Creek trout.

The park features short trails, including a nature trail, and is conveniently located near various Coconino National Forest hiking trails. It operates on a pack-it-in, pack-it-out basis, and the use of any glass containers is strictly prohibited.

Pendley Homestead Trail: Covering a distance of 0.25 miles with an easy difficulty rating, this paved and level trail is suitable for all visitors. It passes through a portion of the historic Pendley Homestead within Slide Rock State Park. Along the trail, visitors can explore original apple orchards, the Pendley Homestead house, tourist cabins, the apple packing barn, various historical farming implements, a new orchard featuring semi-dwarf apple trees, and enjoy spectacular views of the canyon walls in Oak Creek Canyon.

Slide Rock Route: Spanning 0.3 miles with a moderate difficulty rating, this primitive route along Oak Creek serves as the primary access to the Slide Rock Swim Area. The area is renowned for its natural water slide along Oak Creek. The trail starts near the apple packing barn, descends to the creek via steps, crosses the creek using a small footbridge (not in place during high runoff), and proceeds north along sandstone shelves. During summer, sunbathers may occupy parts of the route, requiring consideration. Along the way, a historic rock cabin on the west side of the creek may be observed, which the original homesteader used in conjunction with a flume and water wheel for generating electricity. The route reaches an eight-foot wall, serving as a potential turn-around point. Adventurous hikers may negotiate the wall to explore more primitive areas upstream.

Clifftop Nature Trail: Covering 0.25 miles, this trail starts near the apple barn and provides scenic views of the Slide Rock swim area.

APPLE ORCHARD

For centuries, individuals have employed creativity and hard work to cultivate and shape domestic apple trees, ensuring the continuation of diverse and remarkable apple varieties. The apple orchard at Slide Rock State Park traces its roots back to 1912 when Frank Pendley initiated the first plantings. Apples served as the primary cash crop for the Pendley family homestead, which eventually became Slide Rock State Park in 1987.

Orchard maintenance at Slide Rock has undergone changes over the years, with contracted services for over a decade. In the spring of 2007, the responsibility for maintenance returned to State Parks. The preservation of the historic trees and the quality of upcoming harvests rely significantly on ranger involvement. Over three hundred apple trees demand consistent care and attention.

Winter in Oak Creek Canyon brings freezing temperatures, causing deciduous trees to shed their leaves. As the apple trees enter dormancy, pruning becomes a crucial task. Key objectives include removing dead wood, allowing sunlight and aeration, promoting high-quality fruit, and shaping the trees for easier harvest and passage. The pruning process involves the use of loppers, handsaws, and chainsaws, with three-legged aluminum ladders enabling access to high sections of the trees. Each cut contributes to the completion of a tree, ultimately leading to a well-trained orchard.

As the days lengthen with the arrival of early spring, blossoms and bud growth become prominent. Apple flowers, small and white with pink highlights, emit a delightful sweet aroma. With the assistance of bees, other insects, and wind, the flowers undergo cross-pollination. After fertilization, the petals fall, and the apples begin to take shape, initiating the cycle of growth in Slide Rock State Park's apple orchard.

Spring poses a delicate phase for apple trees, where a late freeze can potentially harm the blossoms. It is also the time when the codling moth lays its eggs in the trees, with the hatched eggs turning into worms that can damage the fruit and seeds. Monitoring the codling moth is essential, involving the use of pheromone traps. When moth numbers increase, the trees require insecticide spraying to prevent further infestation. As the apples grow, the process of thinning becomes necessary, involving the removal of excess fruit to enhance the size and quality of the remaining apples on the tree.

In the scorching Arizona summer, fruit trees, including the apple orchard, demand irrigation. Electric pumps draw water from Oak Creek, and long aluminum pipes with sprinklers are arranged to distribute water across each section of the orchard.

With well-watered and properly thinned trees, the apples continue to mature. Branches weighed down by the fruit may need support with cull lumber. Harvesting becomes a laborious yet rewarding task in the orchard, usually commencing in late August or early September. Indicators of maturity include size, color, firmness, and, of course, taste. Careful consideration is necessary during picking to prevent bruising, as apples are susceptible to damage. The harvested fruit undergoes sorting and boxing before being transported to cold storage.

The historic "Apple Packing Shed" built by Frank Pendley is still utilized at Slide Rock for sorting, polishing, packaging, and storing the apple harvests. The Pendley family had used this shed for their operations.

The culmination of the harvest is celebrated with the Slide Rock Apple Festival, featuring activities such as a pick-your-own apple program, games, entertainment, vendors, and display booths. Following the festival, orchard cleanup and preparations for the next year's crop begin. Ranger efforts continue to strengthen the connection between apples and humans, enhancing the visitor experience and preserving the historical integrity of the orchard.

PARK HISTORY

Most of the land in Oak Creek Canyon is under the management of the U.S. Forest Service. The Slide Rock area within Oak Creek Canyon stands out as a highly recognized and frequented tourist destination in the state, featuring prominently in various local, national, and international media.

In the early 1900s, Frank Pendley homesteaded the land immediately south of Slide Rock, establishing a substantial apple orchard and cultivating vegetable crops. The property continued to be operated and managed by his son, Tom Pendley, who, by the 1980s, held one of the largest privately-owned parcels in Oak Creek Canyon. In 1982, the Pendley family decided to sell the property. Governor Babbitt, having personal ties to

Flagstaff and Slide Rock, where he grew up and had visited numerous times, learned about the potential sale. Familiar with the Pendley family, he expressed interest in acquiring the land for a State Park. However, Tom Pendley, having faced challenges with the Forest Service, was initially hesitant to sell to a governmental entity.

Around the same time, William G. Roe from the Nature Conservancy contacted State Parks Director Mike Ramnes, informing him of the availability of the property adjacent to Slide Rock. In response to the situation, Governor Babbitt established the Arizona Parklands Foundation in 1983, a non-profit corporation tasked with acquiring properties and receiving gifts for State Parks. This move aligned with recommendations from the Governor's Task Force on Parks and Recreation in Arizona, formed a year earlier. The Foundation, composed of business, political, and community leaders, aimed to acquire and donate land to Arizona State Parks.

Through two years of negotiations and collaboration with the Parks Board, an agreement was eventually reached with the Pendley family for the sale of the property, marking the inaugural acquisition by the Arizona Parklands Foundation.

Following the acquisition agreement, the Arizona Parklands Foundation faced the challenge of securing the necessary funding for the transaction. With the Governor's assistance, the Foundation collaborated with four major banks—Valley National Bank, First InterState Bank, Arizona Bank, and United Bank of Arizona—to secure a $4,000,000 loan for the property purchase. Subsequently, on February 7, 1985, the Foundation successfully acquired the Pendley property for $3,600,000.

However, the anticipated donations to support the acquisition did not materialize as expected. Faced with this shortfall, the Foundation, in collaboration with the Arizona State Parks Board and the Governor, sought legislative funding for the acquisition. During the early 1985 legislative session, House Bill 2391 was introduced. This bill established a State Park Acquisition and Development Fund, authorized the acquisition, development, and operation of various sites, including the Pendley Homestead, and allocated appropriations accordingly.

The introduction of House Bill 2391 faced criticism from some legislators, notably Senator "Hal" Runyan, Chairman of Senate Appropriations. Senator Runyan expressed dissatisfaction, stating that he had been led to believe the Parklands Foundation would be responsible for funding its acquisitions without legislative appropriations. Despite the criticism, the bill passed, and State Parks promptly proceeded with the acquisition of the Pendley property.

On June 21, 1985, a celebratory event took place on the Pendley property, with attendees including Governor Babbitt, the Parks Board, the Foundation Board, legislators, local officials, Pendley family members, community representatives, and State Parks staff. Subsequently, on July 9, 1985, the State Parks Board successfully acquired the Pendley homestead for $3,757,324.65 from the Arizona Parklands

Foundation. This acquisition encompassed the homestead house (1927), an apple packing shed (1932), three tourist cabins (1933), the Brown house (1926), and the historic apple orchard.

With the acquisition of the property adjacent to Slide Rock, State Parks collaborated with the Forest Service to formalize the integrated management concept initiated by Governor Bruce Babbitt and Regional Forester Jean Hassell. This collaboration culminated in the signing of a Memorandum of Understanding between the two agencies in August 1986.

A small private inholding situated between the Park and Forest Service land was generously donated to State Parks by Burns International, Inc. on September 9, 1987, thanks to the efforts of the Foundation and Parks Board members.

The initial development of the park included essential elements such as a new entrance, paved interior roads, parking areas, walking paths, and the renovation/restoration of several existing buildings. With these improvements completed, Slide Rock State Park officially opened to the public in October 1987, under the management of the first Park Manager, John Schreiber.

During the negotiations for the Pendley homestead acquisition, a strong friendship developed between Tom Pendley and Charles Eatherly. Grateful for this friendship, Mr. Pendley generously donated irrigation pipe, equipment, and farming equipment to State Parks. In recognition of these contributions, Tom Pendley was honored with a Lifetime Pass to State Parks by Executive Director Don Charpio.

AREA ATTRACTIONS

Slide Rock is nestled in the heart of Oak Creek Canyon, a picturesque haven featuring sandstone bluffs, diverse flora and fauna, and the flowing waters of Oak Creek. The town of Sedona, located seven miles south of Slide Rock, provides amenities such as food, lodging, shopping, and various recreational opportunities. Heading 25 miles north, Flagstaff sits at the base of the San Francisco Peaks and serves as a gateway to the Grand Canyon. Within the Coconino National Forest, Slide Rock borders the Secret Mountain Wilderness Area, offering a range of outdoor activities in different tranquil settings.

Riordan Mansion Group Tours (Flagstaff, AZ): Accommodates groups of up to 60 with reservations made at least two weeks in advance. Plan for a two-hour visit, with groups divided into smaller units for guided tours and self-guided exploration. Opportunities to visit the Visitor Center, gift shop, and take a self-guided walk around the grounds.

Montezuma Castle National Monument: Explore one of the best-preserved cliff dwellings in North America, showcasing 20 rooms in a high-rise apartment within a limestone cliff. Reveals the enduring story of the Sinagua culture's ingenuity and survival in the desert landscape.

Montezuma Well: Located 11 miles from the park, formed by the collapse of a limestone cavern. Flows over a million gallons of water daily, creating a unique aquatic habitat and serving as an oasis for wildlife and humans for millennia.

Sunset Crater Volcano: Born in eruptions between 1040 and 1100, with powerful explosions impacting local lives and transforming the landscape. Lava flows and cinders, along with signs of wildlife, present a dramatic geological spectacle.

Walnut Canyon National Monument: Walk in the footsteps of people who lived over 700 years ago, exploring cliff dwellings within canyon walls. The canyon's water source made it valuable to early inhabitants and remains a crucial habitat today.

Coconino National Forest: One of the most diverse National Forests, boasting landscapes from Sedona's Red Rocks to Ponderosa Pine Forests and alpine tundra. Offers opportunities for exploration, fishing in forest lakes, and enjoying lazy creeks and streams.

Prescott National Forest: Spans about 1.25 million acres, bordering other National Forests in Arizona. Features diverse landscapes, including the Juniper, Santa Maria, Sierra Prieta, and Bradshaw Mountains, as well as the Black Hills, Mingus Mountain, Black Mesa, and the Verde River headwaters.

SOUTH KAIBAB TRAIL

COUNTY: COCONINO   **CITY:** FLAGSTAFF *n.c.*

DATE VISITED: **WHO I WENT WITH:**

RATING: ☆ ☆ ☆ ☆ ☆   **WILL I RETURN?**   YES / NO

For hikers in search of unparalleled panoramic views along a trail at the Grand Canyon, the South Kaibab Trail presents itself as a compelling choice. It stands out as the sole trail in Grand Canyon National Park that adheres dramatically to a ridgeline descent. However, the thrilling exposure to the canyon's vastness comes with a trade-off: minimal shade and an absence of water along the entire trail. During the winter months, the consistent exposure to sunlight typically keeps most sections of the trail relatively free from ice and snow.

Despite its reputation as the quickest route to the bottom, especially described as "a trail in a hurry to get to the river," hiking the South Kaibab Trail during the summer is not recommended due to the lack of water sources. This absence of hydration points makes ascending the trail a potentially hazardous undertaking. The South Kaibab Trail represents a modern pathway, designed as an alternative to Ralph Cameron's Bright Angel Trail. Cameron, the owner of the Bright Angel Trail, imposed tolls on users and engaged in numerous legal battles over several decades to maintain his business rights. These legal disputes prompted the construction of an alternative trail, the Hermit Trail, by the Santa Fe Railroad in 1911. Subsequently, in 1924, the National Park Service built the South Kaibab Trail. In this unexpected way, Cameron unintentionally contributed significantly to the broader network of trails now available for canyon visitors.

The South Kaibab Trail lacks water sources along its route. Between early May and mid-October, water is accessible near the trailhead, specifically from a spigot near the bus stop. While potable water is consistently available at Bright Angel Campground throughout the year, it's crucial to be aware that occasional pipeline breaks can disrupt the water supply at Bright Angel Campground. To ensure access to water, it is advisable to bring an alternative form of water treatment, such as iodine tablets or a water filter. Particularly in hot weather, hikers should carry at least 4 liters of water.

Camping freely on Corridor Trails is prohibited, necessitating visitors to camp in designated campgrounds. Along the South Kaibab Trail, the sole camping option is at Bright Angel Campground (CBG), situated directly adjacent to the Colorado River at the canyon's bottom.

Situated near Yaki Point, the South Kaibab Trail faces restrictions on parking at the trailhead due to the area's high popularity and extremely limited space. Instead, hikers are required to utilize the park's complimentary shuttle bus system to access the trailhead. Each morning, three hiker express buses depart from the Bright Angel Lodge, followed by stops at the Backcountry Information Center (departure times vary based on the month). Alternatively, hikers can opt for the village bus (Blue Line) to Canyon View

Information Plaza and transfer to the Orange Line for access to the South Kaibab Trail.

Many campers at Bright Angel Campground choose to embark on a hike using the South Kaibab Trail for the descent and the Bright Angel Trail for the ascent. Although the South Kaibab Trail shares an almost identical maximum grade with the Bright Angel Trail, it maintains a more consistently sloped path without offering water or shade. The descent along the South Kaibab Trail typically spans 4-6 hours.

Starting with a set of tight north-facing switchbacks, this section is prone to encountering ice during the winter months. Following these initial switchbacks, the trail moves across a west-facing slope until reaching the summit of the Coconino Sandstone, marked by the aptly named Ooh Ah Point, providing the first panoramic view of the canyon. The trail then follows the dominant ridgeline, descending on its east and west sides before reaching Cedar Ridge. At Cedar Ridge, there are pit toilets but no water or emergency phone.

Continuing from Cedar Ridge, the South Kaibab Trail traverses below O'Neill Butte without employing a single switchback until reaching Skeleton Point. Situated three miles from the rim, Skeleton Point is the recommended maximum distance for a day hike. Here, the trail descends dramatically, passing the end of Skeleton Point where the trail is carved directly out of the limestone cliffs, creating an intense sense of exposure. The descent continues rapidly through a series of switchbacks to the Tonto Platform and Tipoff. Pit toilets and an emergency phone are available at Tipoff, but no water. Hikers planning to use the Tonto Trail to the east or west can find the intersection approximately fifty feet up-trail from the pit toilets.

Below Tipoff, the South Kaibab Trail loosely follows the path of an earlier trail known as the Cable Trail, built in 1907 to facilitate access to the old cable car system across the river before the construction of the current suspension bridge. As the South Kaibab Trail descends toward the Colorado River, remnants of this earlier trail become visible. Access to Bright Angel Campground is achieved by crossing the black bridge, constructed in 1921.

The Grand Canyon, first and foremost, is characterized by its extremes. To ensure safety, it's crucial to adopt appropriate precautions based on seasonal changes in trail conditions. In winter months, the set of tight switchbacks near the top of the South Kaibab Trail may remain icy for an extended period after snowfall. For hikers entering the canyon between May and September, it is imperative to start the hike well before dawn or in the late afternoon. Success hinges on avoiding the trail between 10 in the morning and 3 in the afternoon, with the average descent time ranging from 4 to 6 hours.

Failing to reach Bright Angel Campground by 10 in the morning during hot weather can lead to a challenging experience, with some hikers requiring medical assistance and rescue. The likelihood of encountering issues exponentially increases with every hour spent on the trail past 10 am. Ascending the South Kaibab Trail in hot weather is strongly discouraged. It's essential to thoroughly review the National Park Service's "Hike Smart" pamphlet, provided with summer permits, and consistently practice Leave No Trace principles.

SOUTH MOUNTAIN PARK

COUNTY: MARICOPA   CITY: PHOENIX

DATE VISITED: WHO I WENT WITH:

RATING: ☆ ☆ ☆ ☆ ☆   WILL I RETURN?   YES / NO

South Mountain Park stands out as one of the largest city parks globally, encompassing nearly 17,000 acres. However, it deviates from the typical park concept featuring grassy areas, playgrounds, lakes, and ducks. Instead, South Mountain Park serves as a desert mountain preserve, offering over 50 miles of trails, and there is no entry fee to access the park.

Key facilities like gated roadways, trailhead parking areas, restrooms, and ramadas are open from 5 a.m. to 7 p.m., with the park gates closing at that time. Trails remain accessible until 11 p.m. However, on one Sunday each month, known as Silent Sunday, South Mountain Park prohibits all vehicular traffic. It's advised to check the South Mountain website for any scheduled park closures and specific Sundays when vehicles are not allowed.

The pinnacle accessible to visitors is Dobbins Peak, standing at an elevation of 2,330 feet. This height is moderate enough to accommodate hikers and cyclists who may not be ready for steep trails while still offering splendid city views.

The park attracts more visitors for its scenic drives and panoramic views than any other feature. However, if you're a nervous driver or passenger, it's crucial to note that the drive involves navigating a winding mountain road that isn't overly spacious. Sharing the road with bikers and tourists, alongside limited parking space, demands a cautious and unhurried approach. Dobbins Point provides a breathtaking view on clear days, accessible by picking up a map at the main gate and continuing the drive.

For those interested in a southern view, heading towards the towers is recommended, with clear road signage guiding the way. The South Mountain Park Environmental Education Center, open Wednesday through Sunday from 8 a.m. to 2 p.m., offers insights into the park's flora, fauna, and history. As you ascend South Mountain, you'll quickly encounter spectacular views of downtown Phoenix to the north and Camelback Mountain to the east of downtown. Gila Valley Lookout provides beautiful vistas of Tempe, Chandler, and the south side of South Mountain, including Ahwatukee Foothills and Mountain Park Ranch. Further upward past Dobbins Point, visitors can approach the South Mountain towers for a closer experience.

South Mountain Park offers versatile meeting areas and ramadas suitable for family outings or gatherings of up to 5,000 people. The Piedra Grandes Ramadas operate on a first-come, first-served basis, catering to small groups and those with up to 50 individuals. Alcohol permits are necessary, and regulations prohibit amplified or live music. Conveniently, restrooms are available nearby. For larger groups exceeding 50 people, reservations are mandatory and should be arranged in advance by calling (602) 495-0222.

Beyond being an event space, South Mountain Park provides a picturesque setting for horseback riding. Guided trail rides, accommodating riders of all skill levels, are offered, although riding is restricted during the summer months. Those interested in trail rides, breakfast rides, and cookout rides can reach out to Ponderosa Stables for further information.

Situated in South Phoenix, South Mountain Park is easily accessible. If approaching from Baseline Road and Central Avenue, head south on Central until reaching the park entrance. For those on I-17 heading south, exit at 7th Avenue/Central Avenue, continue on Frontage Road to Central, turn right to proceed south. If traveling on I-10 towards the east, exit at 7th Avenue, head south to Baseline Road, then east on Baseline to Central Avenue, turning right to go south. Lastly, if on I-10 heading west, exit at Baseline Road, turn left, proceed to Central Avenue, and turn left to head south.

It's possible to come across desert wildlife, such as rattlesnakes, during your visit. Ensure you maintain a safe distance and continue on your way. Remember to carry an ample supply of water, wear durable shoes, a hat, and sunscreen for your safety.

----

84 SUNSET CRATER VOLCANO NATIONAL MONUMENT

COUNTY: COCONINO   CITY: FLAGSTAFF *n.c.*

DATE VISITED: WHO I WENT WITH:

RATING: ☆ ☆ ☆ ☆ ☆   WILL I RETURN? YES / NO

About a millennium ago, a volcanic eruption expelled flames 850 feet into the air, giving rise to Sunset Crater. Alongside this, its smaller and older counterpart, Lenox Crater, serves as a remarkable testament to the incredible forces of nature. A trip to Sunset Crater Volcano National Monument offers a view of both craters, along with solidified lava flows and cinder fields. While hiking takes precedence in the 3,040-acre park, off-highway vehicle (OHV) enthusiasts are drawn to the cinder fields in the neighboring Coconino National Forest. Conveniently, both Sunset Crater and Wupatki National Monument can be visited in a single day, as they are situated along a 34-mile loop drive off US-89. It's recommended to start with exploring the lava fields at Sunset Crater and then proceed to the Ancient Puebloan ruins at Wupatki.

While the 34-mile loop provides scenic stops to observe the cinder fields and craters, hiking remains the most immersive way to truly appreciate the landscape. Commence your visit at the visitor center, offering insights into volcanoes, the historical presence of the Puebloan people in the region, and the unique lunar landscape where astronauts trained for the 1969 lunar landing. The visitor center is also the hub for information on ranger-led programs, including seasonal stargazing activities. While not officially part of the park, the Cinder Hills OHV Area is a magnet for off-roading enthusiasts navigating dirt bikes, quads, and other vehicles through the loose cinders, once the testing ground for lunar vehicles. Although not part of the park, the Cinder Hills OHV Area draws off-roading enthusiasts who ride dirt bikes, quads, and other vehicles through loose cinders where the astronauts once tested lunar vehicles. For the testing, NASA created small craters that, today, have eroded into divots. To see them or ride your OHV through them, turn off US 89 at FS 776 and drive about 1.5 miles to the OHV area.

Hiking trails in the park take you through loose cinders and along hardened lava flows. Unfortunately, climbing to the summit of Sunset Crater has been prohibited since 1973 to prevent further damage from visitors. However, you can hike to the top of Lenox Crater and O'Leary Peak, which offers a view into Sunset Crater.

Apart from the self-guided hikes, park rangers lead backcountry hikes and a roughly 2.5-mile Volcanology Hike exploring the Bonito Lava Field. To make reservations, contact (928) 526-0502.

Lenox Crater Trail: This 1.6-mile, moderately strenuous trail provides panoramic views of Sunset Crater, the Bonito Lava Flow, and O'Leary Peak from its summit.

Lava Flow Trail: A partially paved, easy 1-mile loop leading to the base of Sunset Crater.

Allocate about an hour for exploration, delving into the Bonito Lava Flow.

Lava's Edge Trail: Commencing at the visitor center, this 3.4-mile trail traces the Bonito Lava Flow's edge under pine trees and across loose cinders. It links to Lenox Crater Trail, A'a Trail, Bonito Vista Trail, and Lava Flow Trail.

O'Leary Peak Trail: While not within the park, this 9.6-mile trail (just under 5 miles each way) offers glimpses into Sunset Crater's cinder cone. Access the trail from FS 545A off the Sunset Crater-Wupatki Loop Road.

Sunset Crater is situated along the 34-mile Sunset Crater-Wupatki Loop Road, linking it with Wupatki National Monument. The scenic drive initiates 12 miles north of Flagstaff, marked by a right turn at the Sunset Crater Volcano National Park sign. Commence your exploration at Sunset Crater's visitor center and venture onto one of the hiking trails. If time is limited, the Lava Flow Trail, distinct from the lengthier Lava's Edge Trail, offers a convenient option. The journey then progresses to the Wupatki Visitor Center. Park at the center, embark on the 0.5-mile loop around the 104-room pueblo and ball court. The Sunset Crater-Wupatki Loop Road concludes at US-89, approximately 15 miles north of its starting point. The entire route takes about an hour without stops, but plan for a full day if you intend to explore both parks.

The $25 entrance fee to Sunset Crater Volcano National Monument includes admission to Wupatki National Monument. Similar to Sunset Crater, hiking takes precedence at Wupatki. The Wupatki Pueblo Trail, a half-mile loop around the largest free-standing pueblo in northern Arizona, is a popular choice. Additional trails lead to nearby pueblos for those with more time. For a deeper understanding of the ancient Puebloans predating the volcanic eruption that formed Sunset Crater, the visitor center provides educational displays and artifacts discovered in the area.

While camping is not officially permitted within the park, the U.S. Forest Service manages the Bonito Campground situated across the street from Sunset Crater's visitor center. Further camping options are available throughout the adjacent Coconino National Forest, and camping in both areas follows a seasonal schedule.

Bonito Campground: Typically open from late May to mid-October, this campground offers amenities such as picnic tables, grills, fire rings, flush toilets, and drinking water. Campsites operate on a first-come, first-served basis with a nightly fee of $26. However, there are no hookups available at this campground.

Cinder Hills Dispersed Camping: For those open to dispersed camping, this scenic recreation area near Sunset Crater Volcano provides an alternative. Note that it can get noisy due to the popularity of off-highway vehicles (OHVs), and the ground is covered with rocky volcanic cinder. Camping here is free of charge.

Flagstaff KOA: In the winter months, this KOA on the west side of Flagstaff may be the primary camping option. With 200 sites, it offers amenities such as free Wi-Fi, laundry facilities, flush toilets, showers, a dog park, bike rentals, and hiking trails.

Flagstaff, being the nearest city to Sunset Crater Volcano National Monument, boasts a variety of hotels ranging from budget to luxury options. It's advisable to secure accommodations early, as rooms tend to fill up quickly at popular hotels.

Little America: As the sole AAA Four Diamond hotel in Flagstaff, Little America provides an excellent home base for exploring Sunset Crater. Nestled on 500 acres of private forest, each room features floor-to-ceiling windows for a picturesque stay.

Drury Inn & Suites Flagstaff: A great choice for chain hotel enthusiasts, this establishment near the university offers complimentary breakfast, three free drinks, and evening food service at the bar from 5:30 to 7:30 p.m.

DoubleTree by Hilton Hotel Flagstaff: Positioned on historic Route 66, this DoubleTree by Hilton property boasts two onsite restaurants, a welcoming lounge in the lobby, and three electric vehicle (EV) charging stations. It is also a pet-friendly option.

Directions: To reach Sunset Crater Volcano National Monument from Flagstaff, take US-89 north. There's an exit for US-89 on the east side of the city if you're coming from I-40. Drive approximately 12 miles from Flagstaff and then turn right at the sign indicating Sunset Crater Volcano National Monument. The visitor center is situated 2 miles past the park's entrance. After exploring Sunset Crater, you have the option to continue for 21 miles to the Wupatki Visitor Center and eventually reach US-89. Alternatively, you can return using the same route you took initially.

Tips:

1) A fee of $25 per vehicle grants access to both Sunset Crater Volcano and Wupatki national monuments, and it remains valid for a period of seven days.
2) Sunset Crater, a result of volcanic activity, contrasts with Meteor Crater nearby, which is a site of meteor impact.
3) For insights into Sunset Crater's role in the lunar landing, a visit to Lowell Observatory in Flagstaff is recommended, where the discovery of Pluto also took place.
4) Well-behaved pets on leashes are allowed on the paved section of the Lava Flow Trail and a segment of the Lava's Edge Trail.
5) It is advisable to wear closed-toe shoes, particularly if planning to hike on unpaved trails. Carry an ample water supply, apply sunscreen, dress in layers, and stay updated on weather conditions. Seek shelter in case of lightning.
6) Cell phone reception is inconsistent in the area. Depending on your service provider, reception is available at the Bonito Park pullout and the Lava Flow Trail parking lot.
7) GPS reliability is questionable, so avoid venturing onto forest service roads without a paper map.

TALIESIN WEST

COUNTY: MARICOPA   CITY: SCOTTSDALE

DATE VISITED: WHO I WENT WITH:

RATING: ☆ ☆ ☆ ☆ ☆   WILL I RETURN? YES / NO

Situated in the northeastern region of Scottsdale, Arizona, there stands a living tribute to the renowned American architect Frank Lloyd Wright. Spanning 600 acres in the foothills of the McDowell Mountains and enveloped by the breathtaking Sonoran Desert, this expansive complex bears the name Taliesin West (pronounced: tal-ee-ess-in). Frank Lloyd Wright, the visionary architect, designed and constructed this National Historic Landmark, where buildings and landscape coexist harmoniously, seamlessly blending form and color, beauty and grace, and the interplay of nature and science.

Born in 1867, Frank Lloyd Wright spent his early years in rural Wisconsin, imbibing the values of hard work and developing a profound love for the natural landscape. At the age of 18, he embarked on a journey into higher education, studying civil engineering at the university, marking the beginning of his architectural career. Wright earned a reputation as a revolutionary and nonconformist architect, expressing disdain for what he deemed as the stagnant and backward-looking ideas of his contemporaries, who predominantly drew inspiration from Greek, Roman, Gothic, and Tudor architectural models. Instead, he envisioned creating a vibrant American architectural landscape, unrestricted by existing materials and designs.

In his pursuit of innovative architecture, Frank Lloyd Wright championed the concept of "organic architecture," emphasizing site-specific construction where "form and function were one." He articulated the principles of the Prairie House, advocating for open expanses and minimizing architectural subdivisions, which he disparagingly referred to as "boxes." Although his architectural principles gained acclaim internationally, Wright faced ridicule and skepticism at home. Over time, however, his following grew as more individuals recognized the revolutionary nature of his ideas and designs.

In 1911, Taliesin I was constructed in Wisconsin by Frank Lloyd Wright. The term "Taliesin" translates to "a shining brow," potentially referencing the picturesque location and expansive views. This architectural masterpiece was intended to serve as a residence, workplace, school, and cultural center for Wright's students. Every aspect, down to the furniture, was meticulously designed by Wright himself. Unfortunately, in 1914, Taliesin I experienced significant damage from a fire. In response, Taliesin II was promptly erected on the same site. However, it too suffered fire damage, leading to its reconstruction as Taliesin III.

In 1927, architect Albert Chase McArthur, a former student of Wright, sought his assistance in designing the Arizona Biltmore Hotel. Wright accepted the challenge, traveled to Phoenix, and proposed plans based on his distinctive architectural principles. Despite facing opposition to the unconventional design, some compromises were made, resulting in what is now known as The Arizona Biltmore Resort & Spa—a property acclaimed as "the only existing hotel in the world with a Frank Lloyd Wright-influenced design."

Having left his mark on the Arizona landscape, Wright and his apprentices planned and built Taliesin West. The construction predominantly utilized indigenous materials, with Wright's students contributing to the build by hand. Taliesin West captivates visitors with its expansive site and intricate structures featuring massive walls crafted from desert rock embedded in masonry. These structures, topped with canvas flaps for ceilings affixed to redwood beams, possess a tent-like quality while maintaining a sense of weight and permanence. The units are arranged at varying distances and angles, interconnected by terraces, lawns, pools, and stairways.

Reflecting on Taliesin West, Wright expressed, "Our new desert camp belonged to the Arizona desert as though it had stood there during creation."

In 1932, Frank Lloyd Wright established the Frank Lloyd Wright School of Architecture with the aim of imparting his architectural theories and practices to aspiring young men and women. Later on, recognizing the need for a retreat from the harsh Wisconsin winters, the seventy-year-old architect returned to Arizona five years after founding the school. There, he acquired the land where Taliesin West would be constructed. Initially conceived as a winter camp, Taliesin West evolved into much more than its intended purpose. Over the next 22 years until his passing in 1959, Frank Lloyd Wright garnered recognition, accolades, decorations, and celebrations both locally and internationally. Aside from being a prolific writer, inventor, and world traveler, he continued to make a significant mark as an architect.

During his time in Arizona, Wright designed and executed numerous projects, including notable ones in the Phoenix area. Among these is the awe-inspiring Grady Gammage Memorial Auditorium, now known as A.S.U. Gammage, situated on the Arizona State University campus. Notably, the completion of this building occurred posthumously.

Exploring the Taliesin West complex is exclusively available through guided tours, providing access to various entities like The Frank Lloyd Wright Foundation (focused on fundraising), The Frank Lloyd Wright Memorial Foundation (housing archives), The Frank Lloyd Wright School of Architecture, and Wright's residence. Additionally, the Taliesin Association of Artists, a group committed to preserving the founder's spirit, operates on-site at Taliesin West.

Taliesin West presents several tour options for visitors:

1) Panorama Tour (1 hour): This tour encompasses the Cabaret Theater, Music Pavilion, Kiva, Wright's private office, outdoor spaces, terraces, gardens, and walkways. Available year-round.
2) Insights Tour (90 minutes): Similar to the Panorama Tour, with the addition of Frank

Lloyd Wright's living quarters. Offered year-round.

3) Behind-the-Scenes Tour (3 hours): A comprehensive exploration of Taliesin West, equivalent to the Insights Tour but with the opportunity to engage with Wright associates. This tour is particularly appealing to architecture enthusiasts and is available year-round.

4) Desert Walk (90 minutes): Conducted from November through April, this tour involves a guided nature walk through the desert at Taliesin West, providing a detailed explanation of native materials found on the site and utilized by Wright.

5) Desert/Insights Tour: A combination tour offered exclusively from November through April.

6) Night Lights in the Desert (2 hours): This tour includes everything from the Insights Tour but takes on a unique perspective during twilight. Light refreshments are provided. Available in February, March, April, May, October, and November. In December, the Night Lights Tour adopts a festive theme for the holidays, featuring music and holiday refreshments.

The Frank Lloyd Wright School of Architecture provides both academically and professionally accredited undergraduate and graduate degree programs, with students and faculty actively engaged on the premises throughout the year. Within the same property, The Frank Lloyd Wright Foundation Archives boasts the distinction of being "the largest and most complete collection of materials related to a single artist housed under one roof anywhere in the world."

In addition to its educational and archival functions, Taliesin West occasionally hosts special events. The primary goal of The Frank Lloyd Wright Foundation's Arts & Culture Program is to offer the public various performances, exhibitions, and workshops in the realm of arts and culture. This program aims to enhance public awareness of Taliesin as a National Historic Landmark and highlights the unique historical intersection of architecture, arts, and agriculture found on the Taliesin campus.

Tips:

1) Independent exploration is not allowed; visitors must participate in guided tours.

2) Tour reservations can be made at the gift shop, but it is advisable to book in advance.

3) Various tours are available year-round, including the summer months. Tours differ in terms of outdoor activities, but it is recommended to carry a water bottle regardless of the chosen tour or the time of year, as there are no refreshment stops during the tours.

4) Photography is allowed at Taliesin West, except in the gift shop.

5) The tours may not be suitable for young children, as there are no specific activities for them.

6) There is no admission fee for those only interested in visiting the Book Store, which is renowned as one of the best and most distinctive gift shops in the Valley of the Sun.

Taliesin West serves as the Arizona residence for the Frank Lloyd Wright Foundation and is situated in the city of Scottsdale, to the east of Phoenix, Arizona. The entrance to

Taliesin West is positioned at the intersection of Cactus Road and Frank Lloyd Wright Boulevard (equivalent to 114th Street) in the northeastern part of Scottsdale.

Parking at Taliesin West is complimentary, and discounts are available for seniors, active military personnel, students, and youth for most tours. The site is open every day, except on Thanksgiving, Christmas, and Easter.

For those using The Loop 101 (Pima Loop) in Scottsdale, the recommended route is to exit at Cactus Road and head east to Frank Lloyd Wright Blvd. After crossing over Frank Lloyd Wright Blvd, which transforms into Taliesin Drive, follow this road to reach Taliesin West.

TITAN MISSILE MUSEUM

COUNTY: PIMA

CITY: SAHUARITA

DATE VISITED: WHO I WENT WITH:

RATING: ☆ ☆ ☆ ☆ ☆   WILL I RETURN?   YES / NO

The Titan Missile Museum offers a unique opportunity for the public to step back in time and experience an era when the threat of nuclear warfare between the U.S. and the former Soviet Union was a palpable reality. As the sole remaining Titan II site accessible to visitors, the museum provides insight into the historical context of this tense period.

The Titan II possessed the capability to launch from its subterranean silo within a mere 58 seconds, carrying a nine-megaton thermonuclear warhead to a target over 6,000 miles (approximately 10,000 km) away in less than thirty minutes. For a span of over two decades, 54 Titan II missile complexes were in a constant state of "alert" across the United States, operating 24 hours a day, seven days a week. This continuous readiness either heightened the threat of nuclear conflict or served as a deterrent, depending on one's perspective.

Designated as an Arizona Treasure by former Governor Janet Napolitano, the Titan Missile Museum comprises two integral components: The Count Ferdinand von Galen Titan Missile Museum Education and Research Center and the Titan Missile National Historic Landmark. Positioned directly adjacent to the launch complex, The Count Ferdinand von Galen Titan Missile Museum Education and Research Center encompasses an exhibit gallery, museum store, classroom, and an archival storage area. On the other hand, the Titan Missile National Historic Landmark represents the former Titan II launch complex 571-7. Initially part of the 571st Strategic Missile Squadron (SMS), 390th Strategic Missile Wing (SMW) at Davis-Monthan Air Force Base (AFB) in Arizona, this operational missile site is the solitary surviving Titan II Intercontinental Ballistic Missile (ICBM) complex among the 54 that were on alert during the Cold War era from 1963 to 1987.

On November 11, 1982, launch complex 571-7 was deactivated, marking the initiation of efforts to transform it into a museum. In February 1983, Col Paul Comeaux, the commander of the 390th SMW, reached out to Charles Niblett, the president of the Tucson Air Museum Foundation (now the Arizona Aerospace Foundation), proposing the idea of converting one of the soon-to-be-deactivated missile sites around Tucson into a museum. Niblett, along with Col Hugh Matheson, USAF (Ret.), the former deputy commander for maintenance at the 390th SMW, and Lt Col Orville Doughty, USAF (Ret.), the former commander of the 390th Missile Maintenance Squadron, took on the significant task of convincing the Foundation Board, the Air Force, and the Tucson community of the project's worthiness and feasibility.

By September 1985, all involved parties reached an agreement, and the necessary paperwork was finalized. While the Air Force retained ownership of missile site 571-7, it was leased to Pima County. Subsequently, Pima County subleased the site to the Foundation, allowing the operation of the Titan Missile Museum. Prior to its public opening on May 21, 1986, several modifications were made to demonstrate that launch complex 571-7 was no longer operational. For instance, missile N-10 underwent specific modifications, such as cutting holes in its propellant tanks and the heat shield of the Reentry Vehicle. The missile was then displayed on the surface for 30 days to confirm its inoperability through satellite observation. Once installed in the launch duct, the silo closure door was permanently set in a half-open position (secured by six concrete blocks), and a large window was added over the open portion of the launch duct to facilitate visitor and satellite viewing.

In April 1994, the site attained the status of a National Historic Landmark, acknowledging the pivotal role played by the Titan II in American history. This distinction is granted to fewer than 3,000 historic places in the United States, with such recognition typically reserved for sites older than 50 years. Remarkably, launch complex 571-7 achieved this landmark status at just 31 years old. Notably, it stands as one of only two preserved Intercontinental Ballistic Missile (ICBM) sites worldwide accessible to the public.

Since its inauguration, the museum has welcomed over 1.5 million visitors globally. The Titan Missile Museum gained cinematic recognition when portions of the Star Trek movie First Contact were filmed on its premises. Additionally, the museum was featured in two History Channel series in August 2007: Lost Worlds: Secret A-Bomb Factories and Mega Movers: Army Mega Moves. In 2012, it was showcased on TNT's reality TV show, The Great Escape. National Geographic produced a short documentary on nuclear tourism featuring the museum, and PBS included it in two documentaries as part of the American Experience series: Uranium, Twisting the Dragon's Tail, and Command and Control. The Travel Channel's Mysteries at the Museum series also featured the Titan Missile Museum, most recently in a segment titled "The Man Who Saved the World," recounting the story of Stanislav Petrov, the Soviet officer credited with potentially preventing World War III. The museum serves as a poignant exhibit of the Cold War's dramatic remnants between the U.S. and the former Soviet Union, offering a compelling educational experience on the history of nuclear conflict—a history marked by efforts to maintain peace.

Please be aware that every individual in your group must have the ability to safely navigate both the descent and ascent of 55 stairs, as there is no elevator access available to the underground silo.

TOMBSTONE

COUNTY: COCHISE   **CITY:** TOMBSTONE

DATE VISITED: **WHO I WENT WITH:**

RATING: ☆ ☆ ☆ ☆ ☆   **WILL I RETURN?**   YES / NO

Nestled in Cochise County, Tombstone embraces its authentic Wild West heritage by featuring daily re-enactments, actors dressed in period attire, and the preservation of significant landmarks. The town's atmosphere is both genuine and cherished, offering an enjoyable experience for visitors.

Transport yourself back to the 1800s, a time when cowboys and outlaws dominated the scene, with the jingle of spurs and the whinnying of horses at the anticipation of a gunfight. Recapturing this era is made easy on Allen Street, the central thoroughfare of downtown Tombstone, which has retained much of its historic charm that made it renowned decades ago. At The Streets of Tombstone Theater, particularly at the O.K. Corral, actors portraying the Earps and Doc Holliday re-enact the infamous feud against the Cowboys, immortalizing 30 seconds of history for hundreds of weekly visitors. Widely considered one of the most renowned shootouts in the American Wild West, Tombstone keeps this event at the forefront of its attractions, ensuring it remains etched in the minds of all who visit.

Wyatt Earp's residence has been transformed into a museum and gallery, showcasing an impressive collection of memorabilia associated with Earp. Explore the house where Earp resided with his common-law wife, Mattie, and envision the conversations that unfolded regarding the tensions among the Cowboys, Earps, and Doc Holliday. The Boothill Cemetery, while delving into the town's tumultuous history, features lighthearted tombstones that offer a departure from the somber atmosphere.

Take a step into Big Nose Kate's to further immerse yourself in Tombstone's history. Functioning as a bar, former brothel, and an entrance to the town's former silver mine shafts, Big Nose Kate's provides a setting for drinks, dining, and occasional bar dances.

In Tombstone, the intersection of living and departed history is palpable. The Bird Cage Theater and The Crystal Palace stand as places where both the living and the spirits linger. The Bird Cage Theater, hosting the apparitions of former brothel workers, seems to echo with laughter and music, continuing the revelries of the Old West as if time stood still. Meanwhile, at the Crystal Palace, the audible echoes of boots and spurs, along with the roulette wheel's independent spin, contribute to the lively ambiance.

Surprisingly, Tombstone is also home to one of Arizona's finest craft breweries. Stop by the Tombstone Brewing Company to experience the impressive brewing skills of this small town, where hops, yeast, water, and barley come together in delightful combinations.

Explore Tombstone's rich history and attractions:

O. K. Corral: Tour the actual site of Tombstone's legendary gunfight. Witness daily reenactments of the famous shootout. Enjoy 100 captivating photos by photographer C. S. Fly. Experience a multimedia history show narrated by Vincent Price.

The Saloon Theatre: Watch historical gunfight shows written by researchers. Enjoy fully narrated half-hour presentations in an Old West Theatre.

Old Tombstone Western Theme Park: Tombstone's longest-running professional gunfight show (three performances daily). Family-friendly activities like Mini Golf, Panning for Gold, and Shoot 'n Gallery. Explore the charming Cantina, the sweetest little saloon in town.

Rose Tree Inn Museum: Visit the World's Largest Rose Tree. Stay in suites or explore the Rose Tree Museum with 1880s collections. Discover excellent mining dioramas and more.

Tombstone Courthouse State Historic Park: Explore Tombstone and Cochise County's historic museum. View colorful frontier exhibits, from Geronimo to the O.K. Corral gun battle.

Tombstone Epitaph Museum: Founded in 1880 by John Clum, explore this successful newspaper's history. Pick up a souvenir historical edition and see linotype machines from yesteryear.

Tombstone Western Heritage Museum: Specializing in Wyatt Earp memorabilia and unique items from Cochise County Cow-Boys. A must-visit for lawmen and outlaw history enthusiasts.

Wyatt Earp's Oriental Saloon & Theatre: Have a drink in Wyatt Earp's original gambling hall. Experience family-friendly historical gunfights and live music.

The Bird Cage Theatre: Opened in 1881, perfectly preserved with historic artifacts. Explore daily from 9 am to 6 pm and enjoy nightly ghost tours.

Boothill Graveyard: Since 1878, the resting place of those who "died with their boots on." Visit the graves of historic figures like Marshal Fred White and O.K. Corral participants.

Gunfighter Hall of Fame: A must-see museum with historic artifacts, photographs, and new items. View Kurt Russell's revolver from the movie 'Tombstone' and original weapons of famous Western actors.

E Bar 5 Stagelines: Narrated Stagecoach tour of the town "Too Tough to Die."

Good Enough Underground Mine Tours: Venture into a real 1870s Silver Mine, exploring Tombstone from 100 feet below. Group and family discounts available.

Good Enough Mine Trolley Tours: A 6-mile historical tour covering 66 landmarks in Tombstone, Mining Districts, Cemeteries, and the Schieffelin Monument. Package options combining the trolley tour with the Good Enough Mine Tour.

Gunfighter & Ghost Tour: Guided Ghost Tours departing nightly from Downtown Tombstone. Explore haunted spots in Tombstone's Historic District, learning about its history and paranormal tales.

House of Howard Blacksmith: Watch a working blacksmith create items, including brands and knives, inside the O.K. Corral attraction.

Ike Clanton's Haunted Hotel: Thrilling 15-minute walk-through 'Tombstone Ghosts & Legends Tour.' Combines fantasy, history, adventure, and learning with special effects.

Old Butterfield Stagecoach Tours: Ride the Old Butterfield Stage Coach for a 20-minute narrated tour of Historic Old Tombstone.

Old Tombstone Historical Tours: Fully narrated tours operating daily throughout the Historic District, using stagecoaches or covered wagons.

Outlaw Zipline: Experience the World's Only Laser Shooting Zipline at the corner of S. 7th Street and Toughnut Street.

Ponyland Trail Rides: Horseback Riding in Tombstone with guided trail rides, wagon rides, a Petting Zoo, Pony Rides, and Horse Sales.

The Shootout Arena: Event arena hosting Bull Ridings, Bull & Horse sales, Weddings, Live Entertainment, and more.

Tombstone Adventure Co.: Guides you from the ordinary to the EXTRA-ordinary, offering a new way to experience the old west.

Tombstone Trolley Tours: Expert conductors from Old Tombstone Western Theme Park showcasing the historic ins and outs of the "Town Too Tough to Die."

Can Can Old Time Photos: Old-time photography with a choice of 1880s costumes and authentic props. Different picture sizes and packages available in one of Tombstone's historic buildings.

Lady L's Creations: Old-time photo studio where you can dress up like Wild West characters for unique and fun photos. Located between 5th & 6th streets, across from the Bird Cage.

TONTO NATIONAL MONUMENT

COUNTY: GILA   **CITY:** GLOBE *n.c.*

DATE VISITED: _____   **WHO I WENT WITH:** _____

RATING: ☆ ☆ ☆ ☆ ☆   **WILL I RETURN?** YES / NO

Tonto National Monument, situated within an easy day trip from Phoenix, stands out as one of Arizona's most remarkable prehistoric sites. What distinguishes it from other national parks and monuments is the unique opportunity it provides to hike independently to the well-preserved Lower Cliff Dwelling. Visitors can explore its 20 rooms without the need for a guide. Moreover, the Lower Cliff Dwelling offers stunning panoramic views of the Tonto Valley Basin below and Roosevelt Lake in the distance.

The mystery surrounding the Salado people's decision to construct their homes here 700 years ago adds an intriguing layer to the site. Archaeologists offer varied speculations, suggesting that the caves may have provided protection from the elements or potential threats from neighbors. Some propose the idea that inhabitants sought refuge from the congested Tonto Basin floor. Equally perplexing is the enigma of their departure between 1400 and 1450 CE. Regardless of the reasons, the Salado people had vacated the area long before the arrival of American settlers. Concerns about potential damage from increasing tourist visits led to the establishment of Tonto National Monument in 1907, aiming to preserve these cliff dwellings.

The primary attraction at Tonto National Monument is the Lower Cliff Dwelling. Before embarking on the hike to reach it, it's advisable to check in at the visitor center. Take some time to explore the small museum, where you can gain insights into the Salado people and view artifacts, including pottery. Watching the 18-minute film provides a useful introduction before starting the trail. Despite being paved, the Lower Cliff Dwelling Trail is steep, ascending 350 feet in just half a mile. For individuals with knee issues or those who are not physically fit, it might be wise to limit the experience to the view from ground level. If you choose to ascend, anticipate spending about an hour on your journey up and back, depending on breaks and the time spent at the ruins.

Inside the Lower Cliff Dwelling, you'll encounter partially intact rooms, some retaining their original pine and juniper roofs, and walls darkened by smoke from cooking fires. Access is granted to all rooms except Rooms 14 and 15. The former is the only entirely intact room in Tonto National Monument, while the latter boasts its original clay floor and a fire pit. Apart from the Lower Cliff Dwelling, the monument also features a 40-room Upper Cliff Dwelling, accessible through guided tours. Due to the uneven terrain and a 600-foot elevation gain, this tour is recommended only for experienced hikers (children 8 and under are not permitted). For the 3-mile round-trip journey to the ruins, ensure you have an ample water supply and wear sturdy, closed-toe shoes. Throughout the trek, the guide will provide information about the Sonoran Desert and the Salado people, making it essential to stay hydrated, even if you don't feel thirsty. Inside the cave, you'll encounter two-story structures, partially intact roofs, parapet walls functioning as balconies, and two large rooms believed to have been used for gatherings or ceremonies.

Tonto National Monument and its visitor center operate daily from 8 a.m. to 5 p.m. throughout the year, with the exception of December 25. Although the Lower Cliff Dwelling Trail opens at 8 a.m., its closing time varies: from September through May, it closes at 4 p.m., and during June through August, it shuts down at 12 p.m. It's crucial to begin your trek before the specified closing time. Additionally, please be aware that the Lower Cliff Dwelling Trail may be temporarily closed due to lightning, flooding, bee activity, or other safety concerns.

Guided tours of the Upper Cliff Dwelling are available at 10 a.m. every Friday, Saturday, Sunday, and Monday from November through April. Reservations are mandatory and can be made starting on October 1 for the upcoming season. To secure a reservation, you can call (928) 467-2241. The admission fee for the national monument is $10 per person, with children under 16 enjoying free entry. All America the Beautiful passes, including annual, senior, and military passes, are accepted. While you are welcome to bring your pet, they must be leashed at all times and are only allowed on the Lower Cliff Dwelling Trail. Pets are not permitted in the actual cliff dwellings, on the Upper Cliff Dwelling Trail, or inside the visitor center. Leaving your pet unattended in your car for any reason is against the law.

Apart from the visitor center, Tonto National Monument provides shaded picnic tables but lacks additional amenities. The visitor center offers free spring water for refilling water bottles, but it is advisable to bring your own snacks, beverages, and lunch as the monument does not feature a restaurant or café. In case of forgetfulness, there are grocery stores and restaurants conveniently located in Globe and Roosevelt Estates. While camping is not permitted within the monument, options are available at Roosevelt Lake, just 15 minutes away. Additionally, there are campgrounds spread across Tonto National Forest.

To preserve the delicate environment and archaeological significance of Tonto National Monument, it is crucial to adhere to these guidelines to minimize any adverse impact on the cliff dwellings:

1) Avoid climbing, leaning, sitting, or standing on the walls.
2) Refrain from touching the walls as oils from hands can contribute to deterioration.
3) Do not disturb or move rocks that are part of a wall, regardless of their size.
4) Resist the temptation to dig for artifacts or remove any items from the site.
5) Refrain from consuming food within the cliff dwellings, as crumbs and trash can contaminate the site and attract wildlife.
6) Stick to designated trails to prevent damage to the soil and desert plants caused by venturing off the path.
7) Smoking, lighting fires, or using candles is strictly prohibited to ensure the safety and preservation of the site.

Tonto National Monument is situated near Roosevelt Lake, approximately a 30-minute drive from Globe and two hours from downtown Phoenix. Access to the monument is available through two main routes: SR 87 (Beeline Highway) or US 60. For most visitors, SR 87 offers a slightly shorter drive. Take SR 87 north towards Payson, make a right at SR 188, and continue for 39 miles to reach the monument. Alternatively, if you are coming from the East Valley, US 60 may be a more time-efficient option. Head east on US 60 towards Globe, turn left on SR 188, and travel 25 miles to Tonto National Monument.

Historically, the Apache Trail (SR 88) was a route to Tonto National Monument, but due to a fire and flooding in 2019, the segment from Fish Creek Hill Overlook to Apache Lake Marina is indefinitely closed. Even if SR 88 were to reopen in the future, it includes dirt sections with blind turns and drop-offs lacking guardrails. For a safer journey, it is recommended to choose either SR 87 or US 60 instead.

Nearby attractions:

Roosevelt Lake: As the largest lake in central Arizona, Roosevelt Lake provides opportunities for fishing, boating, and camping. Make sure to stop at Roosevelt Dam to witness the world's highest masonry dam, completed in 1911.

Besh-Ba-Gowah Archaeological Park: Situated one mile south of Globe, Besh-Ba-Gowah is another Salado site. Visitors can explore the ruins, visit the museum with a substantial collection of Salado pottery and artifacts, and enjoy features like a botanical garden and gift shop.

Boyce Thompson Arboretum State Park: If you choose to take US 60 to Tonto National Monument, you'll pass by Boyce Thompson Arboretum. Covering 392 acres, the arboretum showcases over 3,000 different plant species. Check the calendar for seasonal hours and plan your visit accordingly.

TONTO NATURAL BRIDGE STATE PARK

COUNTY: GILA   CITY: PAYSON   *n.c.*

DATE VISITED: WHO I WENT WITH:

RATING: ☆ ☆ ☆ ☆ ☆   WILL I RETURN?   YES / NO

Tonto Natural Bridge State Park, situated in central Arizona near Payson, is home to what is believed to be the largest natural travertine bridge globally. This majestic bridge towers 183 feet above a 400-foot-long tunnel, with a width of 150 feet at its broadest point. The park boasts three hiking trails, a designated picnic area, and a group use area. In addition to offering a habitat for various animals, insects, and birds, the park features interpretive exhibits within the historic Goodfellow Lodge. These exhibits showcase artifacts related to the history of Tonto Natural Bridge, information about travertine, details about prehistoric inhabitants, and the significance of the historic Goodfellow Lodge.

The Tonto Natural Bridge Visitor Center, situated inside the historic Goodfellow Lodge, serves as an information hub and park store. The lodge is also available for group reservations. The park store offers a range of books about the region and the area, along with snacks, water, soda, walking sticks, and T-shirts. The Visitor Center operates from 8 am to 5 pm. Visitors have the opportunity to view the Natural Bridge from four different parking lot viewpoints without the need to hike down to the bottom. The Lodge's interpretive exhibits include not only artifacts but also information about the bridge's history, travertine, prehistoric inhabitants, and the significance of the Tonto Lodge. Additionally, visitors can enjoy photographs, a painting of the Natural Bridge, and a scenic slideshow within the Lodge.

Goodfellow Lodge, located within Tonto Natural Bridge State Park, is a unique and rustic retreat situated amidst the breathtaking landscapes of Arizona's Rim Country. This three-story cabin-style lodge, constructed in the 1920s, retains much of its early 20th-century charm. Nestled deep in Pine Canyon, the lodge offers 10 furnished bedrooms equipped with both private and communal restrooms. Additionally, there is a furnished basement suite featuring a private kitchenette with a sink and refrigerator.

On the first floor, guests can enjoy a beautiful wood cabin group dining area adorned with picnic table seating, a fireplace, and a spacious kitchen suitable for accommodating large groups or catering services. The lodge's outdoor amenities include an inviting veranda and a grass event area, providing ideal spaces for entertainment or relaxation. Visitors can take in the natural surroundings and may even spot local wildlife such as deer and javelina.

The Dining Room and Outdoor Veranda at Goodfellow Lodge offer complete furnishings with picnic bench-style seating and small two-person tables strategically placed near the dining room windows, providing a scenic view of the park surroundings. Within the

Dining Room, guests can find amenities such as a fireplace, an old-time stove, and a piano (please note that the piano may not be regularly tuned). The Kitchen is well-equipped with various cooking items, including pots, pans, and utensils, as well as dishes, glassware, and silverware. For outdoor events, the Goodfellow Lawn, accommodating 100-150 people, is ADA accessible. This event area features freestanding restrooms with tiled floors and running water. Guests have the option to rent a wood BBQ or two propane grills for their gatherings. The Roosevelt Suite, designed for private use, includes a restroom with a shower, vanity, a small refrigerator, microwave, cabinets, and a kitchen counter. This suite is available for rental and is ADA accessible. Recent renovations to the lodge have introduced modern conveniences such as heating and air conditioning, indoor plumbing, and enhancements to comply with the Americans with Disabilities Act.

To reserve a day-use ramada, individuals can contact the park directly. The park offers a new Group Ramada, measuring 20x40 feet, equipped with tables and grills. Additionally, the Cypress Group Ramada, sized at 20x30 feet and featuring picnic tables and BBQ grills, is available on a first-come, first-served basis. For those seeking smaller ramadas, there are three 10x10 Ramadas with a picnic table and BBQ grill, which are also available on a first-come, first-served basis, and no reservations are accepted for these. The park provides numerous unsheltered picnic tables throughout the area for general enjoyment.

Bird enthusiasts can explore the diverse bird species that visit the park, including a lively hummingbird community depending on the season. A park bird list is available upon payment of the entrance fee at the entrance station. In addition to birds, the park is home to deer, rabbits, and javelina.

While swimming is prohibited under the Natural Bridge, visitors are allowed to swim downstream in Pine Creek. It is essential to note that there is no lifeguard on duty, and swimming is undertaken at one's own risk.

The park offers several hiking trails, each marked by its steep and strenuous nature, with a reminder that pets and glass containers are not allowed on any trails.

Pine Creek Trail, approximately ½ mile in length (400 feet developed, with an undeveloped section in the creek bottom), guides hikers to the Pine Creek natural area. Hiking shoes are recommended, and the trail takes about one hour to complete.

Waterfall Trail, spanning about 300 feet, concludes at a waterfall cave and includes uneven steps. Allowing 15–20 minutes for completion.

Gowan Trail, extending approximately 2,200 feet down and back, leads to an observation deck in the creek bottom. The trail is steep and rough, with no trash cans available. Hiking shoes are recommended, and the trail takes about one hour.

Anna Mae Trail, around 500 feet in length, connects to Pine Creek Trail and the Natural Bridge, requiring approximately one hour for completion.

Visitors can view what may be the world's largest travertine bridge from multiple angles within the park. The paved paths on top provide access to four great viewpoints, offering a comprehensive understanding of the bridge's scale and a vast view of Arizona's rim country. Quick facts about the immense size of the natural bridge include:

Height of the bridge: 183 feet
Width of the tunnel: 150 feet
Length of the tunnel: 393 feet
Thickness of travertine above the tunnel: 60 feet

Notably, Tonto Natural Bridge stands out as unique and special because, unlike most natural bridges made of sandstone or limestone, it is composed of travertine. The size and the history of its creation make this particular bridge visually stunning, leaving viewers awestruck by its grandeur.

PARK HISTORY

Since its establishment in 1957, the State Parks Board has prioritized the acquisition of Tonto Natural Bridge as a significant project. In July 1967, a revised development program was adopted by the Parks Board, designating Tonto Natural Bridge as the top priority. A letter dated July 31, 1967, was sent to Director Dennis McCarthy, informing the agency that Mrs. Randall, the Executrix for the Glen Randall estate, had set the selling price for Tonto Natural Bridge at $500,000.

During the Parks Board meeting on November 15, 1967, a unanimous motion was adopted. The motion, proposed by Member Fireman and seconded by Member Rarick, authorized the Director to meet with the relevant legislative committees (Natural Resources in the Senate and House) to request the drafting and introduction of legislation for the acquisition of Tonto Natural Bridge as a State Park, pending legislative approval.

On February 13, 1968, House Bill 272 (HB 272) was introduced by Representatives Lyman, Getzwiller, Rosenbaum, Farley, Jones, Shaghnessy, and Shelly. The Act granted authorization to the Park and allocated $250,000 from the State General Fund to the Arizona State Parks Board for acquiring Tonto Natural Bridge. Although HB 272 successfully passed the Natural Resources and the Game and Fish Committee, it faced amendments in the Appropriations Committee, reducing the appropriation to $20,000 for appraisals and planning studies. The Second Regular Session of the Twenty-eighth Legislature concluded without further action on HB 272.

At the behest of State Parks, property owners agreed to hold the property until after the next Legislative session. The Agency explored alternative funding sources such as the Four Corners Regional Commission and The Nature Conservancy. The acquisition, along with limited development and operation of Tonto Natural Bridge, was included in the Agency's budget request for the 1969-1970 Fiscal Year, submitted to the Commissioner of Finance on September 1, 1968, during Jack Williams' tenure as Governor.

On November 7, 1968, the New Starts Committee, a Subcommittee of the State Parks Board, consisting of Chairman A.C. Williams, Duane Miller, and Ralph Burgbacher, convened at the Tonto Natural Bridge. Director McCarthy and Assistant Director Paul Crandall were also in attendance for the meeting. The committee conducted a tour of the grounds and buildings, observed the Bridge, and had lunch at the lodge.

In a letter dated November 29, 1968, Director McCarthy informed Representative Stan Turley that the Tonto Natural Bridge was the top-priority project for the Parks Board. The acquisition and development of the site had been incorporated into the 1969-1970 budget request. The Parks Board intended to seek the introduction of legislation to acquire and develop the location as a State Park. Since Representative Turley had been appointed Chairman of the Natural Resources Committee, the Director requested him to establish a sub-committee on State Parks within the Committee.

In December 1968, Director McCarthy held discussions with representatives of The Nature Conservancy and officials of the Bureau of Outdoor Recreation (BOR) in San Francisco regarding the negotiations for acquiring the Tonto Natural Bridge. The Nature Conservancy expressed willingness to assist, and Frank Sylvester, the Regional Director of the BOR, indicated that if the Arizona Outdoor Recreation Coordinating Commission approved the acquisition project, funds from the Federal Land and Water Conservation Fund would be approved by BOR in fiscal year 1970.

Mrs. Randall was updated on this information, and she conveyed her willingness to wait and see the Legislature's actions. She expressed enthusiasm about the prospect of acquiring the Tonto Natural Bridge as a State Park, either through legislative action or with The Nature Conservancy's involvement.

In a letter dated December 6, 1968, Speaker of the House Stan Turley expressed to the Director that acquiring the Tonto Natural Bridge was likely one of the most logical projects for the Board's top priority. He pledged to do everything in his capacity to achieve this objective. Speaker Turley authorized the Director to have Legislative Council draft the necessary legislation for acquiring Tonto Natural Bridge, intending to introduce it at the beginning of the legislative session.

In January 1969, the Arizona Conservation Council, the Governor's Commission on Arizona Beauty, the Arizona Parks and Recreation Association, and the Arizona Wildlife Federation unanimously endorsed the acquisition and development of the Tonto Natural Bridge as a State Park.

On January 21, 1969, the House Natural Resources Committee agreed to introduce legislation known as House Bill 65 for the acquisition of Tonto Natural Bridge. This bill proposed an appropriation of $175,000 from State funds, to be matched by a grant from the Federal Land and Water Conservation Fund. The Natural Resources Committee heard and approved the bill on January 28, 1969. The bill passed in the House on March 21, 1969, but with a reduced appropriation of $55,000. The Legislature believed that the necessary additional $120,000 could be obtained through matches from The Nature Conservancy and the Land and Water Conservation Fund.

House Bill 65 (Chapter 63) successfully passed the Legislature and received Governor Jack Williams' approval on April 9, 1969. This legislation granted the authority to purchase Tonto Natural Bridge and appropriated $55,000, which would be matched with Land and Water Conservation Funds for a partial payment toward acquiring the property. This appropriation was effective until June 30, 1971.

In May 1969, the Director authorized the commencement of the appraisal process by Mr. Burke, an MIA appraiser based in Phoenix. By June 1969, the Agency prepared the Project Proposal, submitted to the Arizona Outdoor Recreation Coordinating Commission on July 1, 1969. The appraisal was completed by August 12, 1969, valuing the Tonto Natural Bridge at $125,000. However, Mrs. Randall rejected this appraisal and declined to fund another one. In mid-September, the Parks Board obtained a new appraisal from Mr. Veldon Naylor, MIA, setting the value at $325,000. The Parks Board approved sending a letter to Mrs. Randall with an offer of $225,000, but this offer was also rejected. The owners insisted on $390,000, a request the Parks Board rejected. On November 14, 1969, the Parks Board made a formal offer of $250,000 to purchase the 160 acres, including the Tonto Natural Bridge.

In March 1970, the Parks Board learned that the North Star Development Company of Flagstaff had acquired an option to purchase the Tonto Natural Bridge. Board Member Duane Miller was tasked with contacting the owners of the North Star Development Company, emphasizing the Board's continued interest in acquiring the site as a State Park.

In February 1971, the Parks Board directed the Director to send a letter expressing the Board's ongoing interest in Tonto Natural Bridge to the principals of North Star Development Company. On August 19 and 20, 1971, the Parks Board convened a meeting at the lodge to discuss the project and proposals thoroughly. Following extensive deliberations, the Board decided to conclude negotiations with the owners of Tonto Natural Bridge.

Despite the public announcement of ending negotiations, the Parks Board, throughout the early 1970s, continued to have staff explore alternative methods for acquiring Tonto Natural Bridge. These alternatives included seeking authorization to exchange the property for State Trust land outside Gila County, establishing a Revolving Fund in the

Governor's Office, and contemplating possible condemnation. In the late 1970s and throughout the 1980s, the owners periodically approached the Board, inquiring about the potential for securing funding. However, the presence of a very clouded title posed complications, hindering any efforts to pursue acquisition.

By the late 1980s, the courts determined that the Wolfswinkle family held legal ownership of Tonto Natural Bridge. In 1987, the Wolfswinkles undertook the renovation of the lodge, restoring it to its original condition. In 1989, a member of the Wolfswinkle family contacted Director Travous to inquire about the Parks Board's continued interest in acquiring Tonto Natural Bridge. The opportunity to explore this acquisition arose in January 1990 during a presentation on the status of State Parks to the Senate Natural Resources Committee. Following the presentation, Senator Leo Corbet expressed the view that Tonto Natural Bridge should become a State Park and sought ways to facilitate its inclusion in the system. The Committee showed strong support for this idea, prompting the agency to engage in subsequent meetings with various legislators and budget analysts to formulate an acceptable course of action.

Initially, the Senate Natural Resources Committee and the Governor initiated correspondence with each member of the Arizona Congressional Delegation to explore the possibility of federal assistance in acquiring the Arizona landmark. Upon discovering that federal participation was not feasible, the Parks staff collaborated closely with legislative leadership to formulate a bill that could serve as a means to pursue the purchase. Senator Pat Wright, Chairman of Senate Appropriations, expressed her preference for one of her bills to be used for this purpose. By March 8, 1990, a "Strike Everything" amendment had been prepared and gained approval for Senate Bill 1030 (SB 1030). The amendment was introduced and successfully passed the Senate Appropriations Committee on March 9, 1990.

SB 1030, through its amendment, granted authorization to the State Parks Board for the acquisition, development, and operation of Tonto Natural Bridge as a State Park. The bill allocated an appropriation for the initial year of operation and sanctioned the utilization of a Certificate of Participation (COP) to procure the property. Additionally, it mandated the use of the State Park Acquisition and Development Fund (later renamed the Enhancement Fund) for annual lease-purchase payments. The bill received substantial backing from legislators directly impacted by the addition of a State Park in their area, including Senator Bill Hardt, Senator Tony Gabaldon, and Representatives Jack Brown, Polly Rosenbaum, Karan English, and John Wettaw (Chairman of House Appropriations). Within a fortnight, SB 1030 successfully passed the Senate, the House Appropriations, and Rules Committees, positioning it for final approval by the House.

Simultaneously, during this period, the Joint Committee on Capital Review (JCCR) convened and sanctioned the use of a lease-purchase mechanism to acquire the Tonto Natural Bridge. The House endorsed the measure, and on April 12, 1990, Governor Rose Mofford signed SB 1030 into law as Chapter 48 of that legislative session.

The Purchase Agreement between the State Parks Board and Tonto Natural Bridge, Inc., was officially executed on July 19, 1990. Following this, the Lease Purchase Agreement, identifying the Tonto Natural Bridge as Project Unit No. 3, Docket 813, and page 378, was signed on October 1, 1990. The Warranty Deed, completing the transfer of property to the Trustee, was then signed on October 10, 1990. An Amended and Restated Lease-Purchase Agreement was later finalized on December 1, 1993, involving Bank One, Arizona, NA, Trustee as Lessor, and the State of Arizona, represented by the Director of the Department of Administration, as Lessee. This document, consisting of 52 pages, was recorded in Gila County on December 29, 1993, under Fee # 93-641916, with the Tonto Natural Bridge (160 acres) specified as paragraph VIII, Project Unit No. 8 on page A-7 of the recorded documents.

Before the Park was opened to the public, several enhancements and developments took place. The entrance and interior roads, along with parking areas, underwent realignment and paving. Additional picnic facilities were constructed, an entrance station was installed, and landscape improvements were carried out. The official Grand Opening Celebration occurred on June 29, 1991, featuring a full day of activities. Ken Travous, State Parks Executive Director, served as the master of ceremony, introducing notable figures such as U.S. Senator John McCain, Governor Symington, special guests, Parks Board members, legislators, John Boeck (Park Manager), and park staff. During the Dedication Ceremony at 6:30 PM, Ken Travous introduced Parks Board Chairman Ron Pies, who, in turn, presented Governor Fife Symington, jointly cutting the ribbon to signify the official opening of Tonto Natural Bridge State Park.

To address infrastructural needs, an additional 1.04 acres of land was procured from the U.S. Forest Service on September 9, 1999. This acquisition was essential as part of the roadway to the residence area traversed this particular property.

AREA ATTRACTIONS

Explore Payson and the Mogollon Rim, situated in the heart of Arizona's "Alpine Region," northeast of the Greater Phoenix metropolitan area. The town of Payson, along with Pine and Strawberry communities, offers a picturesque drive on State Route 87 through stunning desert and mountain landscapes. Rim Country encompasses different altitudes, with Payson at 5,000', and Pine and Strawberry ranging from 5,400' to 6,000'.

Rim County Chamber of Commerce: Represents towns of Payson, Pine, Strawberry, Star Valley, and Christopher Creek. Address: 100 W. Main St. Payson. Phone: (800) 6-PAYSON.

Rim Country Museums including Zane Grey Cabin: Operated by the Northern Gila County Historical Society. Features the Rim Country Museum and the Zane Grey Cabin.

Payson Ranger Station: Located 1/2 mile east of Payson to the Mogollon Rim on Highway 260. Provides information on camping, hiking, fishing, and hunting in the Rim Country.

Features a short exercise trail adjacent to the station.

Shoofly Native American Ruins: Found 2.3 miles north of Payson on Highway 87, turn right on Houston Mesa Road. Approximately three miles to the ruins with a marked trail and scenic views of the rim.

Pine Trailhead: Located 14 miles north of Payson on Highway 87. Serves as the west end of the 51-mile-long Highline National Recreational Trail, with trails ascending to the Mogollon Rim.

Christopher Creek Campground: Situated 21 miles east of Payson to the Mogollon Rim on Highway 260. Offers fishing and wading in Christopher Creek running through the middle of the campground. A full-service campground.

Rim Visitor Center: Located 30 miles east of Payson to the Mogollon Rim on Highway 260. Provides information on vista points, lakes, fishing, picnicking, camping, boating, hiking, and wildlife.

Tonto Creek Fish Hatchery: North of Payson, allows visitors to feed the fish, take a self-guided tour, photograph, or enjoy birding. Forest Rd. 289. Contact Arizona Game and Fish, Tonto Creek, at (928) 478-4200.

Highline National Recreation Trails (West Entrance): Found 14 miles north of Payson on Highway 87. Includes Pine trailhead, Geronimo trailhead, Washington Park trailhead, and the Highline trailhead. Contact the Payson Ranger Station at (928) 474-7900 for maps and brochures.

The Arizona Trail: A 790-mile border-to-border route between Utah and Mexico. For information, contact the Payson Ranger Station at (928) 474-7900 or (602)-252-4794.

Fossil Creek Trailhead: Offers a trail to Fossil Springs, suitable for hiking, swimming, photography, and birding. Contact the Payson Ranger Station at (928) 474-7900.

TRAIL OF TIME

COUNTY: COCONINO   CITY: FLAGSTAFF *n.c.*

DATE VISITED: WHO I WENT WITH:

RATING: ☆ ☆ ☆ ☆ ☆   WILL I RETURN? YES / NO

The Trail of Time is a 4.56 km (2.83 mile) long paved walk that offers a relatively flat terrain. Its purpose is to serve as a representation of the geologic timeline of the Grand Canyon. Each meter walked on this trail corresponds to one million years of the Grand Canyon's geologic history. As you progress along the trail, bronze markers indicate your position in time, with every tenth marker labeled in millions of years. The trail features rocks and exhibits explaining the formation of the Grand Canyon and its rocks.

This interpretive walking trail focuses on the panoramic views and rocks of the Grand Canyon, encouraging visitors to contemplate, explore, and comprehend the vastness of geologic time. The Trail of Time begins at the Yavapai Geology Museum, which is a half-hour walk from Mather Point and the Canyon View Visitor Center. The trail extends to Grand Canyon Village and beyond, providing the option to stop in the Village or continue walking towards Hermits Rest.

Embark on a journey into the past by walking backward in time between Yavapai Geology Museum and Grand Canyon Village (2.1 km or 1.3 miles). This westward walk covers Grand Canyon's entire geologic history, starting with the "Million Year Trail," which transitions from human time scales to geologic ones. The "Million Year Trail" is immediately followed by the main Trail of Time, where each meter represents one million years of the Grand Canyon's geologic history. This fully accessible one-hour walking trip offers breathtaking views of the Grand Canyon, allowing you to contemplate and understand the profound dimensions of geologic space and time.

Conversely, walking east from Grand Canyon Village provides a journey from the past to the present, moving forward in time. This route encompasses the same experience, leading from the Grand Canyon's oldest rocks to the carving of the canyon and the human history associated with it.

Grand Canyon National Park attracts around six million visitors annually, with a significant portion unable to undertake hikes into the canyon itself. The Trail of Time exhibit serves as an accessible alternative, allowing people to appreciate the Grand Canyon and capture individuals at a moment when they are awestruck by the magnificence of the canyon and wish to gain a deeper understanding of how the landscape evolved due to geological events.

Entrance Portals to the Trail of Time:

The Million Year Walk Portal: The Trail of Time commences at the Yavapai Geology Museum. Upon walking west along the paved trail from the museum, you'll first encounter the Million Year Trail, a brief path covering 150 yards (136 meters). This short trail acts as a transition from human time scales to geologic ones and serves as an "on-ramp" to the main trail, which spans 2 billion years of geologic time over 2.83 miles (4.56 km).

The Main Trail of Time Portal: After traversing the short Million Year Trail of 150 yards (136 m), you will reach the second Trail of Time portal. This marks the beginning of the main Trail of Time, a timeline spanning two billion years of the Grand Canyon's geologic history, covering approximately 2.83 miles (4.56 km). This fully accessible one-hour walking journey provides stunning views of the Grand Canyon, offering an opportunity to contemplate and comprehend the vastness of geologic space and time.

Verkamp's Visitor Center Portal: Starting from the flagpole outside Verkamp's Visitor Center, follow the rim trail to the right and locate the Trail of Time bronze markers embedded in the pavement. From the 2,000 million year marker, the western entry portal for the Trail of Time becomes visible. This marks the "old" end of the main Trail of Time. Walking east from Grand Canyon Village allows you to progress forward in time, from the Grand Canyon's oldest rocks to the carving of the canyon and the human history associated with it.

Headquarters Portal (Parking Lot A): Accessing this portal involves walking the spur trail near Park Headquarters and parking lot A. The trail spans 0.4 miles (0.65 km) to the portal at the junction with the Canyon Rim Trail (Trail of Time). Positioned at 1,000 million (1 billion) years ago along the Trail of Time, this portal corresponds to a period in Grand Canyon history marked by the deposition of rocks belonging to the Grand Canyon Supergroup, some of the oldest sedimentary rocks in the Grand Canyon.

TUCSON

COUNTY: PIMA   **CITY:** TUCSON

DATE VISITED: **WHO I WENT WITH:**

RATING: ☆ ☆ ☆ ☆ ☆   **WILL I RETURN?** YES / NO

Tucson, Arizona, is renowned for its cultural diversity and extensive history, making it a must-visit destination for enthusiasts of Mexican cuisine, historical architecture, and lively nightlife. The city is home to the University of Arizona's main campus and holds the prestigious designation of being a UNESCO City of Gastronomy. Nestled within the Sonoran Desert, Tucson offers an ideal setting for outdoor enthusiasts seeking exploration opportunities. The city's mild winter temperatures make it a magnet for snowbirds from the northern regions, and its abundance of spas and resorts ensures a restful and rejuvenating stay. While many visitors opt for day trips from Phoenix, Tucson has so much to offer that a weekend stay might not be enough to see everything it has to offer.

Explore an Aircraft Boneyard: Tucson, owing to its arid climate, hosts the world's largest aircraft storage and preservation facility known as the Tucson Airplane Graveyard, located on the Davis-Monthan Air Force Base. Accessible through the Pima Air & Space Museum, a guided tour of "the Boneyard" is available, with tram tours departing multiple times daily, showcasing around 4,000 decommissioned planes. It's advisable to make advance reservations. For history and military enthusiasts, a visit to the affiliated Titan Missile Museum, just half an hour away in Green Valley, is recommended. The museum features an unarmed missile still housed in the silo.

Indulge in Craft Beer: Tucson is a well-kept secret in the world of craft beer, boasting local brewers who blend traditional recipes with a Southwestern flair. Ales with cactus fruit and Mexican spices are among the unique offerings. Explore various taphouses in the area to savor the local flavors. Barrio Brewing, established by native Arizonans Dennis and Tauna Arnold, serves favorites like the Tucson Blonde and the Hipsterville IPA. Another noteworthy stop is 1912 Brewing Company, collaborating with the Tucson Tamale Company to provide a delightful pairing of beers and bites.

Mountain Biking at Tucson Mountain Park: Tucson Mountain Park is a haven for mountain biking enthusiasts, offering an extensive network of 104 miles of trails suitable for all skill levels. Beginner-friendly trails like Ironwood, Kerr Jarr, Mariposa, Triple C, and Gates Pass offer flat and swoopy rides, while intermediate riders can explore the base of Brown Mountain or climb Starr Pass on the Golden Gate Trail. Brown Mountain presents trails with tight switchbacks, rock gardens, and varying levels of exposure. Some trails are multi-use, so it's important to adhere to proper trail etiquette, giving ample space to horseback riders or hikers.

Golf on Premier Courses: Nestled in the foothills of the Santa Catalina Mountains,

Ventana Canyon Golf Resort is a lush desert oasis with two 18-hole championship golf courses designed by architect Tom Fazio. The Mountain Course features a par 3 hole, one of the most photographed in the west of the Mississippi, offering breathtaking views of the Sonoran Desert and into Mexico. The Canyon Course winds through Esperero Canyon, passing by the iconic Whaleback Rock. Staying at the resort's lodge provides access to country-club amenities, including a pool, spa, fitness center, and two restaurants, making it an ideal choice for a post-golf retreat.

Step into the Past at San Xavier del Bac Mission: Established by Father Eusebio Kino in 1692, San Xavier del Bac Mission stands as a national historic landmark and the oldest intact European structure in Arizona. Situated 9 miles south of downtown Tucson, the Catholic mission and its grounds are open for exploration. Visitors can delve into its history through a walk in the onsite museum, which narrates the story of the mission's Tohono O'odham people and highlights ongoing restoration efforts. In the parking lot, encounters with members of this Native American Nation selling crafts and fry bread are likely.

Explore Tucson's UNESCO City of Gastronomy Status: Tucson secured the title of the first UNESCO City of Gastronomy in the United States in 2015, celebrating its diverse culinary history. To immerse yourself in the city's gastronomic roots, begin with a visit to the Mission Garden, the oldest continuously farmed land in the nation. Explore the heirloom seed collection and learn about the mission of Tucson-based nonprofit Native Seeds/SEARCH. Dive into the culinary scene with a visit to El Charro Café, the oldest Mexican restaurant in the U.S., or savor the local favorite Sonoran hot dog at El Guero Canelo, acclaimed with a James Beard award for its version of the iconic dish.

Discover Desert Life at the Arizona-Sonora Desert Museum: Renowned as one of Tucson's top attractions, the Arizona-Sonora Desert Museum delves into the intricate web of life within the challenging environment surrounding the city. Its gardens, ranking among the nation's top 10 public gardens, showcase over 1,200 plant species. The zoo introduces visitors to native animals like the Mexican gray wolf, javelina, mountain lion, bobcats, and bighorn sheep. The museum also features a walk-in aviary, an aquarium, and displays on the region's geology, all surrounded by hiking trails. A recommended visit duration is at least two hours, though exploring the grounds could easily extend to most of the day.

Backpack in Saguaro National Park: Saguaro National Park, just outside Tucson, boasts some of the most impressive stands of saguaro cacti—towering, multi-armed giants that can live up to 200 years. Explore the 8-mile Cactus Forest Loop Drive in the Rincon Mountain District or the Bajada Loop Drive in the Tucson Mountain District for an optimal sampling of the park's offerings. Both loops collectively offer over 175 miles of hiking trails, including a short 0.3-mile trek to petroglyphs. Each district features its own visitor center with remarkable cactus gardens. For the more adventurous, the backcountry beckons for backpacking and camping amidst the iconic desert landscape, provided you embark on your journey during cooler weather conditions.

Embark on a Scenic Hike in Sabino Canyon: Positioned at the foothills of the Santa Catalina Mountains in Tucson, Sabino Canyon Recreation Area offers picturesque landscapes with a flowing creek, waterfalls, and diverse wildlife. Spend your day exploring the extensive 30-plus miles of trails or opt for an open-air electric tram ride, which provides a narrated journey through the canyon. Alternatively, engage in activities like jogging, trail running, or biking, making sure to pause at scenic spots for photographs. Ensure you're well-equipped with ample water, sunscreen, and a hat, keeping in mind that bicycles are permitted in the park only until 5 p.m.

Indulge in Relaxation at a Resort Spa: Tucson is home to over half a dozen acclaimed resorts, making it a sought-after getaway for residents of Phoenix. If you have the luxury of booking a stay, take advantage of lounging by beautiful pools with panoramic views in between your city explorations. Enhance your indulgence by scheduling a spa treatment, such as a massage or facial, at the resort's spa. Many resorts extend an invitation for guests to enjoy the entire spa for the day, complete with amenities like a steam room and private pools. For a cutting-edge relaxation experience, check out El Conquistador, Tucson's salt therapy lounge, at SpaWell.

Experience Ranch Life at Tucson Guest Ranches: For a taste of ranch life, Tucson offers two historic guest ranches within the metropolitan area: Tanque Verde Ranch and White Stallion Ranch. These establishments provide horseback riding suitable for all ages and skill levels, team penning, and a range of activities, including nature programs, hiking, tennis, and mountain biking. Following a day filled with adventure, savor a hearty meal accompanied by stories and songs around the campfire. Alternatively, indulge in a spa treatment or unwind by the pool. Both ranches extend the option for visitors to book a ride without staying overnight, offering full-day and half-day trail riding options.

Explore the Depths at Colossal Cave Mountain Park: When the aboveground temperatures soar in Tucson, escape to the cool depths of Colossal Cave Mountain Park, located 15 miles away in Vail. The cave boasts over 3 miles of underground trails accessible to the public through guided tours. Choose from options like the Classic Cave Tour, descending approximately six stories with 363 stair steps, the Ladder Tour with narrow passages, or the Wild Cave Tour, equipped with a headlamp to explore the darkest sections. While underground, keep an eye out for various bat species, including the Mexican long-tongued bat, the Pallid bat, and the Pipistrelle Bat. Above ground, enjoy a horseback trail ride through the scenic La Posta Quemada Ranch or opt for camping and picnicking directly on-site.

Explore the Artistic Legacy at Gallery in the Sun: In a unique twist, Ettore "Ted" DeGrazia, faced with challenges getting his art displayed in traditional galleries, decided to construct his own in Tucson. Taking a hands-on approach, DeGrazia personally poured footers, shaped adobe bricks, and plastered the walls that now form the Gallery in the Sun, which has transformed into a museum. The space showcases around 800 of the museum's vast collection of 15,000 DeGrazia originals, featuring the vibrant paintings of Native Americans that brought him fame. A highlight is the "Dinner with DeGrazia" exhibit, celebrating regional Southwestern cuisine through drawings and paintings. Additionally, don't miss the on-site adobe chapel and gift shop before leaving.

Stroll Along the Turquoise Trail: The Turquoise Trail provides a cultural and historical exploration of downtown Tucson. Initiated by former Presidio Museum board members, this 2.5-mile loop, marked by a painted turquoise line beginning at the museum, guides visitors through downtown's significant historic sites. Obtain a printed self-guided walking brochure at various downtown locations, including the Presidio Museum, or opt for the Turquoise Trail app for phone-guided navigation. Guided walking tours of the trail are also offered twice a month by the museum.

Enter Another Dimension at Biosphere 2: Operated by the University of Arizona, Biosphere 2 is a self-contained, futuristic facility dedicated to research on Earth's ecosystems within a controlled indoor environment. Visitors can embark on a guided tour, approximately 1.5 hours long, exploring the rainforest, desert, mangrove, and savanna ecosystems. Utilizing the Biosphere 2 Experience app, the tour incorporates videos and slideshows relevant to the observed environments. It is advisable to secure tickets in advance, as daily visitor numbers are limited. Comfortable walking shoes and a camera are recommended for an immersive experience inside this otherworldly facility.

TUMACÁCORI NATIONAL HISTORICAL PARK

COUNTY: SANTA CRUZ   CITY: NOGALES *n.c.*

DATE VISITED:	WHO I WENT WITH:

RATING: ☆ ☆ ☆ ☆ ☆	WILL I RETURN? YES / NO

Travel back in time as you explore the 19th-century Franciscan mission of Tumacácori, a remarkable historical site within the National Historical Park. Constructed under the guidance of a master mason, the mission involved the collaboration of American Indian and Spanish laborers. Despite the church's incomplete status, it stands as a prominent landmark within the park's boundaries. Originally designated a national monument in 1908, Tumacácori became one of the oldest national park sites in the U.S., gaining National Historical Park status 80 years later.

Preceding the arrival of missionaries, the land was inhabited by the O'odham's five sister nations: Tohono, Pima, Yaki, Apache, and Mexican people. In the 1600s, Spanish missionaries named the region Pimería Alta, signifying "place of the upper Pimas," with "Pima" being one of the names given to the O'odham. The Jesuit priest Father Francisco Kino established Tumacácori as a mission in January 1691, marking it as Arizona's oldest mission site.

After the Pima rebellion of 1751 and subsequent relocations, the mission settled in its present location, formalized as San José de Tumacácori. Church construction began around 1800 under Franciscan management, with the intention of resembling the San Xavier del Bac Mission near Tucson. Due to delays, the church was only completed in 1823. Following Mexico's expulsion of the remaining Spanish residents in 1828, Tumacácori lost its last resident priest.

Upon achieving national monument status, the original church structure faced deterioration, with the roof gone and brick erosion due to annual rains. Preservation efforts have maintained the ruins, and a visitor center, incorporating original mission elements, was added in the late 1930s to showcase exhibits. Today, Tumacácori stands as a captivating testament to the region's rich history and cultural heritage.

The primary attraction in the park is the San José de Tumacácori church from the Franciscan era, drawing most visitors; however, the site comprises various structures, including a museum, a Melhok ki (a replica of a traditional O'odham dwelling from the era), and the remnants of the mission convent and cemetery. Additionally, the park oversees two more remote missions—Missions Guevavi and Calabazas—that are accessible only through reserved tours held from January to April.

Begin your exploration at the visitor center, where a 17-minute video offers a concise history of the mission. Visitors can continue through the park independently, use a self-guided tour book, or follow an audio tour. Adjacent to the visitor center, a vibrant garden area, an orchard, and a trail leading to the Juan Batista de Anza National Historic

Trail and Santa Cruz River await exploration. The trail includes a mile-long riparian area, perfect for bird watching (keep an eye out for the Vermilion Flycatcher, a striking red bird with black wings). If possible, plan your visit to coincide with cultural demonstrations, showcasing various connections to native cultures in the region. From O'odham basket weavers to painters and cooks, each participant shares their unique narrative through the crafts and food they produce. Immerse yourself in their stories while savoring freshly made corn or flour tortillas over a mesquite fire, prepared in the traditional manner.

The visitor center, museum, restrooms, and the mission grounds are entirely wheelchair accessible, ensuring ease of movement for individuals with mobility challenges. For visitors who are deaf or have hearing impairments, a personal amplifier is provided for use during the park film, which also includes subtitles for enhanced understanding. Moreover, the film has been adapted with audio descriptions to cater to the needs of the visually impaired, and headsets for audio descriptions can be borrowed at the visitor center for an enriched experience.

Situated 45 miles to the south of Tucson, 18 miles north of Nogales, and just 3 miles from the charming community of Tubac, the surrounding area offers an extensive range of lodging options. Whether you prefer hotels, motels, inns, bed and breakfasts, or upscale resorts, there are various accommodations available in all directions after your visit to the mission, ensuring you can find a comfortable place to stay.

TUZIGOOT NATIONAL MONUMENT

COUNTY: YAVAPAI	CITY: COTTONWOOD *n.c.*

DATE VISITED:	WHO I WENT WITH:

RATING: ☆ ☆ ☆ ☆ ☆   WILL I RETURN?   YES / NO

Situated 40 miles southwest of Flagstaff, Arizona, on a 120-foot high limestone ridge overlooking the Verde Valley, Tuzigoot National Monument is a significant archaeological site. The monument centers around the remains of a 110-room pueblo built by the Sinagua culture. Constructed around A.D. 1000, the pueblo is believed to have housed approximately 300 people.

The Sinagua culture, which also left its mark at the nearby Montezuma Castle National Monument, abandoned the Tuzigoot pueblo in the early 1400s for reasons that remain uncertain. Theories propose factors such as disease, extended drought, and conflict as possible causes. Visitors can explore a 1/3-mile trail leading through the ruins and offering views of Tavasci Marsh from an overlook. Open year-round, Tuzigoot National Monument is a convenient stop en route to the Grand Canyon.

Tuzigoot stands out with its unique stone ruins, differing from the cliff dwellings at Montezuma Castle and Well. The pueblo, positioned on a long limestone ridge 150 feet above the Verde River floodplain, consists of 110 rooms. History enthusiasts can appreciate the opportunity to closely inspect the dwelling and even enter some of the rooms. The term "Tuzigoot," derived from Apache, translates to "crooked water," aptly describing the zigzag appearance of the remaining walls. While the original stones remain, the National Park Service has reinforced deteriorating mortar with cement.

To fully experience the pueblo, visitors can ascend the circular trail winding up the hill, offering a panoramic view of the expansive Verde Valley. The Tuzigoot visitor center supplements the visit with additional information about these historically significant ruins.

The mystery surrounding the abandonment of these stone villages by the Southern Sinaguans, with no existing Sinagua tribe today, adds to the allure of the site. The remnants, delicate and irreplaceable, provide a glimpse into America's cultural heritage, inviting curious travelers to explore these captivating ruins and appreciate their historical significance.

Tuzigoot National Monument boasts a partially reconstructed pueblo that was crafted by the Sinagua people in central Arizona. This pueblo featured over a hundred rooms and had the capacity to accommodate hundreds of individuals on a temporary basis. Constructed and continuously inhabited between the 12th and late-15th centuries, Tuzigoot occupies a hillside overlooking the Verde River, which eventually joins other rivers en route to the Gulf of California.

The construction methods employed at Tuzigoot bear similarities to larger and more well-known structures like the cliff dwellings at Mesa Verde or the expansive Pueblo Bonito great house. Notably, Mesa Verde and Pueblo Bonito were built by Ancestral Puebloans, while Tuzigoot was constructed by the Sinagua. While sharing a similar architectural style, Tuzigoot differs in its choice of building materials. Positioned on the extreme southwestern edge of the Colorado Plateau, Tuzigoot utilized different materials compared to Chacoan groups nearer the interior of the plateau.

The pueblo at Tuzigoot is primarily built with sandstone, a common geological feature across the Colorado Plateau. Additionally, the Sinagua incorporated limestone into the construction of Tuzigoot. The building blocks were hewn from sandstone beds and limestone deposits that originated from an ancient inland sea. The Western Interior Seaway, existing millions of years ago, experienced fluctuations in size over extended periods. Shifting shorelines resulted in layers of sand and soil, which, under pressure and over time, transformed into sandstone. Furthermore, the accumulation of crushed crustaceans over millions of years contributed to the formation of limestone. Both of these abundant sedimentary rocks were skillfully shaped, stacked, and interlocked by the Sinagua to create the remarkable structure of Tuzigoot.

The Sinagua people likely arrived in central Arizona around 650 CE, as evidenced by excavations and analyses of Sinagua pit houses in the Verde Valley. Archaeologists have determined this timeline by examining artifacts from pit houses and Tuzigoot, revealing the Sinagua's participation in a vast trade network. This network facilitated the exchange of ideas, including architectural concepts. Tuzigoot, modeled after Ancestral Puebloan architecture that predates it by over a century, stands as a testament to these cultural exchanges. By the early 14th century, the Sinagua population in the Tuzigoot area had diminished, possibly influenced by factors like drought-induced out-migration, a phenomenon affecting numerous Colorado Plateau groups in the late 1100s. Ongoing climatic changes may have further contributed to the Sinagua's departure from Tuzigoot in the mid-14th century. Despite their departure, the Sinagua left a rich legacy through various artifacts, including intricate baskets, pottery, jewelry, and crystals discovered at Tuzigoot.

The first recorded encounter with Tuzigoot by an American occurred after the Mexican-American War (1846-1848) when Antoine Leroux, a respected mountain man, guided US military surveyors exploring potential routes for the transcontinental railroad in 1854. Leroux described the Tuzigoot ruins, noting their impressive but deteriorating walls atop a hill. Official explorations of archaeological sites were temporarily halted during the Civil War and Reconstruction. After Reconstruction ended in 1877, academic adventurers, sponsored by the Smithsonian, embarked on expeditions to the Southwest. These ventures brought the Sinagua, their history, and Tuzigoot to national attention. The meticulous reconstruction of the topmost portions of the pueblo was undertaken, allowing visitors today to walk into the highest room and observe the unique joinery and ladders characteristic of Sinagua construction. An available ladder permits climbing to the rooftop, offering a panoramic view of the Verde River and the rare birds inhabiting the surrounding scrubland.

Numerous waves of archaeologists conducted excavations at Tuzigoot, publishing their findings widely. During the Great Depression, government-funded digs were organized under the Works Project Administration (WPA). Additionally, the Civil Works Administration (CWA) played a role in constructing a visitors center. The growing number of field reports on Tuzigoot intensified the push to designate it as a national monument, reaching its culmination in 1939. At the close of the Great Depression, President Franklin Delano Roosevelt officially established Tuzigoot National Monument. Since its designation in 1939, millions of visitors have explored this unique pueblo, standing out among the numerous prehistoric structures across the Colorado Plateau. Built by the Sinagua using sandstone and limestone blocks, Tuzigoot remains a small but significant national monument, inviting short visits to explore the site, admire intricate artifacts, and enter its ancient rooms.

Tuzigoot National Monument has an entrance fee of $10.00 per person, with children aged 15 and under entering for free. For those interested in visiting both Montezuma Castle and Tuzigoot, an annual pass is available for $40.00, covering the cardholder and three other adults (aged 16 and over) for one year from the date of purchase, with children 15 and under being free. Travelers planning a National Park vacation may consider the America the Beautiful/National Park Pass, which provides entrance fee coverage for an entire year to all US National Park Sites and over 2,000 Federal Recreation Fee Sites. The pass covers everyone in the car for per-vehicle sites and up to four adults for per-person sites.

Dogs are allowed on the trail but must be on a leash no longer than 6 feet. Cell service is unreliable in the area, and the park operates from 8 am to 5 pm daily, with the last car allowed at the gate by 4:45 pm. The park is closed on December 25th and January 1st. There is no public Wi-Fi available at Tuzigoot National Monument. Carrying insect repellent is advisable, particularly when outdoors and around bodies of water. The park features a small/medium-sized parking lot in front of the visitor center, but no restaurants are within the park itself; the nearest ones are located in Cottonwood.

National Park Passport stamps can be obtained in the visitor center. The visitor center, restrooms, and the trail to the Tavasci Marsh Overlook are fully wheelchair accessible. Spring and Fall are optimal times to visit Tuzigoot due to comfortable weather. The park's year-round water source fosters a diverse environment for animals and birds, with most wildlife being nocturnal, including woodrats, mice, skunks, bobcats, pocket gophers, owls, and bats. Daytime sightings may include deer, elk, coyotes, black-tailed jackrabbits, desert cottontails, ground squirrels, and songbirds. Tuzigoot NM is home to around 50 species of mammals, with mountain lions being very rare but occasionally spotted on the property.

COUNTY: COCONINO   CITY: PAGE n.c.

DATE VISITED: WHO I WENT WITH:

RATING: ☆ ☆ ☆ ☆ ☆   WILL I RETURN? YES / NO

Managed by the Bureau of Land Management (BLM), Vermilion Cliffs National Monument sprawls across 280,000 acres within the Colorado Plateau, straddling the border between Arizona and Utah. You may have come across images of the monument or its iconic feature, The Wave, characterized by its layered hues of red, rust, and gold on the desert floor. While hiking is the primary attraction, visitors also engage in camping, photography, and wildlife observation.

The Wave, renowned as one of the country's most exclusive hikes, draws a significant number of visitors. Alternative trails within the monument exist, but some necessitate permits. Due to the undeveloped nature of the trails, proficiency in map and compass navigation is essential. Summer temperatures can soar above 120 degrees F (49 degrees C), while winter may bring snow on the ground. The optimal times to explore are typically in April, May, September, and October. Vermilion Cliffs National Monument lacks visitor centers or designated scenic drives. For permits and information, individuals must visit the Paria Contact Station on Highway 89, the BLM Visitor Center in Kanab, or the Interagency Information Center in St. George, Utah.

If venturing into the monument by car, even on the maintained House Rock Valley Road (BLM 1065), caution is advised during rain. The clay dirt transforms into a slippery surface akin to ice when wet, rendering the road impassable. Hikers with permits can camp in Paria Canyon or at either of the two first-come, first-served campsites at Vermilion Cliffs. However, for non-hikers, camping may not be an ideal destination due to the rugged and remote nature of the area, offering little else to do except observe the once nearly extinct California Condor gracefully gliding overhead.

Vermilion Cliffs National Monument lacks well-defined trails; instead, there are popular hiking areas requiring permits for access. To hike in these areas, individuals may need to participate in a lottery, either online, in person, or by purchasing a permit through a QR code at the trailhead.

When embarking on a hike, it is crucial to bring a gallon of water per person, ensuring each member consumes the entire gallon, even in winter. Understanding the physical limitations of each group member is vital, and pushing beyond these limits should be avoided. Tragically, deaths occur in the Vermilion Cliffs wilderness, often due to heat exhaustion and dehydration.

Highlighted hiking areas include:

Coyote Buttes North (The Wave): A challenging 6.4-mile roundtrip hike starting at a riverbed, traversing rugged terrain with no marked trail. Wayfinding tools such as a map and compass are necessary. The destination, The Wave, offers additional features like a second wave formation, natural arches, petroglyphs, and dinosaur tracks.

Coyote Buttes South: This area lacks marked trails, demanding strong navigation skills. Accessible by high-clearance, four-wheel-drive vehicles due to sandy roads. Inexperienced drivers often become stranded on these roads, emphasizing the importance of preparation.

Paria Canyon: Hikers follow the Paria River, utilizing trails alongside or through the water, requiring preparation for wet conditions. The journey's length is flexible, with experienced backpackers extending it to a 5-day trip. Overnight stays require permits obtained through a lottery.

Buckskin Gulch: Covering 20 miles, this hike spans several days through the longest and deepest slot canyon in the Southwest. Hikers should be ready for obstacles such as rocks, pools, escapable quicksand, and potential flash floods.

White Pocket: With no marked trails leading to these whitish-grey sandstone formations, strong wayfinding skills are essential. Accessible by high-clearance, four-wheel-drive vehicles, the unique landscape of White Pocket justifies the effort.

Many sections of the national monument mandate hiking permits, with availability either on demand or through a lottery system designed to preserve the delicate geological features. Coyote Butte North, famously known as The Wave, can only be accessed through a lottery, with a limited daily allowance of 64 individuals. Obtaining a permit is challenging, as only 48 are awarded through the online system, and an additional 16 through a next-day walk-in lottery held at the Kanab Center Gymnasium. Coyote Butte South follows a similar permitting process with advance reservations.

For Paria Canyon and other designated hiking regions, a day-use permit can be acquired by scanning a QR code. However, if planning to stay overnight in Paria Canyon, obtaining a permit in person is necessary, available at the Interagency Information Center in St. George or the Paria Contact Station on US Highway 89. Overnight permits are limited to 20 people. Permit fees are $6 per person for day hiking and $5 per person for overnight camping. When participating in the lottery application, a nonrefundable $9 administrative fee is required.

Camping is permitted in dispersed areas outside the wilderness region, particularly in previously disturbed locations. Additionally, there are two established campgrounds within Vermilion Cliffs: Stateline and White House.

Stateline: Situated near House Rock Valley Road, Stateline offers seven campsites equipped with a pit toilet, shaded structures, and picnic tables. Camping spots are allocated on a first-come, first-served basis, and no water facilities are available.

White House: Nestled in a sandstone cove along the Paria River, this campground provides seven drive-in sites, five walk-in sites, two vault toilets, fire rings, grills, and picnic tables. Campsites are also assigned on a first-come, first-served basis, with a fee of $5.

Staying in Kanab is the most practical choice, particularly if you need to acquire permits from the BLM Visitor Center or plan to participate in the next-day lottery for the Wave. The town offers various major hotel chains such as Hampton Inn, La Quinta Inn & Suites, Holiday Inn Express & Suites, and Days Inn & Suites. Another appealing option is the historic Parry Lodge. However, if you don't require a permit, Page, Arizona, is equally convenient, offering similar chain hotels and a diverse selection of restaurants along with its proximity to Lake Powell.

Directions: The primary access route is House Rock Valley Road, accessible from Highway 89 between mile markers 25 and 26, when traveling from Kanab to Page. Alternatively, you can take Highway 89A from Marble Canyon toward Jacob Lake and watch for a dirt road between mile markers 565 and 566. While there might not be a sign for House Rock Valley Road, you should look for one indicating "BLM 1065."

Tips:

1) Dress in layers and bring essentials such as sunscreen, a hat, and sunglasses.
2) Ensure you have an ample supply of food, water, and clothing for an extended stay in case of unforeseen issues.
3) If you intend to participate in the walk-in lottery, bring exact cash or a check for permit payment, as credit cards are not accepted, and staff cannot provide change.
4) Check the weather forecast before embarking on your journey. Rain in the area or north of Vermilion Cliffs may lead to floods. When uncertain about weather conditions, consult the BLM for guidance.

COUNTY: COCONINO   **CITY:** FLAGSTAFF   *n.c.*

DATE VISITED: **WHO I WENT WITH:**

RATING: ☆ ☆ ☆ ☆ ☆   **WILL I RETURN?** YES / NO

Situated near Flagstaff, Arizona, Walnut Canyon National Monument encompasses 232 prehistoric sites originating from the 1100s. This region served as the dwelling place for the Sinagua people, who constructed over 80 cliff dwellings over several centuries. In the 1800s, many of these dwellings were damaged by pot-hunters using dynamite to search for artifacts. To safeguard the remaining structures, President Woodrow Wilson established the national monument in 1915. Presently, the monument's trails showcase 25 cliff dwellings, offering a window into the ancient canyon life of the Sinagua people.

Walnut Canyon National Monument is primarily centered around the exploration of cliff dwellings. The visitor center hosts a museum with numerous exhibits dedicated to the Sinagua people, showcasing the artifacts they left behind. Visitors can also view a 20-minute introductory film that delves into the history of Walnut Canyon. Children have the opportunity to engage with a Junior Ranger booklet, completing various activities. While the ruins are visible from the visitor center, the most optimal views are obtained by embarking on a self-guided hike along the rim or into the canyon. The park organizes ranger-led discovery hikes, requiring advance reservations, and conducts daily ranger talks. Furthermore, each March, local archaeologists commemorate Arizona Archaeology and Heritage Awareness month with a series of events, lectures, walks, and activities tailored for children.

The park features two self-guided trails: the Rim Trail and the Island Trail. The Rim Trail, as its name suggests, follows the canyon rim, while the Island Trail descends into the canyon, offering views of cliff dwellings.

Rim Trail: This easy, partially-paved trail spans 0.75 miles round trip along the canyon rim. Two overlooks provide scenic views of Walnut Canyon and the cliff dwellings below. Along the trail, there's a partially rebuilt pithouse and pueblo set back from the canyon's edge. In the summer, the demonstration garden showcases traditional Sinagua crops. Plan to dedicate approximately 30 minutes to complete this trail.

Island Trail: This strenuous hike involves navigating 736 stairs and descending 185 vertical feet into the canyon. The nearly mile-long trail, which runs along the canyon wall with steep drop-offs at certain points, passes by 25 cliff dwellings. It is recommended to budget around an hour for this hike. Note that during winter, the Island Trail might be closed due to snowy or icy conditions, and entry to the trail closes at 3:30 p.m.

Camping is not permitted at Walnut Canyon National Monument, but there are several public campgrounds in the Coconino National Forest nearby. Most of these forest service campgrounds are seasonal, so it's advisable to check their availability, especially if you plan to visit during the winter.

Bonito Campground: Situated next to Sunset Crater Volcano National Monument, this seasonal forest service campground is located 21 miles north of Walnut Canyon. Featuring 44 campsites, Bonito provides amenities such as picnic tables, grills, fire rings, flush toilets, and drinking water, but no hookups. The campground operates on a first-come, first-served basis, and there is a fee of $26 per night.

Canyon Vista Campground: Located south of Flagstaff, this seasonal forest service campground offers 14 single-unit sites equipped with fire rings, cooking grills, drinking water, and picnic tables. There are no hookups, and the toilets are vault-type, not flush. The sites are available on a first-come, first-served basis, with a fee of $22 per night.

Flagstaff KOA: Positioned on the western edge of Flagstaff, KOA provides 200 campsites suitable for tents and RVs. The amenities include free Wi-Fi, 50-amp hookups, laundry facilities, flush toilets, showers, a dog park, bike rentals, and hiking trails. During the period from Memorial Day to Labor Day, the campground hosts family-friendly movie nights and other activities. The cost for a tent site in summer is typically at least $45 per night.

Flagstaff offers the nearest lodging options to the Walnut Canyon National Monument. Due to the presence of Northern Arizona University, hotels in Flagstaff may experience high demand, especially at the beginning of the school year, during college football season, and around winter and spring graduations. Summers can also witness increased bookings, particularly on weekends when residents from Phoenix visit to escape the heat. It is advisable to book accommodations in advance, if possible.

Little America: Recognized as the sole AAA Four Diamond hotel in Flagstaff, Little America boasts 247 recently renovated guest rooms with scenic views of the private 500-acre forest. Conveniently located just off I-40, the hotel serves as an excellent base for exploring the surrounding area. However, it's essential to note that the hotel has a no-pet policy.

Drury Inn & Suites Flagstaff: Popular among parents of university students, Drury Inn & Suites adheres to standard chain amenities such as free Wi-Fi, complimentary parking, and a complimentary breakfast. In addition, guests receive three free drinks and complimentary food at the bar between 5:30 p.m. and 7:30 p.m. This includes a range of food options from hot dogs and chicken nuggets to tacos and pasta, providing enough for a meal. Popcorn is also available in the lobby as a snack.

Hotel Monte Vista: A historic hotel, Hotel Monte Vista is ideal for those who prefer exploring historic downtown on foot. While the rooms may be smaller by today's standards, the hotel offers an on-site restaurant, a cocktail/coffee bar, and a cocktail lounge with live music three days a week. Some reports suggest that certain rooms are believed to be haunted.

DoubleTree by Hilton Hotel Flagstaff: Positioned on historic Route 66 on the west side of the city, DoubleTree by Hilton Hotel Flagstaff features two on-site restaurants, a welcoming lounge off the lobby, and three electric vehicle (EV) charging stations. The hotel is pet-friendly, catering to guests with pets.

Walnut Canyon National Monument is conveniently located just 7.5 miles east of downtown Flagstaff. To reach the monument from I-40, travelers can take Exit 204 and proceed 3 miles south to the visitor center.

It is important for visitors not to solely rely on GPS for navigation to the park, as GPS systems might guide drivers down Forest Road 303, an unmaintained dirt road suitable only for high-clearance vehicles. Additionally, the National Park Service advises against driving vehicles longer than 40 feet into the park, as the available turnaround space is limited.

The visitor center at Walnut Canyon National Monument is equipped with two accessible lifts, facilitating access to the park's museum, gift shop, and both indoor and outdoor observation areas. The restrooms at the visitor center are also designed to be accessible. Regarding the trails, accessibility options are somewhat limited. The Rim Trail is wheelchair-accessible up to the first overlook, covering approximately 150 feet. However, beyond that point, the trail does not fully comply with ADA accessibility standards. Although the trail is relatively flat, some visitors may be able to manage it with assistance. It is advisable to inquire at the visitor center about the feasibility of continuing before starting the trail. The Island Trail, unfortunately, is not accessible due to its steep incline and the presence of 736 stairs.

Tips:

1) Walnut Canyon National Monument operates daily from 9 a.m. to 4:30 p.m.
2) For entry, Walnut Canyon National Monument charges a fee of $15 per person for individuals aged 16 and older, while admission is free for those 15 and younger.
3) Visitors also have the option to purchase a Flagstaff Area National Monuments Annual Pass at a cost of $45. This pass grants admission for up to four adults and includes free entry for all occupants of one vehicle at nearby Sunset Crater Volcano and Wupatki national monuments.
4) Leashed pets are permitted at Walnut Canyon National Park. However, their access is restricted to the Rim Trail and the visitor center parking lot, with no entry allowed into the visitor center or on the Island Trail.
5) Regardless of the chosen trail, visitors are urged to adhere to the designated routes and follow the Leave No Trace principles. Avoid touching, climbing, or leaning on the cliff dwellings. Preserve the natural environment by leaving rocks, plants, and other items undisturbed. It is advised not to feed any encountered animals, and pet owners should responsibly pick up after their pets during their visit.

WATSON LAKE

COUNTY: YAVAPAI   CITY: PRESCOTT

DATE VISITED: WHO I WENT WITH:

RATING: ☆ ☆ ☆ ☆ ☆   WILL I RETURN?   YES / NO

Discover a captivating landscape of boulders surrounding a serene lake just four miles northeast of Prescott. In the elevated city of Prescott, where all four seasons offer a range of outdoor activities, Watson Lake stands out as a unique attraction. Visitors flock to this destination to marvel at the Granite Dells, an extraordinary collection of rock formations encircling the water, appearing as if defying gravity. The parking area boasts a spacious covered ramada that provides a panoramic view of this remarkable natural area, while granite slabs along the shoreline offer ideal spots for picnics. Watson Lake serves as a hub for outdoor enthusiasts engaging in activities such as hiking, mountain biking, and rock climbing, serving as a gateway to the Prescott National Forest. An added attraction is an 18-hole disc golf course along the picturesque shoreline.

For locals and visitors alike, Watson Lake serves as a launch site for kayaks, canoes, and stand-up paddleboards, offering an opportunity to exercise amidst a breathtaking setting. Fishing enthusiasts explore the scenic lake, seeking out prime spots for rainbow trout, largemouth bass, and channel catfish. Canoes and kayaks are available for rent from nearby outfitters, allowing visitors to embark on a journey across the lake, maneuvering through coves and islands formed by the protruding boulders. This surprising riparian habitat attracts a variety of waterfowl, gracefully gliding across the water or wading along the shorelines in search of sustenance.

Granite Mountain Guides takes the lead in organizing rock-climbing adventures within the Granite Dells. Prior to ascending the remarkable rock face of Pavillion Wall, participants receive comprehensive safety instructions. Beyond climbing, many visitors are drawn to the area for hiking through its otherworldly landscape. The Watson Lake Loop offers an extensive nearly 5-mile trek, navigating over boulders on a complete circuit around the lake. Additionally, the Prescott Peavine National Recreation Trail, a converted rails-to-trails project, features a segment along the lake's east shore, attracting mountain bikers.

Prescott, with its rich history, pays tribute to its pioneer heritage by preserving the charm of turn-of-the-20th-century structures on Whiskey Row, which buzzed with activity during the gold rush. Anchoring the city square today, the impressive granite courthouse stands as a testament to Prescott's past prominence when it was the state's largest city and governmental hub. This historic landmark serves as a backdrop to downtown establishments, including restaurants, shops, and bars, inviting visitors to immerse themselves in a city with deep historical roots and a proud Wild West legacy.

COUNTY: COCONINO   CITY: SEDONA *n.c.*

DATE VISITED: WHO I WENT WITH:

RATING: ☆ ☆ ☆ ☆ ☆   WILL I RETURN?   YES / NO

The West Fork Trail presents a captivating hiking experience along Oak Creek, offering 13 river crossings, a striking subway tunnel climax, and a more serene atmosphere compared to other popular trails in Sedona. Positioned over 10 miles north of the desert city, the West Fork of Oak Creek Trail is ideally included in a Sedona itinerary for those with three days or more, allowing visitors to avoid larger crowds.

Key Hiking Details:

Trail Distance: 6.6 miles roundtrip
Elevation Gain: 500 feet
Hike Difficulty: Easy / Moderate
Time Required: 3-4 hours

The West Fork Trail is characterized by an easy to moderately difficult path, featuring mostly flat and undulating terrain within the captivating Coconino National Forest landscape. Navigating the trail involves a total of 13 river crossings, requiring the use of stepping stones and possibly resulting in dampened feet. The scenic beauty is best appreciated by gazing up at the towering red rocks lining Oak Creek River. One notable feature is the trail's conclusion at a subway tunnel-like formation, offering a stunning, though smaller-scale, resemblance to The Subway Cave in Sedona or Zion National Park's Subway Hike.

The West Fork Trail offers an extended adventure beyond the conventional 3.3 miles one way (6.6 miles roundtrip), attracting the attention of the more daring hikers. For those seeking an extraordinary journey, the trail allows an extensive hike of 14 miles one way, totaling 28 miles roundtrip, leading into the Red Rock Wilderness via Oak Creek. This extended trek is best suited for experienced hikers comfortable with elements like bouldering, scrambling, and even swimming. Undertaking the longer version requires ample time in your Sedona itinerary, potentially spanning one long day or even two days for completion.

The West Fork Trail features a designated parking lot located approximately 10 miles north of Sedona on AZ-89A, a significant route connecting Sedona with Flagstaff and the Grand Canyon South Rim. Use Google Maps or Apple Maps to navigate to "West Fork Oak Creek Trailhead" or "Call of the Canyon Picnic Site," both sharing the same parking lot and requiring entrance fees.

While quieter compared to major trails in town, West Fork of Oak Creek remains a popular hiking destination. To enhance your chances of securing a parking space, consider the following tips:

1) Arrive early or late in the day (open 8 am – dusk)
2) Opt for a weekday hike and avoid weekends
3) Plan your visit during the off-season (Summer and Winter)

While the West Fork Trail doesn't require a standard hiking pass, an entry fee is applicable. Sedona stands out as a hiker's theme park, among favorite destinations in the US. However, it comes with certain challenges for both locals and visitors, such as parking at trailheads, congestion, and parking passes. In Sedona, the primary passes accepted are the Red Rock Pass and the America the Beautiful interagency annual pass.

West Fork Trail falls under the category of privately owned areas in Sedona, leading to distinct entry requirements compared to most other hikes in the region. To access the West Fork Trailhead parking lot, there's a fee of $11 per vehicle, covering up to 5 individuals in one vehicle for a single day. Individuals with disabilities holding the Access Interagency Pass are eligible for a 50% discount on the $11 fee, resulting in an entry cost of $5.50. It's essential to note that no Red Rock Pass, except the Grand Annual Red Rock Pass, is valid for West Fork Trail, and the Grand Annual Pass costs $40 for a 12-month period.

For an optimal hiking experience with fewer crowds, consider arriving early morning or late afternoon. Access to the parking lot involves paying at a kiosk, with credit card payment accepted. The parking area also provides facilities such as toilets and picnic tables for visitors' convenience.

Exit the parking lot through the rear upon entering, connecting to the Call of the Canyon Trail, a narrow paved and accessible path. This trail leads to a charming bridge that spans Oak Creek. Turn left and follow the riverside until reaching a set of ancient ruins that can be explored briefly. The Call of the Canyon Trail seamlessly transitions into the West Fork Trail, merging with Oak Creek, marking the commencement of the actual hike.

Over the next 3 miles, hikers will encounter thirteen river crossings. The landscape is breathtaking, offering opportunities to spot wildlife along the way. Utilize stepping stones and larger rocks for assistance during the river crossings. While heavy rainfall or snowmelt can lead to a slight rise in water levels, they typically remain shallow.

Throughout the hike, remember to look up and appreciate the towering red rock cliffs that intermittently grace the upstream path. Keep an eye out for picturesque arches in the cliff faces and the presence of smooth semi-subway tunnels carved into the lower rock faces next to Oak Creek.

The conclusion of the West Fork Trail is signaled when the water suddenly becomes deeper, reaching a point where it's impassable without submerging to shin depth. To extend the hike, one can proceed by wading into the water and entering the subway-like tunnel visible ahead. While not as remarkable as Zion's Subway, this tunnel is still an impressive formation, curving slightly to the right like a fade in golf.

Take a break and enjoy a snack or lunch at the trail's end before retracing your steps back along the same route. Heading back offers a familiar journey, allowing for a relaxed and leisurely return. Quick hikers might complete the West Fork Trail in approximately 2 hours and 30 minutes, but most individuals prefer a slower pace to savor the surroundings, resulting in a hiking time of 3-4 hours.

During the peak tourist seasons in Spring and Fall, especially in Sedona, it's crucial to arrive early at trailheads to secure parking, as it can become challenging later in the day. Winter and Summer, on the other hand, are quieter periods in Sedona, offering better chances of finding parking spaces without issues. Regardless of the season, it's advisable to avoid weekends and holidays.

For a more pleasant and cooler experience, the best times to hike the West Fork Trail are early morning or late afternoon. Although much of the trail is shaded by trees, providing relief from the sun during hotter parts of the day.

Essentials to pack for hiking the West Fork Trail include:

1) Footwear: Choose shoes with good grips and traction for navigating the numerous river crossings.
2) Water: Carry an ample supply of water, considering the 2-3 hours spent on the trail. In the summer, additional water or electrolyte drinks may be necessary.
3) Sun Protection: Sunglasses, sun hats, long layers, and sunscreen are essential, especially during the summer. While much of the trail is shaded, intermittent exposure to the sun is inevitable.
4) Winter Clothing: In colder months, early mornings and late evenings can be chilly. Wearing long pants and light coats is advisable to stay comfortable during the hike.

COUNTY: PIMA   CITY: TUCSON *n.c.*

DATE VISITED:	WHO I WENT WITH:

RATING: ☆ ☆ ☆ ☆ ☆   WILL I RETURN? YES / NO

When considering prominent wine grape growing regions worldwide, Arizona may not immediately come to mind. However, it might surprise you to learn that several wine grape varieties thrive in the state, including Cabernet Sauvignon, Merlot, Syrah, Chardonnay, Sauvignon Blanc, and Sangiovese. The roots of vineyards in Arizona trace back to the 17th century when Franciscan missionaries first planted them. The state boasts three distinct growing regions, each characterized by a concentration of wine tasting rooms.

The earliest and inaugural region in Arizona is located in the Sonoita/Elgin area in Southern Arizona, recognized as a federally-approved growing region or American Viticultural Area (AVA). The second, and the largest, is situated in the southeastern part of the state, encompassing Willcox and its surroundings. Although more secluded, this region features numerous tasting rooms in Southern and Northern Arizona, showcasing wines crafted from grapes cultivated in Willcox. The third and most recent region is found in the north-central part of the state, known as the wine region of the Verde Valley.

Sonoita Vineyards, Ltd., situated in Elgin, approximately 50 miles away from Tucson. Founded in 1983 by Dr. Gordon Dutt, widely regarded as the father of Arizona viticulture, this vineyard has played a pivotal role in shaping the local wine scene. The region's soil is likened to that of Burgundy, France, a characteristic emphasized by the vineyard. Sonoita Vineyards has gained recognition for producing several award-winning wines, particularly excelling in the Cabernet Sauvignon category. Wine-tasting experiences are offered daily at Sonoita Vineyards, excluding holidays. Visitors have the option to bring a picnic lunch, savoring wines on the patio or enjoying scenic views of the vineyard and surrounding mountains from the balcony. A unique feature is the allowance to bring your own glass, potentially garnering a discount on the tasting charge.

Village of Elgin Winery, positioned in Elgin and located approximately 55 miles from Tucson, stands about 5 miles from Sonoita. This winery specializes in classic Claret varietals and Syrahs, employing traditional methods that include grape stomping and the exclusive use of wooden casks. As a family-owned establishment, the winery's production capacity is limited to 120,000 bottles. The wine varieties predominantly feature Cabernet Sauvignon, Chardonnay, Colombard, Merlot, Sangiovese, Sauvignon Blanc, and Syrah, utilizing grapes from the Sonoita AVA. Since 2077, all their wines are bottled with screw caps. The ambiance of the property is somewhat rustic, and they actively host and participate in various festivals throughout the year.

Callaghan Vineyards, located just a short distance east of Elgin Winery, was established in 1990. The vineyard draws grapes from two distinct locations: the Buena Suerte Vineyard in Elgin and the Dos Cabezas Vineyard near Willcox, Arizona.

Visitors to Callaghan Vineyards are provided with a quality wine glass as part of the tasting charge. Alternatively, bringing your own glass qualifies for a discount on the wine tasting experience. The tasting room is open Thursday through Sunday, offering a diverse selection of eleven wines for patrons to choose from.

Situated at an elevation exceeding 4,000 feet between the Santa Rita Mountains and the Patagonia Mountains, Patagonia is a small town with a population of about 1,000. While it boasts charming shops, a pleasant park, local bars, and a modern high school, it has gained international recognition as a prime bird-watching destination. Notably, the Patagonia-Sonoita Creek Preserve, managed by The Nature Conservancy, showcases a cottonwood-willow riparian forest where over 290 bird species have been documented. The preserve offers guided tours every Saturday morning, making it a must-visit for those keen on bird watching in Arizona.

COUNTY: COCONINO

CITY: FLAGSTAFF *n.c.*

DATE VISITED:

WHO I WENT WITH:

RATING: ☆ ☆ ☆ ☆ ☆

WILL I RETURN? YES / NO

Wupatki, once the tallest, largest, and possibly the wealthiest pueblo in the region, accommodated up to 100 people in northern Arizona. However, around 1085 A.D., the nearby Sunset Crater Volcano erupted, blanketing the area with lava pellets, rendering it uninhabitable. The Ancient Puebloans, who had previously inhabited Wupatki, were compelled to leave. Many years later, ranchers exploring the region stumbled upon Wupatki and other pueblos. In 1924, President Calvin Coolidge established Wupatki National Monument to safeguard it and other pueblos within the park's 35,422 acres.

A visit to Wupatki can conveniently be combined with a trip to Sunset Crater Volcano National Monument, as the two parks are connected by a 34-mile loop drive off US-89.

The starting point for all activities is the park's visitor center, where visitors can delve into information about the Ancient Puebloans and view various artifacts. Additionally, children have the opportunity to engage in Junior Ranger activities at this location. Beyond the visitor center, the Wupatki Pueblo Trail guides visitors to the primary ruins of the park, which happen to be the largest freestanding pueblo in northern Arizona.

In close proximity, the Wukoki Pueblo stands at a height of three stories, offering panoramic views of the desert extending to the San Francisco Peaks. The remaining four pueblos are situated several miles away. Citadel and Nalakihu pueblos seem to be designed as single-family residences, while the Lomaki and Box Canyon pueblos exhibit construction using limestone and sandstone.

Hiking options in this park are divided into two main categories: easy walks and backcountry adventures led by rangers. As reservations are necessary for the backcountry hikes, the majority of visitors typically opt for the four easy trails, all of which are under half a mile in length. Rangers conduct three moderately challenging hikes on most Saturdays from October to April. During the initial and final months of this period, individuals can also secure a spot on the demanding two-day Crack-in-the-Rock trek.

Wupatki Pueblo Trail: This 0.5-mile trail, the park's most popular, forms a loop around a 104-room pueblo featuring a ball court and a blowhole. It provides access to a scenic overlook and usually takes about an hour to complete.

Wukoki Pueblo Trail: Covering a distance of 0.2 miles, this trail leads to a pueblo constructed on a sandstone outcrop. Accessible up to the trail's base, exploration typically takes around 15 minutes.

Discovery Hikes: Conducted on select Saturdays from October to April, these ranger-led hikes depart from the visitor center at noon, venturing to backcountry pueblos normally off-limits to the general public. Reservations are mandatory, and each group is limited to 12 participants. The three hikes—Kaibab House, Antelope House, and East Mesa—are moderately strenuous, requiring approximately three hours to complete.

Crack-in-Rock: Offered on specific weekends in October and April, this guided 18- to 20-mile roundtrip hike follows an unmarked route, necessitating an overnight stay in the backcountry. Reservations are mandatory, with a $75 fee. Hikers should be prepared for extreme temperatures, wind, and challenging terrain, and carry a minimum of one gallon of water per day along with their backpack.

The park itself is situated along the Sunset Crater-Wupatki Loop Road, an idyllic drive that commences 12 miles north of Flagstaff. If you're traveling on US-89, make a right turn at the sign indicating Sunset Crater Volcano National Monument. After covering a few miles, you'll encounter the visitor center for Sunset Crater Volcano National Monument. If time permits, it's worth stopping here and exploring one of the trails.

The journey proceeds past the Kana-a Lava Flow before entering Wupatki National Monument. Overall, the Sunset Crater-Wupatki Loop Road meanders for 34 miles through pine forests before reconnecting with US-89, roughly 15 miles north of its starting point. Without factoring in stops, the drive typically takes about an hour to complete.

Before reaching Wupatki, you will pass by Sunset Crater Volcano National Monument. This crater was formed following an eruption in 1085 A.D., and the resulting cinder-covered landscape compelled the Ancient Puebloans residing in the Wupatki region to relocate.

A visit to Sunset Crater Volcano National Monument today offers insights into the volcano, local geology, and the history of astronauts who trained for the lunar landing in the area. While you can catch a glimpse of the crater from the road, hiking presents the optimal way to truly experience it. You can opt for the 3.4-mile Lava's Edge Trail, traversing loose cinders and rugged basalt along the Bonito Lava Flow, or embark on the 1-mile Lava Flow trail encircling the base of Sunset Crater.

Camping opportunities are abundant in the vicinity of Wupatki National Monument within the expansive Coconino National Forest. However, it's important to note that some of the forest service campgrounds may close during the winter season. Prior to embarking on your camping trip, ensure that the campground you intend to stay at is operational. In the event of closures, the Flagstaff KOA remains open throughout the year.

Bonito Campground: Situated next to Sunset Crater Volcano National Monument, this seasonal forest service campground offers amenities such as picnic tables, grills, fire rings, flush toilets, and drinking water. With 44 camping sites available on a first-come, first-served basis, there are no hookups. A nightly fee of $26 is applicable.

Cinder Hills Dispersed Camping: If you're open to dispersed camping, this picturesque recreation area near Sunset Crater Volcano is a viable option, especially if you have an off-highway vehicle. It's important to be aware that the ground is covered with volcanic cinder, which may stick to your shoes and be tracked into your tent or trailer. No fees are charged for staying in this area.

Flagstaff KOA: Positioned on the western edge of Flagstaff, this family-friendly KOA offers 200 campsites along with options for tents and cabins. Amenities include free Wi-Fi, laundry facilities, flush toilets, showers, a dog park, bike rentals, and hiking trails. During the summer season, anticipate a minimum nightly fee of $45 for a tent site.

Flagstaff stands as the nearest city to Wupatki, boasting a range of excellent hotels that cater to various budgets, from affordable options to luxurious establishments. It's advisable to secure accommodations in advance if possible. The city draws in parents and fans of Northern Arizona University on weekends for games, while residents from Phoenix visit during the summer to escape the heat.

Little America: Situated just off I-40 on a vast expanse of 500 private forest acres, Little America holds the distinction of being the only AAA Four Diamond hotel in Flagstaff. Despite its status as one of the top hotels in the area, it strictly adheres to a no-pet policy.

Drury Inn & Suites Flagstaff: This chain hotel, located in proximity to the university, not only provides complimentary breakfast but also offers guests three free drinks and food at the bar between 5:30 and 7:30 p.m. The food options are substantial and include items like pasta, tacos, and baked potatoes.

Hotel Monte Vista: Following a day at Wupatki, this historic hotel serves as an ideal base for exploring downtown Flagstaff on foot. However, it's worth noting that the rooms may be considered small by contemporary standards, and some guests claim the hotel is haunted.

Directions: Depart from Flagstaff and head north on US-89. (Access to US-89 is available from I-40 on the east side of the city.) Make a right turn at the sign indicating Sunset Crater Volcano and Wupatki National Monuments. Following this route, you will encounter Sunset Crater Volcano initially, followed by the Wupatki Visitor Center situated 21 miles from the highway. Eventually, the route will lead you back to US-89, approximately 15 miles north of your initial entry point onto the 34-mile loop.

The majority of trails within the park are designed to be partially accessible. The primary trail, Wupatki Pueblo Trail, provides accessibility up to an overlook approximately 200 feet from the starting point at the visitor center. Similarly, the Citadel and Nalakihu Pueblos Trail is accessible beyond both pueblos, concluding at the base of a cinder hill, while the Wukoki Pueblo Trail is reachable up to the pueblo. The only exception is the Lomaki and Box Canyon Pueblos Trail, which is not accessible.

Furthermore, the Wupatki Visitor Center is designed to be accessible. Equipped with restrooms, ramps, and automatic entry and exit doors, the visitor center offers additional amenities, including a film with closed captioning and versions of the park brochure in Braille, as well as large text for enhanced readability.

The admission fee for both Sunset Crater Volcano and Wupatki National Monuments is $25 per vehicle, and it remains valid for a period of seven days.

Pets are permitted exclusively on a leash within the parking lot, and they are strictly prohibited on all trails, including the Wupatki Pueblo Trail located behind the visitor center. It is crucial not to leave your pet unattended in your vehicle.

For those interested in exploring nearby cliff dwellings, a recommended day trip is to Walnut Canyon National Monument, situated just 7.5 miles east of downtown Flagstaff. To delve deeper into the history of the ancient people who inhabited the region, a visit to the Museum of Northern Arizona in Flagstaff is highly recommended.

YUMA

DATE VISITED: WHO I WENT WITH:

RATING: ☆ ☆ ☆ ☆ ☆   WILL I RETURN?   YES / NO

Yuma, situated in the southwest corner of Arizona along the Colorado River near the borders of Mexico and California, holds the distinction of being the largest city in Arizona outside the metropolitan areas of Phoenix and Tucson. While summers in Yuma are characterized by heat, the city enjoys a pleasantly temperate winter climate with average temperatures in the low 70s, making it a sought-after destination for northern "snowbirds."

The range of activities in and around Yuma is diverse and plentiful. The city boasts six golf courses, several museums, and historic parks, along with three casinos. Visitors can partake in a variety of tours, including fishing, tubing, boating on the Colorado River, exploring local history, farm visits, or experiencing a hot air balloon flight. Yuma's old downtown area is adorned with a historic theatre hosting shows year-round, art galleries, boutique shops, and locally-owned restaurants, bars, and clubs. Festivals and events, such as the Spirit of Yuma fest in January, Yuma River Daze in February, and a seasonal Farmer's Market from December to March, add to the vibrant atmosphere.

During the summer, water recreation on the Colorado River north of town to Martinez Lake is a popular choice, and nearby desert sand dunes attract off-road enthusiasts and campers. Hiking trails are available in town, the surrounding desert wilderness, or at nearby national wildlife refuges. Visitors can also engage in water sports, hunting, fishing, and camping year-round. Two sites near Yuma showcase petroglyphs, while other areas display messages from pioneers or Spanish explorers.

Yuma's significance in Arizona's old west history is evident in two historic parks within the city. The Yuma Territorial Prison, featured in films like "3:10 to Yuma," was a real prison until 1909. The prison, constructed from local granite, stands partially preserved, offering exhibits in the prison museum. The Yuma Quartermaster Depot, a 10-acre historic park dating back to 1864, served as a military warehouse for two decades, storing ammunition, clothing, and food. The visitor's center serves as a starting point for exploring the historic buildings and grounds.

These activities represent just a sampling of the options available to visitors in Yuma. The city provides a myriad of lodging, dining, and shopping choices and is located approximately 185 miles southwest of Phoenix and 240 miles northwest of Tucson, near the California and Mexico borders.

Top accommodations in Yuma:

La Fuente Inn & Suites: For a relaxing stay, La Fuente Inn & Suites stands out, providing guests with the opportunity to unwind around its mid-century modern pool adorned with vibrant lime-green loungers perfect for sunbathing. Accommodation options include courtyard or pool view rooms, with several ADA-compliant choices available. The hotel offers complimentary breakfast in the lobby and hosts an evening happy hour, fostering a social atmosphere among guests.

The Dandy House: Yuma boasts an impressive array of vacation rentals, among which The Dandy House shines. This three-bedroom home, conveniently located in town, accommodates up to six guests and features ample communal spaces such as a backyard fire pit, a spacious kitchen, and a living room equipped with comfortable furniture and a fireplace.

Townhouse in Yuma: Another highly regarded rental option is the townhouse in Yuma, earning praise as an Airbnb guest favorite. This stylish residence accommodates up to six guests and is pet-friendly, ensuring every member of the group feels welcome. The property includes a chef's kitchen for preparing delightful meals, a dining area by the fireplace, and a pleasant grassy backyard for additional outdoor enjoyment.

Best things to do:

Explore the Colorado River by Kayak: Embrace one of Yuma's finest activities by embarking on a journey along the Colorado River with the assistance of 3:10 Kayak and Paddleboard Rentals. The company conveniently delivers equipment to the water's edge, offering rental options for two, four, or six-hour sessions, or even entire days.

Tour Castle Dome Mine Museum: History enthusiasts will find delight in a visit to the Castle Dome Mine Museum, providing insights into life in this 19th-century mining town. Wander through over 50 preserved buildings and venture into caves adorned with a spectrum of colors, courtesy of natural fluorescent and phosphorescent minerals lining the walls.

ATV Adventure in the Imperial Sand Dunes Recreation Area: Experience an adrenaline rush with an ATV ride through the Imperial Sand Dunes Recreation Area, located in close proximity to Yuma. The expansive landscape, featuring rolling sand dunes, serves as an ideal setting for thrilling adventures with friends. Outfitters like Jet Rent offer guided tours and rental services.

Yuma Territorial Prison State Historic Park Visit: Take a step back into the Wild West era with a visit to the Yuma Territorial Prison State Historic Park. Explore well-preserved prison cells, guard towers, and delve into the history of the inmates who occupied this space in the 1800s. The park is open daily, excluding Christmas.

Hiking Expedition at Telegraph Pass: Embark on an afternoon hike down Telegraph Pass, a trail rated as moderately difficult. Spanning a 5.7-mile loop through rugged terrain, the hike promises breathtaking views at every twist and turn. Allocate approximately three to four hours for the trek, and be sure to carry ample water, given the region's hot and sunny conditions.

Best restaurants:

The Garden Cafe: Escape the hustle and bustle at The Garden Cafe, a charming establishment perfect for a relaxing cup of coffee or a delightful breakfast. True to its name, the cafe is situated within a garden, offering a picturesque setting. Indulge in dishes like the Country Scramble, featuring ham, cheese, green onions, tomato, and garden-grown potatoes.

The Chile Pepper: For those who savor a bit of spice, The Chile Pepper is a must-visit family-run restaurant celebrated for its Mexican cuisine. Explore a Sonoran-style burrito with a choice of various salsas or opt for tacos, including options like carne asada, adobo chicken, and whole bean varieties.

Naked Dates: Venture on a 30-minute drive from Yuma to Wellton to experience Naked Dates. This certified organic farm produces medjool dates on its eight-acre property, available for bulk purchase or tasting at the farm's cafe. The menu at Naked Dates includes everything from sandwiches like the bacon date melt to flatbreads adorned with dates and tacos featuring, you guessed it, dates.

Best time to Visit:

If you seek a more relaxed atmosphere with fewer crowds, the period from April through October is recommended. The warmer summer months provide an excellent opportunity for sunrise hikes followed by a refreshing dip in the lake or river. Afternoons can be spent cooling off while exploring the town, shopping, or visiting a museum. The Sanguinetti House Museum & Gardens offer air-conditioning and delightful "refreshing Shirley Temple drinks" for visitors. For summer evenings it is recommended a visit to "Lute's Casino to enjoy the Summer Jazz Series while savoring a Lute's Special or potato tacos. Note: During the summer, it's advisable to call ahead before visiting museums or attractions.

How to reach Yuma:

Air: For those opting to fly, Yuma International Airport is the direct gateway, with daily service provided by American Airlines.

Train: Travelers who prefer train travel can reach Yuma via two Amtrak lines: the Sunset Limited and Texas Eagle, both leading directly to the Yuma train station.

Car: Yuma is also easily accessible for road trippers, particularly those traveling from the

American West. It's a mere 2.5-hour drive from San Diego or a three-hour drive from Phoenix, making it an ideal destination for a weekend getaway.

PHOTOS   PARK NAME...

PHOTOS   PARK NAME...

PHOTOS   PARK NAME...

PHOTOS   PARK NAME...

PHOTOS   PARK NAME..

PHOTOS   PARK NAME...

PHOTOS   PARK NAME...

PHOTOS   PARK NAME..

PHOTOS   PARK NAME...

PHOTOS   PARK NAME...

Thank you for taking the time to read my book. I hope you found it enjoyable.

Your feedback is important to me, and I would greatly appreciate it if you could take a moment to share your thoughts by leaving an online review.

Your review will not only help me improve as an author but also assist other potential readers in making informed decisions.

Once again, thank you for your support and for considering leaving a review.

Warm regards,

Max Kukis Galgan

Write to me if you think I should improve anything in my book:

maxkukisgalgan@gmail.com

ARIZONA
STATE PARKS BUCKET LIST

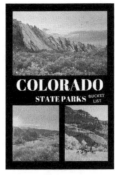

COLORADO
STATE PARKS BUCKET LIST

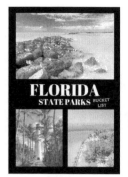

FLORIDA
STATE PARKS BUCKET LIST

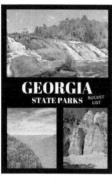

GEORGIA
STATE PARKS BUCKET LIST

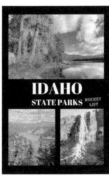

IDAHO
STATE PARKS BUCKET LIST

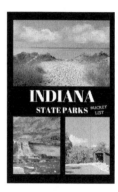

INDIANA
STATE PARKS BUCKET LIST

KANSAS
STATE PARKS BUCKET LIST

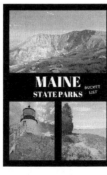

MAINE
STATE PARKS BUCKET LIST

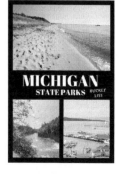

MICHIGAN
STATE PARKS BUCKET LIST

MINNESOTA STATE PARKS BUCKET LIST

MISSOURI STATE PARKS BUCKET LIST

NEW YORK STATE PARKS BUCKET LIST

OHIO STATE PARKS BUCKET LIST

OREGON STATE PARKS BUCKET LIST

PENNSYLVANIA STATE PARKS BUCKET JOURNAL

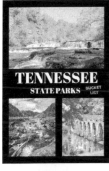

TENNESSEE STATE PARKS BUCKET LIST

TEXAS STATE PARKS BUCKET LIST

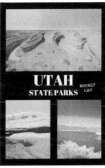

UTAH STATE PARKS BUCKET LIST

VIRGINIA
STATE PARKS BUCKET LIST

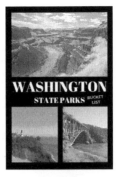

WASHINGTON
STATE PARKS BUCKET LIST

WISCONSIN
STATE PARKS BUCKET LIST

FLORIDA
100 BEST PLACES TO VISIT
BUCKET LIST

TEXAS BUCKET LIST
100 BEST PLACES TO VISIT

Thank you for buying my book!
I hope you like it.

Your feedback is important to me, and I
would greatly appreciate it if you could take
a moment to share your thoughts by leaving
an online review.

Your review will not only help me improve
as an author but also assist other potential
readers in making informed decisions.

Warm regards,

Max Kukis Galgan

Write to me if you think I should improve
anything in my book:

maxkukisgalgan@gmail.com

Made in the USA
Las Vegas, NV
04 December 2024

13326250R00221